THE
AMERICAN
WOMAN
1994-95

*Edited by Cynthia Costello and Anne J. Stone
for the Women's Research and Education Institute
Betty Dooley, Executive Director*

W. W. NORTON & COMPANY

NEW YORK / LONDON

THE
AMERICAN
WOMAN
1994-95

WHERE WE STAND
WOMEN AND HEALTH

The text of this book is composed in 11/13 Bembo,
with the display set in Centaur.
Composition and Manufacturing by The Haddon Craftsmen, Inc.
Book design by JAM Design.

ISBN 0-393-03625-1
ISBN 0-393-31185-6 (pbk.)

W. W. Norton & Company, Inc., 500 Fifth Avenue, New York, N.Y. 10110
W. W. Norton & Company Ltd., 10 Coptic Street, London WC1A 1PU

1 2 3 4 5 6 7 8 9 0

CONTENTS

List of Tables and Figures   7
Acknowledgments   17
Preface *by* Jean Stapleton   21
Introduction *by* Betty Dooley, Cynthia Costello, *and* Anne J. Stone   23

IN REVIEW JULY 1991–JUNE 1993   37

WOMEN AND HEALTH

The Politics of Women's Health *by* the Honorable Patricia
Schroeder *and* the Honorable Olympia Snowe   91

1. Assessing and Improving Women's Health *by* Karen Scott
   Collins, Diane Rowland, Alina Salganicoff, *and* Elizabeth Chait   109
2. The Health Status of Women of Color *by* Wilhelmina A. Leigh   154
3. Securing American Women's Reproductive Health *by*
   Rachel Benson Gold *and* Cory L. Richards   197
4. Women and Long-Term Care *by* Marilyn Moon   223

**AMERICAN WOMEN TODAY:
A STATISTICAL PORTRAIT**

1. Demographics   253
2. Education   265
3. Employment   281
4. Earnings and Benefits   307

5. Economic Security   327
6. Elections and Officials   345

Women in the 103rd Congress   353
Congressional Caucus for Women's Issues   381
References   385
Notes on the Contributors   407
About the Women's Research and Education Institute   409

Index   411
About the Editors   443

List of Tables and Figures

WOMEN AND HEALTH

CHAPTER 1 **Assessing and Improving Women's Health**

Table 1   Life Expectancy at Birth and at Age 65 by Race and Sex,   112
             1900–1989

Figure 1   Female Life Expectancy at Birth in Selected Industrialized   113
             Countries

Table 2   Leading Causes of Death for Whites and Blacks by Sex, 1990   114

Figure 2   AIDS Cases in Females Age 13 and Over by Race and   117
             Hispanic Origin, 1984–1990

Figure 3   New AIDS Cases in Females Age 13 and Over by Race and   118
             Hispanic Origin, 1990

Table 3   Incidence and Death Rates for Selected Cancers Among   123
             Women by Cancer Site, 1989

Figure 4   Female Mortality From Lung Cancer and Breast Cancer,   124
             1979–1990

Figure 5   Cervical Cancer: Incidence and Mortality Rates for White   125
             and Black Women, 1989

Figure 6   Breast Cancer: Incidence and Mortality Rates for White   127
             and Black Women, 1989

Figure 7   White and Black Women With Breast Cancer: Percentage   128
             Early Diagnosis and Five-Year Survival, 1981–1987

Figure 8   Prevalence of Diabetes Among Women Age 45 to 74,   129
             Selected Races and Hispanic Origins

Table 4   Early Detection and Preventive Services for Women: 132
               Guidelines and Usage, 1990

Figure 9   Women Smokers by Age, 1990   133

Table 5   Women Who Had Selected Preventive Services in the Past   135
               Year by Selected Characteristics, 1990

Figure 10   Women Who Had a Pap Smear in the Past Year by Age   136
               and Income, 1990

Figure 11   Women Reporting Ever Having Had a Mammogram by   137
               Selected Characteristics, 1990

Table 6   Physician Visits and Usual Source of Care by Sex and Age,   141
               1987

Figure 12   Hospital Discharge Rates by Sex and Age, 1990   141

Table 7   Poverty Status of Women and Men by Age, Race, and   143
               Hispanic Origin, 1990

Table 8   Health Insurance Coverage Status of Women and Men   145
               Age 18 to 64 by Age and Income, 1990

Table 9   Health Insurance Coverage Status of the Elderly Population   148
               by Sex and Income, 1990

CHAPTER 2 **The Health Status of Women of Color**

Table 1   Life Expectancy at Birth by Sex, Race, and Hispanic Origin   171

Table 2   Overweight Women Age 20 to 74 by Race and Hispanic   172
               Origin, 1976–1980 and 1982–1984

Table 3   Cigarette Smokers Among Women Age 18 and Over by   173
               Race and Hispanic Origin, 1985 and 1987

Table 4   Prenatal Care for Mothers With Live Births by Race and   176
               Hispanic Origin of Mothers, 1989

Table 5   Hypertension Among Women Age 20 to 74 by Race and   179
               Hispanic Origin, 1976–1980 and 1982–1984

Table 6   Distribution of HIV/AIDS Cases Among Women Age 15 to   180
               44 by Race and Hispanic Origin, 1981–1989

Table 7   Sources of AIDS Infection Among Women by Race and   181
               Hispanic Origin, Through October 1991

Table 8   Infant, Neonatal, and Postneonatal Mortality Rates by Mother's   186
               Race and Hispanic Origin, for Birth Cohorts 1984–1986

Table 9   Mortality Rates From AIDS for Black and White Women   187
                by Age, 1990 and 1991

CHAPTER 3 **Securing American Women's Reproductive Health**

Figure 1   Stages of a Typical Woman's Reproductive Life   198

Table 1   Women at Risk of Unintended Pregnancy by Selected   201
                Contraceptive Type and Age, 1988

Table 2   Contraceptive Users Age 15 to 44 Who Rely on Various   202
                Methods by Age, 1988

Table 3   Women Experiencing Types of Contraceptive Failure   204
                During the First 12 Months of Use by Marital Status,
                Poverty Status, and Age, 1988

Table 4   Pregnancy Outcome by Age of Woman, 1988   205

Table 5   Live Births by Month Prenatal Care Began and Age of   207
                Mother, 1990

Table 6   Abortions by Week of Gestation, 1988   208

CHAPTER 4 **Women and Long-Term Care**

Table 1   Health and Functional Status of Elderly Women and Men   229
                by Age, 1984

Table 2   Prevalence of Selected Chronic Conditions by Sex, 1985   230

Figure 1   Number of Men Per 100 Women by Age, 1990   231

Table 3   Living Arrangements of Women Age 65 and Over by Age,   231
                Race, and Hispanic Origin, 1992

Table 4   Relationship of Caregivers to Elderly Women and Men   232
                Receiving Care by Age of Care Recipient, 1982

Table 5   Elderly Women With Incomes Below Twice the Poverty   235
                Threshold by Age, Race, and Hispanic Origin, 1991

Figure 2   Sources of Funding for Nursing Home Care and Home   237
                Health Care

Table 6   Nursing Home Residents Over Age 55 by Sex, Race, and   241
                Age, 1985 and 1977

Table 7   Use of Formal Home- and Community-Based Services by   243
                Women Age 65 and Over Who Have Functional Limitations
                by Selected Characteristics, 1987

AMERICAN WOMEN TODAY: A STATISTICAL PORTRAIT

SECTION 1   Demographics

Table 1-1   Population of the United States in 1990 by Race and   254
             Sex, According to the Decennial Census of 1990

Figure 1-1   Population of the United States by Age and Sex, 1992   255

Figure 1-2   Population of the United States by Sex, Race, and Hispanic   256
             Origin, 1992

Figure 1-3   U.S. Fertility Rates by Race, 1960–1990   256

Table 1-2   Marital Status by Sex, Race, and Hispanic Origin, March   257
             1992

Figure 1-4   Currently Married and Never Married Adults by Sex,   258
             Race, and Hispanic Origin, March 1992

Figure 1-5   Median Age at First Marriage by Sex, 1970–1992   258

Table 1-3   Families by Family Type, Race, and Hispanic Origin, 1970,   259
             1980, 1990, and 1991

Table 1-4   Households With Unrelated Partners by Sex of Partners and   260
             Presence of Children, 1992

Figure 1-6   The Divorce Rate, 1970, 1980, 1990, and 1992   261

Table 1-5   Divorce Ratios by Sex, Race, and Hispanic Origin, 1970,   261
             1980, 1990, and 1992

Table 1-6   Children's Living Arrangements by Race and Hispanic   262
             Origin, 1970, 1980, and 1992

Figure 1-7   Households With Female Householders by Tenure, Type,   263
             and Presence of Children, March 1991

Figure 1-8   Living Arrangements of Persons Age 65 and Over by Sex,   264
             March 1991

SECTION 2   Education

Table 2-1   Educational Attainment by Sex, Race, and Hispanic   267
             Origin, 1991

Figure 2-1   White, Black, and Hispanic Women Age 25 and Over   268
             With 12 or More Years of Education, 1970, 1980, and 1991

Table 2-2   Educational Attainment of U.S.- and Foreign-Born   269
             Women Age 25 to 54 by Race and Hispanic Origin, 1989

Table 2-3   College Enrollment by Sex, Race, and Hispanic Origin,   270
1976, 1984, and 1990

Figure 2-2   Women Enrolled in Colleges and Universities by Age,   271
1970, 1980, and 1990

Figure 2-3   Students Enrolled in Colleges and Universities by Sex and   271
Full- or Part-Time Status, 1970, 1980, and 1990

Table 2-4   Women Awarded Undergraduate Degrees in Selected   272
Fields, 1959/60–1989/90

Table 2-5   Ten Most Popular Majors Among Bachelor's Degree   273
Recipients by Sex, and by Race and Hispanic Origin for
Women, 1989/90

Table 2-6   Women Graduates of U.S. Service Academies, 1980, 1990,   274
and 1993

Figure 2-4   Recipients of Postsecondary Degrees by Sex,   275
1959/60–1989/90

Figure 2-5   First Professional Degrees Awarded in Selected Fields by Sex   276
of Recipients, 1989/90

Table 2-7   Women Awarded First Professional Degrees in Selected   277
Fields by Race and Hispanic Origin, 1976/77 and 1989/90

Table 2-8   New Entrants to and Graduates From U.S. Medical Schools   278
by Sex, 1986–1992

Figure 2-6   Graduates From U.S. Medical Schools by Sex, 1986–1992   278

Figure 2-7   Faculty With Tenure by Sex and Type of Institution,   279
1980/81 and 1990/91

Figure 2-8   Women Heads of Public and Private Colleges and   280
Universities, Selected Years, 1975–1992

SECTION 3   Employment

Figure 3-1   Women in the Labor Force, 1960–1992   283

Table 3-1   Women's Labor Force Participation Rate and Women as a   283
Percentage of the Labor Force, 1960–1992

Table 3-2   Women's Labor Force Participation Rates by Age,   284
1960–1992 and Projected 2005

Table 3-3   Labor Force Participation Rates by Sex, Race, and Hispanic   285
Origin, 1975, 1990, 1992, and Projected 2005

Table 3-4   Labor Force Participation and Unemployment Rates of   286
              Persons of Hispanic Origin by Sex and Origin, 1992

Figure 3-2   The Hispanic Labor Force by Sex and Origin, 1992   287

Table 3-5   Labor Force Participation and Unemployment Rates of   287
              Foreign-Born Women, by Language Spoken at Home and
              English Fluency, November 1989

Table 3-6   Unemployment Rates by Sex, Race, and Hispanic Origin,   288
              1980–1992

Figure 3-3   Women's Unemployment Rates by Race and Hispanic   289
              Origin, 1980–1992

Figure 3-4   Unemployed Workers Age 20 and Over by Sex and Reason   290
              for Unemployment, 1990 and 1992

Figure 3-5   Employed Women, 1971–1991   291

Table 3-7   Workers by Full- or Part-Time Status, Sex, and Race,   291
              1992

Table 3-8   Full- and Part-Time Workers by Sex and Age, 1992   292

Figure 3-6   Workers Holding Multiple Jobs by Sex, 1970, 1980,   292
              and 1991

Figure 3-7   Workers on Goods-Producing and Service-Producing   293
              Nonfarm Payrolls by Sex, 1970–1992

Figure 3-8   Workers With Union Affiliation by Sex, 1984 and 1992   294

Table 3-9   White, Black, and Hispanic Workers With Union Affiliation   294
              by Sex, 1984 and 1992

Figure 3-9   Employed Women and Men by Industry, 1992   295

Figure 3-10 Employed Women and Men by Occupation, 1992   296

Figure 3-11 Employed White, Black, and Hispanic Women by   297
              Occupation, 1992

Table 3-10   Women as a Percentage of Workers in Selected Occupations,   298
              1975, 1984, and 1992

Table 3-11   Women Employed in Selected Health Care Industries, 1982   299
              and 1992

Table 3-12   Women Employed in Selected Health Care Industries by   299
              Race and Hispanic Origin, 1992

Table 3-13   Women Employed in Selected Health Care Occupations   300
              by Race and Hispanic Origin, 1992

Table 3-14   U.S. Active Duty Servicewomen by Branch of Service,   301
Rank, Race, and Hispanic Origin, Fiscal Year 1992

Figure 3-12   Wives in the Paid Labor Force by Race and Hispanic Origin,   302
1981–1991

Figure 3-13   Labor Force Participation of Mothers With Young Children   302
by Marital Status, 1980–1992

Figure 3-14   Children With Mothers in the Workforce by Age of   303
Children, 1972–1992

Table 3-15   Children Under Age 18 With Working Parents by Living   303
Arrangements and Age of Children, 1992

Table 3-16   Employed Mothers by Full-Time Work Status and Age of   304
Children, 1982 and 1992

Table 3-17   Child Care Arrangements for the Young Children of Working   305
Mothers by Race and Hispanic Origin, 1988

Table 3-18   Child Care Expenditures of Families With Working   306
Mothers by Income and Poverty Status, 1988

Figure 3-15   Volunteer Workers by Sex and Type of Organization They   306
Serve, 1989

SECTION 4   **Earnings and Benefits**

Figure 4-1   Median Weekly Earnings by Sex, 1980–1992   309

Table 4-1   Female-to-Male Earnings Ratios by Race and Hispanic   309
Origin, 1980–1992

Table 4-2   Median Weekly Earnings by Sex and Female-to-Male   310
Earnings Ratios by Occupation, 1984 and 1992

Figure 4-2   Percent Change in Real Earnings by Sex and Occupational   312
Group, 1984–1992

Figure 4-3   Median Annual Earnings by Sex and Race, 1971–1991   313

Figure 4-4   Median Annual Earnings by Sex and Hispanic Origin,   314
1976–1991

Table 4-3   Median Annual Earnings by Sex, Race, and Hispanic Origin,   314
1971–1991

Table 4-4   Median Weekly Earnings by Sex and Female-to-Male   315
Earnings Ratios in Selected Health Care Occupations, 1992

Figure 4-5   Median Weekly Earnings of Female Registered Nurses and   316
Licensed Practical Nurses, 1983–1992

Table 4-5   Availability of Parental Leave to Full-Time   316
Employees by Size and Type of Employer, 1989 and 1990

Table 4-6   Workers on Flexible Work Schedules by Occupation and   317
Sex, 1991

Table 4-7   Pension Plan Coverage of Workers by Sex, and of Women   318
Workers by Race and Hispanic Origin, 1991

Table 4-8   All Workers and Workers With Pension Plan Coverage by   319
Sex and Employer Size, 1991

Figure 4-6   Workers With Health Insurance Through Their Own Jobs by   320
Sex and Employer Size, 1991

Table 4-9   Full-Time, Year-Round Workers With and Without Health   321
Insurance Through Their Own Jobs by Sex, Race, and
Hispanic Origin, 1991

Figure 4-7   Women Workers With and Without Health Insurance   322
Through Their Own Jobs by Employer Size, 1991

Figure 4-8   Persons Age 18 to 64 With Private Health Insurance by Sex   322
and Source of Coverage, 1991

Figure 4-9   Women Age 18 to 64 With Private Health Insurance by Age   323
and Source of Coverage, 1991

Figure 4-10 Health Insurance Coverage by Sex and Type of Insurance,   324
1991

Figure 4-11 Persons With and Without Health Insurance Coverage by   324
Sex and Age, 1991

Figure 4-12 Persons Age 18 to 64 With No Health Insurance Coverage   325
by Sex and Age, 1991

Figure 4-13 Persons Age 16 to 64 With No Health Insurance Coverage   325
by Sex and Work Experience, 1991

Table 4-10   Persons With No Health Insurance Coverage by Family   326
Relationship, 1991

SECTION 5   **Economic Security**

Figure 5-1   Median Family Income by Family Type, 1971–1991   329

Table 5-1   Median Income of White, Black, and Hispanic Families   330
by Family Type, 1981 and 1991

Figure 5-2   Median Family Income by Age of Householder, 1971–1991   331

Figure 5-3   Median Income of Families With Children by Family Type,   332
1976–1991

Table 5-2   Sources of Income for Women Age 15 to 64 by Race and   333
Hispanic Origin, 1991

Table 5-3   Receipt of Child Support Payments by Mothers Awarded   335
Support, 1978 and 1989

Table 5-4   Women With Child Support Awards by Race and Hispanic   335
Origin, 1989

Table 5-5   Women Eligible for Child Support by Poverty Status, Race,   335
and Hispanic Origin, 1989

Figure 5-4   Poverty Rates of Families by Family Type and Presence of   336
Children, 1991

Figure 5-5   Homeownership by Age of Householder, 1981 and 1991   336

Table 5-6   Poverty Rates of White, Black, and Hispanic Families by   337
Family Type and Presence of Children, 1991

Table 5-7   Labor Market Problems Among Women Workers Who   338
Maintain Families by Poverty Status, 1990

Table 5-8   Poverty Rates of Unrelated Individuals by Sex and Age,   338
1991

Table 5-9   Sources of Income for Persons Age 65 and Over by Sex,   339
1991

Table 5-10   Sources of Income for White, Black, and Hispanic Women   340
Age 65 and Over, 1991

Figure 5-6   Homeownership by Family Type, Presence of Children,   342
Race, and Hispanic Origin, March 1991

Table 5-11   The Housing Cost Burden by Household Type and Tenure,   343
Selected Age Groups, 1989

SECTION 6   **Elections and Officials**

Figure 6-1   Voter Participation in the 1992 National Election by Sex,   346
Race, and Hispanic Origin

Table 6-1   Voter Participation in National Elections by Sex, Race, and   347
Hispanic Origin, 1976–1992

Figure 6-2   Voters in the 1992 National Election by Sex and Age   348

Table 6-2   Voter Participation in National Elections by Sex and Age,   349
               1976–1992

Table 6-3   Women in Elective Office, Selected Years, 1975–1993   350

Table 6-4   Women on the Federal Bench   351

Table 6-5   Women Presidential Appointees to Senate-Confirmed   351
               Positions, 1977–May 1993

Acknowledgments

THE FIFTH EDITION OF *The American Woman,* like the first four, has enjoyed a broad base of support from foundations, corporations, and individuals who have made generous financial or in-kind contributions to WREI and its work.

The American Woman series was launched with a grant from the Ford Foundation, and supported by contributions from other donors. We are extremely grateful to the Ford Foundation both for its past assistance and for providing a grant to help in the preparation of this edition of *The American Woman.* June Zeitlin, in particular, has earned our gratitude for her support and ongoing advice. Alison Bernstein of the Ford Foundation also deserves special thanks for her encouragement of *The American Woman* series.

The other funders without whose assistance we could not have prepared this book are the American Express Company, AT&T, Juanita Kreps, and the Charles H. Revson Foundation. To each we extend our thanks. We would also like to acknowledge the support of Akin, Gump, Strauss, Hauer and Feld; AFL-CIO; American Income Life Insurance Company; Association of Flight Attendants; ARCO; Chevron U.S.A., Inc.; Chrysler Corporation; Communications Workers of America; Fluor Corporation; Ford Motor Company; Guinness America, Inc.; International Brotherhood of Teamsters; Johnson & Johnson; Lehman Brothers; Martin Marietta Corporation; National Education Association; Pfizer Inc.; Prudential Foundation; Sara Lee Corporation; Schering-Plough Corporation; Sea-Land Service, Inc.; Sears, Roebuck and Co.; Sheet Metal Workers International Association; United Auto Workers; Upjohn Company; UST; Warner-Lambert Company; Xerox Corporation; and Peg Yorkin Foundation.

Members of WREI's board of directors have offered extensive practical help as well as continuing encouragement throughout all of the editions of *The American Woman*. Board president Jean Stapleton has tirelessly spoken about every edition of *The American Woman* in towns and cities across the country. JoAnn Heffernan Heisen and Martina L. Bradford have promoted the book enthusiastically in the corporate community. Thanks to Alma Rangel's initiative, *The American Woman* reached many African American women's organizations in New York. Matina Horner and Juanita Kreps were especially helpful with respect to funding for the book. Indeed, the WREI staff is grateful to the entire board for their belief in the book and for their moral support.

Our editor at Norton, Mary Cunnane, and her assistant, Caroline Crawford, consistently provided constructive advice and guidance, for which we are extremely appreciative.

A stellar advisory committee has been generous with wisdom, expertise, and encouragement. That committee, many of whose members have served since *The American Woman* was first conceived, consists of Mariam Chamberlain, Jane Chapman, Beverly Guy-Sheftall, Cynthia Harrison, Anne Kasper, Harriette McAdoo, Irene Natividad, Brenda Pillors, Sarah Pritchard, Sara Rix, Ida G. Ruben, Ann Schmidt, Margaret Simms, Ronnie Steinberg, and Susanne Stoiber. Sara Rix, who edited the first three volumes of *The American Woman,* deserves special thanks—her recommendations for this edition were, as always, right on target.

WREI's excellent and supportive Health Care Advisory Committee provided guidance, expertise, authors, and reviewers for the textual chapters in this edition. For their help with this volume of *The American Woman,* we want especially to thank Hortensia Amaro, Judith Feder, Vanessa Northington Gamble, Charles Hammond, Karen Ignagni, Dave Kennell, Wilhelmina Leigh, Marilyn Moon, Diane Rowland, Julia Scott, Edward E. Wallach, Judith Waxman, and Sheila Zedlewski.

The writing and editorial assistance of Judith Dollenmayer, Azar Kattan, Sarah Orrick, Allison Porter, and Kitty Stone have been invaluable. We wish to thank the individuals at the Bureau of the Census and the Bureau of Labor Statistics, especially Howard Hayghe at BLS, who so generously shared their time and expertise. Lesley Primmer and Laura Lorenzen, legislative staff for the Congressional Caucus for Women's Issues, were always generous with information, time, and expertise. Karen Davis and Evelyn Katz also deserve our thanks for their recommendations. I would like to thank Jill Miller for her support of *The American Woman* series, and especially Wendy Blum for her wonderful messenger service.

No book of this kind could have been produced without the hard work of WREI's entire staff. The core editorial team, led by Cynthia Costello and

Anne Stone, dedicated countless hours to the research, writing, and editing of *The American Woman*. Cynthia Costello's editorial leadership, organizational skills, tact, and grace under pressure have been central to producing this book. I cannot adequately express my appreciation and admiration of Anne Stone, who has devoted a phenomenal amount of her time, effort, and brilliant editorial skills to all five volumes of the book. The quality of *The American Woman* series is, in no small part, the result of Anne Stone's contributions.

Bridget Rice, WREI's research assistant, worked tirelessly to gather the statistics and prepare the tables and figures, and she ably assisted with the preparation of the textual chapters. Two WREI interns—Christy Chandler and Stacie Leimas—were invaluable, and without their energy and enterprise there would be no "In Review" section. Shari Miles, WREI's fellowship director, offered suggestions on the chapters and assisted in their preparation. Carolyn Becraft, our expert on women in the military, assisted with information on the Tailhook scandal. And Kathleen Pagano helped in many ways with the preparation of this volume and the fundraising efforts that made *The American Woman* possible.

Finally, I want to underscore that our funders, advisers, reviewers, and independent editors are not responsible for any errors or misstatements that may appear in the book. The opinions expressed in the book do not necessarily reflect the opinions of anyone other than the authors of the chapters.

BETTY DOOLEY
Executive Director
Women's Research and Education Institute

PREFACE

Jean Stapleton

THIS VOLUME IS THE FIFTH in a series of comprehensive reports on the status of women in the United States prepared by the Women's Research and Education Institute (WREI). Published every other year, *The American Woman* assembles the latest available information about women's successes and setbacks in many aspects of their lives. The series has become a reliable almanac summarizing where American women are and reflecting upon where they are going.

Beginning and nurturing the series from the first volume's appearance in 1987, Betty Dooley, executive director of WREI, has made *The American Woman* a vehicle for assessing women's status in the policymaking process and politics, as well as in society. These books have reinforced Betty's own persistent contribution to improving the status of American women in all three areas, and they offer solid testimony to the effectiveness of her leadership of WREI.

A brief look backward. The first three editions of *The American Woman* covered a broad array of topics, highlighting—for example—the educational status of women of color, the legacy of the women's movement of the past three decades, and women's status in the military. The fourth edition, published in the Spring of 1992, hit the mark by covering women's roles as political players—candidates, officeholders, and voters—in what became a breakthrough year for women in American politics. A record 48 women were elected to the U.S. House of Representatives and five to the Senate—four on November 8, 1992, and the fifth in the spring of 1993, when Kay Bailey Hutchison won the Texas seat vacated by Lloyd Bentsen, now secretary of the treasury. We may pause to take pleasure from these victories, but there is still far to go when women comprise only about 10 percent of the Congress while we are more than half of the U.S. population.

This fifth edition of *The American Woman* turns to a topic of urgent concern to women and their families: health care. This volume explores the contradictions and omissions in our present health care system that mean inadequate attention to the real needs of all too many American women. Probably no issue looms larger, or carries more paradoxes and ironies for women, than their relationship to the health care system. Women have traditionally been the nurturers and caregivers of family life, yet large numbers of women lack health insurance coverage and find that their health care needs go unmet. The unique health problems of women have been given insufficient attention, yet no group has been so stereotyped by myths and misapprehensions about the effect of women's physical conditions on their behavior and job performance. Wives, mothers, daughters, sisters—American women in these roles are not only people who give care to children, aging parents, and even siblings—they are women who need care themselves.

By investigating women's relationship to the American health care system, this volume does not mean to denigrate the contributions of the holistic and spiritual health movements that are helping Americans to redefine the meaning of "health" throughout their lives. Furthermore, we trust that health care reform will include free choice for women who rely on other proven alternative systems of care and treatment. WREI's aim is to analyze the status of American women in our health care system, especially as the country anticipates a difficult struggle to create major changes in the delivery of health care during the years ahead.

Despite his fondness for large brandies and long cigars, Winston Churchill rightly understood the relation of personal health to national well-being. The contributors to *The American Woman* would agree with him that "There is no finer investment for any community than putting milk into babies. Healthy citizens are the greatest asset any country can have." *A votre santé.*

INTRODUCTION

Betty Dooley, Cynthia Costello,
and Anne J. Stone

As THIS BOOK GOES TO PRESS, a new administration has promised a legislative program of major change in American health care delivery. For most of the past decade, women's advocates have grasped and moved forward the idea that women's health has unique characteristics that require specific new research, preventive and primary care, and focused action. Mainstream medicine and research have been slow to acknowledge that "health" for women may have its own distinct profile. Most research long excluded the possibility that women could react differently than men to the same diseases, as well as to the aging process. Badly understood and poorly researched, sometimes neglected altogether, women's health needs are only slowly coming into focus.

The possibility of major positive change in the health care system makes women's health a natural theme for *The American Woman 1994-95*. This edition assesses women's health today, reporting also about the public policies that will be needed to make women's health a fully equal, well-researched concern of the American health care system and biomedical community.

Women's health has many dimensions. In almost all of them, our knowledge has been limited by lack of research and, it must be said, by lack of the scientific imagination to conceive that the male body may not be the only reliable model on which to base treatment for disease, aging, and stress. Only recently—due in large part to the efforts of the Congressional Caucus for Women's Issues and dedicated allies—have women become a mandatory focus of gender-specific research into how the nation's major life-threatening diseases, from cardiological problems to cancer, may affect them differently.

For women and men alike, health has many facets. The purely physical dimensions of health are difficult to fully achieve, partly because there are more mysteries than certainties in medicine. All of us also hold different cards in a genetic lottery that affects health; as one cardiologist says, "the most effective way to avoid heart disease is to pick the right parents." Mental and emotional health must contend with a fast-break society bombarded by overstimulation, economic stress, violence, and family schism. Getting adequate nutrition, exercise, and rest are not inevitable even for more affluent Americans, and these factors offer no guarantees against disease. Americans increasingly believe that the many faces of health are adequately recognized only by augmenting traditional clinical medicine and remediation with personal programs for wellness; preventive, holistic medicine; and practices from other cultures' traditions of healing.

For women, however, the economic and political dimensions of becoming and staying healthy are especially difficult. There are distinct health challenges, too, among different communities of women from diverse economic backgrounds, cultures, and age groups. Who informs us of available treatments, and how do we find help in choosing the most appropriate? Who has access to care? Who pays? Who has the umbrella of insurance to help bear the costs? And, who cares for the family or elderly parents when the traditional caregiver, usually a woman, needs care herself? Although the contributors to this volume may address the dilemmas of women's health in the language of policy and statistics, they all realize that women's health raises some of the most difficult issues of daily life. Good public policy on women's health is indispensable to improving their lives and opportunities.

Health questions are far from abstract for women, as the following chapters report. Problems of availability, access, and affordability cross class and racial lines. Knowledge and money give one a better chance to remain healthy; just-published studies confirm the commonsensical conclusion that death rates are lower among women and men with more than 12 years of education and incomes above the poverty level. Yet, where women are concerned, even the professional medical community's knowledge of the gender-specific aspects of health has often been minimal, or inadequately applied.

OVERVIEW OF THE CHAPTERS

The American Woman opens with a message from the bipartisan Congressional Caucus for Women's Issues, followed by four chapters that address a broad array of women's health concerns. In **"The Politics of Women's**

Health," the cochairs of the Congressional Caucus for Women's Issues relate the federal struggle of the past decade to bring women's health care issues into the light. Rep. Patricia Schroeder (D-CO) and Rep. Olympia J. Snowe (R-ME) discuss the group's addition of health to its early focus in the 1970s and 1980s on legal and economic equity for women. Working through the congressional budget, reauthorization, and appropriations processes, the caucus and its allies in recent years have significantly expanded the resources devoted to women's health research and intervention, and have ensured that gender variables will be investigated thoroughly.

As Schroeder and Snowe illustrate, there was much to correct. One study of aspirin's preventive effect on heart disease failed to include a single woman in its sample of 20,000 physicians—although 10 percent of American physicians at the time were women. The largest federal study of aging, which began in 1958 and continues today, excluded women from the research until 1978—ostensibly because there was no women's bathroom at the site where study participants were medically assessed. A more recent large study of heart disease risk factors was conducted on 13,000 men at a cost of $115 million; the study's acronym (Mr. Fit) said it all where women were concerned.

Besides piecemeal battles to improve federal research and increase resources devoted to women's special health problems, the caucus and others developed the comprehensive Women's Health Equity Act (WHEA), first introduced in both the House and the Senate in July 1990. The act was a package of 20 separate bills that addressed deficiencies in the treatment of women's health in three critical fields—research, services, and prevention.

Although many pieces of the WHEA were incorporated into other legislation and appropriations measures, mere introduction of the omnibus bill sped up policy changes at the National Institutes of Health (NIH) and other federal agencies with major responsibilities for women's health.

Although there are still problems, especially in the medical and research communities, progress can be reported. An NIH Office of Research on Women's Health opened in the fall of 1990. (Its appropriations have climbed steadily since then.) When Dr. Bernadine Healy took over as NIH director in the spring of 1991, she unveiled plans for a Women's Health Initiative, a 14-year study of 150,000 women that is focusing on preventing breast cancer, osteoporosis, and heart disease in older women. The Women's Health Equity Act also led to the creation of five centers for contraceptive and infertility research under NIH auspices.

Reps. Schroeder and Snowe conclude in their report that the caucus "has a solid record of accomplishment . . . including a new emphasis on women's health issues at NIH, the creation of important disease prevention programs aimed at women, and a more receptive climate that has led to increased funds for women's health programs across the board."

Today the 43 congresswomen from both parties on the caucus's executive committee are working to ensure that a set of eight principles are incorporated into any new national program of health care. Schroeder and Snowe describe the caucus's goals on issues such as access to health care coverage, a basic benefits package, expansion of primary care (as opposed to specialty medicine), the elimination of gender stereotyping in treatment and research, preventive and diagnostic screening, and a continuing focus on the women-specific aspects of health: infertility, contraception, and diseases that disproportionately afflict older women.

CHAPTER ONE, **"Assessing and Improving Women's Health,"** is written by a team of women researchers who at one time or another have been associated with the Kaiser Commission on the Future of Medicaid: Karen Scott Collins, Diane Rowland, Alina Salganicoff, and Elizabeth Chait.

The authors first highlight facts on the most rapidly growing health problems of American women today. They report that:

- Heart disease, accounting for about 31 percent of women's deaths, is the leading cause of death for both women and men.
- Lung cancer has surpassed breast cancer as the leading cause of women's deaths from cancer. Yet more than 28 percent of women age 25 to 34 still smoke.
- Invasive cervical and breast cancers can be greatly reduced by Pap smears and mammography. Yet many women, especially those with low incomes and little education, still fail to receive these tests routinely.
- Domestic violence is an epidemic, victimizing an estimated four million women annually; 170,000 of these women are assaulted in their fifth to ninth months of pregnancy.
- Acquired Immune Deficiency Syndrome (AIDS) is spreading more rapidly among women than men. In the single year from 1989 to 1990, the number of women diagnosed with AIDS rose 34 percent; in New York City, AIDS is now the leading cause of death for black women age 24 to 44.
- Although it is more and more clear that menopause alters the risk of certain conditions such as heart disease, much more research is needed to understand its effects on women's long-term health.

Chapter One also profiles American women's health at different stages of life. Life expectancy in the United States has increased steadily since the turn-of-the-century, and the gap between females and males has widened to the point where gender is a more important factor than race in life expectancy. Both black and white women have longer life expectancies than men. Yet the United States, for all its advanced medicine, lags behind other industrialized countries in life expectancy rates for women. Leading causes of women's mortality are heart disease, cancer, and stroke—accounting for 67 percent of American women's deaths. Across the life span, women's health concerns differ. The authors discuss issues for younger women, from sexually transmitted diseases such as pelvic inflammatory disease and AIDS to depression, eating disorders, and violence—which is as much a public health problem as a problem of law enforcement. During and after menopause, women's concerns turn to conditions associated with aging and changes in hormones, such as heart disease, cancer, cerebrovascular diseases, diabetes, and osteoporosis. Alzheimer's disease, whose cause is unknown, appears to be more prevalent among women, even after accounting for the higher proportion of females among the aged.

How to improve women's health? First, the authors recommend a massive campaign to emphasize preventive measures such as stopping smoking, cancer screening, hormone replacement therapy, increasing calcium intake, and exercising (to prevent osteoporosis). Much more research is needed on preventive measures against heart disease. Failures of education and motivation, too, raise barriers to women's health that need attention.

Access to preventive services is a major obstacle for many women. The authors identify three key factors determining whether women take advantage of such services: having a regular source of care; knowing—or having a physician who knows—what services are available; and having either the personal means or insurance to cover the costs. Women typically use more health care services than men, so barriers to access impede them more often. For poor women, the problems of access to needed preventive services are particularly acute.

Beyond the inadequately insured, the authors report, more than 35 million Americans—14 percent of our people—had no health insurance of any kind in 1991. An unknown number more, we can assume, go in and out from under the umbrella of health coverage, as they move in and out of employment. Women are disproportionately employed in temporary or non-benefits-paying jobs, which expose them to further risk of noninsurance. Of the uninsured, almost 12 million are adult women between the ages of 18 and 65—but nearly three million are under 25, in the primary childbearing years. One-third of poor, nonelderly adult women are uninsured.

Finally, the authors state that health care reform, to be effective, must provide universal access to care. Effective reform will need to eliminate problems associated with employment-based insurance and Medicaid, while covering prescription drugs and long-term care. Positive reforms should include preventive services—counseling as well as procedures—and provide quality care in convenient settings geared to the reality of women's daily lives, which frequently include large responsibilities for children, elderly parents, and sometimes grandchildren. The supply of primary-care physicians must increase, and a good plan will need to address cultural barriers to care in communities. "Finally," they conclude, "a more personal level of reform [is needed] to empower women with knowledge of their health status and risks, and to train physicians to use greater sensitivity in communicating with women on topics such as sexual behavior and violence."

CHAPTER TWO, "The Health Status of Women of Color" hones in on the health problems of minority women. Wilhelmina A. Leigh, senior research associate at Washington's Joint Center for Political and Economic Studies, graphically demonstrates that not all women relate to the health care system in the same way. She covers the special health problems of different communities of women: Native Americans, Hispanics, blacks, and Asian and Pacific Islanders. These four groups, she points out, embrace many subpopulations whose health status varies from better than the U.S. average (for Japanese and Cuban Americans with prenatal care) to far worse than that (such as black and Native American women with amputations due to diabetes).

It is common knowledge that the health status of black Americans differs from that of whites. Blacks suffer from more undiagnosed diseases, higher rates of disease and illness, and a larger number of chronic conditions (such as hypertension and diabetes). Mortality rates for many conditions exceed those of whites.

Racism, poverty, and discrimination have shaped the health experience of women of color as a group. But even among the groups, significant differences exist in health status, reports Dr. Leigh. Hispanic women have the longest life expectancies of all women of color, followed by Native American and black women. Black women below the age of 50 are disproportionately suffering in the AIDS epidemic. Alcoholism and its effects through successive generations of Native American women appear in their higher death rates from alcohol-related syndromes, cirrhosis, and liver disease.

Leigh reminds us that many people of color lack insurance coverage: Hispanics and Asian and Pacific Islanders are two and a half times as likely to be without insurance as whites, while blacks are almost two times as likely. Regarding overall figures for these populations, 32.4 percent of all Hispanics, about 20 percent of blacks, and nearly 13 percent of whites lack insurance. The working poor, Leigh observes, face double jeopardy in the U.S. health care system: they can't afford to pay costly medical bills out-of-pocket, yet they do not qualify for federal programs such as Medicaid. Women of color without citizenship face additional eligibility barriers.

Access to health care means not only the ability to pay, but also the presence of nearby services, transportation to reach those services, and child care arrangements so that mothers can seek care. Leigh would add to this the need for providers who have learned to offer sensitive, competent care to people from diverse backgrounds. Asian and Pacific Islanders, for example, confront linguistic barriers as well as economic ones. Many women are employed in small businesses or factories with unsafe working conditions and no fringe benefits such as health care. Others are reluctant—for cultural reasons—to be examined for various medical conditions.

Leigh reports severe underutilization of preventive care among women of color. Less than half of these women regularly undergo screening tests such as Pap smears or mammograms. The incidence of cervical cancer among black women is twice that among white women; rates for Hispanics and Native Americans also exceed those of whites. And, although breast, lung, and cervical cancers are the most commonly occurring cancers in Asian and Pacific Islander women, about two-thirds have never had a Pap smear and 70 percent have never had a mammogram. Due in part to high-fat diets, obesity is a problem for women of color. In 1987, about 60 percent of all Native American women—both on reservations and in urban areas—were identified as obese.

Infant mortality statistics are especially troubling, for they reflect not only the standard of living of each population but also the health of the mothers. Infant mortality rates are highest for black women, at 18.3 deaths per 1,000 live births—more than double the death rates for white infants. Native American babies have the second highest total mortality rate, followed by Puerto Rican babies.

Leigh warns against generalizations that attempt to create health profiles for these women. Exceptions to ethnic generalizations are numerous. The challenge instead, she concludes, is to refine our knowledge about these groups to the point where individualized care can reach women of color across undeniable cultural and ethnic barriers. Programs that respect cultural norms and differences, and find effective ways around structural problems of daily life—from inadequate employment and transportation to child care—have the best chance to deliver good care to women of color.

In CHAPTER THREE, "Securing American Women's Reproductive Health" Rachel Benson Gold and Cory L. Richards of the Alan Guttmacher Institute survey the most contentious matters in women's health care. The facts of American women's reproductive lives today offer sobering challenges to the health care system, and to the nation's future.

Each year, 6.4 million women in the United States become pregnant. Of these pregnancies, 2.8 million are intended. That means 56 percent are unintentional, caused by either failure to use contraception or by contraceptives that don't work.

It is sobering that nearly half of American women will have had an abortion by the time they reach 45 years of age. Thus, the problem created by government-imposed restrictions on women's right to choose affects many more American women than we commonly believe. Each year, three percent of American women of reproductive age terminate their pregnancies by abortion, most because of unintentional pregnancy. Research shows that this decision is not taken lightly; on average, most women who have abortions cite at least four reasons for doing so, including youth and unpreparedness for the responsibilities of parenthood.

About four million U.S. women give birth each year. Yet six in 10 women experience some health problems during pregnancy or delivery, half of them major problems. Proper prenatal care helps women to take steps that will avoid the problems of prematurity and low birth weight. Yet a startling one-quarter of all women who gave birth in 1990 received no prenatal care in the first three months of pregnancy. The lack of care for pregnant women shows in the stark statistic that 19 countries had lower rates of infant mortality—death before one year of age—than the richest nation, the United States, in 1989.

Unfortunately, the number of childless women 35 to 44 years old who have an impaired ability to have children grew by 37 percent from 1982 to 1988. Thirteen percent of women of reproductive age are either infertile or have problems conceiving. Sexually transmitted diseases (STDs) are a leading cause of infertility. Each year, up to an estimated 150,000 women become infertile due to STDs. In one instance out of seven, just a single episode of pelvic inflammatory disease results in infertility. At current rates, at least one in four Americans will contract an STD at some point. Yet only a third of sexually active teenage girls is screened for STDs each year.

Gold and Richards believe that our current health care system is inadequate and "inherently coercive." It often makes maternity care available and pays for it, but not contraceptives and abortion. It often provides access to sterilization procedures, but not to abortion. Further, fear of malpractice litigation has sharply curbed the availability of prenatal care and other obstetrical services—whole areas of the nation are underserved or lacking in providers.

Access is a particular problem for Medicaid patients, who face both an overall shortage of health care providers and the reluctance of many to serve low-income patients. At most, 5,400 U.S. clinics deliver prenatal care to poor women, and no prenatal clinics exist in more than one-fourth of all counties. The number of abortion providers has fallen since 1985, and clinical training in the procedures has been inadequate for medical residents and interns. Services are unevenly distributed geographically, too; more than a quarter of the women who had abortions in 1988 had to travel at least 50 miles from home.

What of the future? The authors argue that "America's failure to make a commitment to reproductive health care has meant inadequate sex education of the young." Young people receive too little information, too late to help them much. National health care reform, Gold and Richards urge, must include the full range of reproductive health services and all contraceptives. The authors are concerned that if managed care—with its "gatekeeper" feature of requiring screening examinations before providing special services—becomes the building block of health care reform, women may be denied access to needed reproductive services. Health care reform must allow individuals to seek reproductive care outside the managed care system, and be reimbursed for it.

Gold and Richards also argue for basing reproductive services eligibility on the individual, not the family unit, in order to safeguard confidentiality. Finally, even if universal care becomes a reality, to ensure women's access to facilities, they believe the nation must maintain a network of supplementary maternal-child and family planning clinics and special education programs, as other countries have done under their national health systems.

CHAPTER FOUR, "Women and Long-Term Care," by Marilyn Moon of the Urban Institute, argues that women are particularly vulnerable with respect to long-term care because of their longer life expectancy and because, at any age, women are also more likely than men to suffer functional limitations, especially problems that limit movement such as arthritis and osteoporosis. Long-term care needs increase dramatically for people over age 80, when American women in particular face a loss of independence and lower quality of life because the services and support they need are absent. Consider these facts:

• The typical woman age 75 and over has an annual income of $9,170—less than one-third the yearly cost of a nursing home. In 1991, more than a quarter of all elderly women living alone were poor. More than two-thirds of elderly women living alone had incomes less than twice the poverty level (a scanty $13,064). The picture is far worse for minority women—almost nine out of 10 black women living alone had incomes below $13,064.

· Women are more than three times likelier to serve as caregivers to their husbands than vice versa. And wives can expect to live for 17 years beyond their husbands, on average. The irony of women's longer life expectancy is that, when they in turn need supportive services, no family member is there; hence our conventional image of old age as "an old lady in a nursing home."

· Contrary to what many believe, Medicare (the government program for the elderly and disabled) pays less than two percent of the costs of nursing home care; it's mostly an acute care program covering hospital and doctor bills. And a year in a nursing home costs about $30,000—in high-cost regions, as much as $45,000.

· In-home and community-based services are expanding rapidly, but many older women receive no formal care at home despite substantial disabilities.

Dr. Moon notes that even defining long-term care is difficult, when needs vary greatly: when do acute medical services blur into long-term care? Are the services needed by women as much for support (housework, bathing, cooking) as for medical care? Given the variety of needs, and swift change as women age, Moon thinks an ideal long-term care setting requires three things:

· maximum flexibility and individual choice;
· a focus on nonhospital settings, since hospitals are arranged for the convenience of providers in the short-term, not for the long-term comfort of the population that is served; and
· allowance for informal care by relatives and friends.

Moon analyzes the flaws in the current public programs for long-term care, concluding that both Medicaid and Medicare are inadequate, and that the patchwork of other programs with elderly care components are not widely available nor adequately funded. States are already reeling under the impact of Medicaid costs, which rose 14.3 percent in 1992 alone; long-term care now absorbs about 34 percent of Medicaid program costs.

As to private insurance, fewer than two million Americans have purchased long-term care policies, which are prohibitively expensive and limited, with deductibles as well. Insurers also screen for severely disabling conditions, which makes the people who need care most the least eligible. For a 79-year-old, the average premium may be more than $4,000; only six percent of the elderly population could afford such a policy without spending more than five percent of their income on this limited insurance.

"If the current picture for long-term care financing looks bleak," writes Moon, "the future looks even worse." The elderly population will likely grow by 73 percent in the next 30 years, while the population of those over 85, who are most likely to need long-term care, will rise by 115 percent. Even optimistic projections of private insurance growth suggest that, 30 years from now, only half the nation's elderly will have long-term care protection. As a result, with no government policy change, Medicaid expenditures on long-term care, net of inflation, would triple.

What are the options for reform? Long-term care is a classically good candidate for a public program: almost no one can bear the costs out of income and savings alone. But, shared across a whole population, adequate long-term care will cost any individual quite little. However, Moon thinks a full social insurance program for long-term care is unlikely, as it would add up to $60 billion annually to the national budget at a time when many other social needs clamor for attention. Moon concludes that the most likely direction for reform is some form of limited social insurance, beginning with a large expansion of home care and support services as opposed to far more costly institutional care.

TRENDS TO WATCH

The American Woman's statistical chapters explore demographics first, followed by a look at women's educational status. The economic status of American women is examined through the numbers on employment; earnings and benefits; and income and poverty. Elections and Officials has its own section.

The lights and shadows of American women's situation appear in the statistics. Let us mention a few of them:

• Although as of 1991 white women remained the most likely to have had 12 or more years of schooling, it was among black women that the proportion with at least 12 years of schooling increased most dramatically between 1970 and 1991.
• Unfortunately, lack of education is a particular problem among foreign-born Hispanic women between the ages of 25 and 54, over 40 percent of whom had no more than eight years of schooling as of 1989.
• Female labor force participation is at an all-time high. In 1992, nearly six

out of every 10 women were working or looking for work. From 1960 to 1992, the female proportion of the labor force grew from 33 percent to 45 percent.

- Most working mothers work full time, and the proportion who do has increased even among women with toddlers. In 1992, nearly 70 percent of employed mothers who had children under age three worked full time, up from 64 percent in 1982.

- Through the 1980s and into the early 1990s, the unemployment rate for black women was more than twice that for white women. The rate increased between 1990 and 1992 for women in every group, but the increase was sharpest for Hispanic women.

- Between 1975 and 1992, women's presence increased noticeably in professional jobs (e.g., architect and physician), but in skilled blue-collar trades (e.g., carpenter and welder), the proportions of women—small in 1975—remained small in 1992.

- American women are now earning 75 cents for every dollar earned by men, up from 64 cents in 1980. However, this is as much a result of declines in men's wages as increases in women's wages.

- The net increase in family incomes between 1971 and 1991 was driven almost entirely by the gains for married couples with working wives, the only family type for which real income increased both significantly and steadily over the period.

- A family headed by a woman is more likely to be poor than a married couple or one headed by a man. When a family with children is headed by a woman, the odds that it is in poverty approach one in two.

- Black women are only half as likely as white women to be awarded child support. Poverty rates are very high among mothers who have not been awarded child support.

- When personal income from all sources was counted, men age 65 and over received an average of $20,381 in 1991, about 80 percent more than women in that age group averaged.

- In 1991, women age 65 and over were less than half as likely as the men in that age group to be receiving pensions and, if they were, the average amount ($5,186) was far lower than for men ($9,855).

- A greater proportion of males than of females lacked health insurance of any kind in 1991, mostly due to the fact that a larger proportion of females than of males had Medicaid coverage. Still, over half of all uninsured women are in their prime reproductive years.

- More than a fifth of those with no health insurance are children under age 18. Another 15 percent are children over age 18 who live with their parents.

LOOKING AHEAD

The statistics on women's status paint a mixed picture. Whether the picture is hopeful or shadowed is ambiguous, depending in part on the borders where a woman stands—borders of income, race, occupation, class, and family responsibility.

One thing we know for sure: improving women's health status does matter. Two of the largest barriers to women's economic security are low incomes and limited access to health care. Of course, the two are integrally related: women's lower incomes impede their ability to get the health care they need. We at WREI believe that once the nation solves the problems of access for women and children, we will have gone a long way toward solving the health care problems of the country as a whole.

The goal of feminists' continuing efforts to improve women's health has been to expand knowledge, access, and availability of care for all women. This volume is part of that ongoing campaign for awareness and action.

In Review
July 1991–
June 1993

IN REVIEW:
JULY 1991–JUNE 1993[1]

THE PERIOD BETWEEN July 1, 1991 and June 30, 1993 was a stunningly eventful one for American women. So much happened that to include every significant occurrence or trend—every state court decision or legislative initiative that could affect women, every newsworthy research development with implications for women—would have meant a book-length "In Review."

One of the dominant issues was sexual harassment and the efforts to conceal it or deny it. It was as if, over the 24 months, the corners of the national rug were lifted one by one and there turned out to be sexual harassment under them all. Outrage about sexual harassment helped boost a record number of women into Congress, another of the most significant developments of the period. A third was surely the survival of the constitutional right to abortion despite years of state challenges and growing suspense as the make-up of the Supreme Court changed. To be sure, the right is currently more restricted than under *Roe* v. *Wade,* but its future seems fundamentally secure.

The presidential election campaigns, and Hillary Rodham Clinton's role in her husband's campaign, are absent from these pages. Hillary Clinton was an important issue from the beginning. Controversy about her and about what people hoped—or feared—she represented surfaced early in the cam-

[1]Much of the credit for In Review in this edition of *The American Woman* belongs to Christy Chandler, who tackled a monumental task with spirit, intelligence, and determination, not to mention superb organization. The editors also wish to thank Stacie Leimas, whose many contributions to In Review included invaluable assistance and admirable persistence in readying the material for publication.

paign and persisted throughout, powerfully illustrating just how much ambivalence there still is in America about women's proper place.

The editors hope that what has been included in "In Review" in *The American Woman 1994-95* will stir the reader's memory of an extraordinary time.

1991

July 1 / President Bush nominates Clarence Thomas, a conservative Republican judge, to replace retiring Justice Thurgood Marshall on the Supreme Court. Thomas, who is black, is presently a judge on the U.S. Court of Appeals for the District of Columbia Circuit.

July 1 / *Time* magazine's parent company announces that Elizabeth P. Valk will be *Time's* new publisher. She will be the first woman to hold that position.

July 5 / The National Organization for Women (NOW), which is celebrating its twenty-fifth anniversary this year, opens its annual convention in New York City. Patricia Ireland, NOW's vice president, vows an all-out effort to stop the confirmation of Clarence Thomas to the Supreme Court.

July 14 / The National Women's Political Caucus, which celebrates its twentieth birthday this year, winds up its four-day convention in Washington, DC. The group has adopted a unanimous resolution opposing the confirmation of Clarence Thomas as a Supreme Court justice.

July 15 / Operation Rescue's anti-abortion activists begin demonstrations outside clinics in Wichita, Kansas.

July 15 / The August issue of *Vanity Fair* appears on newsstands. A brown paper wrapper conceals the cover, a photograph of Demi Moore, very pregnant and naked except for her strategically placed hands. The photo stimulates much public discussion and some punditry by feminist columnists on the subject of how society perceives women's sexuality and pregnancy.

July 16 / The Michigan Supreme Court lets stand a lower court decision holding that a woman who took drugs while she was pregnant could not be charged with violating the state's law against delivering drugs to a minor.

July 17 / The General Accounting Office (GAO), a congressional watchdog agency, reports that nearly 20 percent of federally sponsored programs under the Job Training Partnership Act (JTPA) discriminate against women and blacks. The $4 billion JTPA program is the largest single job training program in the federal government. In testimony prepared for a hearing today, Assistant Comptroller General Lawrence H. Thompson reports that while women are receiving more classroom training than men, the evidence suggests that "many women receive classroom training for lower-wage occupations." Proposed amendments to the JTPA address many of the GAO findings.

July 17 / The largest cash settlement ever awarded in a discrimination case is announced today by the Equal Employment Opportunity Commission (EEOC). The case involves women telephone workers employed by Western Electric between 1965 and 1977. Under the settlement worked out with AT&T Technologies, Inc., a $66 million award will be shared by at least 13,000 women who, when they became pregnant, were denied benefits—such as retaining accrued seniority and reinstatement in their jobs—that the company provided to workers on medical leave for other conditions. A spokesman for AT&T tells reporters, "The practices that were challenged . . . were common in business and industry at the time . . . It is a far different place at AT&T today."

July 22 / The *New York Times* notes that the July/August issue of *Ms.* magazine marks the beginning of its second year as an ad-free, fully reader-supported publication, with a circulation of 150,000—enough to put the magazine in healthy financial shape.

July 23 / In Wichita, U.S. district judge Patrick Kelly issues a court order barring Operation Rescue's anti-abortion demonstrators from blocking the entrances to clinics or physically harassing staff and patients.

July 23 / A major study released today by the Manpower Demonstration Research Corporation (MDRC) found that the $1 billion-a-year "From Welfare to Work" experimental program to train welfare-recipient parents represents a solid investment for the states, and that program participants generally earned hundreds of dollars more than nonparticipants. MDRC president Judith Gueron reports that seven of the nine programs studied provided welfare recipients (mostly mothers) with organized job searches and unpaid work experience, not with education or training. However, the state programs that will be established under the 1988 welfare reform law will include more remedial education and job training than in the programs included in this study.

July 23 / An $18 million, five-year survey on teenage sexual activity has been canceled by Secretary of Health and Human Services Louis Sullivan, aides to Sullivan tell reporters. Conservative groups have complained that the questions are too explicit. The government-funded survey was designed to gather information needed for developing policies to combat AIDS, teen pregnancy, alcohol and drug use, and other problems.

July 24 / "Workers Find It Tough Going Filing Lawsuits Over Job Bias," according to today's *New York Times*. Steven Holmes writes that people who believe they have suffered race or sex discrimination on the job have a very hard time finding lawyers to represent them. The reason: "The cases are time-consuming, difficult to win, and bring far less money than other civil litigation like personal injury suits, which permit punitive damages."

July 24 / Officials of Skull and Bones announce that women will be allowed to join the oldest and most famous of the secret societies at Yale. The decision to admit women was narrowly agreed to by a vote of alumni members after undergraduate members urged that women be permitted to join. Bonesman President Bush declines to comment.

July 25 / Two studies published in today's *New England Journal of Medicine* found that women are much less likely than men to receive high-tech diagnostic and treatment procedures for heart disease even when they are as ill as men. The researchers report that among women and men with similarly severe conditions, the men were significantly more likely to have angiography, coronary bypass surgery, or balloon angioplasty.

July 29 / A study released today suggests that the relatively small proportion of women among executive headhunters may partially account for the "glass ceiling"—the barrier that prevents women and minorities from reaching top management positions. James H. Kennedy of *Executive Recruiter News,* which did the study, says that only 22.5 percent of the key principals in the 2,286 search firms are women, but he also notes that the number of women is increasing dramatically.

July 30 / House Speaker Thomas Foley dedicates Room H-235 in the U.S. Capitol—known for three decades as the Congresswomen's Reading Room—as the Lindy Claiborne Boggs Reading Room. Boggs, who served in the House of Representatives (D-LA) for 17 years, was one of the founders of the Congresswomen's Caucus (now the Congressional Caucus for Women's Issues) and of WREI, on whose board she now serves.

August 1 / The U.S. Court of Appeals in St. Louis, ruling in *Michelson* v. *Leser,* holds that in a bankruptcy case local governments can get all of the child support arrearage assigned to them by the custodial parent before unsecured creditors get anything.

August 6 / The Justice Department files a motion on behalf of Operation Rescue, the anti-abortion group that is fighting Judge Patrick Kelly's court order of July 23. Judge Kelly calls the Justice Department's action political, and refers to the "mayhem and distress" that Operation Rescue's activities have unleashed on Wichita. Hundreds of anti-abortion protesters trying to block access to clinics have been arrested on charges of trespassing and loitering.

August 8 / Secretary of Labor Lynn Martin releases her department's report on the glass ceiling. The findings are not encouraging: only 6.6 percent of employees at the executive level nationwide are women and only 2.6 percent are members of minority groups. The report was compiled from surveys of businesses—including nine Fortune 500 companies—as well as discussions with representatives of management, and business, labor, civil rights, and women's groups.

August 12 / The Justice Department announces that it will appeal U.S. district judge Jackson Kiser's ruling (June 17, 1991) that Virginia Military Institute (VMI) can continue to exclude women even though it is partially supported by taxpayers. VMI maintains that admitting women would destroy the mystique of male bonding that is the essence of its educational program.

August 15 / U.S. district judge George Wood rules that the Detroit public school system cannot exclude girls from the new schools it designed for male inner-city, at-risk youths. The judge orders that the schools, which are scheduled to open in a few weeks, may open only when a compromise is reached to allow girls to attend.

August 18 / Wilma Mankiller, chief of the Cherokee Nation of Oklahoma, is the subject of *Parade* magazine's cover story.

August 20 / Ortho Pharmaceuticals announces the results of its latest survey of the contraceptive choices of American women—the first time since the annual survey was first conducted 23 years ago that Ortho has made the results public. Findings included a large increase in the number of women—particularly women over age 35—using birth control pills.

August 20 / Marcia Greenberger, co-president of the National Women's Law Center, announces that the center is opposing the confirmation of Clarence Thomas to the Supreme Court. Greenberger tells reporters that Thomas's record "shows no commitment to core constitutional rights or statutory protections for women."

August 20 / Rep. Thomas Downey (D-NY) announces that he will hold hearings next month on the Bush administration's proposed child care regulations. Controversy centers on the regulation that would bar a state from imposing any requirements on government-subsidized day care providers that the state does not also impose on similar categories of unsubsidized day care providers. In effect, the regulation seems to mean that if a state wants to regulate any child care providers it must regulate them all.

August 25 / An article in today's *New York Times* says that a little-known amendment authored by Rep. Louise Slaughter (D-NY) and enacted by Congress in 1990 may help thousands of immigrant women escape from domestic violence without risking deportation. The amendment allows the spouse or child of an abuser to file for permanent residence without having to get the agreement of the abusive spouse or parent.

August 25 / The Families and Work Institute releases a survey showing that state governments have been at the forefront in making workplace changes to help employees accommodate the demands of family and work. The institute found that policies such as onsite day care, flextime, and family leave were more often found in state governments than in the private sector.

August 25 / Less than three percent of the Fortune 500 companies' top executive positions, and less than five percent of those companies' directorships, were held by women in 1990, according to a study released today by the Feminist Majority Foundation.

August 25 / Operation Rescue ends its demonstrations in Wichita.

August 26 / The *New York Times* reports on a new survey of 600 college coaches which found that male coaches are paid, on average, $9,900 more than female coaches. The average gap is about $7,400 when football and basketball are excluded. The study was conducted by Ellen Staurowsky, director of athletics and physical education at William Smith College in Geneva, New York.

August 26 / The National Center for Health Statistics reports that marriage rates have fallen to their lowest point in two decades, largely because people are waiting longer to marry for the first time and divorced people are waiting longer to remarry.

August 29 / Young teenage girls who became pregnant in 1988 were more likely to have their babies than to have abortions, according to a report released today by the Centers for Disease Control (CDC). The CDC found that of the girls under age 15 who became pregnant, 1,000 had live births for every 949 who had abortions.

September 5 / The *Washington Post* reports that the president has selected Elaine L. Chao to be the director of the Peace Corps. She is the highest ranking Asian American in the Bush administration.

September 7 / Lieutenant Paula Coughlin, a helicopter pilot and admiral's aide who is attending the Tailhook Symposium, a convention of naval aviators, is assaulted by drunken aviators who grab and paw her and try to remove her panties as she attempts to walk down a hall at the Las Vegas hotel where the convention is being held.

September 8 / Lieutenant Coughlin reports to her boss, Rear Admiral John W. Snyder, who is head of the Patuxent River Naval Air Test Center, about what happened to her last night.

September 9 / A study released today found that the medical profession is overwhelmingly sex-segregated, and that disproportionate numbers of women physicians are in positions with low status and low pay. According to the Feminist Majority Foundation and the American Medical Women's

Association, sponsors of the study, not one of the country's medical schools is headed by a woman. Moreover, men hold 98 percent of the department chairs and account for 79 percent of the faculty of medical schools. The study also found that women who are doctors make only 63.2 cents for every dollar made by male doctors.

September 16 / A nationwide campaign to provide pregnant teenagers with support and counseling on health and nutrition is launched today by the National Commission to Prevent Infant Mortality. The privately funded program provides "resource mothers"—volunteers from the community—who give advice and support to young mothers.

September 17 / The October 1991 issue of *Working Mother* magazine, released today, contains the magazine's annual ranking of the best companies for working parents and reports a great increase in the number of companies that provide child care programs and other family-related benefits. The criteria used to assess the companies included pay, advancement for women, child care support, and such benefits as job sharing and flextime.

September 19 / Convinced that Clarence Thomas would support overturning *Roe* v. *Wade,* pro-choice advocates Madeleine Kunin, Kate Michelman, Faye Wattleton, and Sarah Weddington testify before the Senate Judiciary Committee urging that Thomas not be confirmed as a Supreme Court justice.

September 20 / The *New York Times* reports that more and more rape victims are filing civil suits in an effort to seek damages for their suffering. The newspaper cites among others the case of a Texas woman who was raped in her home, which lacked a security lock because the management of her townhouse complex had not allowed her to install one. The woman won a $17 million judgment—reported to be the largest to date in a case of this type—against the management company.

September 25 / WREI presents the 1991 American Woman Award to White House correspondent Sarah McClendon.

October 1 / According to "The Growing Presence of Women in Psychiatry," an article in the Health section of today's *Washington Post,* women now make up 24 percent of all practicing psychiatrists in the United States, and 39 percent of those under age 35.

October 2 / Girls Inc. reports that its project aimed at reducing teenage pregnancy succeeded in cutting them by 50 percent. Dr. Heather Johnston Nicholson of Girls Inc. in Indianapolis directed the three-year project, in which 750 girls considered at high risk for teenage pregnancy participated. They worked on strengthening parent-daughter support systems, improving assertiveness skills, and learning about sexuality and health services.

October 2 / Peg Yorkin announces that she will give $10 million to the

Feminist Majority Foundation, the largest single donation ever made to a women's rights organization. The money will be used for the Feminist Empowerment Center, whose first project will be to campaign for RU–486, the so-called abortion pill.

October 2 / The Senate approves the Family and Medical Leave Act by a margin that would be sufficient to override a presidential veto. President Bush has promised to veto the bill, which would require employers with 50 or more employees to grant their workers up to 12 weeks unpaid leave to care for a new baby; a newly adopted child; a child or elderly parent who is ill; or in case of a worker's own serious illness.

October 3 / In Los Angeles, a superior court jury awards Janella Sue Martin, an employee of Texaco, Inc., $15 million in punitive damages and $2.67 million in compensatory damages in a sex-discrimination suit. Martin filed suit when she was rejected twice for the position of credit manager for Texaco's western region. The jury also found that Texaco had retaliated against her when she sued in 1986; the judge, Ronald Cappai, orders the company to promote Martin.

October 6 / National Public Radio breaks the story that Anita Hill, a professor of law at the University of Oklahoma's law school, last month gave Senate Judiciary Committee staffers an affidavit stating that Clarence Thomas sexually harassed her when she worked for him in the Department of Education in the early 1980s. The charge was not brought up during the committee's confirmation hearings on Thomas, which have been completed. The full Senate is scheduled to vote on the confirmation in two days.

October 7 / Controversy both about Anita Hill's allegations regarding the conduct of Clarence Thomas and about how those charges have been handled by the Senate Judiciary Committee dominates the news. Angered by what they perceive as a failure by the all-male committee to take Hill's charges seriously, female lawmakers and others urge the Senate to postpone the Thomas confirmation vote until Hill's allegations can be thoroughly aired and the truth established.

October 8 / To dramatize their demand that the Thomas confirmation vote be postponed, seven female Democratic House members march to the Senate side of the Capitol and ask to be admitted to the room where Democratic senators are caucusing. The congresswomen are denied entrance. Thomas releases a sworn statement saying that there is no truth to Hill's charges, and asks for time to clear his name. Late in the day, the Senate votes to put the vote off for a week so that the Judiciary Committee can hold hearings on the Hill allegations.

October 8 / The Congressional Caucus for Women's Issues introduces the Economic Equity Act (EEA) of 1991, a legislative package of 24 individual bills designed to promote economic equality and opportunity for women. The EEA has four sections (titles): employment opportunities, women in business, economic justice, and retirement equity.

October 9 / Findings published in today's *Journal of the American Medical Association* suggest that cocaine may attach itself to the sperm of a man who uses the drug, and enter an egg to do damage at the moment of conception. If subsequent tests confirm these results, fathers who use cocaine, as well as mothers who use the drug, may be implicated in causing birth defects in their children. The researchers say that other toxins to which fathers are exposed could also be hitchhiking on sperm.

October 10 / The National Women's Political Caucus presents its 1991 "Good Guy" awards. The recipients are Michael Tucker, star of "L.A. Law," Reps. John Lewis (D-GA) and Vic Fazio (D-CA), Senator John H. Chafee (R-RI), and political consultant Frank Greer.

October 10 / Lieutenant Paula Coughlin's complaint about the behavior of naval aviators at the Tailhook convention in September has reached Admiral J. L. Johnson, the vice chief of naval operations, who today orders the Naval Investigative Service to start an inquiry. Coughlin has been troubled by what she regards as an off-hand response to her complaint by her boss, Admiral John W. Snyder. The incidents at Tailhook are not yet public knowledge.

October 11 / Millions of Americans are riveted to their television sets today and this weekend as first Clarence Thomas and then Anita Hill testify under oath before the Senate Judiciary Committee. Their accounts are so at odds with one another that it is clear to most observers that only one of them can be telling the truth.

October 12 / Republicans on the Senate Judiciary Committee raise questions about Anita Hill's veracity and mental stability, suggesting that she fantasized or fabricated her charges against Thomas. Thomas again asserts that he has been wronged and that his life has been made "a living hell."

October 13 / Four witnesses testify to the Judiciary Committee that Anita Hill told them of Thomas's sexual harassment at the time it was occurring or shortly thereafter. They also testify as to Hill's good character and emotional stability. They are closely questioned by Senator Arlen Specter (R-PA), who asks whether Hill gave them the detailed descriptions that she gave the committee. He also demands to know why they did not urge her to quit her job or protest. These witnesses are followed by four female witnesses for Thomas, who paint Hill as a combative, self-centered woman. One says that Hill wanted a more than professional relationship with Thomas and was disappointed when he did not respond.

October 14 / Back in Oklahoma, Anita Hill makes a brief statement: "It was suggested that I had fantasies, that I was a spurned woman, and that I had a martyr complex. I will not dignify those theories except to assure you that I did not imagine the conduct to which I testified. I have been deeply hurt and offended by the nature of the attacks on my character."

October 15 / The Senate votes 52 to 48 to confirm Clarence Thomas as a Supreme Court justice. Results of a poll taken on the evening of October 13 and published today show that many more of the people surveyed believe Clarence Thomas than believe Anita Hill. This is apparently true of both men and women and of both blacks and whites.

October 16 / Feminists react to the Senate's handling of Hill's allegations and the conduct of the hearings themselves with a vow to put more women in Congress.

October 16 / At a news conference in the emergency room of Chicago's Cook County Hospital, the American Medical Association launches a campaign to combat domestic violence. Dr. Antonia C. Novello, the U.S. surgeon general, notes that domestic violence is the single largest cause of injury to women in the United States.

October 21 / According to today's edition of *Roll Call,* the unofficial newspaper of Congress, 1992 is expected to be an exciting year for women candidates. Quoting Jane Danowitz of the Women's Campaign Fund and Ellen Malcolm of EMILY's List, *Roll Call* reports that redistricting and the country's anti-incumbent mood, as well as the anger sparked by the Senate's handling of the Clarence Thomas hearings, have produced unprecedented opportunities to elect women to office next year.

October 24 / Rep. Barbara-Rose Collins (D-MI) introduces a bill to require the Bureau of Labor Statistics to calculate the dollar value of the unpaid housework that women and men do. She proposes that when its dollar value is established, housework be included in the Gross National Product.

October 29 / The secretary of the Navy, H. Lawrence Garrett, learns that five women in addition to Coughlin have complained of being assaulted at the Tailhook convention and orders the Navy's inspector general to begin an investigation. The public first learns about Tailhook when newspapers report today that the Navy is investigating incidents at a convention of naval aviators in Las Vegas last month.

November 4 / The Navy relieves Admiral Snyder of his command of the Patuxent Naval Air Station "for his apparent failure" to take action on Lieutenant Coughlin's complaint.

November 7 / A study described as the most comprehensive survey of the child care market since the mid-1970s is released. The study, which was funded by the Department of Health and Human Services, the Department of Education, and the National Association for the Education of Young Children, found that while enrollment in child care centers has increased fourfold in the past 15 years, "quality"—as measured by child-staff ratios, group size, and staff turnover—has decreased.

November 7 / A memorial to honor the estimated 10,000 women who served in the Vietnam War receives final approval for construction. The memorial, a bronze sculpture by Glenna Goodacre of New Mexico, will be placed near the Vietnam Memorial wall. The scheduled dedication date is Veterans Day 1993.

November 12 / The U.S. Merit Systems Protection Board reports that a number of federal departments and agencies have programs to try to meet the needs of employees caring for children and elders. The programs offered include 65 onsite child care centers, the use of flextime and flexplace, and educational programs that prepare employees for elder care and make referrals to community resources.

November 13 / The House passes the Family and Medical Leave Act, but the majority is more than 30 votes short of the two-thirds that would be needed to override an expected presidential veto.

November 14 / *The Corporate Reference Guide to Work-Family Programs*, a 437-page documentation of work and family policies in corporate America, is released by the Families and Work Institute. Johnson & Johnson, IBM, Aetna Life and Casualty, and Corning scored highest on the overall scale of the institute's "Family Friendly" index, a yardstick by which companies can assess their own work-family policies and programs.

November 15 / The Justice Department files papers asking the U.S. Court of Appeals for the Fourth Circuit to overturn the June 1991 ruling upholding the Virginia Military Institute's admission policy excluding women.

November 22 / President Bush signs the Civil Rights Act of 1991 into law. The product of two years of negotiations and compromise between Congress and the White House, the legislation is designed to restore and strengthen laws protecting women and minorities from job discrimination. It also expands the remedies for women who are victims of intentional discrimination.

November 29 / Norplant, the contraceptive implant that is inserted into a woman's upper arm, is becoming more and more widely used in the United States, reports today's *New York Times*. Over 25,000 doctors and nurses are trained to insert Norplant and upwards of 100,000 women are now using it.

November 30 / In Guangzhou, China, the U.S. women's soccer team defeats Norway's team to win the World Cup trophy for women. This is the first international soccer championship to be won by a U.S. team of either sex.

December 4 / A study released today by the Times Mirror Center for the People and the Press found that 59 percent of the 2,020 adults surveyed about current political issues agreed that "the country would be better off if there were more women serving in Congress in the future." Seventy-one percent of the survey respondents said they had a favorable view of the women's movement (an increase from the 63 percent who were favorable when asked the same question in 1985).

December 5 / President Bush signs Public Law 102-190, repealing the statutes that prohibited women in the Air Force and Navy from being assigned to combat aircraft.

December 5 / This year, 112 American women earned Ph.D.'s in mathematics, accounting for nearly one in four of all math doctorates granted to U.S. citizens in 1991, according to today's *Washington Post*. The information came from the November 1991 issue of *Notices*, published by the American Mathematical Society.

December 7 / Helen Thomas is elected vice president of the Gridiron Club of Washington, a social organization for Washington-based journalists. United Press International's long-time White House correspondent, Thomas is the first woman to hold one of the top four offices in the club, which first admitted women in 1975—90 years after it was founded.

December 9 / A survey of Senate staffers released today by the Congressional Management Foundation finds that women fill 31 percent of the higher-paying jobs—administrative assistants, legislative directors, press secretaries, and state directors. The female/male earnings ratio among Senate staffers is 78 percent—narrower than in either the federal civil service or the private sector.

December 10 / In today's *Washington Post*, Don Colburn sums up the findings of a new study on the detection of depression in men and women: "[It] helps explain why depression appears to be about twice as prevalent among women as among men: mental health specialists tend to overdiagnose it in women, and doctors tend to underdiagnose it in men."

December 11 / A woman's chances of surviving breast cancer are not significantly better today than they were 20 years ago, concludes a study released today by the General Accounting Office. Survival rates after detection have increased somewhat, but not enough to counter the increasing incidence of breast cancer cases, according to the report.

December 15 / Patricia Ireland takes office as president of the National Organization for Women (NOW), succeeding Molly Yard. Ireland says that her philosophy is the same as Yard's and that NOW's agenda will continue to include protecting legal abortion and publicizing the increase in rapes and violence against women in the home.

December 17 / A Minnesota court decision filed today has granted Karen Thompson, a lesbian, legal guardianship of her partner, Sharon Kowalski, who has been disabled since suffering brain injuries in an auto accident in 1983. The decision overturns a lower court ruling that appointed a friend of the disabled woman's family as guardian.

December 18 / Forty states froze or cut benefits under the Aid to Families with Dependent Children Program in 1991, according to a study issued today by the Center for Budget and Policy Priorities and the Center for the Study of the States.

1992

January 7 / Susan Bianchi-Sand is named executive director of the National Committee on Pay Equity, a Washington-based coalition of labor, women's, and civil rights groups. Bianchi-Sand spent 18 years as a union organizer before joining the committee.

January 15 / *Daughters of the Dust,* which was written, produced, and directed by Julie Dash, opens today in New York City. Reported to be the first feature length film by a black woman to get commercial release, the film is booked in more than 20 cities.

January 17 / The income growth rate of dual-earner families (adjusted for inflation) was less than one percent per year during the 1980s, according to a report released today by Congress's Joint Economic Committee. The report attributes what gains there were to more working wives and wives working more hours.

January 17 / It is not an offense to the dignity and decorum of court proceedings for women lawyers to wear pantsuits in the courtroom, opines the New York County Lawyers' Association's ethics committee. According to today's *New York Times,* the committee was responding to a query by a Manhattan law firm.

January 21 / The U.S. Supreme Court agrees to review a challenge to the constitutionality of the 1989 Pennsylvania law that tightly restricts access to abortion. Many see this case, *Planned Parenthood of Southeastern Pennsylvania* v. *Casey,* as providing an opportunity for the Court to overturn the 1973 *Roe* v. *Wade* decision that legalized abortion.

January 21 / New Jersey's governor Jim Florio signs into law a bill that will make a number of changes in the state's welfare system. One is to deny an automatic increase in aid to a mother who has another baby after joining welfare. Other changes will allow a welfare family to retain more of its earnings from a job and will allow a family that gets off welfare because of employment to keep Medicaid health benefits for 24 months instead of 12 months. Some of the reforms will require waivers of federal regulations.

January 22 / On the nineteenth anniversary of *Roe* v. *Wade,* 70,000 people opposed to legal abortion march on Capitol Hill in protest. President Bush speaks to the crowd by telephone and commends their efforts to make abortion illegal.

January 31 / A condom for women gets tentative approval as a disease prevention device from an expert panel convened by the Food and Drug Administration. Cynthia A. Pearson of the National Women's Health Network says that the device, called a vaginal pouch, would "give women more control over their exposure to sexually transmitted diseases, including AIDS."

February 1 / Breaking a 24-year-old record that was set by her father, John Somogyi, Kristen Somogyi becomes New Jersey's leading high school basketball scorer. She is a student at St. Peter's High School in New Brunswick.

February 2 / Today's *New York Times* reports that since the Anita Hill–Clarence Thomas hearings last October, the organization 9to5 has been getting about 200 telephone calls a day from working women, nearly all of them concerning sexual harassment. Calls averaged about 200 a week before the hearings, according to Karen Nussbaum, executive director of 9to5.

February 3 / Shirley D. Peterson, President Bush's choice for the position of commissioner of the Internal Revenue Service (IRS), is confirmed by the Senate. She will be the first woman to head the IRS in its 129-year history.

February 6 / On the sixth annual National Girls and Women in Sports Day, the Women's Sports Foundation honors golfer Nancy Lopez with its Flo Hyman Award, which was established in memory of the late Olympic volleyball player.

February 7 / Nannerl Overholser Keohane, president of Wellesley College, a women's college in Wellesley, Massachusetts, announces that its recently completed fundraising drive raised $167 million—a record for a private liberal arts college.

February 12 / The American Association of University Women releases *How Schools Shortchange Girls,* a report synthesizing the major studies of girls in education. The report concludes that girls still face discrimination, unequal treatment, and sexual harassment in school, and that girls' skills and self-confidence suffer as a result—especially once they reach high school.

February 18 / The Refugee Women Council in New York holds a conference, "Refugee and Immigrant Women's Right to Know," at the Hunter College School of Social Work. According to Le Lieu Browne, founder of the council, problems for newly arrived women include isolation, illiteracy, and domestic abuse.

February 18 / The Conference Board releases a new report, *The Emerging Role of the Work-Family Manager.* According to the report, during the past two years several hundred U.S. firms have initiated work-family positions to develop, coordinate, and promote such policies as child care, elderly care, maternity and paternity leave, and flextime.

February 18 / A Food and Drug Administration advisory panel begins analyzing the research that has been done on silicone breast implants, and especially on the risks and consequences of ruptures and leaks. Case studies have shown leaks in silicone implants to be associated with autoimmune diseases such as lupus or scleroderma, but none of the evidence presented so far is regarded as conclusive.

February 19 / The Census Bureau releases a report showing that the percentage of Americans in the middle-income category shrank from 71.2 percent in 1969 to 63.3 percent in 1989. Over the same period, the percentage in the high-income category grew from 10.9 percent to 14.7 percent; the percentage in the low-income category grew from 17.9 percent to 22.1 percent.

February 19 / The U.S. Navy announces a new policy on sexual harassment in which violators of certain anti-harassment rules will be automatically fired "on the first substantiated incident." A Navy spokeswoman says that until now commanders have had the option but were not required to dismiss personnel who violate the most serious anti-harassment rules.

February 19 / A federal appeals court decision overturning a federal policy that gave special preference to women in obtaining radio and television broadcasting licenses is issued today—long after its author, Clarence Thomas, left the appellate bench for a seat on the Supreme Court. The decision, written when Thomas was on the appeals court, is based on the premise that the policy discriminates against men.

February 23 / The 1992 Winter Olympics in Albertville, France, come to an end and American women take home nine of the 11 medals won by U.S. athletes. All five of the gold medals won by Americans at Albertville were captured by women.

February 26 / In a unanimous ruling handed down today in *Franklin* v. *Gwinnett County Public Schools,* the U.S. Supreme Court holds that students can sue for monetary damages for sexual harassment and other forms of sex discrimination under Title IX of the 1972 Education Act, which bars sex discrimination in schools and colleges that receive federal funds. Women's advocates predict that the ruling will convert Title IX into a powerful new weapon against sex discrimination on campus.

February 27 / The Senate confirms the nomination of Barbara Franklin to be secretary of commerce. She is the second woman ever to hold that position—Juanita Kreps, appointed by President Carter, was the first. Franklin joins two other women currently serving as cabinet officials in the Bush administration: Lynn Martin, secretary of labor, and Carla Hills, U.S. trade representative.

February 27 / Korn/Ferry International, a worldwide executive search firm based in New York and Los Angeles, reports that the number of its female placements at the senior corporate level rose from five percent in 1981 to 16 percent in 1991.

March 1 / The world record for the women's 100-meter freestyle swimming event is broken at the U.S. Olympic trials by 19-year-old Jenny Thompson, a first-year student at Stanford University. It has been 59 years since an American woman last held the world record.

March 2 / Derrick Bell, who was the first black professor to be tenured at Harvard Law School, files a discrimination complaint against Harvard for its failure to hire black women and other minorities for tenured positions at the law school. Bell's action, filed with the Education Department's Office of Civil Rights, comes a few days after the law school voted to grant tenure to four more white men. In 1990, Bell began an unpaid leave of absence from the university, vowing not to teach another day at the law school until it put a black woman on its faculty.

March 3 / A report released today by Catalyst, a New York–based research organization, finds that women in corporate America face not only glass ceilings that inhibit upward mobility, but also glass walls that prevent lateral movement within companies. The result is that women are deprived of the broad management experience necessary to move upward.

March 5 / Nearly 50 U.S. senators and their spouses attend the second in a series of seminars on "gender dynamics." The event, held in the U.S. Capitol, includes a two-hour discussion led by professor Deborah Tannen, author of the book *You Just Don't Understand: Women and Men in Conversation*. Senators Al Gore of Tennessee and Barbara Mikulski of Maryland are the hosts of the event.

March 11 / The Senate Labor and Human Resources Committee approves legislation amending the Civil Rights Act to remove the cap on monetary damages that women can receive for job discrimination.

March 11 / A study released today by the National Collegiate Athletic Association indicates that men's collegiate athletic programs are still getting more money than women's programs—this despite the fact that Title IX, barring sex discrimination in education, has been the law for 20 years.

March 14 / Today's *New York Times* reports on a team of AIDS educators that visits beauty salons in New York's Harlem neighborhoods, where team members talk to the customers about AIDS, answer questions about the disease, and distribute educational materials and condoms. The team, which has reportedly reached more than 8,000 women since the project began in 1988, works for Women in Crisis, an organization that also concerns itself with drug and alcohol addiction in women.

March 16 / Effective today, Dade County, Florida has a family and medical leave law. It requires Dade companies with 50 or more employees (and any company that does business with the county) to allow workers unpaid leave of up to 90 days for childbirth, adoption, or caring for a sick relative.

March 17 / Carol Moseley-Braun wins the Illinois Democratic Senate primary, beating incumbent Alan Dixon. The fact that Dixon was among the senators who voted to confirm Clarence Thomas to the Supreme Court is believed to have had a lot to do with Moseley-Braun's success today— exit polls reportedly show that women are voting for her in droves. If she wins the general election in November, she will be the first black woman and the fourth black person ever to serve in the U.S. Senate.

March 19 / United Nations Secretary General Boutros Ghali receives Julie Andrews at a luncheon today. Andrews has been named goodwill ambassador by the United Nations Development Fund for Women, known as "Unifem." Her responsibilities will include traveling around the world to promote Unifem's projects for women.

March 19 / The number of female drivers involved in fatal traffic accidents is on the rise, according to a report released today by the Centers for Disease Control. A study conducted by Maria Vegega of the National Highway Traffic Safety Administration found that compared with 1982, fatalities in 1990 were 13 percent higher for women and three percent lower for men.

March 20 / The Bush administration issues revised regulations implementing the so-called gag rule—the rule that bars family planning clinics which receive federal funds from giving women any information about abortion. (Because of court challenges, the rule has yet to go into effect.) The guidelines announced today allow physicians—but not nurses or other clinic personnel—to discuss abortion with patients but not to refer women to abortion clinics.

March 24 / Donna Redel is elected chair of the Commodity Exchange of New York, becoming the first woman to head a U.S. futures exchange.

March 29 / Home sewing seems to be enjoying something of a renaissance, according to today's *New York Times*. The *Times* reports that after two decades of slow or no growth, 1991 sales of patterns and sewing machines were up significantly compared to 1990.

March 31 / The National Aeronautics and Space Administration announces its newly selected astronauts. Among them is Lieutenant Commander Wendy B. Lawrence, who is the first female Navy aviator to become an astronaut. Lawrence's father, retired Vice Admiral William P. Lawrence, is a long-time advocate of equity for military women.

April 5 / Half a million people march in Washington, DC in support of abortion rights. Today's March for Women's Lives is reported to be one of the largest political events in the city's history.

April 6 / The Communications Workers of America elect Barbara J. Easterling secretary-treasurer, the union's second highest office. Easterling is the first woman to be made secretary-treasurer of a major industrial union.

April 12 / Today's *Washington Post* publishes the findings from the National Women's Political Caucus's annual survey of women in appointed state cabinet positions. For the first time in the survey's six-year history, the governor with the largest percentage of women in his or her cabinet is a Republican—Governor William Weld of Massachusetts, whose cabinet is 45.5 percent female.

April 16 / The Food and Drug Administration orders sharp restrictions on the use of silicone gel breast implants while studies of their safety are carried out. Women who have had breast cancer surgery will be able to get the implants, but only a few thousand women seeking cosmetic implants will be allowed to have them, and those women will have to agree to participate in clinical studies.

April 19 / Violent crimes, including rapes, rose dramatically in 1991, according to findings released today by the Justice Department. The department's report, which was based on a survey of crime victims, found that the number of rapes and attempted rapes was 207,610 in 1991 compared to 130,260 in 1990—a 59 percent increase in reported incidents.

April 23 / Two studies published in today's *New England Journal of Medicine* found large regional differences in the rate at which women with early stage breast cancer and their physicians opted for lumpectomies rather than mastectomies. The data on which the studies were based were gathered in 1986, after publication of a study showing that lumpectomies and mastectomies are equally effective for early stage cancer. An editorial accompanying the studies notes that the breast-sparing alternative was most often used in states with laws requiring physicians to describe treatment choices to patients.

April 23 / The General Accounting Office (GAO) issues a report finding that the federal government, once a pacesetter in developing "family friendly" policies for its employees, is now lagging behind employers in the private sector. The GAO warns that unless the government keeps up with the private sector, it will have trouble attracting and retaining qualified employees.

April 23 / The Food and Drug Administration tells birth control pill makers to simplify their directions and make them less confusing. According to the National Academy of Sciences, about 250,000 women become pregnant each year because they do not properly follow the directions for taking contraceptive pills.

April 23 / Judging by findings in the National Women's Study, a government-financed survey made public today, the Justice Department's survey of violent crime victims (*see* April 19, 1992) grossly underestimates the number of rapes in the United States. The National Women's Study reports that at least 12.1 million adult women were forcibly raped in 1990.

April 25 / More than 2,000 women attend "Women Tell the Truth: A Conference on Parity, Power and Sexual Harassment," with Anita Hill as the keynote speaker, in New York today. Another 1,500 people reportedly had to be turned away. Introduced by Gloria Steinem, Anita Hill speaks about sexual harassment, which she calls "an abuse of power." Other speakers include Bella Abzug, Carol Bellamy, Geraldine Ferraro, Elizabeth Holtzman, and Ruth Messinger.

April 28 / The National Academy of Sciences announces 59 new members. Only five of them are women.

April 28 / In Los Angeles, a sex discrimination lawsuit filed 13 years ago against State Farm Insurance of California is settled today for $157 million—the largest total amount of damages ever paid in a civil rights case. The plaintiffs in the case, 814 women who sued State Farm over discriminatory hiring and promotion practices, will receive an average of $193,000. Muriel Kraszewski initially filed the suit in 1979 after she was told she would not be promoted to agent because she did not have a college degree. Kraszewski, who was then a secretary at State Farm, knew that the male agents she worked for did not have college degrees.

April 28 / Lynn Yeakel, virtually unknown in Pennsylvania political circles a month ago, wins the state's Democratic Senate primary. She will face Republican incumbent Arlen Specter in the general election. Yeakel's television ads feature clips of Senator Specter's aggressive questioning of Anita Hill during the Senate Judiciary Committee's hearings last October.

April 29 / The Naval Investigative Service and the Navy's inspector general release their report on Tailhook. They found that at least 26 women—more than half of them officers—were assaulted on the third floor of the

hotel in Las Vegas. Investigators learned that groups of drunken male officers in civilian clothes formed into a "gauntlet" through which women
were shoved while the men grabbed at the women's breasts and buttocks
and tore at their clothing. The report says that many naval aviators have
refused to cooperate with the investigation.

April 30 / In today's *New York Times,* Harriett Woods, president of the
National Women's Political Caucus, is quoted on the subject of the current
political climate: "This will be a unique year for the outsider—and women
are seen as outsiders even when they're inside." A record number of
women are running for House and Senate seats this year, and many have
made the Anita Hill hearings a campaign issue. (Women are candidates in
21 of the 34 Senate races and in 173 of the 435 House races.)

April 30 / Supporters of abortion rights claim a victory today when the
House of Representatives approves legislation that repeals the so-called gag
rule, the Bush administration's rule that bars the staff of family planning
clinics from telling clients about the availability of abortion services or referring them to doctors, hospitals, or clinics that provide abortions. However,
the vote falls short of the two-thirds majority that would be needed to
override an expected presidential veto.

April 30 / "Women in the Military: International Perspectives," a conference sponsored by WREI, is held in Washington, DC. Participants include women from Canada, Israel, the United Kingdom, and South Africa,
as well as the United States. It is the first international conference on
women in the military.

May 2 / Operation Rescue ends its two-week anti-abortion campaign in
Buffalo, New York, having failed to shut down any clinics. The campaign
was reportedly overwhelmed by the strong showing of pro-choice advocates who organized to defend clinics, and had difficulty finding enough
anti-abortion volunteers willing to risk arrest.

May 4 / At the second annual James Beard Awards ceremony in New
York, Alice Waters of Chez Panisse in Berkeley, California, is named Chef
of the Year. Fourteen women were among the 43 chefs who were nominated for the award this year, compared to only three women last year. The
evening celebrates the achievements of women in a profession that was long
considered a male preserve.

May 5 / The U.S. Navy's commander of aviation, Vice Admiral Richard
M. Dunleavy, says he has long supported the idea of women flying combat
aircraft and that he and another admiral mapped out a strategy to put
women in combat aircraft more than a year ago. On the subject of the
Tailhook scandal, Dunleavy admits to reporters that "naval aviation leadership failed in its responsibility to provide guidance and leadership to junior
and mid-grade officers."

May 11 / The percentage of full-time, year-round workers with low earnings grew sharply in the last decade, according to a Census Bureau report released today. The report indicates that the percentage of 40-hour per week, 50-weeks per year workers with real earnings of less than $12,195 per year in 1990 dollars (i.e., inflation-adjusted dollars) declined in the 1960s, was steady in the 1970s, and rose significantly in the 1980s.

May 12 / The United Methodist Church, which has nearly nine million members, announces at its quadrennial general conference that it has approved a new book of worship with more inclusive ways of referring to God and prayers that draw on many cultures. Some prayers refer to the deity in both male and female terms, like "God, our Father and Mother."

May 19 / Vice President Dan Quayle causes a flap when he publicly deplores the single motherhood of the character played by Candice Bergen on the TV sitcom "Murphy Brown." Remarks Quayle, "It doesn't help matters when prime-time TV has Murphy Brown mocking the importance of fathers by bearing a child and calling it just another life style choice."

May 22 / The Job Training Partnership Act, the federal government's largest job training program, does improve educational progress for some participants, according to results released today from an ongoing national study. Findings show that 19.1 percent of the adult women who had dropped out of school went on to complete high school or obtain a General Equivalency Diploma after participating in the program, compared to 10.8 percent of the women who did not participate.

May 26 / Members of the Republican platform committee, meeting in Salt Lake City, hear from Mary Dent Crisp, chair of the National Republican Coalition for Choice, and Phyllis Schlafly, chair of the National Coalition for Life. Crisp urges that the party adopt a pro-choice platform; Schlafly urges that the party retain its uncompromising anti-abortion plank.

May 27 / The National Capital Memorial Commission approves the revised design of the memorial to honor women who have served in the U.S. military. Retired General Wilma Vaught, the president of the Women in Military Service for America Memorial Foundation, says that $4.5 million of the needed $14 million has been raised for the memorial, which is to stand at the gateway of Arlington National Cemetery.

May 28 / The U.S. Army dismisses Colonel Margarethe Cammermeyer, the chief nurse of the National Guard in the state of Washington, after nearly 27 years of service because she is a lesbian. Cammermeyer hoped to become the nation's chief military nurse. Now she will challenge her dismissal in federal court with the hope of overturning the 49-year-old ban on gays in the military.

May 28 / President Bush signs a bill reauthorizing the only federal program specifically designed to help victims of domestic violence. The Family

Violence Prevention and Services Act provides grants to states to establish and maintain shelters, child care programs, counseling, and other services to victims of domestic violence and their families.

May 29 / The *New York Times* publishes an open letter from Beverly B. Hudnut and William H. Hudnut 3d to the Republican National Committee. Headlined "We're Good Republicans—and Pro-Choice," the letter tells of the Hudnuts' own decision to terminate a pregnancy after tests found grave defects in the fetus. "We would have been terribly upset if an outside force, namely government, had prevented us from following the dictates of our conscience in this matter." The Hudnuts urge the Republican party not to take any stand on abortion. William Hudnut, a Presbyterian minister, is a former Republican member of Congress and mayor of Indianapolis.

June 2 / A survey of people leaving the polls after voting in the California, Ohio, and New Jersey primaries indicates that most people believe abortion should be made legal or kept off of the party platform. More than six in 10 Democrats and more than four in 10 Republicans said their party should support legal abortion. Two in 10 voters in both parties said their party should not take an official position on abortion.

June 4 / The promotions of 4,000 U.S. Navy and Marine Corps officers are held up by the Senate Armed Services Committee in an effort to break the stonewalling tactics of the aviators who refuse to cooperate with investigations into the Tailhook affair.

June 8 / The Presbyterian Church (U.S.A.) adopts an official policy that discourages abortions but supports a woman's right to obtain one.

June 11 / Two women veterans sue the Citadel, an all-male state-supported military college in Charleston, South Carolina, for admission into the college's day program, in which male veterans are permitted to enroll. Currently, women veterans may attend the Citadel's night and summer programs, which offer three degrees, but women are excluded from the day program, which offers 17 degrees.

June 12 / The Evangelical Lutheran Church, America's largest Lutheran denomination, elects its first female bishop, the Reverend April Ulring Larson, making her the second woman to hold such a post in the history of Lutheranism worldwide. Larson will head a synod of 80 congregations with 40,000 members.

June 13 / Ross Perot's lack of popularity among women is the subject of Ellen Goodman's syndicated column today. Goodman notes that in the *Time*-Cable News Network poll, 45 percent of the men but only 31 percent of the women chose Perot.

June 16 / The American Medical Association issues guidelines advising physicians to routinely ask female patients if they have been abused. The widespread incidence of domestic violence is documented in studies to be published in the *Journal of the American Medical Association* tomorrow.

June 18 / At the request of Secretary of the Navy Garrett, the Department of Defense takes over the Tailhook investigation.

June 18 / The president of the Cook County (Illinois) Board of Supervisors, Richard J. Phelan, announces that Cook County Hospital, which is the major provider of health care to poor people in Chicago, will provide first trimester abortions. Phelan says that his order is an attempt to furnish the same medical services to the poor and uninsured that are available to the affluent and the insured. Until it stopped performing abortions in 1980, the hospital performed 3,500 abortions per year.

June 22 / The National Coalition of 100 Black Women honors Camille Cosby, Kathleen Battle, Julie Dash, Queen Latifah, and Maxine Waters. This year marks the tenth anniversary of the coalition's Candace Awards.

June 23 / Twenty years ago today Congress enacted Title IX of the Education Amendments of 1972, the landmark law that prohibits sex discrimination in all federally funded school programs.

June 23 / President Bush vetoes legislation that would provide $5.4 billion in spending authority to the National Institutes of Health and would mandate greater efforts on cancer research and women's health issues. The president objects to the bill because it contains a provision allowing federal financing of research using the tissue of aborted fetuses.

June 23 / Lieutenant Paula Coughlin, the female naval aviator whose complaint about being assaulted at the Tailhook convention in 1991 finally led to an investigation, goes public. Lieutenant Coughlin, who has not previously allowed her name to be used, tells the *Washington Post* that she decided to come forward because she feels she has not been able to bring her attackers to justice through military channels.

June 25 / A study released today by the Commonwealth Fund estimates that some 12.7 million men are among the Americans over age 55 who look after children or grandchildren, or provide hands-on care for relatives and friends. Although women are still the major providers of care, men are taking a more active role in this respect than they used to, according to the report.

June 26 / Navy Secretary Garrett resigns. In a letter to President Bush, he takes "full responsibility" for the "leadership failure which allowed the egregious conduct at Tailhook to occur in the first place." Garrett's credibility was damaged when it became known recently that he had "come by" one of the hospitality suites off the corridor where the assaults took place. While Garrett's presence at the Tailhook convention party area was not news, he has previously maintained that he stayed on an outdoor patio and was entirely unaware of what was going on inside.

June 29 / The U.S. Supreme Court hands down its decision in *Planned Parenthood of Southeastern Pennsylvania* v. *Casey*. The Court affirms by 5 to 4 a woman's right to have an abortion, but upholds most of the restrictions in the Pennsylvania law, allowing those restrictions that do not, in the Court's opinion, impose an "undue burden." An undue burden is defined as "a substantial obstacle in the path of a woman seeking an abortion before the fetus attains viability." Justices O'Connor, Kennedy, and Souter wrote the opinion, in which they were joined in part by Justices Blackmun and Stevens. Justices Rehnquist, White, Scalia, and Thomas dissented. Neither abortion rights supporters nor abortion opponents are happy with the decision.

June 29 / In an interview published in today's *New York Times,* Army Major Rhonda Cornum deplored "the big deal" that was made about the indecent assault she suffered when she was first captured during the Persian Gulf War. "There's a phenomenal amount of focus on this for the women but not for the men [POWs]" who, she said, suffered far worse treatment than she did. Cornum, one of two servicewomen taken prisoner by the Iraqis, testified before the Presidential Commission on the Assignment of Women in the Armed Forces on June 8 that she had been manually violated vaginally and rectally.

June 30 / Muriel F. Siebert, a member of the New York Stock Exchange since 1967, when she became the first woman allowed to buy a seat on the exchange, is honored for her work on behalf of Wall Street's women with the 1992 Veuve Clicquot Business Woman of the Year Award.

July 1 / Acting Secretary of the Navy Daniel Howard tells high-ranking Navy and Marine Corps officers that he is establishing a standing committee on women in the Navy and the Marine Corps to be chaired by the assistant secretary for manpower and reserve affairs, Barbara Pope. Howard says, "My purpose . . . is to dismantle a decaying culture, a residual fabric of counterproductive and unworthy attitudes that is preventing this organization from getting on with its mission. . . . Anyone in this department who is still wasting time disparaging women, fighting their integration, or subjecting them to sexual harassment, is a dragging anchor. . . . Anyone who still believes in the image of a drunken, skirt chasing warrior back from the sea is about a half a century out of date. If that's you, we don't need you because we've got places we need to go, and not much time to get there."

July 1 / Herma Hill Kay becomes dean of Boalt Hall, the University of California at Berkeley's school of law. Kay, who has been on the Boalt Hall faculty for 32 years, is the first woman to hold the position of dean.

July 1 / U.S. Customs officials at Kennedy Airport seize one dose of

RU-486 from an American woman who brought the abortifacient drug to the United States from London in a deliberate attempt to challenge publicly the federal restrictions on importing it. The woman, who gives only her first name—Leona—is six weeks pregnant. RU-486 is not recommended for use after the eighth week of pregnancy. The drug, which is manufactured by a French company, Roussel-Uclaf, is legal in Britain and France, but the U.S. government bars its importation into this country.

July 1 / As of today, Derrick Bell, who began an unpaid leave of absence in 1990 to protest Harvard Law School's failure to appoint a woman of color to its faculty (*see* March 2, 1992), is considered by the university to have resigned. Harvard's policy is to limit leaves of absence to two years. Bell, a member of the law school faculty since 1969, will argue his case for an extended leave of absence before a special panel of Harvard's top governing board at an unprecedented hearing later this month.

July 1 / Seven women athletes at the University of Texas file a class action Title IX sex discrimination suit against the university. They want to force the university to add softball, soccer, rowing, and gymnastics—which are currently club or intramural sports—to the women's athletic department.

July 2 / The *Washington Post* notes that three novels by black women are currently on the national bestseller lists at the same time—a first. The novels are *Waiting to Exhale* by Terry McMillan, *Jazz* by Toni Morrison, and *Possessing the Secret of Joy* by Alice Walker.

July 8 / The number of children living in poverty increased by 1.1 million during the 1980s, and by another 841,000 just between 1989 and 1990, the Children's Defense Fund reports.

July 9 / The *Washington Post* reports that a Naval Investigative Service agent made "romantic overtures" to Lieutenant Paula Coughlin while he was interviewing her about the incidents at Tailhook. The agent has reportedly been disciplined.

July 12 / Governor Ann Richards of Texas, who is in New York to chair the Democratic convention, throws a pre-convention party where the spotlight is on six Democratic women who have won their party's nominations for the Senate—Barbara Boxer and Dianne Feinstein of California, Jean Jones of Iowa, Carol Moseley-Braun of Illinois, Gloria O'Dell of Kansas, and Lynn Yeakel of Pennsylvania. (Several Senate primary races in which women are candidates have yet to be held—e.g., Washington and New York.) Richards tells the gathering, "This is going to be an interesting Senate. They're going to be saying, 'Hey, there's ladies in here.' "

July 13 / Barbara Jordan of Texas, a former member of the House of Representatives, gives the keynote address at the Democratic convention.

Other women playing prominent roles in this convention include Ann Richards, the convention chair, and Senator Barbara Mikulski (MD), who will place Senator Albert Gore's name in nomination for vice president.

July 15 / A Federal Highway Administration study on travel behavior released today provides evidence that women are driving more than ever, and suggests that women commuting to work and running weekend errands may be a major source of congestion in U.S. metropolitan areas. In 1990, on average, women took their cars out 3.13 times a day, compared to an average for men of 3.04.

July 17 / Judge Ronald Cappai overturns the sex discrimination verdict against Texaco, in which the jury awarded nearly $18 million to Janella Sue Martin in punitive and compensatory damages (*see* October 3, 1991). The judge says the amount is so disproportionate to the injuries suffered that it "shocks the conscience of this court." Cappai also voids his own order that Texaco promote Martin and orders a new trial in the case.

July 17 / In a brief unsigned opinion, the Supreme Court declines to force the federal government to return the RU-486 pills to Leona Benten, the pregnant woman who brought them into the United States on July 1. The High Court's ruling stays a lower court order that the government release the pills to Benten.

July 19 / A study of female entrepreneurs is the subject of an article by Carol Kleiman in today's *Washington Post*. The study by the National Association of Women Business Owners (NAWBO) found that the federal government has underestimated the number of women-owned businesses by about two million. According to NAWBO, 5.4 million women own their own businesses.

July 20 / By approving the necessary waivers of federal regulations, Secretary of Health and Human Services Louis Sullivan gives the go-ahead to New Jersey's new welfare reform law (*see* January 21, 1992).

July 23 / The Higher Education Act reauthorization is signed into law today by President Bush. The provisions liberalizing eligibility for financial aid should be particularly welcome to low-income women students who are struggling to get a college education while they work to support their children. The law allows less-than-half-time students to receive Pell grants, and it allows for more accurate accounting of child care costs in determining eligibility for aid. Also of particular interest to women are the law's requirements that colleges and universities provide sexual assault programs and promote rape awareness.

July 23 / Florida's Supreme Court overturns the 1989 felony conviction of Jennifer C. Johnson, who was found guilty of "delivering" drugs to a minor because she took cocaine shortly before her child's birth. The state's highest court finds that the Florida legislature never intended the word "delivery" to mean the delivery of drugs through the umbilical cord.

August 5 / Gender bias is alive and well in the federal court system in the western states, according to a survey of judges and lawyers in the ninth federal circuit. A report released today says that 60 percent of the female lawyers practicing in the ninth circuit have been sexually harassed by lawyers, clients, judges, or other court personnel. Sex bias also affects female plaintiffs and defendants, whose testimony "may simply be disbelieved or discounted." The report concludes that concerted effort to change attitudes is needed to solve the problem of sexual harassment. The ninth circuit, headquartered in California, comprises Alaska, Arizona, California, Hawaii, Idaho, Montana, Nevada, Oregon, Washington, Guam, and the Northern Mariana Islands.

August 5 / Mississippi becomes the first state to enforce a requirement that a woman seeking an abortion wait 24 hours before having the procedure. The U.S. Supreme Court approved a state's right to impose such a waiting period in *Planned Parenthood of Southeastern Pennsylvania* v. *Casey* (*see* June 29, 1992). Mississippi will also require that doctors inform women of abortion risks and alternatives.

August 9 / The 1992 Summer Olympics in Barcelona, Spain, conclude today. American women won 14 gold medals (of a total of 37 golds won by U.S. athletes), 12 silvers, and 19 bronzes.

August 9 / The American Bar Association (ABA), which is holding its annual convention in San Francisco, honors Anita Hill at a luncheon. The keynote speaker is Hillary Clinton, who says of Hill's testimony before the Senate Judiciary Committee, "All women who care about equality of opportunity, about integrity and morality in the workplace, are in Professor Anita Hill's debt."

August 11 / The ABA's House of Delegates approves an abortion rights resolution that promises to fight any laws that restrict a woman's right to choose. The resolution reverses a resolution of neutrality adopted by the ABA two years ago.

August 11 / The Senate approves the conference report on the Family and Medical Leave Act by a voice vote. This version of the bill—a compromise worked out by the House and Senate—will go to the House for final approval in September. President Bush has said that if Congress passes the bill, he will veto it.

August 11 / Labor Secretary Lynn Martin announces that, regrettably, little has changed since her department released its report on the glass ceiling last year (*see* August 8, 1991). Martin says that only 7.5 percent of the board members of America's 100 biggest companies are women, and that only

11.5 percent of the leadership positions in the country's biggest unions are held by women.

August 11 / The Marine Corps announces that all female lieutenants in the corps will get full combat training this fall, with live firings of M-16s and grenades, and classes with men.

August 12 / In an interview with magazine reporters, Barbara Bush says that abortion is a "personal thing" and that, in her opinion, personal things have no place in party platforms or conventions. (The new platform recently completed by the Republican platform committee retains the old platform's strict anti-abortion plank.)

August 14 / Three senior U.S. Navy officers are relieved of their commands for participating in a skit that included obscene comments about Rep. Patricia Schroeder (D-CO). This is expected to mean the end of the officers' naval careers. The skit occurred at the "Tomcat Follies," an annual event put on by F-14 fliers at Miramar Naval Air Station near San Diego.

August 17 / Although most of the delegates at the Republican convention in Houston reportedly do not subscribe to the rigid anti-abortion plank in their party's platform, the Bush campaign successfully appeals to pro-choice Republicans to avoid an open debate on the issue, lest it hurt the president's chances for reelection.

August 18 / Women who wait until they are in their thirties to have children have a slightly higher risk of stillborn birth than those who have children in their early twenties, according to a study published today in the *Journal of the American Medical Association*.

August 19 / Women in the Bush administration are in the spotlight at the Republican convention, where the theme is "family values." Both Barbara Bush and Marilyn Quayle address the convention and Secretary of Labor Lynn Martin nominates George Bush. However, a number of Republican female candidates and elected officeholders are reported to be disappointed that elected women have not been given more prominent roles in the convention.

Mary Fisher, a prominent Republican who is HIV positive, addresses the delegates about the disease, moving some to tears. She says, "We may take refuge in our stereotypes, but we cannot hide there long. Because HIV asks only one thing of those it attacks: Are you human?. . . . My call to you, my party, is to take a public stand no less compassionate than that of the president and Mrs. Bush," who, she says, have helped and supported her since she learned last year that she had the AIDS virus.

August 21 / Speculating about how the "family values" theme that was sounded at the Republican convention will play with the electorate, commentators discuss the ambivalence in this country about women's roles.

Today's *New York Times* notes "a paradox in tone between the two women the campaign has presented as avatars of Republican family values." In her speech to the convention, Barbara Bush, who has devoted herself to her family and has never pursued a career, said women should be encouraged to do either or both. Marilyn Quayle, a lawyer who has given up her profession, appeared in her speech to criticize women who make a different choice.

August 23 / According to today's *Washington Post,* the Reverend Pat Robertson wrote last month to contributors to his Christian Coalition about Amendment 1, an Iowa ballot initiative that would extend the protection of the state constitution to women. Robertson's letter, an effort to defeat the initiative, reportedly said, "the feminist agenda is not about equal rights for women. It is about a socialist, anti-family political movement that encourages women to leave their husbands, kill their children, practice witchcraft, destroy capitalism and become lesbians."

August 26 / Mary E. Clutter, assistant director for biological sciences at the National Science Foundation, has made it her directorate's policy not to fund meetings or conferences if there are no women scientists involved—or if there are, in Clutter's opinion, too few women among the proposed speakers. According to today's *Washington Post,* when conference organizers cannot come up with any women to speak, Clutter provides them with the names of women doing research in the relevant area.

August 26 / Two weeks before the New York state senatorial primary, candidate Elizabeth Holtzman, who is lagging badly in the polls, has launched a television campaign harshly criticizing the ethics of Geraldine Ferraro, the leading contender for the Democratic nomination. The bitter contest between two of New York's best-known feminist politicians has already aroused dismay and disagreement in the ranks of feminists in the state.

September 2 / Dr. Barbara McClintock, one of the most influential geneticists of the century, dies in a Long Island hospital near the Cold Spring Harbor Laboratory where she conducted research for more than 50 years. McClintock was the first woman to win an unshared Nobel Prize in Physiology or Medicine. She is best known for her discovery that fragments of genetic material move among chromosomes, regulating the way genes control cells' growth and development.

September 4 / Facing a sex discrimination suit for barring female veterans from day classes that are open to male veterans, the Citadel solves the problem by closing the classes to male veterans (*see* June 11, 1992).

September 5 / The Kennedy Center's Friedheim Awards for new works by American composers are awarded and first prize goes to Shulamit Ran for her *Symphony*. This is the first time in the 15-year history of the annual award that a woman composer has won first prize.

September 8 / Four civilian women file suits against the Tailhook Association, claiming that they were sexually accosted during the 1990 and 1991 Tailhook conventions.

September 10 / A new study presented today before the Presidential Commission on the Assignment of Women in the Armed Forces found that the majority of the Army's female officers and enlisted personnel favor repealing the military's regulations that exclude women from combat roles, but only 15 percent say they would volunteer for combat jobs if allowed. The study, by the Army Research Institute, also found that 60 percent of female Army officers and 54 percent of Army enlisted women believe that the combat restrictions hurt their chances of promotion.

September 10 / By a vote of 241 to 161 (less than the two-thirds that would be required to override a veto), the House approves the conference report of the Family and Medical Leave Act. The measure was passed by the Senate last month, and now goes to President Bush, who has said he will veto it.

September 10 / Eleven of the country's leading corporations and more than 100 smaller businesses and private organizations announce that they will collaborate on a $25.4 million project to help provide their workers with care for their children and aging relatives. Most of the money for the project, called the American Business Collaboration for Quality Dependent Care, is reportedly being provided by the 11 big corporations—IBM, American Express, Exxon, Eastman Kodak, Xerox, Travelers, Johnson & Johnson, Amoco, Allstate Insurance, Motorola, and AT&T.

September 12 / U.S. astronaut Mae Carol Jemison, aboard the space shuttle Endeavour, becomes the first African American woman to go into space. Mission tasks for Jemison, a physician and chemical engineer, include an experiment to see if biofeedback techniques can be used to reduce motion sickness in space.

September 14 / A report released today by Rep. Les Aspin (D-WI), chair of the full House Armed Services Committee, and Rep. Beverly Byron (D-MD), chair of the Military Personnel and Compensation Subcommittee, calls for fundamental changes in the way the military culture views women in order to end sexual harassment in the armed services. The report analyzes the patterns of change in the military's successful efforts to end racial discrimination and illegal drug use, in order to understand better the problem of sexual harassment.

September 16 / WREI presents its 1992 American Woman Award to Donna De Varona, long a leading advocate for equity for women in sports.

September 16 / Retired Republican Congresswoman Millicent Fenwick, the woman who inspired the Lacey Davenport character in Garry Trudeau's "Doonesbury" comic strip, dies at age 82 in her home in Bernardsville, New Jersey.

September 17 / IBM issues a warning to its employees that two chemicals commonly used in manufacturing semiconductor chips—and in other industries—may significantly increase the risk of miscarriage. Preliminary results of a study by health researchers at the Johns Hopkins University showed that among 30 women who worked in close contact with the chemicals, 10 had miscarriages—a much higher rate than expected. IBM has reportedly also issued the warning to other computer chip manufacturers and the Environmental Protection Agency.

September 21 / The season premiere of "Murphy Brown" mingles television footage of real events with its fictional world as Murphy Brown replies on camera to Vice President Quayle's charge that she has "glamorized" unwed motherhood (*see* May 19, 1992). Brown, played by Candice Bergen, says, "If there are those who choose to view me as a role model, I would hope to be seen as someone who tries to do her best, sometimes makes mistakes and when she does, accepts responsibility for them. I would ask the vice president to do the same."

September 22 / As expected, President Bush vetoes the Family and Medical Leave Act.

September 22 / The Senate votes to cut $200 million from military projects and use $185 million of it for breast cancer research.

September 24 / Lena Guerrero, who has been widely regarded as a rising political star, resigns as chair of the Texas Railroad Commission after admitting that she falsified her résumé with college credentials that she never earned. Guerrero, a former state legislator who was appointed to the powerful commission by Governor Ann Richards, was the first woman and the first Hispanic ever to be appointed to that body.

September 24 / The report by the Defense Department's inspector general about the Tailhook investigation is made public. The document, a review of the Navy's probe of Tailhook, severely criticizes the Naval Investigative Service (NIS) for not aggressively investigating the sexual assault and misconduct that took place at the Tailhook convention. The report also says that senior Navy officials deliberately undermined their own investigation. As a result of the report, the commander of the NIS has been relieved of his job, and two other senior Navy officials will take early retirement.

September 27 / Alison Leigh Cowan writes in today's *New York Times* that the percentage of women among applicants to leading business schools has dropped. According to Cowan, women's interest in business schools has declined in part because of the growing assumption that would-be MBAs should wait until their late twenties before enrolling in business school. For women who want to have children as well as a career, this is an impractical plan.

September 29 / In a letter to Mattel, Inc., the National Council of Teachers of Mathematics warns about the "negative impact" the company's new Teen Talk Barbie could have on girls' attitudes toward math. The doll's "talk" includes the line "Math class is tough."

September 30 / *The New Our Bodies, Ourselves* reaches bookstores. Compiled by the Boston Women's Health Book Collective, the new edition covers such issues as the debate on the Norplant contraceptive, the RU-486 "abortion pill," health and sexuality issues of concern to disabled women, post-mastectomy decisions, and AIDS. The original *Our Bodies, Ourselves* came out two decades ago.

September 30 / The House of Representatives fails to override President Bush's veto of the Family and Medical Leave bill.

October 1 / Sonia Sotomayor is appointed a judge in the federal southern district of New York. She is the first Hispanic American to be named to the federal bench in the southern district, which has 58 judges (counting Ms. Sotomayor, seven of the 58 are women).

October 2 / The National Institutes of Health (NIH) announces that the Fred Hutchinson Cancer Research Center in Seattle, Washington will coordinate the largest study of women's health ever undertaken in the United States. The $140 million, 15-year project is part of the $625 million NIH "Women's Health Initiative" (*see* "The Politics of Women's Health" in this volume).

October 5 / A federal appeals court overturns a lower court ruling that allowed the Virginia Military Institute (VMI), which is partially supported by the state's taxpayers, to exclude women. The appellate judges do not, however, hold that VMI must admit women to comply with federal laws barring sex discrimination in education. Rather, they suggest that the legal requirements would be satisfied if a program similar to VMI's were offered to women in the state.

October 7 / Economists Heidi Hartmann, director of the Institute for Women's Policy Research, and Barbara Bergman, a professor at the American University, propose a six-point, $1 billion a year national women's policy agenda that is endorsed by 80 economists, including two Nobel Prize winners. They call for guaranteed health care, antidiscrimination measures, abortion rights, improved child care, and welfare reform, and for more taxes to pay for the changes they propose.

October 7 / The Women in Apprenticeship and Nontraditional Occupations Act is passed by the Senate today (it passed the House in September) and is ready for President Bush to sign into law. This act authorizes $1 million for community-based organizations to offer technical assistance to private employers for recruiting, training, and retaining women in jobs and apprenticeships that are traditionally held by men.

October 12 / Columbus Day—and 22 Native American women leaders are in Washington for the fourth annual Leadership Conference of Female Chiefs. Women account for about one-fifth of the leaders of the more than 500 federally recognized tribal nations.

October 14 / Women may be as susceptible as men to inheriting a disposition for alcoholism, according to a study published today in the *Journal of the American Medical Association*. Many doctors and psychiatrists have believed women's alcoholism to be more closely tied to social and psychological factors. This study, using 1,030 pairs of female twins, shows that genetics is the single most important factor in determining whether a woman becomes an alcoholic.

October 17 / According to the Fund for the Feminist Majority, the number of women in congressional races this year is up 64 percent from 1990.

October 26 / Four anti-abortion groups in southern California are charged with misrepresenting themselves as medical clinics offering abortion services in a lawsuit filed today by "Jane Roe" and Planned Parenthood of San Diego and Riverside Counties. The anonymous plaintiff had gone to one of the clinics, which advertised free pregnancy testing, and was presented with information discouraging abortion.

October 28 / The glass ceiling apparently exists in the federal government as well as in the private sector, according to a study released today by the U.S. Merit Systems Protection Board. The board found that even though half of the government's white collar jobs are held by women, they account for only one in four federal supervisors, and only one in nine senior federal executives.

November 2 / Pearl Stewart is named editor of the *Oakland* (California) *Tribune*. When she assumes the post on December 1, she will be the first black woman to have the top editorial job at a major U.S. daily.

November 2 / After two days of deliberation on the Defense Department's recruiting standards and physical requirements, the Presidential Commission on the Assignment of Women in the Armed Forces recommends that there should be no discrimination on the basis of sex in military specialties that are open to both men and women. By a vote of 8 to 7, the commission also says that women should continue to be barred from flying combat missions and to be prohibited from engaging in ground combat, although they should be allowed to serve on combat ships.

November 3 / Election Day brings major gains for women candidates. Five women (four newly elected and one incumbent) win Senate seats (the other incumbent woman senator was not up for reelection this year). Forty-eight women, 24 newly elected and 24 incumbents, win seats in the House. Illinois voters give the Senate its first-ever black woman senator. California voters make their state the first to have two women senators.

There are disappointments, however. None of the six women challenging incumbent senators is elected. In the 103rd Congress women will still hold only six percent of the seats in the Senate and 11 percent in the House, and only 26 states will have women on their congressional delegations.

November 3 / The Bush administration's ban on abortion counseling at federally funded clinics is set aside by a federal appeals court. Were it to go into effect, the ban—commonly known as the "gag rule"—would apply to 3,900 family planning clinics around the country. They would be required to choose between submitting pledges of compliance or refusing federal money.

November 8 / "Female Candidates Got Major Boost from Contributors" says today's *Washington Post*. The heads of EMILY's List, the Women's Campaign Fund, and the National Women's Political Caucus told the *Post* that their memberships surged after the Clarence Thomas-Anita Hill hearings. EMILY's List, which raises funds for selected pro-choice Democratic women, is reported to have given $4.6 million to House and Senate candidates as of the end of September, making it the biggest contributor to congressional candidates.

November 18 / The National Conference of Catholic Bishops refuses to adopt a proposed pastoral letter that, in effect, endorses the traditional role of women in the church, although it affirms the equality of men and women and condemns violence and discrimination against women.

November 20 / Susan J. Insley becomes the highest ranking woman in American automotive manufacturing today when she is named by Honda Motor Company to supervise Honda's engine plant in Anna, Ohio.

November 21 / The public learns today that Senator Bob Packwood (R-OR) has been accused of sexual advances toward female members of his staff and women lobbyists. According to the *Washington Post,* which breaks the story, the newspaper asked Packwood about these allegations late last month—"days before his reelection to a fifth term" in the Senate. Packwood told the *Post* that none of the accounts was true and later provided the newspaper with statements intended to cast doubt on the women's credibility. Yesterday, however, Packwood gave a statement to the *Post* that said, "I will not make an issue of any specific allegation," and went on "If any of my comments or actions have indeed been unwelcome . . . I am sincerely sorry."

November 30 / The U.S. Supreme Court makes it clear that a woman has a constitutional right to abortion. The High Court refuses, by a vote of 6 to 3, to hear an appeal from a federal appellate court decision which held that Guam's broad prohibition on abortion is unconstitutional.

December 1 / President-elect Bill Clinton asks Maya Angelou to compose a poem to read at his swearing-in ceremony. Angelou tells the *Washington Post,* "It is fitting that he asks a woman and a black woman to write a poem about the tenor of the times."

December 1 / The Senate Ethics Committee begins a preliminary inquiry into complaints that Senator Bob Packwood (R-OR) sexually harassed women on his staff as well as some women lobbyists. The ethics probe was formally requested yesterday by a Los Angeles-based women's group, the Women's Equal Rights, Legal Defense and Education Committee.

December 3 / The 21,000 American women who work in computer chip plants across the United States have an unusually high risk of miscarriage, according to a study released today by the Semiconductor Industry Association. This study found a 14 percent miscarriage rate among women who work in the chip factories, compared with a 10 percent rate for women who do not. One major chipmaker, Intel Corp., has responded by saying that it will grant pregnant women transfers to nonfactory jobs at full pay, and will modify its factories to eliminate suspect chemicals. (IBM warned its employees of the risk earlier this year. *See* September 17, 1992.)

December 6 / This year's 32 Rhodes Scholars are announced and 16 are women—the largest percentage of women since the scholarships were opened to females in 1976. The winners of the prestigious scholarship to Oxford University in England were chosen from 1,275 applicants; selection criteria for Rhodes scholarships include academic excellence, integrity, leadership ability, and athletic prowess.

December 7 / To the dismay of abortion rights supporters, the U.S. Supreme Court refuses to hear a challenge to a Mississippi abortion law that requires women to wait 24 hours for an abortion after receiving counseling intended to change their minds.

December 8 / The Labor Department's Glass Ceiling Commission, which was instituted to research barriers that prevent women and minorities from reaching the highest levels in the business world, holds its first public hearing in Kansas City, Kansas. The legislation that created the commission was introduced by Senator Bob Dole (R–KS) and Rep. Susan Molinari (R–NY) after the release in the summer of 1991 of a Department of Labor report on the glass ceiling (*see* August 8, 1991).

December 8 / The past two decades have seen dramatic social change in marriage and divorce, according to a Census Bureau report released today. Highlights of the report show that women age 30 to 44 are more likely to be divorced at some time in their lives than any group in American history. However, the overall divorce rate is expected to decline slightly in the future, with four in 10 marriages ending in divorce rather than the previously projected five in 10.

December 10 / Senator Bob Packwood (R–OR) makes his first public response to the charges that he sexually harassed women members of his staff and women lobbyists. Although Packwood insists that he will not resign under any circumstances, he admits he "was just plain wrong" to make unwanted advances. The senator also takes the opportunity to review his record of supporting women's causes like the Equal Rights Amendment, the family and medical leave bill, and abortion rights legislation.

December 11 / Duke University names Nannerl Overholser Keohane its new president. Keohane, who is currently president of Wellesley College, will be Duke's first woman president.

December 11 / President-elect Clinton names three women to high posts in his new administration: Donna E. Shalala to head the Department of Health and Human Services; Laura D'Andrea Tyson to chair the Council of Economic Advisors; and Carol M. Browner to administer the Environmental Protection Agency. Shalala is currently chancellor of the University of Wisconsin's flagship campus, Tyson teaches economics at the University of California at Berkeley, and Browner was until recently Florida's secretary of environmental regulation.

December 15 / Contending that Senator Packwood won reelection by "fraud on the voters," Oregonians for Ethical Representation, an umbrella organization of women's and other groups, petitions the Senate Rules Committee not to seat Packwood when the 103rd Congress convenes in January.

December 18 / The *Washington Post* publishes the results of a *Post*-ABC News poll, which was conducted last week, on sexual harassment. Eighty-five percent of the women and men surveyed said sexual harassment is a problem in the workplace, 32 percent of the women said they have been sexually harassed on the job, and almost four out of 10 of the men surveyed said they have changed the way they act toward women in the past year.

December 21 / President-elect Clinton has a press conference to announce two nominees for his cabinet. One is a woman, Hazel R. O'Leary, a Minnesota power company executive, who is Clinton's choice for secretary of the Department of Energy. If confirmed, O'Leary will be the first woman and the first black person to head that department.

Clinton also reacts to criticism from women's groups that he has not included enough women among his cabinet nominees. He says his critics are "bean counters" who are "playing quota games and math games" with the selection process.

December 24 / President-elect Clinton says he plans to nominate Jocelyn Elders, a black pediatrician who currently heads the Arkansas Public Health Department, as U.S. surgeon general. Elders is characterized in the *Washington Post* as "brash, charismatic, and never shy of controversy."

December 31 / The House Government Operations Committee's Subcommittee on Human Resources and Intergovernmental Relations, which oversees the Food and Drug Administration, accuses the agency of failing to monitor the use of silicone gel breast implants since restrictions were placed on their use last April (*see* April 16, 1992). According to the subcommittee, abuses with the devices have continued.

1993

January 1 / Nurses suffer from increasingly demanding workloads without proportionate increases in their salaries, according to 10,000 respondents in the National Nurse Survey. The survey, released today, was compiled by the Service Employees International Union (SEIU). SEIU reports that nurses' wages have been rising, but not enough to offset the declines in working conditions, which include inadequate staffing, non-nursing tasks, assignments for which they are unqualified, and stress-related injuries.

January 6 / Senators Dianne Feinstein (D-CA) and Carol Moseley-Braun (D-IL) are assigned to the Senate Judiciary Committee, the formerly all-white, all-male panel that was criticized for its handling of Anita Hill's sexual harassment charges against Clarence Thomas and for the way it conducted the hearings on this matter.

January 6 / For the first time in its history, the Congressional Caucus for Women's Issues takes a position in the abortion debate. On a motion by Rep. Louise Slaughter (D-NY) at an organizational meeting today, the caucus's executive committee votes unanimously to become an officially pro-choice organization.

January 10 / Now that there are six women senators, the Senate will install a restroom for their private use, according to today's *New York Times*. Up to now, women senators have used a public restroom near the Senate chamber.

January 13 / Women who smoke can almost completely eliminate their increased risk of stroke by quitting, according to a study of over 120,000 women. Findings published in today's *Journal of the American Medical Association* indicate that the excess risk of stroke can be largely eliminated within two to four years after quitting, regardless of the age at which a woman started to smoke and how many cigarettes she smoked.

January 13 / In a 6 to 3 decision, the U.S. Supreme Court rules in *Bray* v. *Alexandria Women's Health Clinic* that women seeking abortions are not a protected class under federal civil rights law. The decision means that federal law enforcement authorities cannot be called in to handle the militant tactics of groups like Operation Rescue that physically block access to clinics.

January 21 / The Senate confirms Carol Browner as administrator of the Environmental Protection Agency, Hazel O'Leary as secretary of energy, and Donna Shalala as secretary of health and human services. Browner and O'Leary are the first women in their respective positions; Shalala is the fourth woman in hers.[2]

January 22 / President Clinton, in office for two days, abolishes the abortion-counseling "gag rule" that would have prohibited anyone but physicians at federally funded clinics from providing abortion counseling. He also ends restrictions on U.S. funding for United Nations population programs that provide information or counseling on abortion, returns to U.S. military hospitals the right to perform privately funded abortions, and orders the government to review the Bush-era ban on the private importation of RU-486.

January 22 / The twentieth anniversary of *Roe* v. *Wade* is marked by the march of at least 75,000 abortion opponents from the Ellipse near the White House to Capitol Hill. According to a *Washington Post* survey of 742 randomly selected marchers, the marchers are mostly middle-aged, married with children, and from outside the Washington metropolitan area.

January 23 / Zoe E. Baird, President Clinton's nominee for the post of U.S. attorney general, asks that her name be withdrawn. Baird's Senate and public backing has crumbled since her acknowledgment that she knowingly violated the law both by hiring illegal immigrants to care for

[2]Oveta Culp Hobby held the post during the Eisenhower administration when the department was the health, education and welfare department. Patricia R. Harris (a Carter appointee) and Margaret M. Heckler (a Reagan appointee) were secretaries of health and human services.

her child and by failing to pay Social Security taxes for them.

January 25 / President Clinton appoints his wife, Hillary Rodham Clinton, to chair a task force to prepare legislation to overhaul the nation's health care system. Mrs. Clinton is the first First Lady to hold such an influential policymaking position (at least in public). She is also the first to occupy an office in the West Wing of the White House, alongside the president's senior staff members.

January 27 / The Senate confirms Madeline Albright as U.S. ambassador to the United Nations. She is the second woman to hold the position; the first was Jeane Kirkpatrick, appointed by President Reagan.

February 2 / President Clinton says that he is concentrating on finding a woman to serve as his attorney general because he is concerned about sending the signal that there are no women qualified for the job. As a result of what has been dubbed "Nannygate," Clinton's first choice for the position, corporate lawyer Zoe E. Baird, withdrew her name from nomination (*see* January 23, 1993).

February 2 / In an address to the National Governors' Association, President Clinton pledges to reform welfare. Emphasizing that welfare should only be a temporary solution and not a way of life, the president suggests the expansion of job training and education programs for recipients of Aid to Families with Dependent Children and an increase in the earned income tax credit to supplement the incomes of the working poor.

February 3 / Reps. Constance A. Morella (R-MD) and Charles E. Schumer (D-NY) introduce legislation that would make blockading abortion clinics a federal crime and would permit the women who were prevented from entering clinics to sue the groups that organize the blockades. The legislation, which would reverse the U.S. Supreme Court ruling in *Bray* v. *Alexandria Women's Health Clinic* (*see* January 13, 1993), promises to be one of the most controversial pieces of abortion rights legislation in the 103rd Congress.

February 4 / Both the House and the Senate pass the Family and Medical Leave Act, a bill to require employers with 50 or more workers to grant employees unpaid leave for up to 12 weeks a year for the birth or adoption of a child; for medical treatment; or for the illness of a child, spouse, or parent. President Bush vetoed the bill last year and proponents were unable to muster enough votes to override the veto. President Clinton is expected to sign the bill.

February 4 / A survey of 82 interns and residents in internal medicine at the University of California at San Francisco found that three-fourths of the women and one-fifth of the men believed that they had been sexually harassed during their training. The study, published today in the *New*

England Journal of Medicine, found that most of the incidents involved offensive comments and unwelcome flirtation from male doctors. The authors recommend that schools and hospitals concentrate on preventing sexual harassment, rather than punishing it.

February 4 / The Senate Ethics Committee announces that its probe into allegations of sexual harassment against Senator Bob Packwood (R-OR) will include looking into charges that Packwood and his staff attempted to intimidate and discredit the women who reported his alleged unwanted sexual advances.

February 4 / Women's groups and top female athletes gather in Washington for the seventh annual National Girls and Women in Sports Day. Advocates for equity in sports lobby on Capitol Hill for stricter enforcement of Title IX, the law that requires federally funded institutions to provide equal funds and programming for women's and men's athletics.

February 5 / Surrounded by longtime supporters of the Family and Medical Leave Act (which was first introduced in 1985), President Clinton signs the bill into law, and says he is proud to have it be the first bill he signs in his presidency.

February 5 / The Senate confirms Laura D'Andrea Tyson as chair of the Council of Economic Advisors. She is the first woman to hold the position.

February 5 / Kimba M. Wood, a federal judge who was President Clinton's choice for U.S. attorney general, withdraws her name from consideration after an uproar develops over her having employed an illegal immigrant as her babysitter. According to news reports, Wood said that she had not anticipated that this would cause a problem for her nomination because, unlike Zoe Baird, she hired the babysitter before it was against the law to employ an illegal alien, and she has always paid Social Security taxes for her employees.

February 11 / President Clinton names Janet Reno as his choice for attorney general, the nation's chief law enforcement officer. Reno, who is chief state attorney for Dade County, Florida, comes well qualified for the job—she has had nearly 15 years of experience in dealing with race riots, crime waves, drug cartels, political corruption, and police brutality. Unlike Clinton's earlier choices to head the Justice Department, Reno is single and childless.

February 21 / Women working on Capitol Hill report that sexual harassment, discrimination, and inequitable working conditions are part of their daily lives, according to a survey conducted last month by the *Washington Post* and published in today's edition. The survey questioned 603 women and 200 men who work for members of Congress or congressional committees. Thirty-four percent of the women said they had been sexually harassed on the job; of the women who had been harassed, about a third said the offender was a member of Congress. A majority of the women described the Hill as a male-dominated environment where women are less respected and less valued than their male colleagues and are still considered to be outsiders.

February 23 / Hillary Rodham Clinton meets with the executive committee of the Congressional Caucus for Women's Issues for an hour-long talk about health care reform. She is the first First Lady to meet with the caucus for a working session.

February 23 / Governor Mario Cuomo nominates Judge Judith Kaye to be chief judge of the Court of Appeals of New York State. Kaye will be the first woman to serve in the state's top judicial position.

February 24 / Edouard Sakiz, president of Roussel-Uclaf, the French pharmaceutical company that makes the abortion pill RU-486, says that he believes the drug should be made available in the United States. This marks a change from the company's previous policy not to market the drug in this country because of what it described as the anti-abortion climate here, notably the anti-abortion sentiments expressed by Presidents Reagan and Bush. President Clinton has stated that he believes American women should have the option of using RU-486.

March 1 / The Supreme Court agrees to consider a case, *Harris* v. *Forklift Systems,* that asks the Court to decide whether workers suing for sexual harassment must prove that they were not only offended but also psychologically injured. The case, which will be heard next term, is potentially important for defining the protection federal law gives against sexual harassment in the workplace.

March 4 / Two House subcommittees hold a joint hearing on the need to reform Social Security laws to encourage employers of household workers to comply with the laws. This issue emerged from obscurity with what has come to be known as "Nannygate," when it turned out that Zoe Baird was not the only person in line for an important job in the Clinton administration who had failed to pay Social Security taxes for a household worker. It has been estimated that only 25 percent of all households employing domestic workers abide by the current law, which requires employers who pay a worker more than $50 in any calendar quarter to pay Social Security and Medicare taxes, and requires employers who pay wages of $1,000 or more in a quarter to pay unemployment taxes.

March 10 / Elaine Jones, the new director of the NAACP Legal Defense and Education Fund, and the first woman to head the organization, announces that the group will expand its agenda to include more cases involving environmental and health care discrimination.

March 10 / Dr. David Gunn, a physician who performed abortions in clinics in the South, is shot to death by an abortion protester outside a clinic in Pensacola, Florida. Gunn's killer is said to be Michael Griffin, a fundamentalist Christian who recently joined the anti-abortion group Rescue America. According to press reports, John Burt, the leader of Rescue America, calls Gunn's death unfortunate but says that babies' lives will be saved as a result.

March 11 / The Senate unanimously confirms Janet Reno as attorney general of the United States. She is the first woman to hold that position.

March 11 / Secretary of Veterans Affairs (VA) Jesse Brown orders major changes in the way his department handles harassment complaints and requires all 259,549 VA employees to attend four hours of sexual harassment lectures. Brown's announcement comes a few hours after Senator Barbara A. Mikulski (D-MD) condemns VA administrators for ignoring a decade of sexual harassment by top officials at the VA hospital in Atlanta.

March 17 / Roussel-Uclaf announces that RU-486 will be tested in clinical trials in the United States in about two months. The announcement by the drug's manufacturer comes as a result of the Clinton administration's expressed interest in making the drug available to American women.

March 17 / The Senate Judiciary Committee holds a hearing to discuss a number of proposals for federal antistalking legislation. A stalker is defined as someone who harasses victims by following them home, sending them threatening letters, making obscene phone calls, or making death threats.

March 18 / Differences in the treatment of women and men for heart disease dominate debate at the annual scientific meeting of the American College of Cardiology. Researchers report today that although women with heart disease are less likely than men to benefit from medical advances, the older age at which they tend to have heart attacks and their differing symptoms may partly explain the disparity.

March 23 / Attorney General Janet Reno says the Clinton administration wants to stiffen the proposed Freedom of Access to Clinic Entrances Act, which would make it a federal crime to obstruct access to an abortion clinic. Reno's announcement comes after an internal Justice Department review she previously ordered found that current laws will not permit immediate federal action to prevent clinic violence.

March 24 / President Clinton nominates Pamela Harriman to be U.S. ambassador to France. Harriman, a prominent and active Democrat who is the widow of Averell Harriman, will be the first woman ever to serve in that post.

March 25 / The National Council of Juvenile and Family Court Justices hosts the first national conference for the judiciary on domestic violence.

Attending the three-day conference in San Francisco are more than 400 judges, prosecutors, and victims' advocates who have joined "action teams" from every state in the union plus the District of Columbia, Guam, Puerto Rico, and the Mariana Islands. Conference participants hope to develop specific plans for coping with domestic violence and implement them in jurisdictions across the country.

March 29 / Goldman, Sachs & Company in New York City opens a center where its employees can bring their children for the day, at no charge, when a babysitter gets sick, or a day care center is closed, or regular arrangements fail. The center can accommodate as many as 48 children between the ages of three months and 12 years. Emergency child care centers of this type have recently been opened by Chase Manhattan, Time Warner, and Bankers Trust.

March 29 / President Clinton pledges to abolish the ban on using federal Medicaid funds for abortions. The ban—known as the Hyde amendment after its author, Rep. Henry Hyde (R–IL)—has been in force since 1976; it allows federal funds to be used for abortions only when the life of the mother would be endangered if the fetus were carried to term. Congress will have to agree to lifting the ban.

March 30 / The National Institutes of Health announces a new health research initiative that will involve more than 160,000 women age 50 to 79, one-fifth of whom will be minority women. The project will examine the causes of heart disease, cancer, and osteoporosis, and will look at the role of diet and hormone replacement therapy in disease prevention.

March 30 / A panel of congresswomen testify today before the House Ways and Means Subcommittee on Health on the types of benefits that should be included in the Clinton administration's health care reform plan. Rep. Olympia Snowe (R–ME), cochair of the Congressional Caucus for Women's Issues, says that the many needed services include prenatal and delivery care, mammography, Pap smears, baby care, and a wide range of support services such as transportation or assistance in finding child care.

April 2 / The U.S. Supreme Court rejects a request by North Dakota's only abortion clinic to stop state officials from enforcing a state law that requires women to receive counseling and to wait 24 hours before obtaining an abortion.

April 4 / Roman Catholic feminists gather in Albuquerque, New Mexico, today for the third national Women-Church conference. The meeting includes workshops and lectures on topics like the exclusion of women from the ministry, domestic violence, and sexual abuse by members of the clergy.

April 4 / Admiral Frank Kelso, Jr., chief of naval operations and acting secretary of the Navy, endorses an ambitious plan that would eventually allow women to serve on almost all types of Navy ships including combat vessels.

April 18 / In today's *Washington Post,* Carol Kleiman writes about the contingent workforce—temporary, part-time, subcontracted, and/or independent contract workers. This is a fast growing workforce and a largely female one. But women contingent workers tend to end up at the lower end of the job scale with inferior salaries, fewer benefits, and less chance for training and career advancement, according to the Women's Initiative, the women's advocacy arm of the American Association of Retired Persons (AARP). The AARP group has found not only that contingent work plays a role in keeping women's lifetime earnings lower than men's, but that middle-aged women and older women are disproportionately represented among contingent workers.

April 18 / The first Nancy Drew conference is held this weekend at the University of Iowa and 450 scholars, collectors, and fans gather to discuss the teenage heroine of more than 1,000 books since 1930. Nancy Drew is best known as a smart, adventurous, independent, and free-spirited young woman. According to Nancy Drew scholars, the idea of exploring their heroine as a role model represents a coming of age of popular culture in women's studies.

April 19 / David Swank, dean of the University of Oklahoma Law Center where Anita Hill teaches, is stepping down, reportedly to let a "healing process" begin. Swank has loyally backed Hill, but has declined to comment on whether he is being forced out because of his support for her.

April 19 / Governor Roy Romer of Colorado signs into law a bill to protect clients, doctors, and staff at health clinics and medical facilities from being harassed by anti-abortion protesters. The Colorado law will be the strongest of its kind, creating a "protective zone" around abortion clinics by making it illegal for protesters to get within eight feet of people entering and leaving the facilities, and punishing violators with a $750 fine and six months in jail.

April 19 / Thirty-four percent of Americans say they have witnessed a man beating his wife or girlfriend, and 14 percent of women report that they have been beaten, according to the Family Violence Prevention Fund. The results of the first comprehensive nationwide telephone survey on family violence, released today, are based on a national sampling of 500 men and 500 women age 18 or older.

April 21 / President Clinton announces that Karen Nussbaum is his choice to head the Women's Bureau of the Department of Labor. Nussbaum, a former office worker, has served since 1977 as the executive director of 9to5, the National Association of Working Women. She also serves as president of District 925 of the Service Employees International Union, and on the union's executive board.

April 21 / Roussel-Uclaf, the French manufacturer of RU-486, agrees to license the drug to an American organization, the Population Council, which will find a manufacturer in the United States and sponsor an application to the Food and Drug Administration. RU-486 has been used safely and successfully in Europe to end early pregnancies without surgery and is expected to be on the American market within two years.

April 22 / Children, teachers, and child care providers take time off today to march and rally for higher wages and health care benefits for child care workers in what is being called "Worthy Wage Day," a program sponsored by a group known as the Worthy Wage Coalition. According to the Child Care Employee Project, a research and advocacy project in Oakland, California, the highest paid teachers at child care centers make an average of $15,488 a year, and paid health benefits are offered to less than a third of all teachers.

April 23 / U.S. Surgeon General Antonia C. Novello proposes a federal action plan to improve the health of Hispanic Americans, a large percentage of whom are uninsured and whose health problems include a tuberculosis rate as much as four times higher than that of the rest of the population. The plan calls for better medical data about the Hispanic community, greater access to community-based health care, and an increased Hispanic presence in the health and science professions. It also recommends more attention to the needs of migrant workers and undocumented aliens.

April 23 / The Department of Defense releases the second part of its inspector general's report on Tailhook. (The first was released last year; *see* September 24, 1992.) The report (*Tailhook 91, Part 2*) says that 83 women and seven men were assaulted during the three days of the convention. In total, 117 officers were implicated in one or more incidents of indecent assault, indecent exposure, conduct unbecoming an officer, or failure to act in a proper leadership capacity while at the Tailhook convention. The report also says, "The number of individuals involved in all types of misconduct or other inappropriate behavior was more widespread than these figures would suggest. Furthermore, several hundred other officers were aware of the misconduct and chose to ignore it." The findings of the inspector general's investigation are being turned over to the Navy and Marine Corps, which will be responsible for taking appropriate action against the officers found to have been implicated in the affair.

April 27 / Family-oriented corporate programs such as child care and flexible working hours encourage employees to perform better and boost employees' morale and loyalty, according to findings by researchers at the Families and Work Institute and the University of Chicago, who hold a joint press conference today. The companies studied, Johnson & Johnson and Fel-Pro, Inc., have established reputations for their conscientious attention to family problems.

April 27 / The House of Representatives approves legislation that will establish an independent office within the Department of Veterans Affairs to examine all discrimination complaints, including sexual harassment complaints. The bill also orders the permanent assignment of a staff of trained counselors to the Office of Employment Discrimination Complaints Resolution, and calls for independent administrative law judges to make final decisions on complaints.

April 28 / Defense Secretary Les Aspin announces that he will lift the Pentagon ban on women serving in aerial combat (Congress repealed the statutory bans in 1991), and will ask Congress to repeal the law barring women from Navy combat ships. The decision will permit qualified female pilots to make the shift immediately from trainers and transports to high performance combat aircraft. Aspin has also ordered the services to consider permitting women to be assigned to all other combat jobs except for those in front line infantry and armored units.

April 28 / On the first Take Our Daughters to Work Day, almost one million girls age nine to 15 join their mothers, mentors, and even some fathers at companies and government agencies across the country. The Ms. Foundation for Women is sponsoring the day to help raise girls' self-esteem and to introduce them to the array of workplace opportunities. Although the day was initially planned as a New York event, the idea caught on elsewhere.

May 4 / Bernadine Healy, director of the National Institutes of Health, says that there is some truth to allegations that the agency has discriminated against its employees on the basis of race and sex. Healy announces that she has appointed a task force to investigate the allegations and to set up a disciplinary process for managers who have engaged in discriminatory practices.

May 4 / The House Armed Services Committee begins hearings on President Clinton's plan to lift the ban on homosexuals in the military. Unlike hearings held last month by the Senate Armed Services Committee, which focused on gay men in the military, the House hearings will concentrate on how the ban affects both heterosexual and homosexual military women.

May 6 / New York State's highest court rules that drug treatment programs cannot exclude pregnant women as a matter of policy because the practice constitutes sexual discrimination.

May 10 / The female condom is approved for marketing by the Food and

Drug Administration. The manufacturer, Wisconsin Pharmacal, announces that the device, called Reality, will be shipped to clinics, centers treating people with sexually transmitted diseases, and doctors within eight to 10 weeks, and will be available commercially nationwide by the end of the year.

May 13 / Attorney General Janet Reno testifies in support of the Freedom of Access to Clinic Entrances Act at a hearing before the Senate Labor and Human Resources Committee. Reno says the bill, which would allow federal law enforcement officials to help protect abortion clinics, is needed because local law enforcement agencies are overwhelmed by nationally organized violence against the clinics.

May 13 / Jane Bolin, a retired judge on New York's Domestic Relations Court, is presented with New York City's Corporation Counsel's award for distinguished service. Bolin, age 85, was the first black woman to graduate from Yale Law School, the first black woman to join the New York City Bar Association, and the first black woman in the Corporation Counsel's office, to which she was appointed in 1939 by Mayor Fiorello La Guardia. Since mandatory retirement in 1978, Bolin has continued to work and currently reviews cases for the New York Board of Regents.

May 14 / In a letter sent to Hillary Rodham Clinton, 30 members of the House of Representatives call on the Clinton administration to include abortion services in the new health care plan.

May 16 / Barbara Spyridon Pope has started the Foundation for Prevention of Sexual Harassment and Workplace Discrimination, according to today's *New York Times*. Pope, who was assistant secretary of the Navy for manpower and reserve affairs in the Bush administration, is widely regarded—and respected—as the person who deserves most of the credit for forcing the Navy to get at the truth about Tailhook.

May 17 / Joel Valdez is convicted of aggravated sexual assault in Austin, Texas. The case has drawn national attention because it turned on whether a woman whom Valdez attacked at knife point "consented" to have sex with him when she supplied him with a condom. The victim, Elizabeth Xan Wilson, explained to the court that she gave her attacker the condom because she was afraid of contracting the AIDS virus, and compared her position to that of a victim of robbery giving her assailant her wallet while being held at knife point. Wilson said that in that case, as in her own situation, there should not be a question of whether a crime had been committed.

May 18 / Rita Dove is named the next poet laureate of the United States. A Pulitzer Prize-winning poet who is a professor of poetry at the University of Virginia, Dove will be the first black poet laureate and, at age 40, the youngest person to hold the position.

May 19 / By a vote of 20 to 15, the House Judiciary Committee approves the Freedom of Choice Act, legislation that would codify the Supreme Court's 1973 *Roe* v. *Wade* decision establishing a woman's right to have an abortion.

May 20 / The Senate Rules Committee dismisses a petition that sought to void Senator Bob Packwood's election last November on the grounds that his lying during his reelection campaign about sexually harassing members of his staff and lobbyists constituted fraud (*see* December 15, 1992). The committee's conclusion that Packwood's election in November cannot be overturned does not, however, mean the end of the Senate Ethics Committee's investigation of the sexual harassment charges against the Oregon Republican (*see* December 1, 1992).

May 25 / The Senate approves President Clinton's nomination of gay rights activist Roberta Achtenberg as assistant secretary of housing and urban development in charge of fair housing and equal opportunity. Achtenberg is the first openly lesbian nominee to be confirmed by the Senate for high federal office.

June 1 / The board of the Virginia Military Institute (VMI), which is determined to preserve VMI as an all-male institution, tells its lawyers to draw up a proposal that will bring the institution into compliance with federal anti-sex discrimination laws without having to admit women. This could mean a proposal to start a state-financed military program for women at Virginia Tech or at a private women's college (*see* October 5, 1992).

June 2 / More than three-quarters of teenage girls and 56 percent of teenage boys say they have been the target of unwanted sexual advances, according to a survey by Louis Harris & Associates for the American Association of University Women Foundation, which released the findings today. The study is reported to be the first to quantify both what teenagers do to one another and how they react when it happens. The survey found that girls, far more than boys, said such insolent behavior interferes with their ability to study, and 43 percent of girls said this type of behavior made them feel less confident about themselves.

June 5 / The Reverend Mary Adelia McLeod is elected bishop of the Episcopal Diocese of Vermont, making her the first woman in the United States, and the second in the world, to hold the post of diocesan bishop in the Anglican church.

June 5 / In the special election to replace Lloyd Bentsen (who resigned from the Senate to become President Clinton's treasury secretary), Texas state treasurer Kay Bailey Hutchison, a Republican, defeats Bob Krueger (the incumbent appointed to fill Bentsen's seat until this election). Hutchison's election brings the number of women in the Senate to seven, and the number of Republican women in the Senate to two.

June 6 / Julie Krone rides Colonial Affair to victory in the 125th Belmont Stakes. She is the first woman jockey to win a Triple Crown race.

June 10 / Rep. Maxine Waters (D-CA) introduces a bill to establish a Women's Bureau within the Department of Veterans Affairs (VA). The measure, which would give the VA Women's Bureau the authority to investigate all matters pertaining to the welfare of women veterans, is designed to provide outreach to women veterans and to provide a resource for and consulting services to women's veterans coordinators.

June 12 / The *New York Times* reports that Felice N. Schwartz, the founder and president of Catalyst, a national nonprofit organization that works to help women in business and professional life, has announced that she will step down after 31 years. Although Schwartz is leaving Catalyst, she has pledged to remain an advocate for women. Her successor, who will begin July 5th, is Sheila W. Wellington, currently the secretary of Yale University.

June 15 / President Clinton announces that he will nominate Ruth Bader Ginsburg, a judge on the U.S. Court of Appeals for the District of Columbia Circuit, for the Supreme Court seat being vacated by retiring Justice Byron R. White. Ginsburg is regarded as a pioneer in the development of legal rights for women. If confirmed, she will be the second woman on the High Court and the first Jewish justice since the late Justice Abe Fortas resigned in 1969.

June 15 / Speaking at the "World Conference on Human Rights" in Vienna, Austria, Secretary of State Warren Christopher announces that the United States will press for the appointment of a United Nations Special Rapporteur on Violence Against Women. Christopher also says that the Clinton administration will seek Senate approval of the Convention on the Elimination of All Forms of Discrimination Against Women.

June 22 / The Department of Veterans Affairs (VA) announces that it will begin a series of health care initiatives for women. It will establish four health care centers for women, provide four stress disorder treatment teams, and hire 69 counselors to treat victims of sexual assault and harassment. A survey by the department's inspector general found that senior health officials at the VA have heretofore ignored the needs of the growing number of women veterans.

June 24 / Sonya Tyler, the women's basketball coach at Howard University since 1980, is awarded $2.39 million by a District of Columbia superior court jury in a sex discrimination case against the university. The jury found the university guilty of violating both the District's Human Rights Act and Title IX, the federal law barring sex discrimination in educational institutions that receive federal funds.

June 29 / Executive women have made significant gains in their professional and personal lives over the past decade, but they are paying a price in
terms of the energy needed to juggle work and family obligations. *Decade of
the Executive Woman,* a report released today by the Graduate School of
Management at the University of California at Los Angeles (UCLA) and the
executive search firm Korn/Ferry International, found that today's average
senior woman executive is 44 years old and married with children. A similar
study done in 1982 by UCLA and Korn/Ferry found that most women
executives had sacrificed family for career. Because they report feeling
burned out, three-quarters of today's executive women, compared with
only 30 percent of their male counterparts, say they want to retire before
age 65.

June 30 / For Bernadine Healy, today is the last day on the job as director
of the National Institutes of Health (NIH). She is the first woman to head
NIH and in the two years that she has been director, she has made many
revolutionary changes, including establishing the Women's Health Initiative, a 14-year clinical study on diseases in women as they age.

June 30 / To the dismay of abortion rights proponents in Congress, who
were outflanked in a series of procedural maneuvers, the House adopts a
modified version of the Hyde amendment. The amendment to the Labor-
Health and Human Services appropriations bill prohibits federal funds to be
used for abortions for poor women except in cases of rape, incest, or a threat
to the life of the woman. The Senate is expected to act on the bill in
September. Pro-choice members of Congress reportedly hope that the
amendment, which President Clinton opposes (*see* March 29, 1993), can be
deleted during an anticipated House-Senate conference on the bill.

WOMEN
AND
HEALTH

THE POLITICS OF
WOMEN'S HEALTH

*The Honorable Patricia Schroeder
and the Honorable Olympia Snowe*

MORE THAN A DECADE AGO, the federal government funded a study of 20,000 male physicians to determine if small doses of aspirin would help prevent heart attacks. Physicians were thought to be the ideal subjects, knowledgeable and disciplined, and able to comply with complicated research protocols. Women, who comprised 10 percent of physicians in the United States at the time, were excluded from the study. Nurses, the vast majority of whom were women, apparently weren't considered up to the task.

By 1988, when evidence from this study showed that aspirin indeed lowered heart attack rates in men, the political climate had changed. Two government task force reports on women's health had sounded the alarm about the dearth of research data on women. A year later, when the bipartisan Congressional Caucus for Women's Issues first raised this issue on Capitol Hill, the aspirin study was on its way to becoming a highly charged political symbol of government's failure to address women's health.

After several years of debate, Congress and now President Clinton have taken important steps to give women's health the place it deserves on the nation's research agenda. Signed into law on June 10, 1993, the National Institutes of Health (NIH) Revitalization Act includes the requirement that women be adequately represented in federally funded clinical research studies. The new law also gives statutory authority to the NIH Office of Research on Women's Health and provides dramatic increases in spending for research on women's health issues.

Enactment of the NIH Revitalization Act closed the first chapter of a major campaign launched by the Congressional Caucus for Women's Issues in 1989 to improve the health of American women. But, this campaign is far from over.

This essay examines the role of the caucus in focusing the attention of policymakers, the research community, and the public on women's health, a story that began in 1989 with the introduction of legislation to improve research on contraception and infertility.

CAUCUS EXPANDS AGENDA TO INCLUDE WOMEN'S HEALTH

For its first dozen years, the Congressional Caucus for Women's Issues was best known as an advocate for legal and economic equity for women. Founded in 1977, the new caucus cut its political teeth gaining a three-year extension for states to ratify the Equal Rights Amendment (ERA). As prospects for the ERA grew dimmer, the caucus in 1981 began a legislative push to secure economic equity for women, an effort that continues today.

One issue notably absent from the caucus's agenda was reproductive choice. From its founding until January 1993, the caucus took no position on the issue of abortion. The founding congresswomen had agreed that the organization would work only on the issues that united them, not on those that divided them.

As the Supreme Court moved in the late-1980s to give states more latitude to restrict access to abortion, escalating the debate in Congress and around the country, we, as caucus cochairs, began to look for a new middle ground that could be embraced by congresswomen on both sides of the abortion divide. There had always been broad support among the congresswomen for reducing the need for abortion. We decided to pursue a new, highly visible research effort aimed at preventing unintended pregnancy through improved contraception.

When we began work on our legislation in 1989, we were shocked to learn that American women had fewer contraceptive options available to them than women in Western Europe and indeed, many underdeveloped countries. This situation has improved somewhat with the recent approval of Norplant and Depo Provera. Additionally, only one major U.S. pharmaceutical company was engaged in contraceptive research in 1989, down from 13 in 1970.

Throughout the 1980s, the National Institutes of Health had received only about $8 million a year for applied research in contraceptive development, without any significant funding increases. For a decade, funding for contraceptive development had fallen victim to a political environment that equated contraception with abortion and chilled research on any area of human reproduction—including, ironically, efforts to help infertile couples conceive.

We introduced legislation in 1989 calling for the establishment of three contraceptive and two infertility research centers under the auspices of NIH to conduct clinical and applied research. The legislation also proposed a grant and loan repayment program to attract top scientists to work at the university-based centers.

At the same time several congresswomen began working to focus congressional attention on breast cancer. Following a family tragedy—that of a sister, who like many women underwent a biopsy for a suspicious lump in her breast and awoke to find her breast, lymph nodes, and the muscles in her chest wall removed—former Rep. Mary Rose Oakar (D-OH) introduced legislation to penalize states that failed to require doctors to inform women of their treatment options.

These two initiatives—contraceptive and infertility research and informed consent for breast cancer treatment—were the first components of the Women's Health Equity Act (WHEA), the caucus's omnibus legislation on women's health. We used as our model for this package another successful caucus initiative, the Economic Equity Act (EEA).

First introduced in 1981 and introduced in every Congress since, the Economic Equity Act is a package of individual bills that is reintroduced as one bill to set forward a broad-based agenda for eliminating barriers to economic equity for women. Many important reforms during the 1980s in the area of pensions and child support enforcement received their start as part of the Economic Equity Act. We were eager to apply this legislative model to women's health.

RESEARCH NEED IDENTIFIED

As the caucus began assembling its women's health package, we discovered that much of the groundwork was already in place. The most comprehensive effort was the 1985 *Women's Health Report of the Public Health Service Task Force on Women's Health Issues*. The task force held public meetings in Washington, DC and around the country to examine the status of women's health with an emphasis on the diversity among women and the social factors that affect their health. The report defined women's health issues as diseases or conditions that were unique to women, were more prevalent or more serious in women, or for which specific risk factors or interventions differed for women.

We were particularly struck by one of the 16 recommendations contained in the task force's final report: the need to expand biomedical and behavioral research on women's health. The report identified the lack of data on women as an important factor in limiting our understanding of their health care needs and recommended that ". . . a systematic effort . . . be made to address issues relating to gender bias in research and clinical practice . . ."[1]

The Public Health Service (PHS) task force generated more than a final report to occupy the shelves of policymakers and women's health advocates; it led to the establishment of advisory committees on women's health in each Public Health Service agency. One such advisory committee at NIH began working to remedy the lack of data on women by developing a new policy to encourage researchers to include women in clinical studies.

NIH advised the research community of its new policy in 1986 by publishing it in the *NIH Guide for Grants and Contracts*. Although the policy did not *require* that women be included in clinical trials, researchers were encouraged to provide a clear rationale for their exclusion if an all-male study population was planned. The policy also said that researchers who included women in their trials should note and evaluate gender differences in their research results.

A 1987 report by the Women's Health Advisory Committee called on NIH to implement the policy it had announced a year earlier and to increase its investment in women's health research. The report itself provided an institute-by-institute accounting of resources committed to research on women's health. Based on this inventory, the advisory committee calculated that only 13.5 percent of NIH's overall budget in 1987 went to women's health research.

Although the 1985 Public Health Service report and the 1987 NIH advisory committee report received little attention at the time they were issued, their recommendations for increasing women's health research were kept alive by a small group of advocates from the American Nurses Association, the American Psychiatric Association, and the American College of Obstetricians and Gynecologists who began meeting to develop a strategy for spurring interest in women's health issues in Congress. This group evolved into a new professional association, the Society for the Advancement of Women's Health Research, whose primary purpose is to advocate for increased funding for research on women's health. These advocates were convinced that women's health was an issue ripe for public attention and congressional action.

---

[1]Department of Health and Human Services (DHHS), Public Health Service (PHS). *Women's Health Report of the Public Health Service Task Force on Women's Health Issues*. DHHS Pub. No. (PHS) 85-50206. Washington, DC: DHHS, May 1985.

GENERAL ACCOUNTING OFFICE REPORT
SERVES AS CATALYST FOR ACTION

The issue of women's health research exploded on Capitol Hill on June 18, 1990, when the General Accounting Office (GAO) told the House Subcommittee on Health and the Environment that three years after establishing a policy to encourage the inclusion of women in research studies, NIH had done little to implement it. Although the scope of the GAO report *(National Institutes of Health: Problems in Implementing Policy on Women in Study Populations)* was fairly narrow, it became the "smoking gun" for the government's neglect of women's health research.

We had requested the GAO investigation on behalf of the caucus in December 1989 in an attempt to focus public and congressional attention on the lack of research on women's health. Rep. Henry Waxman (D-CA), chairman of Energy and Commerce's Subcommittee on Health and the Environment, joined us in our request to the GAO and proved to be a powerful ally on women's health.

At the time we made the request to the GAO, we were disturbed by reports of several major studies that, like the aspirin study on physicians, had excluded women. One was the Multiple Risk Factor Intervention Trial, a $115 million study of heart disease risk factors conducted on 13,000 men. Even the acronym for the study—Mr. Fit—seemed to confirm the scientific community's insensitivity to women's health.

NIH's Baltimore Longitudinal Study of Aging—the National Institute on Aging's largest study (started in 1958 and ongoing today)—was another case in point. Women were excluded from the study entirely for its first 20 years, added only after 1978. The major research findings from the study were published by the Department of Health and Human Services in 1984 in a thick tome entitled *Normal Human Aging.* Although women outnumber men dramatically in their senior years, this report contained no research findings on women.

We were outraged that women, who pay their fair share of tax dollars in this country, derived little benefit from these important federally funded research studies. Still, we recognized that these studies had been funded before NIH adopted its 1986 policy on women in clinical trials. Surely the situation had improved, we thought, as we awaited the results of the GAO investigation. We were wrong.

The tone of the hearing on the GAO report, held before Rep. Waxman's Subcommittee on Health and the Environment, was best described by the magazine *Science* when it wrote, "If a federal agency can be hoist by its own petard, then the National Institutes of Health suffered that experience at a congressional hearing . . . on women's health."[2]

The GAO reported to the subcommittee that although the policy was adopted in 1986, NIH had not applied it consistently in reviewing research applications until mid-1990, after the GAO completed its report. It seemed clear to us that the GAO investigation itself had been the primary impetus for NIH to implement its own policy.

According to the GAO, implementation had been hampered by NIH's failure to communicate the policy to the scientific research community. Indeed, even though NIH advised the research community of its policy in the *NIH Guide for Grants and Contracts,* the application booklet that NIH provided to researchers contained no reference to the policy. In addition, the GAO said that NIH had directly undermined the goal of its policy by refusing to consider the gender composition of the study group as a factor in determining the scientific merit of research proposals. Compliance with the inclusion policy was to be stated in the administrative notes filed only after an application had been evaluated on its merits.

In our original request, we also asked the GAO to examine the extent to which grant proposals were being designed to examine gender differences, as specifically addressed in the NIH policy. To us, the token inclusion of women in study populations was meaningless unless the researchers also examined their findings for gender differences. The GAO confirmed that this aspect of the policy had been virtually ignored by NIH and the research community. Although some NIH grant solicitations had begun to cite the importance of including women in study populations, few suggested that studies be designed to analyze differences between the sexes.

While acknowledging the validity of the GAO's findings, NIH Acting Director Dr. William Raub told the subcommittee that, "The NIH system is not badly out of focus, but instead needs only some fine tuning." He pledged to comply with the GAO's modest recommendations, which included informing NIH staff, grant reviewers, and the research community how to carry out the policy; revising the grant application booklet to include a section explaining the policy; and directing NIH institutes to maintain readily accessible data on the gender composition of study participants.

Testifying on behalf of the caucus at the June hearing, we used the opportunity to announce our plan to introduce omnibus legislation on women's health. Among the provisions we described from our soon-to-be introduced Women's Health Equity Act was the creation of an office on

[2]Palca, Joseph. "Women Left Out at NIH." *Science* 248 (June 30, 1990): 1601-2.

women's health research at NIH to oversee enforcement of the inclusion policy and to direct research efforts on women's health. When asked about our proposal, Dr. Raub said that it would be ". . . premature to speculate about whether a specific organizational change would be necessary."

The GAO report addressed just one dimension of a much larger debate on women's health. However, it demonstrated an institution-wide failure on the part of NIH to take action on a policy it had acknowledged was necessary to address significant gaps in knowledge about women's health. The GAO report was quite simply an indictment of NIH and the research community for its callous disregard of women's health. It also served as the catalyst for a number of important policy changes made by Congress and NIH.

AN OFFICE AND A POLICY WITH TEETH

The first Women's Health Equity Act was introduced in the House of Representatives on July 27, 1990. The package contained 20 separate bills that addressed deficiencies in the treatment of women's health in three crucial areas: research, services, and prevention.

The caucus felt strongly that a comprehensive approach to women's health was important. Research into the causes and cures of diseases affecting women was needed to develop effective treatments. Likewise, knowledge about which treatments were most effective was of little use unless women had access to the full range of available health services. Finally, the best way to treat women's health problems was to prevent them from occurring, or to catch them early when they were most treatable. These tenets still apply today.

The research title of the Women's Health Equity Act contained two provisions that responded directly to the GAO's disturbing findings. First, it proposed to write into law NIH's policies regarding the inclusion of women and minorities in clinical research. A parallel policy on minority inclusion in research studies had been issued by NIH a year after its policy on women was announced. While our legislation required researchers to include women and minorities in their studies, exceptions would be permitted where inclusion of these groups would pose a danger to their health or be inappropriate to the purpose of the research, or where there were other compelling reasons as determined by the NIH director. The bill also required clinical trials to be designed so that an analysis of gender differences could be done.

A second provision of the research title proposed the creation of an office of women's health to serve as an overseer and coordinator of efforts to improve women's health research at NIH. This office would identify women's health research needs, supplement existing funds for research on women's health and gender differences, and coordinate research among the various institutes. Finally, the office would be responsible for monitoring the inclusion of women in study populations.

The remaining bills in the title called for increased funding for research on a variety of important women's health issues, including breast and ovarian cancer, acquired immune deficiency syndrome (AIDS), osteoporosis, and contraception and infertility.

Four days later, on August 1, 1990, Sen. Barbara Mikulski (D-MD) introduced the Senate version of the Women's Health Equity Act. On that same day, she won inclusion of several of its key provisions—including the requirement that women be included in clinical trials and the establishment of a women's health office at NIH—in the NIH reauthorization bill approved by the Senate Labor and Human Resources Committee. The House Energy and Commerce Subcommittee on Health and the Environment was prepared to take similar action when Congress reconvened in September.

With growing congressional support for legislative action to remedy the neglect of women's health research, NIH began making its own plans to create a women's health office and to more aggressively enforce its policy of including women in clinical trials.

In late August, NIH reissued its policy on women in clinical trials. Only this time, the policy had teeth. Rather than merely encouraging the inclusion of women in clinical trials, scientists would now be required to include women proportionally to the extent they were affected by the disease being studied. NIH also specifically acknowledged that the underrepresentation of women in a study could hamper the researcher's ability to answer the scientific question being posed. For this reason, the new policy required researchers to provide a compelling justification if their proposals did not include adequate numbers of women to be studied. However, the most significant change was NIH's unequivocal statement that it would refuse to fund grants or contracts to researchers who did not comply with the policy.

To monitor enforcement of the new policy, NIH decided to establish the Office of Research on Women's Health. The official announcement was made at a meeting between members of the Congressional Caucus for Women's Issues and the institute directors held at the Bethesda, Maryland campus of NIH in early September 1990.

That same day, Health and Human Services Secretary Dr. Louis Sullivan made his own news on women's health by announcing his decision to recommend to President Bush that Cleveland Heart Clinic Director Dr.

Bernadine Healy be named as NIH director. Seven months later, Dr. Healy, the first woman ever nominated for this position, was confirmed by the Senate.

The meeting between caucus members and NIH officials—including eight institute directors—was not without fireworks. Tempers flared when the head of the National Institute on Aging acknowledged that women had been excluded from the Baltimore Longitudinal Study on Aging because there was no women's bathroom at the Baltimore hospital where study participants came periodically for medical assessments. For want of a bathroom, women were excluded for 20 years from the most important study of the aging process!

While the meeting was acrimonious at times, we were able to agree on several important steps to advance women's health within NIH and the Public Health Service. First, we agreed on the need for a summit on women's health to gather the opinions of the medical and research community, as well as women's health advocates. In a letter to Secretary Sullivan sent earlier that day, caucus members asked that the summit be held within one year. Additionally, Assistant Secretary for Health Dr. James Mason agreed to prepare an action plan on women's health for each agency of the Public Health Service.

The summit on women's health took place almost exactly one year later in September 1991 at a conference center located in Hunt Valley, Maryland. The 300-page report of the conference, entitled *Opportunities for Research on Women's Health,* summarized hundreds of recommendations for further research made by 10 working groups. These groups looked at women's health issues both across the life span—from birth to the mature years—and in terms of crosscutting issues such as reproductive biology, cardiovascular disease, and malignancy. Although NIH characterized the Hunt Valley report as a research agenda for addressing the gaps in knowledge about women's health, the failure to establish priorities for the needed research and a plan for implementation limited its usefulness.

The second initiative to emerge from the NIH meeting was the Public Health Service's *Action Plan for Women's Health,* presented to the caucus by Health and Human Services Secretary Dr. Louis Sullivan at a February 1991 meeting in the Capitol. The action plan contained 39 specific goals to be pursued by individual agencies and offices within the Public Health Service to advance women's health. Although it appeared that many agencies had merely listed activities related to women's health that were already underway, the action plan is still a valuable compilation of plans and activities for the various PHS offices with responsibility for women's health.

In April 1991, Dr. Bernadine Healy took over as director of NIH. Although the Office of Research on Women's Health was already up and running, Dr. Healy moved quickly to establish her own track record on women's health. She used her first visit to Capitol Hill to unveil plans for the Women's Health Initiative—a $625 million, 14-year study of 150,000 women—which she termed the equivalent of a "moonwalk for women." The focus of the Women's Health Initiative was ambitious: the prevention of breast cancer, osteoporosis, and heart disease in older women.

Bernadine Healy brought new credibility to women's health research at a time when many at NIH viewed the increased congressional and public attention to the issue as a temporary annoyance. However, Dr. Healy alienated many women's health advocates when she opposed the women's health provisions of the NIH reauthorization bill as unnecessary.

Since 1991, there have been an unprecedented number of women's health hearings and conferences, reports and papers, and references to women's health in legislation and administration policies. However, it was the three-month period from June to September of 1990 that firmly established women's health as a potent political issue on Capitol Hill and in the medical research community. Beginning with the release of the GAO report in June—followed by the introduction of the Women's Health Equity Act in July, and House and Senate committee action on the NIH reauthorization bill in August and September—women's health had arrived as an important issue in the minds of policymakers, the press, and most important, American women.

A LEGISLATIVE STRATEGY UNFOLDS

Three separate legislative processes determine which programs get federal dollars and how much they receive. The caucus used all three—the budget, authorization, and appropriations processes—to advance the cause of women's health. These legislative processes were used simultaneously to increase women's health research at NIH and to expand prevention and other services important to women. Although these efforts were legislatively distinct, our success in one area fostered a climate that fueled support for the others.

The two primary vehicles for the passage of women's health legislation have been the NIH reauthorization bill, which finally became law in June 1993, and the annual appropriations bill for the Departments of Labor, Health and Human Services, and Education. Several other provisions of the Women's Health Equity Act were also passed as free-standing bills or incorporated into other pieces of legislation.

Enactment of the National Institutes of Health reauthorization bill represented the culmination of our three-year effort to improve women's health. Although NIH had already adopted many of our proposals by the time the bill was signed in June of 1993—including establishing an Office of Research on Women's Health and strengthening its policy to require the inclusion of women in medical research—it was important to put the force of law behind these hard-fought gains for women's health. Giving statutory authority to the newly created office and the policy on women in clinical trials will ensure that, at some point in the future, these important victories will not be reversed or discarded at whim.

The other WHEA provisions passed as part of the NIH bill increased funding authorization levels for research on breast, ovarian, and cervical cancer; osteoporosis; and contraception and infertility. While authorizing language of this type is one of the primary ways Congress seeks to influence the medical research agenda, the most important measure of our success was in the actual dollars provided for women's health research in the annual appropriations bills.

Using the appropriations process to increase funding for a particular area of medical research, however, can be tricky business. Congress has tended to eschew specific earmarks lest the research agenda be dictated by the lobbying group with the deepest pockets or best connections. The scientific community, too, abhors directives and earmarking of funds from Congress, putting its faith in peer reviewers, not politicians, to determine the research agenda.

Still, under the current system of research funding, women's health research had been sorely neglected. For the most part, the researchers who write the grant proposals are male, as are most of the members of the peer review committees who determine which grants to fund. Moreover, powerful interest groups have developed around entrenched areas of research. And while they may fight each other tooth and nail for a bigger slice of the funding pie, they quickly band together against any newcomer who might force a redivision of the pie. On all counts, women's health research was losing out.

Consider, for example, research on ovarian cancer—one of the deadliest cancers affecting women—as well as research on women and AIDS, which tragically has become one of the leading killers of young women. In 1993, an estimated 22,000 women will be diagnosed with AIDS—of whom more than half will die. The long-term survival rate for ovarian cancer has improved little in the past 30 years. In 1989, when we began looking at funding for research on women's health, the National Cancer Institute had allocated only $7.9 million of its $1.6 billion budget to ovarian cancer research. By 1993, in large part due to a legislative initiative by Rep. Patsy Mink (D-HI), the research budget for ovarian cancer had increased to $26 million.

Two pieces of legislation introduced by Rep. Constance Morella (R-MD) as part of the Women's Health Equity Act sought to improve the odds for women with AIDS. Although the number of women with the AIDS virus began to grow dramatically in the late 1980s, research into how the condition affects women did not. Since the introduction of Rep. Morella's legislation, research at the National Institutes of Health on women and AIDS has increased steadily and new attention will soon be paid to developing substances that can be used by women to prevent infection with the virus that causes AIDS.

Our success in increasing funding for women's health research was not limited to ovarian cancer and women and AIDS. Appropriations for the NIH Office for Research on Women's Health climbed from $2 million in fiscal year 1991 to $10.9 million two years later, the majority of which was used to supplement ongoing research on women's health in the different institutes. The Women's Health Equity Act also resulted in the creation of five centers for contraceptive and infertility research under NIH.

THE POLITICS OF BREAST CANCER

Nowhere was the caucus more successful than in its effort to increase funds for breast cancer research. Although many people had a hand in this success, it was former Rep. Oakar who guided the caucus's early efforts to increase awareness of breast cancer—and who ultimately rounded up votes against her own leadership for failing to act to protect women against this tragic disease.

Congress did not respond to the call for states to adopt informed consent requirements for breast cancer surgery, despite the fact that a panel of experts convened by NIH in June 1990 confirmed that for early breast cancer, lumpectomy (in which only the affected area is removed, rather than the entire breast) followed by radiation, is preferable to mastectomy.

While this effort was not successful, the fight to restore Medicare (the federal health insurance program for the elderly) coverage of screening mammography was. In 1988, Congress passed the Medicare Catastrophic Coverage Act, which sought to protect the elderly and disabled from catastrophic health care costs and included, for the first time, coverage of mammograms every other year for eligible women. The effort to repeal the catastrophic coverage bill began almost as soon as it was passed as angry seniors objected to the use of a new surtax to pay for the program. Despite efforts to forge a compromise that might have saved mammography coverage, in late 1989 Congress decided to scrap the entire act, mammograms and all.

A number of caucus members moved quickly to restore the mammography benefit. In fact, the first version of the Women's Health Equity Act contained three separate bills to restore the mammography benefit, each differing in the level of reimbursement that would be provided.

Legislation to restore mammography coverage under Medicare was added and later struck from the 1991 Omnibus Budget Reconciliation Act. Outraged that mammography benefits were jettisoned once again, Rep. Oakar rounded up other congresswomen willing to vote against the budget reconciliation package if the benefit was not restored. And she took to the House floor, publicly threatening to vote against the bill, a threat the House leadership—facing a close vote on the bill—could ill-afford to ignore.

It was never clear how many congresswomen were prepared to vote against the reconciliation package, which among other things included nearly $20 billion for child care assistance, mostly for needy families. However, the congresswomen held firm and the provision was restored in conference.

The caucus next turned its attention to the need to increase funding for research on breast cancer, the most common form of cancer in women and the second leading cause—after lung cancer—of cancer deaths in women. Particularly troubling to the congresswomen was the inability of cancer researchers to explain the recent increase in breast cancer rates: one in every eight baby girls born today can expect to develop breast cancer in her lifetime, compared with one in every 20 in 1961.

Increasing funding for basic research into the causes of breast cancer was the primary goal of early legislative efforts in this area. With only $17 million of the $77 million budgeted for breast cancer research in 1989 targeted toward basic research, caucus members were concerned that this area was being given short shrift.

The first Women's Health Equity Act in 1990 called for a $25 million increase in funding for basic research, which would have brought the National Cancer Institute (NCI) budget for breast cancer research to just over $100 million. By 1993, the NCI had committed nearly $200 million to breast cancer research, with another $210 million earmarked in the Department of Defense budget as part of its medical research program. In all, total appropriations for breast cancer research have increased fourfold over the past three years.

The Senate vote in 1992 to earmark $210 million from the Department of Defense is perhaps the best illustration of the growing clout of the breast cancer lobby, most of whom are survivors of the disease. They have become increasingly politically active, showering lawmakers with more than 600,000 letters and vowing to adopt the tactics of AIDS activists (such as demanding meetings with NIH officials and challenging existing research priorities) in the fight for more breast cancer research funding.

After twice rejecting a bipartisan effort to transfer money for breast cancer research out of the defense budget and into the domestic budget, many senators expected an amendment to directly earmark $210 million in the defense budget for breast cancer research to fail and opposed it. However, when it became clear that the amendment would succeed, senators who had voted against it returned to the Senate floor to change their votes, fearful of casting a wrong vote on the issue of breast cancer. In the end, the amendment passed by a vote of 89-4.

EARLY SUCCESSES EXTEND BEYOND WOMEN'S HEALTH RESEARCH

Three years after the Women's Health Equity Act was first introduced, the caucus has a solid record of accomplishment to show for its efforts, including a new emphasis on women's health issues at NIH, the creation of important disease prevention programs aimed at women, and a more receptive climate that has led to increased funds for women's health programs across the board.

Although the research provisions of WHEA have received the most attention, several of the provisions to improve access to health care services, especially in the area of prevention and early detection, have become law over the years.

The first provision of the WHEA to become law was the Breast and Cervical Cancer Mortality Prevention Act, approved by Congress in 1990. The act created a program of state grants administered by the Centers for Disease Control (CDC) to make mammograms and Pap smears more accessible to low-income women. This important program has enjoyed steady increases in funding over the past few years, enabling more states to expand cancer screening services to poor women.

Concerned that many mammography facilities in the United States had failed to meet professional accreditation, Congress passed the Mammography Quality Assurance Act in 1992. The law established federal standards for mammography facilities and required them to be accredited. Caucus members were stunned and saddened when one of the bill's principal sponsors, Rep. Marilyn Lloyd (D-TN), was diagnosed with breast cancer shortly after the bill's introduction. Testifying on the legislation, Rep. Lloyd told the House Energy and Commerce Subcommittee on Health and the Environment that access to quality mammography had made her "one of the lucky ones."

A second provision of the prevention title of WHEA became law in 1992. The Infertility Prevention Act authorized $25 million for the CDC to prevent infertility through screening and treatment of chlamydia and other sexually transmitted diseases (STDs). An estimated 125,000 women become infertile each year from STD-related pelvic inflammatory disease. While chlamydia is both treatable and preventable, few women with chlamydia experience any symptoms. Because of this, women rarely seek routine screening and treatment for the disease.

The caucus was also concerned about access to health care coverage and included several bills in the WHEA to improve access to health insurance for part-time workers and displaced homemakers who lost their insurance due to divorce or the death of a spouse. By 1992, we knew it was time to abandon these piecemeal efforts in favor of a more comprehensive approach to health care reform.

HEALTH CARE REFORM: EIGHT PRINCIPLES

The executive committee of our bipartisan caucus is comprised of congress-women with diverse political views from liberal Democrats to moderately conservative Republicans. Although several congresswomen had already introduced bills to reform the health care system, there seemed little possibility that this politically diverse group of congresswomen could reach a consensus on comprehensive health care reform legislation. Still, we felt the issue was so important to women that we wanted to find a way of addressing it as a caucus.

We agreed upon a set of principles on women's health care that we would seek to have incorporated into whatever health care reform proposal became law. For this approach, we must thank the Campaign for Women's Health, a broad-based coalition of organizations that developed its own set of 10 principles, for ensuring that issues of importance to women were included in health care reform. We used the campaign's principles as our starting point, arriving in the end with eight principles upon which the congresswomen agreed.

Our health care reform principles focus both on the need to ensure that women have access to coverage, regardless of their employment or marital status, as well as the need to make sure that coverage responds to the unique and special health care needs of women throughout their life spans.

We endorsed universal access to health coverage and the development of a basic benefits package that included important preventive and treatment services for women. The concept of universal access is particularly important for women, who are more likely than men to be employed part time and are concentrated in service, sales, and household jobs that are less likely to have employer-based health insurance.

Our principles also recognize the importance of primary care services and the necessity of making these services available in a range of settings and through a variety of providers, including nurse midwives and nurse practitioners. Another issue of concern to the caucus is the increasing specialization of health care providers, which has put women at risk when a specialist provides primary care without being trained to fully assess a woman's health status.

We also emphasize the need to eliminate gender stereotyping in the delivery of health care, and the need for further research into the service delivery modes that are best suited to meeting women's health care needs. We know that women often receive less aggressive treatment or appropriate care than men with the same symptoms, particularly with respect to coronary care. The causes of these disparities are less clear, although they probably include underlying gender bias by physicians; lack of proper education and training; and the use of treatments, equipment, and drugs developed on a male research model.

The importance of a continued women's health research effort cannot be overstated. Additional research will help to identify ways to streamline the provision of care, improve health care status, and ultimately reduce costs. The deficiency of research on women's health has led to less appropriate and less effective care for women. The two most common surgical procedures performed in the United States today are cesarean sections and hysterectomies, procedures that in many cases are unwarranted. Particularly for women, a concerted effort to close the health research gap must not be overlooked in the health care reform debate.

WHERE DO WE GO FROM HERE?

The 1992 elections significantly changed the face of Congress, tripling the number of women in the Senate and increasing by two-thirds the number of women in the House of Representatives. But the so-called "Year of the Woman" led to other less visible, but no less important, changes in the power structure on Capitol Hill. The most significant perhaps was the appointment of four new women to the House Appropriations Committee, bringing the total to seven. Of particular importance to the caucus's work on women's health was the naming of four women to the previously all-male appropriations subcommittee responsible for funding the Departments of Labor, Health and Human Services, and Education.

The caucus also moved early to work with the Clinton administration on women's health. Within days of her confirmation, we sat down with the new secretary of health and human services, Donna Shalala, to discuss women's health issues. Shortly after that, we met with First Lady Hillary Rodham Clinton, the head of the President's Health Care Reform Task Force, to present her with our women's health principles. We also discussed the importance of making available the full range of reproductive health care services, including abortion, in the basic benefits package provided to all Americans.

With a record 43 women serving on the caucus's executive committee and so many issues needing attention, we established several task forces to assist in preparing our legislative initiatives. The Women's Health Task Force assumed responsibility for preparing a new Women's Health Equity Act for introduction in the 103rd Congress. As in past years, the bills in the package address both the need to expand research on women's health and to ensure the availability of appropriate health care services for women.

Some of our proposals are updated pieces of legislation introduced in the first or second versions of the Women's Health Equity Act. We have renewed our call for creating interdisciplinary centers of excellence on women's health research and expanding research on women and AIDS, and women and alcoholism. Each of these bills was introduced previously, but failed to become law.

New areas of emphasis include expanded research on lupus, a disease that disproportionately strikes minority women in the prime of their lives, and on the health care needs of women in their postreproductive years. The latter responds to a 1992 report on the dearth of research on menopause prepared by the Congressional Office of Technology Assessment at the request of the caucus, entitled *The Menopause, Hormone Therapy, and Women's Health*.

The new Women's Health Equity Act will also include legislation to create primary and preventive health care packages for active-duty military women as well as women veterans. These brave women have been willing to give their lives to our country, only to discover that neither the Department of Veterans Affairs nor the Department of Defense is capable of treating their gender-specific needs. Our legislation will also increase research on the health of these women.

Well-documented gender disparities in health care delivery have led us to focus on the need to examine medical school curricula and education in this country. A systematic review of existing medical school curricula, as well as demonstration grants to medical schools to assist in the development of new curricula that better address women's health care needs, are important new features of the Women's Health Equity Act.

Another new direction for our women's health effort is smoking prevention. The fastest growing sector of smokers in our country is women under the age of 23. Early in the next century, the number of women dying from smoking-related diseases is expected to exceed that of men. The targeting of adolescent girls and young women by tobacco company advertising is particularly troubling to the caucus.

Significant changes in the treatment of women's health have taken place since the caucus first introduced the Women's Health Equity Act in 1990. Through our efforts, we helped to force NIH and the research community to pay attention to a neglected area of medical research. And we spoke out on behalf of American women who had long suspected that matters relating to their health were taken less seriously by their doctors and their government.

We believe that the caucus's efforts have forever changed the debate on women's health. We do not think that another physicians' aspirin study could happen today. Nor do we believe that NIH will ever again be the old boys network it once was. And above all, we hope that we will be the last generation of women to battle diseases like breast and ovarian cancer with so little information about their causes and so little hope for their cure.

ONE

★

ASSESSING AND IMPROVING WOMEN'S HEALTH

Karen Scott Collins, Diane Rowland,
Alina Salganicoff, and Elizabeth Chait

HIGHLIGHTS

THE SUBJECT OF WOMEN'S HEALTH has broadened in recent years, reflecting women's determination to understand and improve their health and reflecting the recognition that health and disease often affect women and men in different ways—biologically, psychologically, and socially. In addition, a woman's health care needs vary significantly over the course of her lifetime, with the focus typically changing from reproductive health to the care of chronic conditions. Many of these concerns are just beginning to receive the attention necessary to achieve real progress in the delivery of quality health care services to women.

The following points highlight some of the important issues relating to the health status of women today:

- Heart disease, which accounts for about 31 percent of female deaths, is the leading cause of death among American women overall, as it is among American men. However, cancer and diabetes have been gaining on heart disease. The proportion of female deaths from these two causes increased in the past two years.
- Lung cancer has replaced breast cancer as the leading cause of women's deaths from cancer.
- Smoking rates are declining faster for women than for men; however, the women most likely to smoke are those in their childbearing years. More than 28 percent of women age 25 to 34 smoke.
- The risks of developing invasive cervical and breast cancers can be greatly reduced by Pap smears and mammography. Yet many women, especially

those with low incomes and low educational levels, still do not receive
these tests on a routine basis.

- An estimated four million women are victims of domestic violence every
  year. One hundred seventy thousand women are assaulted in their fifth to
  ninth month of pregnancy.
- The spread of AIDS (Acquired Immune Deficiency Syndrome) is growing more rapidly among women than men. From 1989 to 1990, there was
  a 34 percent increase in the number of women diagnosed with AIDS. In
  New York City, AIDS is now the leading cause of death among black
  women age 24 to 44.
- Because females have a longer life expectancy than males, they are more
  likely to acquire the diseases associated with very old age, including Alzheimer's and complications arising from osteoporosis (a loss of normal
  bone density).
- It has become increasingly clear that menopause plays a role in altering
  risks of certain conditions such as heart disease; however, much more
  research is needed to understand this association and what it means.
- Women are more likely than men to use health care services; as a result,
  women's relationship to the health care system tends to have more importance in their lives.
- Largely because women are far more likely than men to be eligible for
  Medicaid, men are more likely than women to lack any kind of health
  insurance coverage.
- Many poor and low-income women are not, however, eligible for Medicaid. Unless she is pregnant, disabled, or elderly, a poor childless woman
  is not eligible for Medicaid regardless of her income. One-third of poor
  women have no health insurance of any kind.
- The current health care system emphasizes highly specialized care, rather
  than comprehensive primary and preventive health care. The result is that
  many women do not receive treatment for problems such as depression or
  counseling that would help them change behaviors that are risky to their
  health.
- Health care reform must ensure that the specific health needs of American
  women are met through greater availability of health care providers who
  are able to meet those needs, through insurance coverage for all Americans, and through the expansion of medical research and education to
  include issues of concern to women.

INTRODUCTION

It is often assumed that, because women live longer than men, they must be healthier. However, living longer does not necessarily imply good health. Though females may have more biological protection than males in some respects, they are still at risk for many of the same conditions. There are also important differences in the health concerns of men and women relating to conditions that are unique to women as well as those that affect both women and men but have been studied primarily in men. In addition, women and men tend to use the health care system in significantly different ways.

Another important issue is that this country's current health care system still presents barriers to care for women, particularly with respect to health insurance coverage. While there has been much overall progress in the effectiveness of health care, there are still significant gaps both in knowledge about female health specifically and in women's access to care.

This chapter presents an overview of women's health issues, including an explanation of conditions that concern women at different times in their lives and a discussion of measures that can be undertaken to prevent disease and disability. The chapter also examines how women interact with the health care system, as measured by their health insurance coverage and by the extent to which they seek or receive care.

A HEALTH PROFILE OF AMERICAN WOMEN

In developing strategies to improve women's health, it is important to take stock of their current status and to identify those areas or conditions where intervention could lead to better health. The following profile discusses major causes of mortality in American women and specific diseases and conditions that can affect them over the course of their lives.

LIFE EXPECTANCY

Progress in improving life expectancy has been one of the notable achievements of the twentieth century. As Table 1 shows, the expected life span of Americans born in 1900 was 47.3 years; in 1989, average life expectancy at birth was 75.3 years. Both males and females have benefitted from the improvements in living conditions and treatment of infectious disease, once

Table 1 • LIFE EXPECTANCY AT BIRTH AND AT AGE 65 BY RACE AND SEX, 1900–1989 (in years)

ALL RACES

	At Birth			At Age 65		
	Both Sexes	Female	Male	Both Sexes	Female	Male
1900	47.3	48.3	46.3	11.9	12.2	11.5
1960	69.7	73.1	66.6	14.3	15.8	12.8
1970	70.9	74.8	67.1	15.2	17.0	13.1
1980	73.7	77.4	70.0	16.4	18.3	14.1
1989	75.3	78.6	71.8	17.2	18.8	15.2

Life Expectancy

WHITES

	At Birth			At Age 65		
	Both Sexes	Female	Male	Both Sexes	Female	Male
1900	47.6	48.7	46.6	—	12.2	11.5
1960	70.6	74.1	67.4	14.4	15.9	12.9
1970	71.7	75.6	68.0	15.2	17.1	13.1
1980	74.4	78.1	70.7	16.5	18.4	14.2
1989	76.0	79.2	72.7	17.3	19.0	15.2

Life Expectancy

BLACKS

	At Birth			At Age 65		
	Both Sexes	Female	Male	Both Sexes	Female	Male
1900	33.0[1]	33.5[1]	32.5[1]	—	11.4	10.4
1960	63.2	65.9	60.7	13.9	15.1	12.7
1970	64.1	68.3	60.0	14.2	15.7	12.5
1980	68.1	72.5	63.8	15.1	16.8	13.0
1989	69.2	73.5	64.8	15.5	17.0	13.6

Life Expectancy

[1]Number is for "all other" population.
Source: National Center for Health Statistics 1992.

a major cause of early death. Women have also been the beneficiaries of advancements that have resulted in a 90 percent decline in maternal mortality—from 73.7 deaths for every 100,000 births in 1950 to 7.3 deaths for every 100,000 births in 1989 (National Center for Health Statistics [NCHS] 1992).

These improvements have contributed to the widening of the life expectancy gap between females and males. In 1989, life expectancy at birth was 78.6 years for a girl and 71.8 years for a boy. Although narrowing, the gap remains in later years. On average, in 1989 a woman who reached age 65 could expect to live 18.8 more years and a man at age 65 could expect to live 15.2 more years.

Gender is a more important factor than race in predicting a person's life expectancy. Although average life expectancy is shorter for black women than for white women, both groups of women have a longer life expectancy than men. A female child born in America in 1989 could be expected to live an average of 79.2 years if she were white and 73.5 years if she were black. However, as can be seen in Table 1, the life expectancy gap between black and white women narrows after age 65.

Despite the significant increase in life expectancy for Americans during the twentieth century, the United States is behind other highly industrialized countries in this regard. Life expectancy at birth is highest for females in Japan (82.5 years for those born in 1990) (Figure 1). In Sweden, Canada,

Figure 1 • FEMALE LIFE EXPECTANCY AT BIRTH IN SELECTED INDUSTRIALIZED COUNTRIES

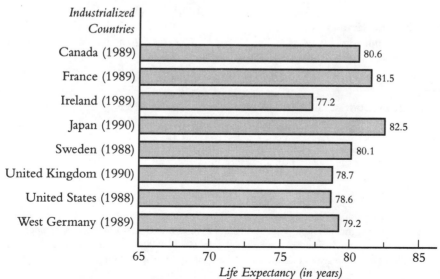

Source: World Health Organization 1992.

and France, girls born at the end of the 1980s also could expect to live to at least age 80. Thus, while American women tend to live longer than American men, a comparison with women in other countries suggests that there is room for improvement in life expectancy for women in the United States.

LEADING CAUSES OF MORTALITY

As in all of the highly industrialized countries, the most common causes of death in the United States are heart disease, cancer, and stroke (World Health Organization 1992). These diseases account for 67 percent of American women's deaths. The percentage is somewhat higher for men (NCHS 1992).

Heart disease, historically the leading cause of death in America among females of all races, has been overtaken by cancer as the leading cause of death among white women. In 1990, among white women, the cancer mortality rate[1] was 111, compared to 103 for heart disease as seen in Table 2.

Table 2 · LEADING CAUSES OF DEATH FOR WHITES AND BLACKS BY SEX, 1990 (number of deaths per 100,000 persons in population)

	Females		*Males*	
	White	*Black*	*White*	*Black*
Malignant neoplasms (cancers)	111.1	137.2	160.3	248.1
Heart diseases	103.1	168.1	202.0	275.9
Cerebrovascular diseases	23.8	42.7	27.7	56.1
Accidents and adverse effects	17.6	20.4	46.4	62.4
Chronic obstructive pulmonary diseases	15.2	10.7	27.4	26.5
Pneumonia and influenza	10.6	13.7	17.5	28.7
Diabetes mellitus	9.5	25.4	11.3	23.6
Chronic liver disease and cirrhosis	4.8	11.5	11.5	20.0
Suicide	4.8	2.4	20.1	12.4
Septicemia	3.1	8.0	4.2	11.6

Source: National Center for Health Statistics 1993.

[1]A mortality rate is the ratio of deaths—overall, or from a specified cause—to the population, or a particular segment of the population, in a given year. Unless otherwise specified, the population unit on which mortality rates are calculated is 100,000. Mortality rates by race, sex, and/or age group are calculated on the basis of the appropriate segment of the population.

Among black women, however, heart disease remains the leading cause of death. Men of both races are more likely to die from heart disease than from cancer.

Proportionally more black women than white women die from all the leading causes of death, except for suicide and chronic obstructive pulmonary disease (a lung condition usually resulting from emphysema, asthma, or chronic bronchitis). Mortality rates among black women are nearly twice as high for stroke and over twice as high for diabetes and septicemia (blood poisoning) as they are among white women.

HEALTH STATUS ACROSS THE LIFE SPAN

In general, the primary health concerns of women who are of reproductive age are different from those of postmenopausal women. This section begins with a discussion of conditions found largely among younger women, and goes on to a review of conditions found mostly in postmenopausal women—that is, women over 50 years old. It should be recognized, however, that most of the conditions discussed in this section can occur at any age.

HEALTH CONCERNS OF YOUNGER WOMEN

Some diseases, while not life threatening, cause impairment and disability and limit one's ability to perform daily functions, including working and caring for family members. Such illnesses often necessitate frequent contact with health care providers. For younger women, conditions in this category include gynecological infections, emotional disorders, and autoimmune diseases. In discussing the health of younger women, it is also essential to consider the impact of illnesses on reproductive health and pregnancy.

Sexually Transmitted Diseases
This country has been experiencing a resurgence of sexually transmitted diseases (STDs), due in part to penicillin-resistant strains of gonorrhea and an epidemic of venereal viruses for which there are currently no cures (Althaus 1991). Rates of infection can only be estimated because not all STDs are required to be reported to health authorities and many cases are asymptomatic (i.e., have no outward symptoms) particularly in women.

In the United States, the most common of these infections are chlamydia, gonorrhea, syphilis, herpes simplex 2 virus, and the human papilloma virus

(HPV) (Horton 1992). Cases of gonorrhea and syphilis are reported by every state. In 1991, the rates (per 100,000) of reported gonorrhea were nearly 263 for men and 202 for women; the rates of reported syphilis were nearly 20 for men, and 15 for women (Centers for Disease Control [CDC] 1992a). Infection rates were higher among adolescent girls than boys, most likely reflecting girls' exposure to infected older men. Among black women, the incidences of gonorrhea and syphilis were four to five times the national rates (CDC 1992a).

STDs are more easily transmitted from males to females than from females to males. Moreover, infection in women is more likely to be asymptomatic and therefore less likely to be identified and treated early. As a result, women are at greater risk than men of suffering long-term consequences from these diseases. This is important because an untreated STD can severely impair a woman's reproductive health, and infection during pregnancy carries a risk for both the mother and the fetus. For example, exposure to chlamydia during birth can result in conjunctivitis (an eye disease) or pneumonia in the newborn, and transmission of herpes simplex 2 virus can lead to newborn infection or death (Althaus 1991).

The STD epidemic is in part driven by increased sexual activity among young people, often in combination with drug and alcohol use. The risk of infection increases when multiple partners and unprotected sex are involved. An individual with a history of STD infection is considered at greater risk of contracting AIDS (Acquired Immune Deficiency Syndrome) because the AIDS virus is more easily transmitted through skin irritated by infection.

Pelvic Inflammatory Disease
Pelvic inflammatory disease (PID) is an acute infection of a woman's upper reproductive tract (uterus, ovaries, and fallopian tubes). The infection may be sexually transmitted (particularly through contact with individuals who have gonorrhea or chlamydia) or may result from an overgrowth of normal bacteria. The risk of having PID is highest for young women. An estimated 10 to 15 percent of American females between the ages of 15 and 44 have had at least one episode of PID. Annually, approximately one million women experience symptomatic PID, resulting in about 210,000 hospitalizations (Althaus 1991).

Moreover, the incidence of PID is believed to be significantly underestimated due to the extent of "silent"—asymptomatic—PID. In such cases, the first evidence of infection may be an ectopic pregnancy (pregnancy occurring outside of the uterus), infertility, or chronic pelvic pain (Althaus 1991; Cates and Wasserheit 1991). At this point, extensive medical attention and treatment are required. Further research on PID must include an evaluation of the efficacy of hospital versus outpatient treatment, a determination of what factors lead to long-term complications, and an effort to detect and assess the prevalence of silent PID (Padian 1992).

Acquired Immune Deficiency Syndrome

AIDS is a disease of the immune system—the body's system for fighting infection. The cause of AIDS is thought to be a virus called HTLV-3, which is believed to be spread through the exchange of body fluids such as semen and blood. Although the initial impact of AIDS in the United States was on men, it is now becoming a leading cause of death among young women. As Figure 2 shows, the number of new cases among females in this country increased by 34 percent from 1989 to 1990, to an estimated 4,544 cases of women with AIDS in 1990.

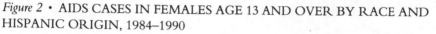

Figure 2 • AIDS CASES IN FEMALES AGE 13 AND OVER BY RACE AND HISPANIC ORIGIN, 1984–1990

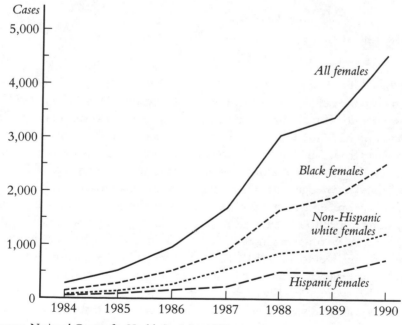

Source: National Center for Health Statistics 1992.

Many more women, while not showing symptoms of the disease, carry the AIDS Human Immunodeficiency Virus (HIV). As AIDS moves from being a disease principally associated with gay men and those who use intravenous drugs to one that threatens the general population, it is disproportionately affecting black and other minority women (see Figure 3). In New York City, for example, AIDS is now the leading cause of death among black women age 25 to 44 (CDC 1992f).

Figure 3 • NEW AIDS CASES IN FEMALES AGE 13 AND OVER BY RACE AND HISPANIC ORIGIN, 1990

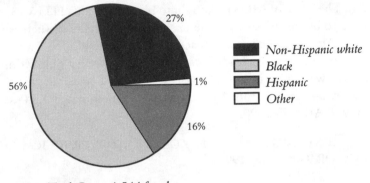

27%

1%

56%

16%

■ *Non-Hispanic white*
▨ *Black*
▦ *Hispanic*
☐ *Other*

Total Cases: 4,544 females

Source: National Center for Health Statistics 1992.

When AIDS first appeared in the United States, it was perceived to be a gay men's disease. The public was not generally aware that AIDS could be transmitted to women through intravenous drug use or sexual contact with infected men. Many women still do not know enough about protecting themselves from AIDS. Others who have the knowledge—those who know about the importance of using condoms, for example—may have difficulty translating knowledge into practice within their sexual relationships.

Until very recently, females were included in the AIDS medical literature only in reference to the transmission of the disease to newborn infants; the effect of AIDS on women themselves was not researched or discussed (Minkoff and DeHovitz 1991). Recent literature suggests, however, that AIDS may progress faster in women than in men. In addition, it is now known that women usually begin to receive medical care for AIDS later in the course of the disease. The Centers for Disease Control recently broadened the definition of AIDS from one that defined symptoms as they were manifested in men to include symptoms that more commonly appear in women with AIDS, such as persistent vaginal yeast infections, severe pelvic inflammatory disease, and cervical cancer (Donovan 1993).

In women, the hallmark symptom of depressed immune function is typically a persistent vaginal yeast infection. Yeast infections of the mouth and esophagus are common as the immune function deteriorates (Minkoff and DeHovitz 1991; Pfeiffer 1991). HIV-positive females are more likely than uninfected women to have severe pelvic inflammatory disease, and are much more likely to have abnormal Pap smears, indicating some stage of cervical cancer (Minkoff and DeHovitz 1991). Since very little is known about how pregnancy affects the course of the disease, an HIV-positive woman must make careful decisions about current or future pregnancies. An infected woman must also weigh the risk of transmitting the infection to an unborn child, a risk now estimated at 25 percent (down from much higher estimates a few years ago but still clearly a concern). In addition, the risk to both the mother and fetus of continuing AIDS therapy during pregnancy is still uncertain (Pfeiffer 1991).

Much work needs to be done to improve the quality of life and medical care of women with AIDS. To date no studies have been conducted to determine whether women respond differently than men to currently available AIDS treatments. It is clear, however, that AIDS has a different effect on women not only with respect to physical symptoms, but socially as well. Women are often the caretakers of others with AIDS, and as a result tend to postpone their own care when they become infected. Those most affected by AIDS are poor and minority women who must rely for care on government programs or the limited health care resources in their communities. Since the consequences of treating pregnant women with AIDS are still unknown, many treatment programs are reluctant to take on patients who are, or may be, pregnant, leaving this group of women without the care they desperately need (Minkoff and DeHovitz 1991).

Major Depression

Nearly five percent of women, compared to two percent of men, suffer from major depression. Studies repeatedly find depression to be two to three times more prevalent among women than men (Weissman et al. 1984; Coryell, Endicott, and Martin 1992). However, although women in every racial, ethnic, and socioeconomic group have a higher rate of depression than their male counterparts, overall rates of depression are lower among black and Hispanic women than among non-Hispanic white women (U.S. Department of Health and Human Services [DHHS] 1991b). Age is a factor as well since depression is most common among women between 25 and 44 years old (Coryell, Endicott, and Martin 1992; Halbreich et al. 1984; Horton 1992). Increasing rates of depressive behaviors among teenage girls and other young women indicate that the age of onset may be declining (Horton 1992).

The clinical symptoms of major depression include sleeplessness, difficulty in concentrating, eating disorders, physical illness, and suicide. Although women are more likely to attempt suicide, more men than women actually commit suicide.

In addition to sex and age, another risk factor for depression is marital separation or divorce (Anthony and Petronis 1991). The risk of depression for women may be increased by a combination of biological factors, as well as by psychosocial factors such as low self-esteem, marital difficulty, and a sense of limited life options (Public Health Service Task Force 1985).

Although many forms of depression are treatable, only about 30 percent of people with depression receive treatment (DHHS 1991a). One reason may be that primary care physicians often do not recognize early symptoms of depression and do not refer their patients for treatment. Another major factor is that coverage for mental health care is very limited under most insurance plans, making comprehensive mental health therapy a luxury that most women cannot afford.

Eating Disorders

The eating disorders anorexia nervosa and bulimia nervosa, both far more likely to affect females than males, have become increasingly prevalent among teenage girls and young women. It has been estimated that five in every 1,000 adolescent and young adult females are anorexic. Females are at 10 times greater risk for anorexia nervosa than males. Young, white adolescents are at greatest risk (U.S. Congress, Office of Technology Assessment [OTA] 1991).

A distorted body image causes anorexics to believe that they are seriously overweight when they are not, and they refuse to eat. In addition to a weight loss of at least 25 percent of original body weight, clinical manifestations of anorexia include dehydration, amenorrhea (cessation of menstruation), cold intolerance, and dry skin and hair (Smith 1984). An estimated nine percent of anorexics die prematurely, either from suicide or starvation, and fewer than half of anorexics are able to recover fully (Horton 1992). Anorexia is difficult to cure because anorexics tend to deny their disorder and often refuse help from medical professionals.

Bulimia nervosa (binge eating followed by vomiting) is more common than anorexia and usually occurs in girls in late adolescence. It is estimated that between one and four percent of young women have bulimia. A national survey of students indicates that at least 4 percent of eighth and tenth graders are bulimic (Horton 1992). Clinical manifestations of bulimia include irregular menstruation as well as a constant sore throat and problems with the stomach and teeth caused by vomiting (Smith 1984). Bulimics are more likely than anorexics to admit that their behavior is abnormal, and are thus more amenable to treatment.

Autoimmune Diseases

Autoimmune diseases, which are far more common among women than among men, are conditions in which the body makes antibodies against some of its own parts, leading to their destruction. Two of the more common autoimmune diseases are systemic lupus erythematosus (SLE) and rheumatoid arthritis. Females are nine times more likely than males to develop lupus (Horton 1992), and three times more likely to develop rheumatoid arthritis (Pritchard 1992). The onset of SLE may occur anywhere between the ages of 20 and 64. In this disease, several parts of the body may become inflamed, including the skin, joints, kidneys, and nervous system. The prevalence of rheumatoid arthritis peaks between the ages of 35 and 45. Also a chronic inflammatory condition, rheumatoid arthritis affects many joints, particularly those of the hands (Condemi 1992). SLE and rheumatoid arthritis are both characterized by progressive physical deterioration, loss of functional abilities, chronic pain, and shortened life span.

A pregnant woman with an autoimmune disorder has reason for additional concern. The condition may be transmitted to the fetus, although long-term effects are rare (Giacoia 1992). There also is an increased risk of miscarriage. Symptoms may subside during pregnancy, but an exacerbation of the condition typically occurs in late pregnancy or right after childbirth. Another concern is whether and how to treat these diseases during pregnancy. Given the prevalence of autoimmune diseases among women, and changes in the illnesses during pregnancy, hormonal factors may play a role in autoimmune diseases although more research is needed to determine exactly what that role might be.

Violence

As violence against women is more widely publicized, reported, and studied, the horrifying dimensions of this epidemic are beginning to be appreciated. There were over 92,000 reported rapes in 1988. An estimated four million women are severely assaulted by their male partners every year. More than half of the women murdered in the United States are killed by current or former male partners (American Medical Association [AMA] 1992). Most rapes, as well as most other types of assault against women, are committed by persons known to the victims.

The psychological impact of sexual and physical abuse may be manifested in feelings of dependency, vulnerability, and betrayal—and by depression and suicide attempts. In addition to psychological damage, women who have been sexually assaulted usually suffer lacerations, bruises, and an increased risk of AIDS and other sexually transmitted diseases, as well as of unwanted pregnancy.

Women who have been battered usually have injuries to parts of their bodies that would not normally be injured in an accident. Among abused pregnant women, for example, bruises to their abdomens are typical. National data from a 1985 survey found that 154 out of every 1,000 pregnant women were assaulted by their partners during the first four months of pregnancy, and an even greater number (170 out of every 1,000) were assaulted during the fifth to ninth months. This abuse is not only very painful for the pregnant women involved but it also increases the risk of placental separation, uterine rupture, fetal fractures, hemorrhage, and preterm labor (AMA 1992).

The American Medical Association recently issued recommendations to help train physicians

- to identify evidence of violence;
- to discuss it with their patients;
- to refer patients for proper treatment; and
- in general to help health professionals become more comfortable in dealing with this complex medical and social issue (AMA 1992; Sugg and Inui 1992).

HEALTH CONCERNS OF OLDER WOMEN

The health concerns of women during and after menopause become primarily the chronic conditions associated with aging and changes in hormones. In some respects, the conditions of concern become more similar to the concerns of their male counterparts. Yet hormonal changes and longevity result in conditions of unique concern to women.

Heart Disease

Coronary heart disease, which includes angina (intermittent chest pain) and heart failure, accounts for about 31 percent of female deaths. Symptoms of heart disease typically develop in women about 10 years later in life than is the case for men. In other words, for females heart disease is largely a postmenopausal disorder. Illness and death resulting from heart disease rise dramatically in women after age 55 (Lerner and Kannel 1986).

Risk factors for heart disease have been found to be similar for men and women, but smoking, diabetes, and systolic hypertension (high blood pressure) appear to be more important risk factors for women than for men. On the other hand, the type of cholesterol known as high density lipoprotein

(HDL) appears to be more protective in women than in men (Lerner and Kannel 1986).

Whereas the first sign that a man has heart disease is likely to be a heart attack, the first sign in a woman is more likely to be angina (Lerner and Kannel 1986). Nevertheless, heart attacks occur in about 30 percent of female heart patients (Hendel 1990). The risk of having a heart attack increases with age. A woman is more likely than a man to die after a heart attack, or to have a second attack (Hendel 1990; Becker 1990).

One reason for these differences may be that the therapies used, which have been tested mainly on males, may not be directly applicable to the care of women. Recent studies find that women respond differently than men to both medical and surgical treatments for heart disease (Clyne 1990; O'Conner 1992). More research is needed to determine why such discrepancies exist and how the treatment of heart disease in women can be improved.

Cancer

Breast cancer and lung cancer are not only the most commonly occurring cancers in women, but together they are also responsible for nearly half of all cancer deaths in women. The gynecological cancers (cancer of the cervix, ovaries, and uterus) are less common (see Table 3) but are of concern to women throughout their lives. Mortality rates for white women are higher than for black women for lung and ovarian cancer, but lower for breast, endometrial, and cervical cancer. These differences by race may be related to the availability of preventive care and access to treatment.

Table 3 · INCIDENCE AND DEATH RATES FOR SELECTED CANCERS AMONG WOMEN BY CANCER SITE, 1989 (per 100,000 women)[1]

	Incidence		Deaths		
Cancer Site	White	Black	All Races	White	Black
Breast	108.2	87.6	23.1	23.1	26.5
Lung and bronchus	40.1	45.2	24.9	25.3	25.0
Endometrial	21.9	16.7	2.6	2.4	4.5
Ovary	15.8	10.6	6.4	6.6	5.0
Cervix	8.2	12.8	2.7	2.3	6.2

[1]Rates are age-adjusted.
Source: National Center for Health Statistics (NCHS) 1992 (incidence rates) and NCHS, unpublished cancer statistics, January 1993 (mortality rates).

Lung Cancer. Twice as many males as females die of lung cancer, but while the death rate for men is leveling off, the death rate for women continues to rise. The lung cancer death rate among women has quintupled in the past 30 years, from a (per 100,000) mortality rate of 5.4 in 1958 to 28.2 in 1988 (American Cancer Society [ACS] 1992). In 1987, for the first time, more women died from lung cancer than from breast cancer as Figure 4 illustrates. Most female lung cancer deaths occur among women who are between the ages of 55 and 74 (NCHS 1989).

In proportion to their numbers in the population, more black women than white women get lung cancer; in 1989 the (per 100,000) incidence rate was 45.2 among black females and 40.1 among white females (see Table 3 above). The incidence rates for breast cancer among females of both races are much higher than for lung cancer; however, lung cancer is the leading killer cancer among white women. Among black women, it lags slightly behind breast cancer.

Figure 4 • FEMALE MORTALITY FROM LUNG CANCER AND BREAST CANCER, 1979–1990 (age-adjusted mortality rates)[1]

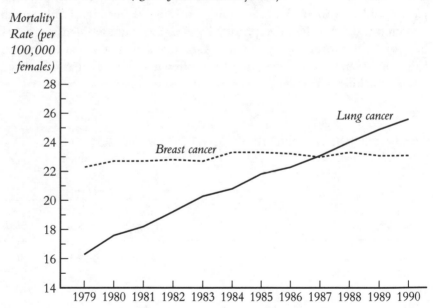

[1]A mortality rate is the number of deaths in a given year per 100,000 persons in the population. An age-adjusted rate is a weighted average of the age-specific rates, where the weights are the proportions of persons in the corresponding age groups of a standard population. This is done to reduce the potential confounding effect of age.
Source: National Center for Health Statistics, unpublished cancer statistics, January 1993.

Approximately 85 percent of lung cancers are attributable to smoking, and the number of years that women smoke during their lives is now approaching that of men. The increase in female lung cancer deaths is not expected to begin to level off until the year 2013 (CDC December 1990).

Cervical Cancer. Cervical cancer is one of the most detectable and treatable cancers. The five-year survival rate for women whose cancer is detected early is 90 to 100 percent (ACS 1992). Mortality rates for cervical cancer have steadily declined in the past 40 years, due almost entirely to the Pap smear, which can detect the cancer before it has begun to spread—thereby allowing for curative treatment. Annually there are an estimated 13,500 cases and 4,400 deaths from cervical cancer. However, as Figure 5 shows, the incidence of cervical cancer among black women is about one-third higher than the incidence among white women. The mortality rate among black women is three times as high as the mortality rate among white women (ACS 1992). Mortality from cervical cancer is also higher among Native American women and low-income elderly women. Lack of

Figure 5 • CERVICAL CANCER: INCIDENCE AND MORTALITY RATES FOR WHITE AND BLACK WOMEN, 1989[1]

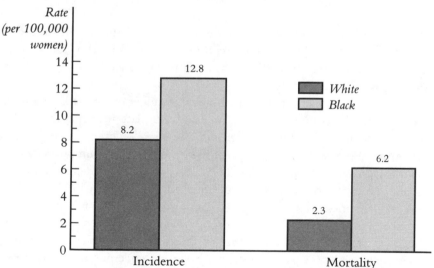

[1]A mortality rate is the number of deaths in a given year per 100,000 persons in the population. An incidence rate is the number of new cases in a given year per 100,000 persons in the population. Rates are age-adjusted.
Source: National Center for Health Statistics (NCHS) 1992 (incidence rates) and NCHS, unpublished cancer statistics, January 1993 (mortality rates).

regular Pap smears, intercourse at an early age, smoking, the presence of the human papilloma virus, and a history of multiple sexual partners are all risk factors for cervical cancer.

Ovarian Cancer. One in 70 women will be diagnosed in her lifetime with ovarian cancer (ACS 1992). Both incidence rates and mortality rates for ovarian cancer are higher among white women than among black women. Because ovarian tumors are typically diagnosed at advanced stages, survival rates for ovarian cancer are the poorest of all the gynecologic cancers; only 39 percent of white women and 36 percent of black women survive for five years after being diagnosed with ovarian cancer. (Although a higher percentage of white women with ovarian cancer survive for five years when compared to black women, white women's overall mortality from ovarian cancer is higher than black women's.)

The risk factors for ovarian cancer are not well understood, and there is currently no effective screening procedure that can be widely applied to identify ovarian cancer at an early, highly treatable stage when the tumor is asymptomatic. Very recent evidence indicates that the use of oral contraceptives that suppress ovulation may help protect against ovarian cancer (Hankinson et al. 1992).

Breast Cancer. One out of every nine women can expect to be diagnosed with breast cancer in her lifetime. According to the American Cancer Society (1992), there were 46,000 deaths from breast cancer and 180,000 new cases of the disease in 1992.

Breast cancer is associated with a history of cancer in a mother or a sister, never having been pregnant, early menstruation, late menopause, and benign breast disease. White women, and women of high socioeconomic status, are also at higher than average risk. Excessive consumption of food with a high fat and caloric content as well as excessive consumption of alcohol appear to increase the risk of breast cancer (Mettlin 1992).

Various combinations of surgery, chemotherapy, and radiation therapy have been used to treat breast cancer; however, survival is closely linked to the stage of the cancer at the time of discovery, as well as to treatment decisions made by the patient and her physician. Screening by clinical exam and mammography has proven very effective in detecting early breast cancer in women over age 50. (Mammography is discussed in greater detail later in this chapter.)

Although the incidence of breast cancer is higher among white women than among black women, the latter are more likely to die from this disease

Figure 6 • BREAST CANCER: INCIDENCE AND MORTALITY RATES FOR WHITE AND BLACK WOMEN, 1989[1]

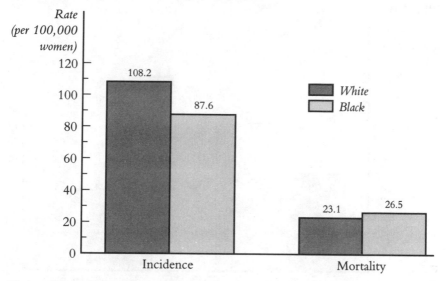

[1]A mortality rate is the number of deaths in a given year per 100,000 persons in the population. An incidence rate is the number of new cases in a given year per 100,000 persons in the population.
Source: National Center for Health Statistics (NCHS) 1992 (incidence rates) and NCHS, unpublished cancer statistics, January 1993 (mortality rates).

(see Figure 6). Part of the problem is that the disease is typically more advanced in black women when they are diagnosed: only 43 percent of black women, compared to 52 percent of white women, are diagnosed at a stage when the disease is still localized (Boring, Squires, and Tong 1992). However, as Figure 7 illustrates, even among black and white women diagnosed at the same stage, five-year survival rates are lower for black women.

Breast cancer also appears to strike black women at an earlier age than their white counterparts, raising questions about variations in the nature of the disease, and about the adequacy of current screening guidelines with respect to minority women. Another concern is that because breast cancer education typically has targeted higher-income white women, the population at greatest risk of breast cancer, many minority women believe they are not at significant risk.

Figure 7 • WHITE AND BLACK WOMEN WITH BREAST CANCER: PERCENTAGE EARLY DIAGNOSIS AND FIVE-YEAR SURVIVAL, 1981–1987

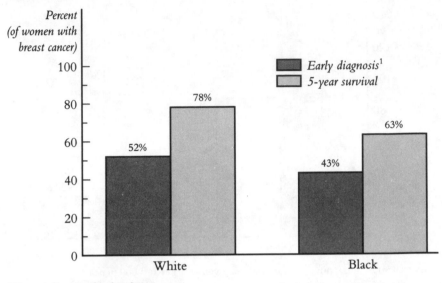

[1]Cancer diagnosed in local stage.
Source: Boring, Squires, and Tong 1992.

Endometrial Cancer. The incidence and mortality rates for endometrial cancer (cancer of the uterus) have remained constant over the past decade (the 1989 rates are shown in Table 3 above). This disease, which typically afflicts women over age 50, generally has a good prognosis. Age, a history of infertility, failure to ovulate, estrogen therapy, and obesity are all considered risk factors for endometrial cancer (ACS 1992). Five-year survival rates are about 85 percent overall, higher if the disease is diagnosed and treated early. Preventive screening for endometrial cancer involves regular checkups, prompt medical attention for abnormal bleeding, and sampling of the endometrial tissue by biopsy at menopause for women who are at high risk for the disease (ACS 1992).

Cerebrovascular Disease
Cerebrovascular disease, the third leading cause of death among females, is the inclusive name for the diseases relating to the blood supply to the brain, including stroke and multi-infarct dementia (a form of brain disease causing a rapid failure of mental functioning). Nine percent of deaths among white women and eight percent of deaths among black women are caused by cerebrovascular disease.

Among women overall, mortality from cerebrovascular disease is less common than it is among men overall. However, mortality rates for blacks of both sexes are much higher than for their white counterparts. As Table 2 shows (see above), in 1990 the rate for black women was 42.7 per 100,000 persons—nearly 80 percent higher than the rate for white women.

Not only is cerebrovascular disease a major killer, it is also a major cause of physical and mental disability. It is largely a disease of the old: 87 percent of deaths from the disease, and 74 percent of hospitalizations due to it, involve people age 65 and over (CDC 1992c).

Diabetes

Diabetes is both a disabling condition and one that can lead to death if untreated or poorly managed. It ranks fourth among the leading causes of death for black women, and seventh for white women (see Table 2). Diabetes is also a condition that disproportionately affects the older age groups, with death nearly four times more likely to occur among women age 65 to 74 than among those age 45 to 64 (NCHS August 1991).

Diabetes is more prevalent among females than males, almost entirely because its incidence is very high among black, Hispanic, and other minority women (CDC November 1990). In the 45 to 74 age group, for example, 11 percent of black women and over 15 percent of Mexican American and Puerto Rican women have diabetes, compared to only six percent of white women (see Figure 8).

Figure 8 • PREVALENCE OF DIABETES AMONG WOMEN AGE 45 TO 74, SELECTED RACES AND HISPANIC ORIGINS[1]

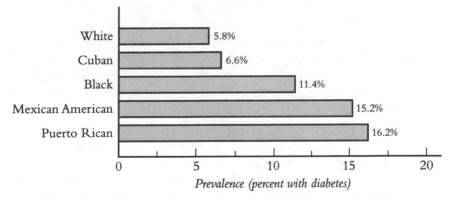

Prevalence (percent with diabetes)

[1]Data for whites and blacks are from the National Health and Nutrition Examination Survey II, 1982–1984. Data for Hispanics are from the Hispanic Health and Nutrition Examination Survey, 1976–1980.
Source: Flegal et al. 1991.

As a chronic disease, diabetes can give rise to many disabling conditions including:

• kidney disease, which can lead to kidney failure;
• eye disease, which can lead to blindness;
• peripheral vascular disease, which affects blood circulation in the extremities and can ultimately lead to amputation of the legs or feet; and
• increased risk of death from coronary heart disease or stroke (Lerner and Kannel 1986).

Risk factors for diabetes include a family history of the disease, obesity, and a history of diabetes during pregnancy. Early control of blood sugar through diet and exercise can retard the development of complications, or the need for medications.

Osteoporosis

Osteoporosis is a condition in which bone density has been reduced, in some cases to the point where fractures can result from minor accidents or even normal physical activity. Women are more likely than men to be affected by osteoporosis because they have less bone mass to begin with, and bone loss is accelerated as estrogen levels decline during and after menopause. While data are not available on the prevalence of this disease nationally, it is estimated that 50 percent of women over age 45, and 90 percent of women over age 70, have some degree of osteoporosis (U.S. DHHS 1991a).

The most common clinical manifestations of osteoporosis are fractures of the vertebrae, hip, and wrist. A total of 1.3 million fractures per year are attributed to osteoporosis. Hip fractures are of great concern because of the attendant high rates of illness and death. Most hip fractures cause some degree of permanent impairment; 25 percent require institutionalization and 20 percent result in death (Resnick and Greenspan 1989). Seventy-five to 80 percent of the approximately 250,000 hip fractures that occur annually are to women (Horton 1992). The consequences of vertebral fractures are not as severe, but vertebral fractures can lead to spinal deformity, chronic back pain, and loss of height.

Because at every age white women typically have less bone mass than either their black counterparts or men, they are at greatest risk for having osteoporotic fractures (Farmer et al. 1984). Other risk factors for osteoporosis include being thin, smoking, having a family history of the disease, and having experienced amenorrhea.

Alzheimer's Disease

Alzheimer's disease is an illness characterized by a gradual loss of memory and cognitive abilities. People in the advanced stages of the disease typically do not recognize even their closest relatives, have lost the ability to manage the simplest tasks involving personal hygiene, and are often fearful about their surroundings. At this point, the cause of the disease is not known.

The incidence of Alzheimer's disease increases dramatically after age 70 (Treves 1991). Some studies have found a higher prevalence of Alzheimer's among women, even after taking into account the higher proportion of females among the aged (Schoenberg, Anderson, and Haerer 1985; Schoenberg, Kokmen, and Okazaki 1987).

Whether women are truly at greater risk than men is one of the many questions about Alzheimer's disease that need to be answered. Other items on the current research agenda include an examination of head trauma and family history as risk factors, the reported association between heart attacks and Alzheimer's in women (Aronson et al. 1990), and the development of early diagnosis methods and new forms of treatment. Alzheimer's disease will increase in prevalence as the population ages.

IMPROVING WOMEN'S HEALTH

PREVENTING DISEASE

Several preventive measures can make a significant difference in the health outlook for women overall. First, women themselves can avoid risky behaviors that are known to cause health problems. Second, early detection and treatment can often arrest a potentially serious disease that is not yet symptomatic. And third, even a disease that is already symptomatic can often be arrested, or its progress retarded, by the right treatment and good management.

Many risk factors, such as age and family history, cannot be altered—but some others can be. Altering these risk factors depends primarily on an individual's willingness to make behavioral changes. The evidence is clear that smoking, dietary habits, and physical activity significantly affect the risk of cardiovascular disease, lung cancer, respiratory disease, and diabetes. Dietary habits also are likely to affect risks for other cancers and for osteoporosis. The health consequences of alcohol and drug abuse are well documented. Nevertheless, it must be recognized that behavioral changes can be very difficult to achieve, often because cultural influences as well as personal decisions are involved.

Certain medical interventions can, however, significantly affect and improve a woman's health. The most notable of these are the Pap smear, mammography, hormone replacement therapy, and blood pressure measurement (see Table 4).

Table 4 • EARLY DETECTION AND PREVENTIVE SERVICES FOR WOMEN: GUIDELINES AND USAGE, 1990

Service	For Early Detection or Prevention of	Screening Guidelines	Percentage of Women Who Had Service in Past Year
Mammography	Breast cancer	From age 40 to 49, every one to two years; annually after age 50	—[1]
Clinical breast exam	Breast cancer	From age 20 to 40, every three years; annually after age 40	53
Pap smear	Cervical cancer	Annually[2]	50
Hormone replacement therapy	Osteoporosis; cardiovascular disease	Physician counseling on risks and benefits to menopausal women	—
Blood pressure check	Hypertension	Every one to two years[3]	91

[1]Data are not available on the percentage of women having mammography in the past year. However, 31 percent of women reported following the American Cancer Society guidelines for frequency.
[2]Frequency may be reduced after three normal tests.
[3]If normotensive, at least once every two years; if borderline (diastolic 85–89 mmHg), every year.
Source: American Cancer Society 1992a; U.S. Preventive Services Task Force 1989; Piani and Schoenborn 1993; and Centers for Disease Control September 14, 1990.

Use of these preventive interventions has increased over the past two decades, but analyses show persistent differences by age and race (Makuc, Freid, and Kleinman 1989) as well as by socioeconomic status (CDC September 1990; Piani and Schoenborn 1993). The following sections discuss some preventive measures and their effectiveness in improving women's health.

Smoking Cessation

Smoking is associated with the major killers of women—heart disease, lung cancer, and cerebrovascular disease. In 1988, the deaths of almost 150,000 women were attributed directly to the effects of smoking (CDC February 1991). Smoking is also linked to osteoporosis, cervical cancer, and poor pregnancy outcomes, including low birth weight and miscarriage (CDC October 1991). Smoking cessation is one of the most important behavioral changes a woman can make to improve her prospects for good health. Quitting can make a difference—after 10 years of smoking cessation, the risk of lung cancer decreases by 30 to 50 percent as compared to the risk among smokers (CDC December 1990).

Smoking rates have been declining for both women and men, although they have been diminishing at a faster rate for women since 1985. Currently about 23 percent of women smoke, compared to 28 percent of men. Smoking rates are about the same for white and black adult women, but they are higher for Native American and Puerto Rican women, at 28 and 30 percent, respectively (Lefkowitz and Underwood 1991; Amaro 1992). White teenage girls are more likely to smoke than their male counterparts, but they are less likely to become long-term smokers. As Figure 9 shows, among

Figure 9 • WOMEN SMOKERS BY AGE, 1990

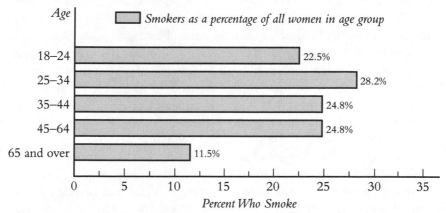

Source: National Center for Health Statistics 1992.

women overall, those between the ages of 25 and 34 are the most likely to smoke.

Passive smoking—exposure to smoke from others' smoking—is another serious concern. Women are exposed to the toxic effects of smoke by being around men who smoke. Although the scientific evidence about the negative effects of passive smoke is building, general public awareness is limited.

Helping women to stop smoking requires an understanding of smoking habits and attitudes. Although younger women are more likely to smoke than older women, the latter tend to be heavier smokers and are less likely to try to quit (CDC October 1991). Poor and less educated women are not as likely as their male counterparts to be informed about the health effects of smoking (Brownson et al. 1992). Many women believe that quitting smoking will cause them to gain weight, although recent studies dispute the hypothesis that there is a connection between the two. Another problem is that women may suffer more severe withdrawal symptoms than men when attempting to quit (Waldron 1991).

Programs need to be developed to inform women about the dangers of smoking. Tobacco ads that portray women who smoke as slim, youthful, and liberated need to be countered with the hard facts about the ill-effects of the habit. Educational programs should focus both on preventing girls and women from starting to smoke and on encouraging smokers to quit. Methods to help smokers stop often include a combination of behavioral and physician counseling, and, more recently, pharmaceutical interventions such as the nicotine patch. These methods are often not fully covered by insurance.

Cancer Screening
Pap Smear. The spread of cervical cancer can be prevented, and the cancer cured, if it is detected during its relatively long preinvasive stage. It can be detected early by the Papanicolaou (Pap) smear. Having a regular Pap smear is considered the most important measure a woman can take to guard against invasive cervical cancer. In 1990, 50 percent of women had received a Pap test in the year past, though rates varied by demographic characteristics (see Table 5 and Figure 10). The women least likely to get regular Pap smears are poor, elderly, and uninsured women (Makuc, Freid, and Kleinman 1989; Haywood et al. 1988; Piani and Schoenborn 1993).

The U.S. Preventive Services Task Force (USPSTF) recommends that all sexually active women be screened every one to three years at their physicians' discretion, based on risk factors. Women at higher risk benefit significantly from having a Pap smear every year. On the other hand, Pap smear screening may be discontinued at age 65 if the patient has a history of

Table 5 · WOMEN WHO HAD SELECTED PREVENTIVE SERVICES IN THE PAST YEAR BY SELECTED CHARACTERISTICS,[1] 1990

| | Percentage Who Had | | |
| | | | |
Characteristics	Pap Smear	Clinical Breast Exam	Blood Pressure Check
Total, age 18 and over	50.1	53.1	90.8
Family income			
Less than $10,000	41.0	45.5	89.5
$10,000–$19,999	44.0	47.0	89.2
$20,000–$34,999	50.1	53.0	90.4
$35,000–$49,999	55.2	58.3	91.0
$50,000 or more	58.9	61.4	92.6
Age			
18–29	63.9	62.2	92.1
30–44	55.2	55.6	89.9
45–64	43.6	49.1	90.0
65 and over	30.4	42.0	91.7
Race			
White	49.7	53.1	90.6
Black	54.3	55.3	92.6
Hispanic origin			
Hispanic	49.1	50.4	88.3
Non-Hispanic	50.1	53.4	90.9
Education			
Less than 12 years	37.9	43.0	88.9
12 years	49.6	52.2	89.9
More than 12 years	57.2	59.7	92.7

[1]Data for mammograms in the past year are not available from the National Center for Health Statistics.
Source: Piani and Schoenborn 1993.

normal tests (USPSTF 1989). The American College of Obstetricians and Gynecologists and the American Cancer Society have made similar recommendations. Pap testing is highly effective, its importance is widely accepted by physicians, it can be done conveniently as part of a regular exam, and its cost is relatively low.

Figure 10 • WOMEN WHO HAD A PAP SMEAR IN THE PAST YEAR BY AGE AND INCOME, 1990

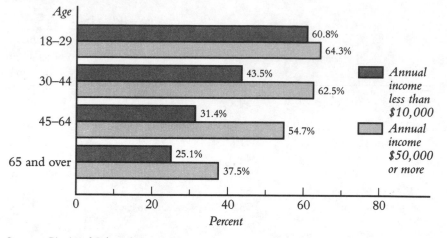

Source: Piani and Schoenborn 1993.

Mammography. Mammography, along with the clinical breast exam, significantly improves survival from breast cancer by detecting tumors at an early stage. For women age 50 and over, the value of mammography is uncontested; but its effectiveness with respect to younger women, particularly those between the ages of 40 and 49, is less certain. Guidelines current in 1993 call for mammograms every year for women age 50 and over, and every other year for women age 40 to 49, depending upon risk factors (ACS 1992). However, the guidelines for women under 50 are being challenged by recent studies that do not show a benefit from mammography in this age group (Miller et al. 1992). These findings may result in revised screening guidelines in the near future.

In 1990, 58 percent of women age 40 and older reported having had a mammogram in the past two years (CDC 1992b), and 64 percent reported having had a mammogram at some time during their adult lives (CDC September 1990). The number of women who had mammograms nearly doubled over a five-year period. Nevertheless, over one-third of women (36 percent) had never received this important, effective screening. Moreover, although in 1990 twice as many women reported ever having had a mammogram than in 1987, only 31 percent of women were following the recommended schedule of screening. In addition, as shown in Figure 11, demographic differences in mammography use persist. Women who were black, over age 70, or of low-income and educational levels were less likely to receive mammograms in 1990.

Figure 11 • WOMEN REPORTING EVER HAVING HAD A
MAMMOGRAM BY SELECTED CHARACTERISTICS, 1990

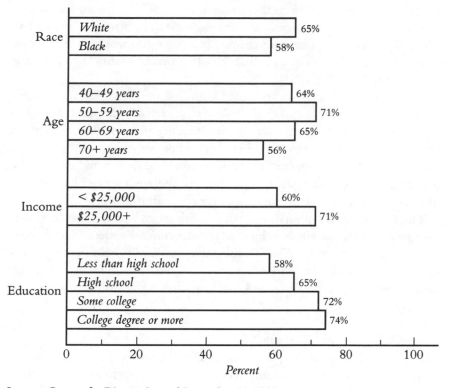

Source: Centers for Disease Control September 14, 1990.

Women report that physicians' advice, cost of mammography, and knowledge of the importance of the screening are leading influences for obtaining regular mammograms. Women are also more likely to have mammograms if they believe that they are at risk for the disease. Some targeted programs have increased the use of mammography by developing coordination between family practitioners, gynecologists, and radiologists—and by making screening available at women's places of employment. Questions that still need to be resolved include the effectiveness of mammography for women under age 50, and whether screening guidelines should be adjusted for black women (who appear to get breast cancer at younger ages than white women). Better data collection to monitor who is getting screened and who remains at risk is also needed.

Hormone Replacement Therapy

Hormone replacement therapy (HRT) is the use of estrogen or an estrogen/progesterone combination to alleviate symptoms of menopause and to prevent conditions that accelerate after menopause. The strongest preventive effect of hormone replacement therapy is to slow the rate of osteoporosis. There is also good evidence that HRT protects against heart disease (Stampfer and Colditz 1991).

There are, however, risks associated with hormone use. Taking estrogen without progesterone increases the risk of endometrial (uterine) cancer, and long-term (15 to 20 years) combination therapy may increase the risk of breast cancer (Kelsey 1992). When counseling women about hormone therapy, therefore, physicians must assess individual factors and explain the benefits and risks to patients, recognizing that there is a greater lifetime risk of osteoporosis or heart disease than of cancer (Pettiti 1992).

There are currently no national data on the use of hormone replacement therapy or on the extent to which physicians counsel patients and recommend it. The role of HRT as a preventive measure is being critically reviewed by the U.S. Preventive Services Task Force, and clinical trials are under way to expand and clarify knowledge about the risks and benefits of therapy.

Prevention of Heart Disease

The potential is great for preventing deaths from heart disease among women as well as men. Programs that encourage people to eat low fat diets, to exercise, and to stop smoking have already contributed to a decline in deaths from heart disease among all groups. Given the increased risk of heart attacks in postmenopausal women, further research is needed on the role of menopause and estrogen. As noted above, one area currently being explored is the role of hormone therapy in preventing heart disease. A low dose of aspirin as a preventive measure against heart attacks has been studied in men but, although observational studies suggest that aspirin may have a similar effect in females, clinical trials are required to establish the appropriateness of this treatment for women (Manson 1991).

Hypertension (high blood pressure) adds significantly to the risk of stroke and coronary heart disease in people of both sexes after age 55 (NCHS 1992). Through regular blood pressure measurement, hypertension can be detected early and treated so that the risks of heart disease and stroke are reduced. The U.S. Preventive Services Task Force recommends that blood pressure be checked every one to two years (USPSTF 1989).

In 1990, about 80 percent of women and 69 percent of men had their blood pressure measured (Piani and Schoenborn 1993). Older women and black women, who are at greatest risk of hypertension, are more likely than younger and white women to have their blood pressure checked (Makuc, Freid, and Kleinman 1989). Since this procedure is a routine part of any contact with a physician or a nurse, it is not surprising that most women have their blood pressure measured at least once a year. And the likelihood that she will have her blood pressure checked can be expected to increase as a woman ages, since physician contact becomes more frequent with age. It is important that people who have high blood pressure maintain treatment and have regular checkups throughout the year.

Prevention of Osteoporosis

Teenagers and young women as well as older women are the targets of efforts to prevent osteoporosis, and women should be counseled on the preventive measures appropriate for their age. Adolescents and young women should be encouraged to make sure their diets include plenty of calcium, and should be informed about the importance of exercise in increasing bone density. Middle-aged women should be counseled about the value of hormone replacement therapy, diet, and weight-bearing exercise in slowing the loss of bone mass after menopause. For elderly women, the focus shifts to helping them prevent falls that can result in hip fracture. Screening for osteoporosis has received considerable attention, and several radiographic methods are available to measure bone density. However, while these may be helpful for high-risk women, some of the tests are expensive and the value of the information they provide is questionable (Cummings and Black 1986; Melton 1990).

ACCESS TO PREVENTIVE SERVICES

There are three key factors that determine whether, and to what extent, people take advantage of preventive services:

- having a regular source of care;
- having the knowledge—or a physician with the knowledge—of the services that are available; and
- having either the personal means to pay for the services or insurance that will cover the costs.

Limited insurance coverage is a major deterrent to the use of preventive services.

Private indemnity insurance, more commonly known as fee-for-service insurance, generally covers diagnostic services but not screening, counseling, or preventive services. Health maintenance organizations (HMOs)—group health care practices that provide a set of services to members for a flat fee—typically offer preventive care at minimal or no cost. Medicaid coverage for breast and cervical cancer screening differs from state to state, with wide variations in reimbursement rates and eligibility criteria (American College of Obstetricians and Gynecologists 1991). Medicare has recently been expanded to cover Pap smears and mammography to a limited extent; however, Pap smears are covered only once every three years and mammography is covered only once every two years (U.S. Congress, House Committee on Ways and Means 1992). Standardizing preventive service coverage among all types of health insurance plans, based upon individual age and risk factors, would increase the chance of all women receiving needed services.

IMPROVING ACCESS TO CARE

Women typically differ from men both in their use of health care services and in the financial and structural barriers to services they confront.

UTILIZATION OF HEALTH CARE SERVICES

As women grow older, concerns related to reproductive health, sexually transmitted diseases, and depression are likely to be gradually replaced by concerns about the risks of cardiovascular disease, cancer, and diabetes that increase with age, especially after menopause. To some extent, women's health needs at various points in their lives are reflected in national statistics on health care utilization. Other needs, such as counseling on AIDS or domestic violence, are not so readily quantified. A look at how much contact women have with the health care system throughout their lifetimes, however, validates concerns about whether the system is really meeting women's needs.

Women use more health services than men at all ages. In 1987, for example, 76 percent of women—compared to 59 percent of men—reported having visited a physician at least once in the preceding 12 months (see Table 6). The contrast is greatest during the ages corresponding to a woman's reproductive years: almost three-quarters of women age 25 to 44, compared to only one-half of men in that age group, reported at least one visit to a physician in the year past.

In addition, women were more likely than men (83 percent as opposed to 73 percent) to report having a regular source of care. Much of the difference between women and men in the use of health care services is undoubtedly related to women's needs for gynecological and obstetrical

Table 6 • PHYSICIAN VISITS AND USUAL SOURCE OF CARE BY SEX AND AGE, 1987

| | *Percentage Reporting* | | | |
| | *At Least One Physician Visit in Past Year* | | *Having Usual Source of Care* | |
	Women	*Men*	*Women*	*Men*
Total, age 18 and over	76	59	83	73
Age				
18–24	68	45	76	64
25–44	74	53	79	67
45–64	77	67	85	82
65 and over	86	80	91	89

Source: Estimates are based on the Agency for Health Care Policy and Research 1987 National Medical Expenditures Survey.

Figure 12 • HOSPITAL DISCHARGE RATES BY SEX AND AGE, 1990[1]

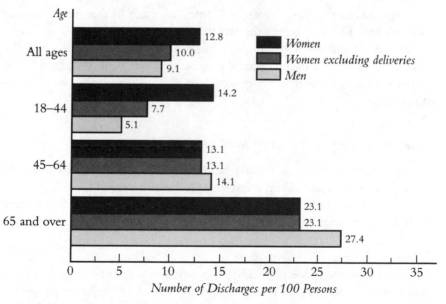

[1]Number of short-stay discharges per 100 persons in the population.
Source: Adams and Benson 1991.

care. In 1990, for example, a much higher proportion of reproductive-age women than of men in the same age group had hospital stays, but as Figure 12 illustrates, the difference narrowed considerably when hospital stays for childbirth were excluded.

This pattern is consistent with medical recommendations that women of reproductive age receive regular gynecological exams and early prenatal care. The need to seek care for pregnancy and gynecological disorders, and for most forms of birth control, also brings women into regular contact with the health care system. Visits to obstetricians/gynecologists account for nearly one-third of all office visits to specialists by women age 18 to 44 (Adams and Benson 1991). Women are more likely than men to have diagnostic procedures performed during visits to physicians, and for women, one-third of these procedures are related to reproductive health (DeLozier and Gagnon 1991).

Among older women, the patterns of health service use are somewhat different, reflecting the ebbing of the reproductive functions and the onset of chronic diseases. By age 45, women are typically already beginning to pay more visits to internists and fewer visits to gynecologists (DeLozier and Gagnon 1991). While older women visit physicians and report a regular source of care more often than men, the gap narrows with age. Among elderly women and men, contact with the health care system is almost comparable.

Hospitalization rates are lower for women after age 45 than for their male counterparts. This may reflect the fact that males are at greater risk of developing acute conditions that require hospital care, while for females the greater risk is of developing chronic conditions that can be managed on an outpatient basis. Women are consistently more likely than men to use outpatient care.

FINANCIAL AND STRUCTURAL BARRIERS TO CARE

In some respects, the U.S. health care system is one of the finest in the world. Nevertheless, millions of Americans do not benefit from it because they lack financial resources, they lack health insurance altogether or have inadequate coverage, or the health care services they need are not available.

Low Income

The poor and near-poor populations are less likely than better-off Americans to be insured and they are less able to afford out-of-pocket expenses for health care. Poverty has repeatedly been found to be associated with poor

Table 7 · POVERTY STATUS OF WOMEN AND MEN BY AGE, RACE, AND HISPANIC ORIGIN, 1990

	Women		*Men*	
	Total Number (in millions)	*Percent Poor*	*Total Number (in millions)*	*Percent Poor*
Total, age 18 and over	95.8	13.3%	87.8	8.4%
Age				
18–24	12.6	19.5%	12.3	12.2%
25–44	41.2	12.6%	40.4	8.1%
45–64	24.4	9.9%	22.6	7.3%
65 and over	17.6	15.4%	12.6	7.6%
Race				
White	81.2	10.8%	75.5	7.0%
Black	11.4	31.0%	9.3	19.0%
Native American[1]	.5	29.1%	.5	16.6%
Asian	2.6	10.9%	2.3	8.8%
Other	.2	18.2%	.2	11.5%
Hispanic origin				
Hispanic	7.0	26.2%	6.9	18.8%
Non-Hispanic	88.8	12.3%	80.8	7.5%

[1]Includes American Indians and Alaskan Natives.
Source: Estimates are based on the Bureau of the Census March 1991 Current Population Survey.

health status and reduced access to care. The authors' analysis of the National Medical Expenditure Survey for 1987 found that one-third of all poor women who were between the ages of 18 and 64, and nearly two-thirds of those who were over age 65, reported either fair or poor health status (Agency for Health Care Policy and Research 1987).

Poverty is a particular problem for women. The authors' analysis of the Current Population Survey of March 1991 found that one-third of all women are either poor or low income compared to 26 percent of men. As seen in Table 7, women are more likely than men to live in poverty at all ages past childhood. By the time a woman is 65 years old, she is almost twice as likely as her male counterpart to be living in poverty (Bureau of the

Census 1991). For minority women, the statistics are even more devastating. Nearly one-third of all black women, 29 percent of Native American women, and 26 percent of Hispanic women live below the poverty level.

Health Insurance Coverage

For most Americans, it is health insurance coverage that provides the means to overcome financial barriers to care. People who lack insurance are far less likely than those who have it to get adequate care. Indeed, the uninsured are up to three times more likely than privately insured individuals to experience low health care utilization, inadequate care, and poor health outcomes (U.S. Congress, OTA 1992). Because the inability to pay frequently delays care, the result is too often emergency hospitalization or hospitalization for conditions that, if diagnosed and treated earlier, could be handled on an outpatient basis.

The fragmented health care system in this country makes any discussion of insurance coverage complex. The majority of Americans are covered by either private or public insurance (including Medicaid and Medicare); however, more than 35 million people—14 percent of Americans—are entirely uninsured, with no coverage of any kind at any time during the year (Bureau of the Census 1992). Another 60 million people are underinsured—that is, their insurance is inadequate; or they risk losing coverage if they become ill; or their policies require them to pay very high out-of-pocket expenses before the insurance coverage begins.

The most significant contrast with respect to insurance coverage is between the elderly (age 65 and over) and the non-elderly. Almost all elderly people (99 percent) are insured, most of them under the Medicare program. As Table 8 shows, among men and women under age 65, equivalent proportions (75 percent) were covered by private insurance in 1990. However, a larger proportion of women than of men (eight percent versus three percent) had coverage under Medicaid. As a result, women were somewhat less likely than men to lack insurance altogether (15 percent compared to 19 percent). Nevertheless, because of the system's patchwork structure, gaps, and inconsistencies, it often fails to meet women's health care needs.

Private Insurance. The majority of Americans have financial access to health care through private health insurance. For most people, coverage is linked to their own full-time employment or that of a family member, with employers providing group health insurance as a benefit to workers and their dependents. In general, large firms are more likely than small firms to have health insurance plans for their employees, and firms in the manufac-

Table 8 · HEALTH INSURANCE COVERAGE STATUS OF WOMEN
AND MEN AGE 18 TO 64 BY AGE AND INCOME, 1990

	Total Number (in millions)	*Total Percent*	*Percent Distribution* Private	Medi- caid	Other Public[1]	None
WOMEN						
Total, age 18–64	78.3	100	75	8	2	15
Age						
18–24	12.6	100	64	11	3	22
25–44	41.2	100	77	8	2	14
45–64	24.4	100	79	6	3	13
Income[2]						
Poor	10.1	100	23	42	3	33
Low-income	12.9	100	57	10	4	28
Middle-income	26.5	100	84	2	3	11
High-income	28.8	100	94	[3]	1	5
MEN						
Total, age 18–64	75.2	100	75	3	3	19
Age						
18–24	12.3	100	64	·4	3	29
25–44	40.4	100	75	3	2	19
45–64	22.6	100	80	3	4	12
Income						
Poor	6.4	100	25	21	5	49
Low-income	11.6	100	51	6	6	37
Middle-income	26.2	100	78	1	3	17
High-income	31.0	100	91	[3]	1	7

[1]Includes Medicare, CHAMPUS, and CHAMPUS-VA.
[2]Income levels: Poor is less than 100 percent of federal poverty level; low-income is 100 to 199 percent of federal poverty level; middle-income is 200 to 399 percent of federal poverty level; high-income is 400 percent or more of federal poverty level.
[3]Indicates sample size too small to make national estimates.
Note: Details may not total to 100 percent due to rounding.
Source: Estimates are based on the Bureau of the Census March 1991 Current Population Survey.

turing industry are more likely to offer coverage than those in the service, agricultural, and retail industries.

The connection between health insurance and full-time employment has important implications for women. Because women often have caregiving responsibilities for children or elderly parents, they are more likely than men to work part time (Piacentini and Foley 1992), and consequently are less likely than men to have health insurance coverage through their own jobs.

The authors' analysis of the March 1991 Current Population Survey found that employed women who are insured through an employer-provided plan are twice as likely as men to have their coverage through a family member—usually a spouse—rather than through their own job. This is true even of women who work year round, full time: 18 percent of those who were insured under an employer-provided plan in 1991 had their coverage through a family member's job. The comparable percentage for men was 9.4 percent (Bureau of the Census 1991).

Even when they participate in the workforce, women are more likely than men to rely on dependent coverage (Older Women's League 1992). Dependence on a spouse's coverage places women at risk of becoming uninsured in the event of divorce or widowhood (Berk and Taylor 1984). When coverage through an employer or spouse is not available, women must choose either to bear the prohibitive cost of purchasing individual policies or become uninsured. Nearly one-quarter of women over age 45 buy individual health insurance, compared with 17 percent of men (Bureau of the Census 1991). In many cases, these costly health insurance policies offer only limited benefits.

Medicaid. Medicaid, the nation's public health insurance program for the poor, plays a critical role in assuring access to health care for many poor women, as well as some near-poor women, but it falls far short of providing comprehensive, uniform coverage across the country. Eligibility for Medicaid, which is jointly financed by the federal and state government, is largely determined by the states under broad federal guidelines. By federal law, Medicaid coverage is automatic for women who meet their states' eligibility criteria for Aid to Families with Dependent Children (AFDC) or Supplemental Security Income (SSI), a public assistance program for the poor, elderly, and disabled. Federal law also now requires Medicaid to cover prenatal and neonatal care for pregnant women with incomes below 133 percent of the poverty threshold. Some states are more generous, covering pregnant women with incomes of up to 185 percent of poverty, but in general, eligibility is highly restricted.

Medicaid's emphasis is on low-income families with children, and, in particular, on poor families that are headed by women. As a result, Medicaid provides coverage for more young adult females than for any other adult age group (see Table 8 above).

Medicaid eligibility is predicated upon passing both an income and a categorical test. Because of this, many poor women do not meet the criteria for coverage. For example, a childless woman who is poor but not pregnant, elderly, or disabled is ineligible for Medicaid. Of the 10.1 million women between the ages of 18 and 65 who were poor in 1990, one-third (33 percent) had no health insurance coverage of any kind during that year (Bureau of the Census 1991).

Although Medicaid can provide coverage for a broad array of services, persons who are publicly insured receive fewer health services than their privately insured counterparts (U.S. Congress, OTA 1992). Some states limit coverage for important preventive services. For example, Medicaid coverage for pregnant women is limited to treatment for pregnancy-related conditions, and benefits end 60 days after the woman gives birth unless she is, or becomes, eligible for cash assistance or AFDC. Moreover, women who have Medicaid coverage often have problems finding physicians who will accept Medicaid payment for services. Because reimbursement rates are low and administrative requirements burdensome, many physicians—particularly obstetricians—refuse to take Medicaid patients. Obstetricians have the lowest Medicaid participation rate of all specialists (Mitchell 1991).

Medicare. Medicare is the federally financed and administered health insurance program for the elderly and persons with permanent disability or end-stage renal (kidney) disease. Unlike Medicaid, it is not means-tested. To qualify for Medicare, persons must be either age 65 or older and eligible for Social Security or railroad retirement insurance, or have been permanently and totally disabled for two years or more.

Medicare Part A provides coverage for inpatient hospital expenses (for up to approximately 90 days) and limited coverage for skilled nursing care at home. Coverage for outpatient expenses (Medicare Part B) may be purchased for an additional premium ($36.60 per month in 1993).

Although Medicare insures the vast majority of the elderly population, there are significant gaps in the coverage it provides. Prescription drugs and long-term care services are not covered. These are critical services for elderly women, who are more likely than elderly men to have limited incomes and to require prescription drugs and long-term care because of chronic health conditions and longer life expectancy.

Most elderly people buy additional private insurance (often known as "Medigap" insurance) to supplement Medicare, primarily to pay for copayments and drugs. Without this additional coverage, Medicare beneficiaries are vulnerable to high out-of-pocket costs. As shown in Table 9, 68 percent of elderly women and 73 percent of elderly men supplement Medicare with private health insurance. Because of their typically lower socioeconomic status and more limited retirement benefit coverage, elderly women are slightly more likely than elderly men to be either solely dependent on

Table 9 · HEALTH INSURANCE COVERAGE STATUS OF THE ELDERLY POPULATION BY SEX AND INCOME, 1990

| | | | | *Percent Distribution* | | |
	Total Number (in millions)	Total Percent	Medicare and/or Private[1]	Medicare and Medicaid	Only	None
WOMEN						
Total, age 65 and over	17.6	100	68	8	23	1
Income[2]						
Poor	2.7	100	37	27	34	2
Low-income	5.2	100	61	9	30	1
Middle-income	5.8	100	77	3	19	1
High-income	3.9	100	85	2	13	[3]
MEN						
Total, age 65 and over	12.6	100	73	5	21	1
Income						
Poor	1.0	100	28	30	38	4
Low-income	3.0	100	57	9	33	1
Middle-income	4.8	100	78	2	19	1
High-income	3.8	100	90	[3]	9	[3]

[1]Medicare and/or private includes those persons with either Medicare and private coverage or private coverage only.

[2]Income levels: Poor is less than 100 percent of federal poverty level; low-income is 100 to 199 percent of federal poverty level; middle-income is 200 to 399 percent of federal poverty level; high-income is 400 percent or more of federal poverty level.

[3]The sample size is too small to make national estimates.

Note: Details may not total to 100 percent due to rounding.

Source: Estimates are based on the Bureau of the Census March 1991 Current Population Survey.

Medicare or to have coverage under Medicaid, which serves as supplemental insurance to Medicare for the low-income elderly persons who are eligible (Piacentini and Foley 1992).

The Uninsured

In 1991 more than 35 million Americans, 14 percent of the population, had no health insurance coverage of any kind at any time during the year. About 11.8 million of the uninsured were adult women between the ages of 18 and 65, and of these, nearly one-fourth (2.8 million) were under 25. Among both women and men, it is this 18 to 24 age group that is most likely to be uninsured. Twenty-two percent of the women and 29 percent of the men in this age group lacked insurance throughout the year. The authors' analysis of the March 1991 Current Population Survey found that of poor non-elderly adult women, 33 percent were uninsured (see Table 8 above) (Bureau of the Census 1991).

Approximately 65 percent of uninsured women of working age had some work experience in 1991, and about a quarter of them were year-round, full-time workers. Poor women who worked were much more likely than poor women who did not work to be uninsured (41 percent versus 29 percent in 1991) (Bureau of the Census 1992). Minority women—especially Hispanics—are heavily overrepresented among uninsured women workers. Indeed, Hispanics of both sexes are the most likely of all Americans to be uninsured (Bureau of the Census 1991). Many more women are at risk of becoming uninsured or underinsured as a result of employer changes in insurance coverage, preexisting condition rules of insurance companies, changing jobs, or serious illnesses.

Moreover, many states have recently been forced to reduce their supplemental state-funded Medicaid coverage because of fiscal crises. For example, in 1992 the precedent was set when a state that had offered coverage to pregnant women at 185 percent of the poverty level dropped back down to the federally mandated level of 133 percent. In general, the current system leaves access to health care for women unstable.

Delivery of Services

Having health insurance does not by itself guarantee access to quality health care. In Chapter Two of this volume, Wilhelmina Leigh discusses the barriers to care that arise from cultural differences. Geographical distances can also be a barrier. The shortage of primary care providers in rural areas and inner cities is well documented. For example, a recent report found that, in

1988, there were 111 nonmetropolitan counties in the United States without a physician, and nearly 1,500 counties without an obstetrician (Summer 1991).

An issue key to improving the delivery of care, especially to women, is better coordination between providers. It is recognized throughout the health care field that a renewed emphasis on comprehensive care, including preventive services, is needed. Coordination of care is a particular problem for women because for them even routine care typically involves both a gynecologist and an internist. This type of fragmentation increases the chances that women will not receive needed services or that other services will be unnecessarily repeated (Clancy and Massion 1992). Most likely to be left out are services like counseling on violence or depression that are outside the strict clinical realm of gynecologists and internists.

NATIONAL HEALTH CARE REFORM

The current national health care reform debate has focused on controlling skyrocketing costs and increasing access to care for the millions of Americans who are uninsured and underinsured. The issue of universal coverage primarily applies to those under age 65, since Medicare covers nearly all elderly persons. The reform debate has focused on three approaches: the single-payer plan; the so-called "play or pay" plan that requires employers to provide coverage; and managed competition. These options are summarized below, along with their possible implications for women.

The Single-Payer Plan

The single-payer approach would provide universal health insurance coverage and replace the current patchwork of multiple public and private insurers with a system in which all health services would be financed through federal government tax revenues. The Canadian health care system is an example of this approach. Under the plan, individuals could go to any provider they chose, with all bills sent to a central "insurer" for payment. Costs would be contained by setting an annual national health care budget. (In Canada, it is up to each province to stay within its allocated budget.) The single-payer plan would standardize benefits for the entire population, and stress primary and preventive care.

Proponents of the single-payer approach believe it is the best way to assure universal coverage, to control costs, and to reduce administrative burdens. Opponents fear that it would lead to rationing of care and discourage continued advances in medical technology. For women, however, a single-payer system could eliminate many of the current barriers to adequate care, since insurance would not be linked to employment or welfare status.

The Employer-Mandate Approach

Widely known as "play or pay," this plan would build on the existing system under which a majority of Americans are covered by health insurance provided through employers. The difference would be that the government would require all employers to participate. Proposals under consideration generally would require all employers to either provide insurance for their employees and, in some cases, their dependents, or pay a tax to a public health insurance fund. The taxes paid would help finance a public plan to cover uninsured workers and those not connected to the workforce, thus achieving universal coverage. Proposals based on this approach have featured basic benefits packages. Some include specific preventive health care services; others neglect preventive services for adults—such services as, for example, mammography and Pap smears.

Managed Competition

Managed competition is an approach to controlling health care spending that is based on the creation of a consumer-driven health care market. Under managed competition, consumers would be given a choice of competing health plans and would be provided with incentives to select the most cost-effective one. A quasi-public intermediary organization would be created to help consumers compare the costs and quality of different health plans. This intermediary would select and offer several different health benefit plans to consumers. Under some proposals, a federal health board would establish standards and certify the health plans selected by the intermediary. All insurance companies would be required to offer a basic benefits package.

Developers of managed competition believe that given sufficient information and incentives, health care consumers would select cost-effective plans. Insurance plans would have to respond to consumer demands for quality and value in order to survive. The plans most likely to be competitive are managed care arrangements such as health maintenance organizations or similar programs. The basic administration of managed competition would be through the quasi-public intermediaries, which would collect information on health plans, distribute information to consumers in their regions, and facilitate the enrollment of beneficiaries.

Concerns with managed competition include the ability to restructure the present health care system, feasibility in areas of the country in which there are too few people or providers to support competition among several plans, and the ability to adequately adjust capitated payments based on risk (Merlis 1993). Risk adjustment (the modification of payment based on the probability of use of health care services) is an important issue because there are also concerns that the poor and low-income would be viewed by managed care plans as "too sick," more likely to use health care services, and therefore too costly. As a result, negative incentives may be created that continue to limit access to care for the poor.

It will be hard to assess how well a managed competition proposal would meet the needs of women and others with special needs until the composition of the basic benefits package is determined. Also critical would be the proposal's ability to monitor and regulate plans and to risk-adjust payment rates to eliminate any negative incentives for underservice. In addition, it would be of great importance, particularly for women who have long-standing ties to physicians and other providers, to be assured that provider choice and continuity would be maintained.

CONCLUSION

In the past, concern about women's health problems as distinct from men's has focused largely on reproductive health. However, it is now understood that there are many other health conditions that, even if not unique to females, are much more likely to affect women than men, or are likely to affect them in quite different ways.

It is now known, for example, that young adult women are much more likely than men to suffer from emotional disorders, autoimmune conditions, and long-term consequences from sexually transmitted infections. As they grow older, women's health concerns change. Chronic conditions that increase with age and hormonal changes after menopause leave women at risk for disability.

The good news is that there are effective preventive services that can have a significant impact on women's health. Unfortunately, not all women who would benefit from these services receive them. The barriers that limit access to preventive services include cost, lack of knowledge about the services, and inconveniently located health care providers.

Limits on access to care, of course, mean more than limits on access to preventive services. Affording care is a major problem for the millions of women who are uninsured, or at risk of losing their insurance in the event of a job change or serious illness. Women with Medicaid coverage may find themselves at risk of receiving reduced benefits when states are faced with difficult budget decisions. A majority of the public, health care providers, and legislators now agree on the overwhelming need for national health care reform to provide everyone with access to quality services and to reduce the astronomical cost of health care in America.

If it is to address the particular needs of women adequately, health care reform will

- provide universal access to care;
- eliminate the problems associated with employment-based insurance and Medicaid;
- cover prescription drugs and long-term care services for the elderly;
- include preventive services (counseling as well as procedures);
- ensure that quality health care is available to women in convenient settings;
- include initiatives to increase the supply of primary care physicians;
- develop a more even distribution of health care providers and hospitals; and
- address cultural barriers to care at the community level.

And finally, a more personal level of reform will be required to empower women with knowledge of their health status and risks, and to train physicians to use greater sensitivity in communicating with women on such topics as sexual behaviors and violence.

There are several factors that emerge as influences on the health status of American women. Those factors that reflect gaps in knowledge about how to prevent and treat illnesses in women and in access to quality health care must be addressed in order to improve the health outcomes and quality of life for women. Further research and a reformed health care system can close these gaps, if the concerns and needs of women are considered.

TWO

★

THE HEALTH STATUS OF WOMEN OF COLOR

Wilhelmina A. Leigh[1]

HIGHLIGHTS

IN THIS CHAPTER THE TERM WOMEN OF COLOR encompasses four major groups of women—Native, Hispanic, Black, and Asian and Pacific Islander Americans—with subgroups within each of the major groups. These four groups include many subpopulations whose health status varies from better than the U.S. average (e.g., Japanese and Cuban Americans with prenatal care) to worse than the U.S. average (e.g., Black and Native American women with amputations due to diabetes).

Because all people of color have experienced both deculturation (relative to their place of origin) and acculturation to American society, women of color have confronted not only the stresses associated with trying to be the preservers of culture and bulwarks of family life—but also the prejudice, discrimination, and racism that seem to come hand-in-hand with minority status in the United States. As a result, women of color experience high rates of poverty and depression as well as inadequate housing—all of which have implications for their health status.

The following points highlight some of the important issues relating to the health status of women of color today:

[1]This analysis is the author's own and should not be attributed to the Joint Center for Political and Economic Studies, its board of governors, or its sponsors. The author would like to thank the following people for their assistance during the preparation of the chapter: Hortensia Amaro, I. Evelyn Baez, Linda Burhansstipanov, Susan Chu, Tylene Harrell, Wendy Hee, Laurin Mayeno, Socorro Sosa, Elena Yu, and Ruth Zambrana. Any errors or other shortcomings of this chapter are, of course, the sole responsibility of its author.

- Hispanic American women have the longest life expectancy of all women of color, followed by Native American and then by Black American women. (Data for Asian and Pacific Islander American women are not available.)
- Obesity, defined as excess body weight for height, is a problem for all women of color, but especially for Native American, Pacific Islander, and Black American women. The high incidence of adult-onset diabetes is a major problem for women of color (especially Native American and Native Hawaiian women), in part because of obesity.
- For a variety of reasons (financial, cultural, informational, and access-related among them), less than half of all women of color regularly avail themselves of preventive tests such as Pap smears or mammograms. This translates into higher death rates from breast and cervical cancer among women of color than among White women. Black and Native Hawaiian women, especially, have higher death rates and lower five-year survival rates than White women for most types of cancer.
- Although the human immunodeficiency virus/acquired immune deficiency syndrome (HIV/AIDS) has infected and killed many women of color, its incidence is much greater among Black and Hispanic (mainly Puerto Rican) American women than among other women of color.
- Heart disease and cancer are the major killers among women of color, as they are among the rest of the population. Other prominent causes of death among women of color include: HIV/AIDS (as mentioned above); homicide and unintentional injuries (especially among Black, Hispanic, and Native American women); and alcohol-related diseases (especially among Native American and Pacific Islander American women).
- Undercounting, failing to collect subpopulation data, and misidentifying women of color are the major problems associated with collecting data on them.
- Guidelines for preventive medical testing and for research often fail to incorporate and reflect the distinct needs of women of color.
- A greater number of community-based medical facilities with culturally sensitive health care providers are needed to serve women of color.

INTRODUCTION

Women in the United States address their health care needs through several filters. Filters imposed outside of their family context include:

- a biomedical knowledge base that presumes that women can be treated the same as men for conditions that afflict them both;
- a health care system oriented to viewing and treating women as vessels for reproduction;
- a federal health insurance program for the elderly (Medicare) that provides better coverage for the acute illnesses more common in men than for the chronic diseases more common in women; and
- a medical profession that has been slow to acknowledge and develop responses to the impacts of domestic violence on both physical and mental health.

In addition to these external filters, women access health care not simply as individuals but in the context of the families in which they perform multiple caregiving roles—as wives, mothers, daughters, widows, etc. These caregiving roles often translate into interrupted employment histories and limited access to health insurance, and place time constraints on women's ability to seek care for themselves. Dependence on a husband for health insurance coverage leaves the caregiver wife vulnerable if the marriage dissolves or if the employer cuts back on or eliminates dependent coverage.

These general problems and characteristics of women as caregivers and consumers of health care services are compounded for women of color by the special circumstances of their lives and those of the men with whom they live. Prejudice, discrimination, poverty, lack of language skills, and varying degrees of acculturation all interact to generate the daily diet of stresses that have further bearing on the health status of women of color.

FACTORS AFFECTING THE HEALTH OF WOMEN OF COLOR

ETHNIC AND RACIAL HERITAGE[2]

Before moving into a discussion of the factors influencing the health of the four primary groups of women of color, the population groups need to be briefly described. Of the nearly 249 million people counted as U.S. residents in the 1990 Census, 51.3 percent of them were women, and over 31 million were women of color. These 31 million women of color are dis-

[2]Women of color are discussed in rough chronological order of the arrival of any member of their group in the United States. Native American refers to American Indians and Alaskan

tributed as follows: 50 percent Black, 35 percent Hispanic, 11.8 percent Asian and Pacific Islander, and three percent Native American (Bureau of the Census 1992d). Women of color are nearly a fourth of all U.S. women; in raw numbers, there are nearly 16 million Black American women, nearly 11 million Hispanic American women, nearly one million Native American women, and over 3.7 million Asian and Pacific Islander women.

The fastest growing minority group is Asian and Pacific Islander Americans, increasing by nearly 108 percent between 1980 and 1990. The group that is a distant second in its growth rate is Hispanic Americans, growing by 53 percent over the 1980-1990 period. The Native American population increased by nearly 38 percent over the decade, while Blacks grew by only 13 percent and Whites by six percent (Bureau of the Census 1992f).

NATIVE AMERICANS

The ancestors of the people known today as Native Americans came across the Bering Strait to live in North America many centuries before Europeans came. Although 12 to 15 million Indians were here when Columbus arrived in 1492, today their progeny number only two million.

Native Americans are the smallest of the four major racial/ethnic subpopulations discussed in this chapter. They are constituted as 300 recognized tribes in seven nations (such as the Navajo or Iroquois) in the lower 48 states and approximately 500 government units in Alaska (Scott and Suagee 1992). The many Native American subpopulations are culturally distinctive, diverse, and complex—and, as noted above, are growing six times more rapidly than the White population. Native Americans speak more than 200 distinct languages, which makes their dialects more diverse than the entire Indo-European language family.

This diversity, coupled with their many small population groups scattered throughout the United States, has made it difficult to provide a uniform, readily accessible health care system for Native Americans. Two-fifths of American Indians, a third of Eskimos, and over half of Aleuts lived in urban

---

Natives (Eskimos and Aleuts). Hispanic refers to the Spanish-surnamed and Spanish-speaking residents of the United States. This term is chosen rather than Latino or Latina because it is used in most of the data sources on which this chapter is based. Black is used instead of African American to signify that this group includes Black West Indians and other members of the African diaspora who might not be both of African descent and American. Asian and Pacific Islander refers to both the Asian subpopulations (Chinese, Japanese, Filipino, Korean, Vietnamese, etc.) and the Pacific Islander subpopulations (Native Hawaiians, Samoans, Guamanians, and Tongans, etc.) who are U.S. residents.

areas (as of the 1980 Census), with sizable numbers remaining in rural areas and/or on reservations (Liu and Yu 1985).

Although Native Americans are culturally diverse to the point that it often becomes meaningless to classify them together for any but the most gross comparisons, their shared experiences include:

- the rapid and forced change from a cooperative, clan-based society to a capitalistic and nuclear family-based system;
- the outlawing of language and spiritual practices;
- the death of generations of elders to infectious diseases or war; and
- the loss of the ability to use the land walked by their ancestors for thousands of years (Scott and Suagee 1992).

In addition, Native Americans are the only ethnic minority group in the United States with which the federal government has treaty obligations to provide health services. The Indian Health Service (IHS)—since 1955 part of the U.S. Public Health Service—provides health care through its clinics and hospitals to all Native Americans living near or on the reservations in its 12 service areas. Although the IHS reports that it serves approximately 60 percent of all Native Americans, services in urban areas and in nonreservation rural areas are often very limited and uncoordinated (Scott and Suagee 1992). For example, there are only two IHS health units east of the Mississippi River (a clinic in Nashville, Tennessee and a hospital in Cherokee, North Carolina) to serve all Native Americans from Maine to Florida (Health Resources and Services Administration [HRSA] 1992a).

How has the legacy of Native Americans in this country influenced the health of Indian women? The major legacy of the forced relocation of Native Americans throughout the United States has been to place them in communities in which they confront racism and hostility from their non-Native neighbors (IHS 1991b).

This racism, coupled with a mistrust of the U.S. government, has engendered low self-esteem among many Native Americans. Racism and discrimination also have contributed to the poverty in which 28 percent of Native Americans live, and this poverty has in turn fostered welfare dependency and diets replete with government commodity foods, high both in fat and calories. Sixty percent of both male and female urban Native Americans are reported to be overweight and, therefore, at risk for diabetes and other illnesses. Poverty also has placed Native Americans at risk of environmental degradation to their health, as the result of living in poor quality housing (often with lead-based paint that poisons the children) and exposure to local toxins. Half of all Native Americans live in areas with uncontrolled toxic waste sites (Alston 1992).

The loss of access to the lands their ancestors roamed freely has extinguished the traditional gender roles for Native American males (as hunters, horsemen, and protectors). Native American men often have channeled their rage about this against Native American women, who must still fulfill the caretaker role for their families. Family violence among Native Americans takes on many forms—child abuse and neglect, elder abuse, spouse battering, spouse abandonment, and sexual abuse of young children (IHS 1991b).

Both the lack of tribal ordinances to deal with family violence and the refusal of local non-Indian law enforcement officials to take seriously rapes reported by Native American women (especially if they are alcoholics or substance abusers) limit the recourse of Native American women who seek help. In addition, many Native American women are reluctant to report mistreatment by the men in their lives to non-Indian authorities because of the history of harsh treatment of Native American men by the U.S. justice system.

Responses of Native American girls and women to their life circumstances often include teen pregnancy, alcoholism, and substance abuse. Low self-esteem among Indian girls frequently translates into teenage pregnancy, as they use their fertility to seek approval from males. Alcoholism and its multigenerational effects is at the root of most health problems experienced by Native American women, as evidenced by their death rates from alcoholism, cirrhosis, and other liver diseases. In addition, alcoholism among their daughters often adds to the stresses of elderly Native American women who wind up parenting their grandchildren and/or great-grandchildren, as well as managing the chronic diseases typical in older women (IHS 1991b).

The prevailing life circumstances for many Native American women jeopardize their health status in a second way as well, because poverty, low self-esteem, alcoholism, and substance abuse may interfere with their ability to seek preventive health care. The necessity of patronizing culturally insensitive providers located at great distances also may limit preventive health practices and place the day when measures such as breast self-examination have been adequately taught and accepted in Native American communities even farther into the future (IHS 1991b).

The response to the human immunodeficiency virus/acquired immune deficiency syndrome (HIV/AIDS) by Native Americans reflects the long history of their mistreatment by the U.S. government and, consequently, the complexities of providing treatment to them. For example, HIV/AIDS has not been given a meaning in local Native American languages. Thus, the condition cannot be discussed in local tongues, nor can indigenous healing processes be applied to HIV/AIDS. Consequently, HIV/AIDS is discussed solely as a "White man's disease," like the many other infectious diseases to which Whites have exposed Native Americans. This perception, coupled with the fact that the federal government does not pay Native Americans to be tested for HIV infection—as it has paid them to participate in other federal health programs—leaves many Native Americans both skeptical of the need for testing and unwilling to get it.

Many Native Americans also view the federal government's emphasis on multicultural outreach in funding for AIDS prevention as favoring Black Americans and as resulting in ethnic minority groups competing among themselves for very limited resources. Native Americans find it difficult to identify HIV/AIDS as something that can affect them, without a spokesperson who is Native American to bring the message home in the way former basketball star Magic Johnson has for many young people and for Black Americans (HRSA 1992a).

Finally, HIV/AIDS is only one of many health problems that Native Americans need to address. And all health problems are subordinated to issues such as the needs for food, housing, and employment that weigh heavily on Native Americans, as they do on all minority groups with large subpopulations in poverty.

HISPANIC AMERICANS

The earliest forebearers of the group known today as Hispanic Americans or Latinos were Spanish colonists in the late 1500s who came from Mexico to live in what is now the southwestern United States. In 1990, the descendants of these forbearers were included among "other Hispanics" and made up seven percent of the 22.4 million Hispanics in the United States (HRSA 1991; General Accounting Office [GAO] 1992). The other major Hispanic subgroups in 1990 were Mexican Americans (60 percent), Central and South Americans (14 percent), Puerto Ricans (12 percent), and Cuban Americans (five percent).

Over 90 percent of the nation's Hispanic population in 1990 was urban, and 70 percent of the population was concentrated in six of the most populous states—California, Texas, New York, Florida, New Jersey, and Illinois. Only 29 percent of all Hispanic Americans were foreign born, and the nearly 11 million Hispanic women were slightly less than half of the total Hispanic population (Bureau of the Census 1992e).

The Hispanic population in the United States is diverse. It includes farmworkers (with a life expectancy of 49 years and infant mortality rates about 25 percent higher than the U.S. average) and people from Spanish-speaking countries (such as certain parts of El Salvador and various southern regions of Mexico) whose primary language is not Spanish (Bastida 1992; Zambrana 1992). The Hispanic population ranges from dark-skinned to light-skinned and all of the shades in between. The population includes Mexican Americans, who enjoy better health than would be predicted, given their socioeconomic status and the fact that they have the lowest utilization rates for health care facilities among all ethnic/racial groups (Higginbotham, Trevino, and Ray 1990). It also encompasses Puerto Ricans and Cuban Americans, whose utilization rates of health care facilities are comparable to the rates of Whites. In short, there is such variation in the health status of the Hispanic American subgroups that looking at aggregated measures can obscure meaningful intra-group differences.

The socioeconomic positions of Hispanic American families, as of all families, influence their access to health insurance, and thereby to health care. In 1990, 28 percent of the U.S. Hispanic population was below the poverty line (National Institutes of Health [NIH] 1991).

Hispanic American families also are more likely than non-Hispanic White families to be headed by females. Among Puerto Rican families, 43 percent are headed by women, as are 26 percent of Cuban American families, and 19 percent of both Mexican American and Central and South American families (Amaro 1992). Overall, nearly half (46 percent) of poor Hispanic American families are female-headed and are likely to face the combined stresses of poverty, lack of health insurance, lack of health care for themselves and their children, and lack of social support—all of which place these women at risk for mental health problems as well as substance and alcohol abuse.

Hispanics are more likely than other Americans to be among the working poor, and partly as a reflection of this, 32 percent of the Hispanic population was not covered by health insurance in 1990 (HRSA 1991). When Hispanic women are employed, they tend to hold jobs of low status and with low pay. Over 28 percent of Hispanic women in the labor force held jobs as service workers, operators, fabricators, and laborers in 1991 (Bureau of the Census 1991).

The working poor face double jeopardy with respect to health care because they cannot afford to pay costly medical bills out-of-pocket and because they do not qualify for federal programs such as Medicaid. Some of the Hispanic working poor have the added disadvantage of lacking U.S. citizenship and thus are ineligible for federal health assistance programs, even if their incomes are low enough.

Along with socioeconomic status, cultural context or acculturation—the process of change that occurs as a result of continuous contact between cultural groups—plays a major role in the access of Hispanic populations to health care in the United States (Solis et al. 1990). More acculturated Hispanics (as reflected by greater use and skill with the English language, lessened contact with their homeland, and greater involvement with the Anglo American culture) would be expected to adopt behaviors and have health outcomes similar to the dominant Anglo culture (Rosenbach and Butrica 1991).

Less acculturated Hispanic immigrants have a significantly lower likelihood of outpatient visits for health problems (either physical or mental). And surprisingly the incidence of low birth weight infants (which is highly correlated with the infant mortality rate) among less acculturated first generation Mexican American women is lower (3.9 percent of live births) than among White non-Hispanic women (5.7 percent of live births) and among second generation Mexican American women (6.1 percent of live births) (Guendelman et al. 1990).

Another aspect of acculturation for the Hispanic American is encountering discrimination, prejudice, and exclusion (based either on language or skin color), perhaps for the first time, and incorporating into her or his identity a newly acquired "minority status." Experiences with discrimination and exclusion can frustrate expectations of improved socioeconomic status when the dominant culture's values are adopted (Amaro 1992). This may explain the fact that highly acculturated Mexican Americans and Puerto Ricans, who have not enjoyed access to the educational resources of the United States, are most likely to report marijuana and cocaine use (Amaro et al. 1990). Also, among more acculturated, younger Hispanic women, alcohol consumption has been found to be greater than among less acculturated, younger Hispanic women (Markides et al. 1990).

Other aspects of culture that can influence health are religion, folk healing, and "familism" or family mores. The health beliefs of many Hispanics relate to their views about God as the omnipotent creator of the universe, with personal behavior subject to God's judgment (Rosenbach and Butrica 1991). Beliefs such as these make it difficult to establish the importance of preventive health behaviors. The reluctance of users of indigenous healers and folk medicines to disclose their use, and the associated delays in seeking biomedical care while using these treatments, also can jeopardize the health of Hispanics (HRSA 1991). Family mores that dictate that Hispanics must seek the advice of family members before getting professional health care also can build delays into the care-seeking process that may be costly in terms of either morbidity or mortality (Rosenbach and Butrica 1991). Thus, low utilization of health care services can result from cultural beliefs as well as from socioeconomic barriers (Scrimshaw, Zambrana, and Dunkel-Schetter 1990).

Finally, HIV/AIDS, as it affects the Hispanic community, illustrates the many barriers to effective care that are socioeconomic, cultural, and political. Puerto Ricans, on the mainland and on the island, have the highest incidence of HIV/AIDS among Hispanics, and also have several characteristics that distinguish them from other Hispanic subgroups (Menendez 1990). All Puerto Ricans have U.S. citizenship and therefore have no need to marry non-Puerto Ricans to maintain residency in the United States. Thus, Puerto Ricans marry each other in greater proportions than do other Hispanic subpopulations in the United States, and are, therefore, more likely to have sex with other Puerto Ricans than they are with non-Puerto Rican Hispanics or non-Hispanics (Menendez 1990). This has contributed to the heterosexual spread of HIV/AIDS among Puerto Ricans, as has the existence of racially and ethnically homogeneous needle-sharing networks. The frequent and relatively cheap flights between New York City and Puerto Rico, and continuous work-related migration between the two, have added to the difficulty in counting and providing continuous care to Puerto Ricans diagnosed with HIV/AIDS.

Cultural factors enter into the picture because Hispanics often are unwilling to discuss intimate and emotional matters such as illness and sex unless they are able to speak to someone in Spanish. Educational programs to prevent HIV/AIDS, which instruct Hispanic women to encourage their sex partners who are intravenous drug users to use condoms, ignore the riskiness of speaking out for Latinas. Suggesting the use of a condom may cause her partner to believe that the Latina either knows too much about sex or is being unfaithful, and may place her at risk of either physical or emotional abuse from her partner. Successful educational programs for poor Hispanic (and Black) women have been difficult to establish, partly because these women need help in surviving in their daily environments before they can become receptive to skill building and informational strategies (Nyamathi et al. 1993).

BLACK AMERICANS

The African ancestors of the group known today as Black Americans or African Americans were brought to the shores of what is now the United States as slaves by Europeans, beginning in 1619. Today, there are 30 million Black Americans in this country, 12.1 percent of the total population, and they are currently the largest minority group (Bureau of the Census 1992d). Over half of all Black Americans (nearly 16 million) are females. Approximately three percent of Black Americans are foreign born, mainly comprised of French-speaking Haitians and other non-Spanish-speaking Caribbean people, some of whom are farmworkers in the United States.

Though seldom studied, marked differences in acculturation exist among Black women and contribute to the diversity of their health (Nyamathi et al. 1993). Black Americans are a largely urban population (84 percent in 1990) but can be found in most parts of the United States (Bureau of the Census 1992f).

Differences in the health status of Blacks and Whites are many and varied. Blacks have more undetected diseases, higher disease and illness rates, and more chronic conditions (such as hypertension and diabetes) than Whites (Leffall 1990). Mortality rates for Blacks from many conditions (cancer, HIV/AIDS, and homicide) exceed those for Whites. Explanations for these racial differences have been sought by experts, and many contributing factors have been identified. The major factors—genetics, poverty, and racism—are discussed below.

The murkiness of race as a concept to define Black Americans, who range from fair-skinned and blue-eyed to dark-skinned with coarse hair, makes purely genetic explanations of the health differences between Blacks and Whites questionable. Biology appears to explain very little of the differences in health status between Blacks and Whites, if the proportion of excess deaths among Blacks—that is, deaths that would not have occurred if Blacks experienced the same age- and sex-related death rates as Whites—due to hereditary conditions is examined. Less than one percent of Black deaths have been attributed to hereditary conditions such as sickle cell anemia, for which genetic patterns have been established (Jaynes and Williams 1989). On the other hand, researchers studying the incidence of hypertension among Blacks have found that it varies with skin color. That is, lighter pigmented Blacks have a lower prevalence of hypertension than darker skinned Blacks, and pigment is related to the degree of admixture with Whites, whose overall incidence of hypertension is lower than that of Blacks (Wilkinson and King 1989).

Instead of looking at population-related genetic differences, others link the racial differences in health status to Black subpopulations that are exposed to multiple risks—such as intravenous drug users, those living and working in hazardous environments, and the like. Those health conditions common among Blacks that are considered to be genetic in origin are likely to receive more public attention and resources than conditions that arise from behavior or life style choices. For example, conditions such as sickle cell anemia receive more research attention and public support than health conditions attributable to accidents, substance abuse, and environmentally caused illnesses (Wilkinson and King 1989).

Poverty affected nearly one-third of all Black Americans (31.9 percent) and 35.5 percent of all Black women in 1990. Single-parent, female-headed households, 44 percent of all Black households in 1990, were mired in poverty to a greater degree than the entire Black population (Bureau of the Census 1992d). Forty-eight percent of all Black female-headed families had incomes below the poverty level in 1990, and 75 percent of the two million Black families in poverty were maintained by women with no husbands present (Bureau of the Census 1992b). Inadequate income carries over into other aspects of daily life that impinge upon health. These include inadequate housing (which may quicken the spread of communicable diseases), malnutrition, the stress of constantly struggling to make ends meet, dangerous jobs, and little or no preventive medical care. Malnutrition in little Black girls may later result in low birth weight babies and high infant mortality rates when these girls become mothers. The stresses of constantly struggling to make ends meet may translate directly into the finding that Blacks below the poverty level have the highest rate of depression for any group (Liu and Yu 1985). Dangerous jobs (and living environments) may expose Blacks to certain cancers to a much greater extent than Whites (Miller 1989). Little or no preventive care may come about for a variety of reasons, including:

- parental ignorance of disease symptoms and when to seek medical care;
- lack of health insurance to enable access to health care;
- lack of neighborhood facilities in which to seek health care;
- persistent use of emergency rooms to treat chronic conditions, which are better managed in other settings; and
- racial discrimination encountered when seeking care (Jaynes and Williams 1989; Headen and Headen 1985-86).

Racial discrimination and racism have remained significant operative factors in the health status and health care of Blacks over time. From as early as 1867, Black spokespersons concluded that racism was a major contributor to the poor health of Black America in two significant ways. First, "structural racism" creates barriers to getting access to adequate care, and second, dealing with both structural barriers and racial insults may contribute to stress-related health problems such as pregnancy-induced hypertension among Black women (Hogue and Hargraves 1993).

"John Henryism," defined as the behavioral predisposition to work hard and strive determinedly against the constraints of one's environment, has been advanced as an explanation for the Black-White differences in hypertension rates. High blood pressure in Blacks is a response to the incongruity between the social position one's work would typically merit and the position one actually occupies (Smith and Egger 1992).

Racial discrimination has limited the access of Blacks to higher incomes, improved health care, adequate housing, and better education—all of which are necessary to achieve modern levels of health and mortality (Ewbank 1989). Racial discrimination probably " . . . exacerbates the mental health-damaging effects of poverty status among Blacks" (Miller 1989: 511). Being Black impinges upon health status, even at higher income levels. A study of stress found its severity highest in lower-class Blacks and lowest in middle-class Whites. Even more notable is the fact that middle-class Blacks and lower-class Whites had similar levels of stress (Miller 1989).

Another example of what may be a physiological response to racism is pregnancy outcome. Mortality rates for infants born to college-educated Black parents (from 1983 to 1985) were 90 percent higher than the rates among infants born to college-educated White parents. This excess mortality was due primarily to higher rates of death associated with premature delivery of Black babies (Schoendorf et al. 1992). In addition, immigrant Black couples have a lower incidence of low birth weight babies when compared to the incidence among native Black couples. The incidence of low birth weight babies among immigrant Blacks is similar to the incidence among White couples. Moreover, Black babies born in more segregated cities have higher rates of infant mortality than their Black counterparts born in less segregated cities (Hogue and Hargraves 1993).

Further, the impact on health of responses to racism can be seen by the high mortality rates for Blacks from cancer and HIV/AIDS. Blacks are both less educated about the danger signs for cancer and more pessimistic about treatment for cancer than are Whites. Both of these facts interact to make cancer the terminal disease Blacks conceive it to be (Manton 1989).

It has been suggested that the experience of fighting HIV/AIDS is different for most Whites than for minorities and the poor. For Whites with HIV/AIDS, the fact that they have education and employment contributes to their sense of outrage about the disease and motivates them to fight for what is being lost. Blacks and members of other minority groups, who may never have had these advantages, lack this sense of loss, the associated drive to fight against the loss, and the educational tools with which to wage the fight. Delays in seeking medical care, differences in preexisting health status, and differences in drugs administered as treatment generate a mean survival time of six months for Blacks after diagnosis with HIV/AIDS, while Whites have a mean survival time of 18 to 24 months (Friedman et al. 1989).

Resentment by others at the unfair advantages presumably accorded Blacks under affirmative action programs contributes to the sense of exclusion from and inequality in mainstream America felt by Blacks, a sense that bears on them economically, socially, and physically. Even if poverty in

America is reduced, as long as economic, social, and political inequalities persist, the health status of Black Americans is likely to remain impaired (Miller 1989).

ASIAN AND PACIFIC ISLANDER AMERICANS

The population known as Asian and Pacific Islander Americans is comprised of immigrants and their descendants from over 43 countries who speak over 100 different languages. Asians come from more than 20 countries (including China, India, Japan, the Philippines, Korea, Laos, Cambodia, Vietnam, and Thailand) with over 60 different ethnicities and a multitude of languages and dialects. Pacific Islanders have immigrated from over 22 territories and nations (including the U.S. territories of Guam, American Samoa, and Tonga) with up to 1,000 different languages (Ponce 1990).

The numbers of Pacific Islanders in the United States have grown from 1.5 million in 1970 to over 7.2 million in 1990; they are currently almost three percent of the total population and 12 percent of the total minority population (Bureau of the Census 1992f; Bureau of the Census 1992d). Asian and Pacific Islander women represent 12 percent of all U.S. minority group women and 51 percent of all Asian and Pacific Islander Americans.

A majority of Asian and Pacific Islander Americans—over 90 percent—reside in metropolitan centers. The states with the largest numbers of Asian and Pacific Islander Americans are California, New York, and Hawaii. Among all the states, Hawaii has the largest proportion of Asian and Pacific Islander Americans—62 percent (Bureau of the Census 1992f).

The many Asian and Pacific Islander subpopulations who have immigrated to the United States (and/or who have become U.S. citizens) have varied histories that have contributed to the wide, bipolar distribution in their socioeconomic positions. For example, the percentage of the population below the poverty level ranged from a national low of six percent among Japanese Americans to a national high of 66 percent among Laotians in 1990 (compared to 12.8 percent for the entire U.S. population in 1990) (Leung and Lu 1990). While 37.4 percent of all Asian and Pacific Islander American households had annual incomes in 1990 of at least $50,000, over five percent had incomes of less than $5,000, and nearly 12 percent had incomes of less than $10,000 (Bureau of the Census 1992a). The resettlement of more than one million Indochinese refugees in the 1970s and 1980s made the bimodal distribution even more pronounced because those refugees arriving after 1979 have had higher rates of unemployment, underemployment, and poverty than other Asian and Pacific Islander Americans and other minorities (Leung and Lu 1990). The histories of two Asian and Pacific Islander groups—the Chinese (the most populous Asian group in the United States today) and Native Hawaiians—are described below.

In the mid-1800s, with the discovery of gold and the decline of the African slave trade, waves of mostly male Chinese were brought to the United States as cheap, docile laborers to work in the mines and railroads in the western states. This new servant class became the new "negro" for the White majority and was even referred to as "nagurs" by some (Hu-DeHart 1992). Later labeled the "yellow peril" or disease-ridden and heathen, in 1882 the Chinese, and shortly thereafter other Asians, were barred from entering the United States on the basis of race alone. This ban remained in effect until 1942, and it was 1952 before immigrant Chinese people were able to become citizens. In 1965, when the Supreme Court struck down immigration quotas based on national origin, approximately one million Asians were in the United States. In the decades since then, Chinese immigrants from more diverse ethnic and social strata than before have come to the United States (Yu 1986).

In many Chinese American communities, unity is an elusive goal because of the differences between foreign born and American born, urban residents and suburbanites, old timers and newcomers, northerners and southerners, Catholics and Protestants, Christians and Buddhists, professionals and laborers, and rich and poor that frequently override a common ethnic identity (Yu 1982).

In 1966, the negative stereotypes applied to the Chinese and other Asian Americans were replaced with the "model minority" image. Coming shortly after the 1965 Watts riots in Los Angeles, the identification of a model minority is viewed by some as an attempt to provide proof that the U.S. social system does work for minorities (Hu-DeHart 1992). However, Asians are often pitted against other minority groups and are made out to be scapegoats by low-income Whites and other minorities who indirectly blame Asians for their failure to succeed and claim that Asians take away their educational and job opportunities. The "model minority" epithet has direct implications for the health and economic status of Asian Americans. It tends to trivialize the health problems of Asians, suggesting that they can take care of these problems on their own, and has led to overlooking the diversity among Asians and the problems of the newest refugees (Liu et al. 1990).

Among Pacific Islander Americans, Native Hawaiians—individuals whose ancestors were natives of the Hawaiian Islands prior to 1778—are the largest subpopulation (Alu Like, Inc. 1985). The health problems of Native Hawaiians today reflect in large measure their socioeconomic situation. During the past 200 years, Native Hawaiians have faced traumatic social changes resulting in the loss of their traditions and threatening their survival as a distinct group. The political and economic transformation of Hawaii associated with statehood and with the development of a modern commercial/service economy has resulted in the loss of land and political power for Native Hawaiians (Alu Like, Inc. 1985). Native Hawaiians are disproportionately in the lower income brackets—nearly 20 percent of Native Hawaiian families earn less than $15,000 per year compared to only 12.5 percent of families from other ethnic groups in Hawaii (Papa Ola Lokahi 1992).

Many Native Hawaiians engage in high risk behaviors, and the group as a whole has poorer health outcomes (such as a lower life expectancy) than other groups in Hawaii. They have diets high in fat and salt, are often overweight, smoke, consume alcohol heavily, and do not get sufficient exercise. In addition, they enter medical treatment at late stages of diseases, often only when self-care and traditional practices have not brought sufficient relief (Alu Like, Inc. 1985).

Efforts to modify behavior among Native Hawaiians and improve their health are fraught with obstacles. For example, obesity is acceptable within Polynesian cultures, where large body size is equated with power and respect (Alu Like, Inc. 1985). In addition, efforts from outsiders to bring about behavior changes in Native Hawaiians are viewed as infringements on their traditions and are resisted for that reason alone. It may not be realistic to expect Native Hawaiians to give up high risk behaviors without first solving the socioeconomic problems and cultural conflicts that contribute to these behaviors (Alu Like, Inc. 1985).

The health problems of all Asian and Pacific Islander Americans are worsened by a complex set of cultural, linguistic, structural, and financial barriers to care. In 1980, a language other than English was spoken at home by nine out of 10 Asian and Pacific Islander Americans who were five years of age or older (Yu and Liu 1987). Nearly three-fifths of Asian and Pacific Islander Americans are foreign born and, if they are illegal aliens, may not seek out medical care for fear that this will expose their illegal status and result in deportation. Since many are unable to communicate in English, they are not readily employable. When employed, it is often in small businesses or sweatshop-type factories with unsafe and unhealthy working conditions and no fringe benefits such as health insurance. Thus, Asian and Pacific Islander Americans are frequent users of hospital emergency rooms. Even with health insurance, culturally accepted medical models such as acupuncture and herbal medicines often are not covered services, a fact that further limits access to health care services (Asian American Health Forum, Inc. [AAHF] 1990).

Fear of difficulties in communicating—compounded by shame, guilt, anger, depression, and other responses to certain stigmatized conditions such as mental retardation, substance abuse, and HIV/AIDS—also may deter Asian and Pacific Islander Americans from seeking care promptly (Leung and Lu 1990). In addition, not all English medical/health terminology can be readily translated into the various Southeast Asian languages, nor can many Southeast Asian expressions describing physical and mental conditions be directly translated for U.S. health care providers. Thus, even if Asian and Pacific Islander Americans get to health care providers and translators are available, communication is still not guaranteed, and appropriate care still may not be received (U.S. Commission on Civil Rights 1992).

Other cultural characteristics that influence the health of Asian and Pacific Islander Americans are familism, reverence for authority, and a sense of shame/pride. Asian and Pacific Islander cultures—like Hispanic cultures—often emphasize family decisionmaking, and the practice may be heightened by necessity in the United States. The reverence for authority common in Asian societies with hierarchical structures, such as in Korea, for example, may result in a Korean American patient not questioning a physician's diagnosis and treatment and indicating understanding, agreement, and compliance when there is none (Leung and Lu 1990). The strong desire to "keep up appearances" within the community has resulted in low utilization of addiction treatment services for alcoholism and substance abuse by Asian and Pacific Islander Americans.

The vast differences between Asian and Pacific Islander societies in the United States mean that the most basic economic and socio-emotional needs of new immigrants cannot be met by existing institutions. The painful process of acculturation produces high levels of stress and may produce a high incidence of mental illness among Asian and Pacific Islander Americans (Liu and Yu 1985). The major mental health problem for Asian and Pacific Islander Americans, though, is racism—which adversely affects their psycho-economic status, as well as the status of other peoples of color (AAHF 1990).

Crosscutting Factors

Each of the groups in the preceding discussion has faced both deculturation and acculturation in the United States. The women in these minority groups often support families alone and on poverty-level incomes. In addition to having many of the socioeconomic risk factors associated with depression (e.g., lower educational or income levels, unemployment or employment in low-status/high-stress jobs, and single parenthood), women of color also face the added burden of discrimination and racism. Although many women of color engage in high risk behaviors that are detrimental to their health (such as overeating, alcoholism, and substance abuse), it is legitimate to ask, "Which factors will improve their health more—improved income and social conditions, or medical interventions and health education?"

HEALTH ASSESSMENT OF WOMEN OF COLOR

LIFE EXPECTANCY

Among both Whites and people of color, life expectancy (or expected remaining years of life) from birth is greater for women than for men. As Table 1 illustrates, among women of color in 1980, Hispanics had the longest life expectancy (77.1 years), followed closely by Native Americans (76.2 years), and then by Blacks (73.5 years). (Data for Asian and Pacific Islander Americans are not available.) The life expectancy for White men exceeded that of all men of color, while the life expectancy of White women exceeded that of all women of color.

Table 1 · LIFE EXPECTANCY AT BIRTH BY SEX, RACE, AND HISPANIC ORIGIN[1]

Race and Hispanic Origin[2]	Females	Males
White	79.2	72.7
Black	73.5	64.8
Hispanic origin[3]	77.1	69.6
Native American[4]	76.2	67.2
All races	78.6	71.8

[1]Life expectancy is the number of expected remaining years of life. Life expectancies are based on population counts by age and sex enumerated during the 1980 Decennial Census and on mortality experienced during the 1986–1988 period.
[2]Data for Asian and Pacific Islander Americans are not available.
[3]Persons of Hispanic origin may be of any race.
[4]Data do not include Native Hawaiians, and are based on Native Americans on reservations only.
Source: National Institutes of Health 1991; Indian Health Service 1992.

HABITS AND LIFE STYLES

Habits and life style patterns influence the health and incidence of disease in all Americans. Among these are overeating (which can lead to obesity and high serum cholesterol), smoking, alcohol consumption, and substance abuse.

Obesity

A condition associated with diabetes, hypertension, and cardiovascular disease, obesity is a problem for all women of color and is related in part to the "diets of poverty"—high in fat and low in fruits and vegetables—that many of these women consume. Defined as excess body weight for height, or being overweight, obesity was found among nearly 60 percent of all Native American women on reservations in 1987 and among 63 percent of urban Native American woman (Lefkowitz and Underwood 1991; Scott 1991). Among Pacific Islanders, Native Hawaiians and Samoans are some of the most obese populations in the world. Based on the data from 1976-1980 and 1982-1984 in Table 2 for women 20 to 74 years of age, the percentage of overweight women ranged from 24 percent for White women, to 44 percent for Black women, with the major Hispanic subpopulations arrayed in between.

Table 2 • OVERWEIGHT WOMEN AGE 20 TO 74 BY RACE AND HISPANIC ORIGIN, 1976–1980 AND 1982–1984

Race and Hispanic Origin	Percentage Overweight
Hispanic origin[1]	
Mexican American	41.6
Puerto Rican	40.2
Cuban American	31.6
Non-Hispanic Black	44.4
Non-Hispanic White	23.9

[1]Persons of Hispanic origin may be of any race.
Source: National Center for Health Statistics 1991.

High Cholesterol

Although sometimes associated with obesity, high serum cholesterol (a factor in cardiovascular disease) is a problem for White women 20 to 74 years of age more than for women of color in that age group. Twenty-eight percent of White non-Hispanic women have high serum cholesterol, nearly double the 14.6 percent of urban Native American women who had it (National Center for Health Statistics [NCHS] 1991; Scott 1991). Seventeen percent of Cuban American women report high cholesterol, with 20 percent of Mexican American and 23 percent of Puerto Rican women reporting high cholesterol. The more acculturated Mexican Americans have greater incidence of high serum cholesterol, while less educated Mexican Americans and those living below the poverty line have lower levels (Delgado and Trevino 1985). Among Black non-Hispanic women, 25 percent have elevated levels of serum cholesterol.

Smoking

Although the data tend to differ slightly from survey to survey, the percentages of women age 18 and over who reported "currently smoking cigarettes" in 1985 and 1987 (see Table 3) ranged from a low of 12 percent (Asian and Pacific Islander American women) to a high of 31 percent (Native American women). Although 31 percent of Native American women smoke cigarettes, 54 percent of Native American women living on reservations have never smoked (Lefkowitz and Underwood 1991). In addition,

Table 3 • CIGARETTE SMOKERS AMONG WOMEN AGE 18 AND OVER BY RACE AND HISPANIC ORIGIN, 1985 AND 1987[1]

Race and Hispanic Origin	Percentage Who Smoked
Hispanic origin[2]	
Mexican American	15.5
Puerto Rican	23.4
Cuban American	20.2
Asian and Pacific Islander American	11.9
Native American	30.6
Non-Hispanic Black	29.1
Non-Hispanic White	28.6

[1]Current smokers.
[2]Persons of Hispanic origin may be of any race.
Source: National Center for Health Statistics 1991.

smoking prevalence varies by reservation for Native Americans, from relatively low percentages in Arizona and New Mexico to highs of 50 percent among Native Americans in the Plains states and over 60 percent among Alaskan Natives. If lifetime use of cigarettes is examined, 73 percent of White females report smoking while only 63 percent of Black females and 52 percent of Hispanic females have ever smoked (Horton 1992). Current cigarette smoking among Black and White females has declined since the late 1980s, while recent cohorts of Hispanic women have made little progress in reducing consumption or have actually increased it (Haynes et al. 1990; Leigh 1992). Targeted advertising to minority groups by the tobacco industry may be associated with these trends.

Alcohol Consumption

Alcohol consumption becomes a factor in women's health if it is frequent and heavy enough to impair their judgment, to place women at risk of accidents and abuse by others, and to result in fetal damage among pregnant women. The high death rates due to alcoholism-related conditions and the high rates of infant births with fetal alcohol syndrome (FAS) attest to the problem among Native American women. The rate of FAS among Native American tribes ranges from 2.2 to 16.7 per 1,000 live births, more than eight times the rate for the total U.S. population. Fetal alcohol syndrome, the leading cause of disability among Native American newborns, can result in malformation, mental retardation, dysfunction of the nervous system, growth deficiencies, and joint abnormalities (IHS 1991a).

Eighty-three percent of White women, 75 percent of Black women, and 70 percent of Hispanic women have used alcohol at some point in their lives (Horton 1992). Black women (46 percent) are more likely to abstain from alcohol than are White women (34 percent), although equal proportions drink heavily (U.S. Department of Health and Human Services n.d.). When looking at Hispanic subpopulations, the percentage of women reporting that they are current alcohol users ranges from 35 percent among Mexican Americans and 33 percent among Puerto Ricans to 23 percent among Cuban Americans. With Asian and Pacific Islander Americans, considerable variation exists in the likelihood both of alcohol consumption and of reporting symptoms of alcoholism. Native Hawaiian women are more likely to drink alcohol than Hawaiian women of Filipino, Chinese, or Japanese descent. In addition, Native Hawaiian women in the youngest (18 to 19) and oldest (over 30) age groups tend to consume more alcohol during pregnancy (Bell, Nordyke, and O'Hagan 1989).

Substance Abuse

Some women of color and White women have used illicit substances, risking their own health and that of their unborn children. More White women (35 percent) and Black women (33 percent) report using illicit drugs at some point in their lives than do Hispanic women (25 percent). Current use of any illicit drug is slightly higher among Black non-Hispanic women (seven percent) than among either White non-Hispanic or Hispanic women (Horton 1992).

PREVENTIVE HEALTH MEASURES

Often women of color, for many of the cultural reasons discussed previously, do not avail themselves of preventive health tests such as Pap smears and breast exams. For example, although breast, lung, and cervical cancer (in that order) are the three most commonly occurring cancers in Asian and Pacific Islander American women, approximately two-thirds of Asian and Pacific Islander immigrant women have never had Pap smears and roughly 70 percent have never had mammograms (Lee 1992). In answer to the question, "When was your last Pap smear," only 43 percent of Asian and Pacific Islander American women reported "less than a year ago," the smallest share among all women of color. Only 47 percent of Asian and Pacific Islander American women (who were 45 years of age and older) reported ever having a mammogram (Communications Consortium Media Center [CCMC] and National Council of Negro Women [NCNW] n.d.).

Although the incidence of cervical cancer among Blacks is twice that among Whites, and the rates for Hispanics and Native Americans also exceed the rates for Whites, these women of color underutilize Pap smears and mammography. Sixty-six percent of Black women report that their last Pap smear was less than a year ago, as do 72 percent of Hispanic women. Seventy-one percent and 78 percent, respectively, of Hispanic and Black women in the 45 years and older age group report ever having had a mammogram (CCMC and NCNW n.d). Although Mexican American women are more likely than either Cuban American or Puerto Rican women to have had a recent Pap smear and breast exam, less than 50 percent of all Mexican American women report having had a routine physical exam within the last two years, and approximately 20 percent report never having had a regular physical exam (Solis et al. 1990).

Nearly 83 percent of Native American women on reservations (as opposed to more than 90 percent of all U.S. women) have had at least one Pap test. For these women and all women, being married and having a high school education are associated with higher screening rates. Among Native American women on reservations, 78 percent report ever having mammography, while 89 percent of urban Native American women report the same (Lefkowitz and Underwood 1991; Scott 1991). Only 10 percent of urban Native American women report never having a Pap smear. For both groups of Native American women and among all women, the likelihood of getting these preventive tests declines as they age.

Another example of preventive care that many believe contributes to the delivery of a healthy baby is prenatal care in the first trimester of pregnancy. In 1989, although over half of all women of color (in the major racial and ethnic groups) received prenatal care in the first trimester, large percentages did not. Over 86 percent of Japanese American women began prenatal care in the first trimester as seen in Table 4. At the other extreme, however, the table shows that only 58 percent of Native American, 57 percent of Mexican American, and 60 percent of Black mothers received early care. Data from California reveals that the following women usually receive late or no prenatal care: 59 percent of Samoans, 48 percent of Laotians, 47 percent of Cambodians, 32 percent of Vietnamese, and 25 percent of women of all racial groups combined (Association of Asian Pacific Community Health Organizations [AAPCHO] n.d.). Women who receive late or no prenatal care are more likely to be poor, adolescent, unmarried, rural dwellers, or over 40 years of age—characteristics that place their pregnancies at high risk from other causes as well (Jaynes and Williams 1989).

Table 4 • PRENATAL CARE FOR MOTHERS WITH LIVE BIRTHS BY RACE AND HISPANIC ORIGIN OF MOTHERS, 1989

	Percentage of Live Births for Which Mothers Received	
Race and Hispanic Origin	*Late or No Prenatal Care*	*Early Prenatal Care*
Hispanic origin[1]		
Mexican American	14.6	56.7
Puerto Rican	11.3	62.7
Cuban American	4.0	83.2
Central and South American	11.9	60.8
Asian and Pacific Islanders		
Chinese American	3.6	81.5
Japanese American	2.7	86.2
Filipino American	4.7	77.6
Native American	13.4	57.9
Black	11.9	60.0
White	5.2	78.9

[1]Persons of Hispanic origin may be of any race.
Source: National Center for Health Statistics 1992a.

DISEASES

Although the incidence of most infectious diseases has been reduced since the 1940s (with the exception of HIV/AIDS), people of color continue to have rates in excess of the national average for such conditions as tuberculosis and hepatitis B. For example, 48 percent of all births to women who were hepatitis B positive were to Asian and Pacific Islander American women, while only three percent of all births were to these women (AAPCHO n.d.). In addition to infectious diseases, conditions such as cancer, diabetes, and hypertension impair the health of people of color.

Cancer

Cancer is the second leading cause of death for women in the United States (second to heart disease). Moreover, breast cancer was the leading cause of death due to cancer among White and Black females age 25 to 54 and for those 85 years and older in 1987. For all other age groups, breast cancer ranked second to lung cancer in 1987 as the leading cause of cancer deaths among women (NCHS 1991). Native Hawaiian women have the highest cancer incidence of all women in Hawaii, while Black and Native Hawaiian women have higher death rates and lower five-year survival rates than White women for most types of cancer.

White and Native Hawaiian women have the highest risk of breast cancer among the major racial/ethnic groups in the United States. Japanese, Shanghai Chinese, Singapore Chinese, and Hawaiian Filipino women have the lowest risk of breast cancer (Petrakis 1988). The five-year survival rate for women with breast cancer is greater than 70 percent in all groups except Native Americans (less than 45 percent) and Blacks (64 percent) (Horton 1992).

Cervical cancer also takes a large toll on women of color. Although the rate of cervical cancer is twice as high for Hispanic women as for White women, Black non-Hispanic, Native American, and Chinese American women have even higher rates than Hispanic women (Delgado and Trevino 1985). The five-year survival rate for Black women is 10 percentage points lower than the comparable rate for White women (57 percent versus 67 percent) (Horton 1992).

Diabetes Mellitus

Diabetes mellitus—a chronic condition characterized by abnormal glucose metabolism—is a major health problem for all women of color. Diabetes primarily affects the circulatory system, and is frequently associated with conditions such as arteriosclerosis (hardening of the arteries) and kidney failure. While the incidence of diabetes among Black non-Hispanic women is double that for White non-Hispanic women, the incidence for Hispanics is 2.5 times the rate for Whites, and the incidence for Native Americans is five times that for Whites (IHS 1991b). Among the populations in Hawaii, Native Hawaiians, Filipinos, Japanese, Koreans, and Chinese Americans have incidence rates for diabetes at least double the rate for Whites (AAPCHO n.d.).

Because compliance with the regimen to treat diabetes requires monitoring by health care providers and family support, treatment poses particular challenges for Native Hawaiians. Treatment practices that focus on the individual rather than others and alter diet and eating times violate many of the cultural practices of Native Hawaiians.

The estimated age-adjusted death rate for all women of color from diabetes in 1987 (18.8 per 100,000) was more than double that for White women (8.1 per 100,000). For Native American women, the rate was 2.7 times that of White women (Horton 1992; IHS 1992).

The manifestations of the disease vary only slightly among women of color. Perinatal mortality (infant mortality at birth) for pregnant Black women with diabetes is three times higher than for pregnant White women with diabetes (Headen and Headen, 1985-86). Gestational diabetes (diabetes occurring in a pregnant woman) is present in one to three percent of all pregnancies in the White and Black populations. However, in one study of Navajos, 6.1 percent of pregnancies were identified with gestational diabetes (IHS 1991b). Among Native American mothers with gestational diabetes, nearly 60 percent will develop freestanding diabetes within 16 years of delivery. For Mexican American women, with greater acculturation comes reduced obesity and a lower incidence of diabetes (Delgado and Trevino 1985).

Hypertension

People are classified as hypertensive if their average systolic blood pressure is greater than 140 mm mercury, or their average diastolic blood pressure is greater than 90 mm mercury, or they report taking high blood pressure medicine. Hypertension, a major risk factor for coronary heart disease and cerebrovascular disease, infringes upon the health of Black women much more than it does upon the health of other women of color.

Using data collected in 1976-1980 and 1982-1984, Table 5 shows that 44 percent of Black non-Hispanic women were found to be hypertensive, more than double the rates for Mexican American women (20 percent) and Puerto Rican women (19 percent), and more than triple the rate among Cuban American women (14 percent). The rate of hypertension among Black females was 1.7 times the rate among non-Hispanic White females. Among Native American women living on or near reservations and eligible for services provided or supported by the Indian Health Service, 22 percent reported hypertension in 1987.

Table 5 • HYPERTENSION AMONG WOMEN AGE 20 TO 74 BY RACE
AND HISPANIC ORIGIN, 1976–1980 AND 1982–1984

Race and Hispanic Origin	Percentage With Hypertension
Hispanic origin[1]	
Mexican American	20.3
Puerto Rican	19.2
Cuban American	14.4
Non–Hispanic Black	43.8
Non–Hispanic White	25.1

[1]Persons of Hispanic origin may be of any race.
Source: National Center for Health Statistics 1991.

Selected Asian and Pacific Islander American populations experience high rates of hypertension and are less likely to be aware that they have the disease or to be under medical supervision than are members of other racial/ethnic groups. Filipino women over 50 years of age who live in California have a slightly higher incidence of hypertension (65 percent) than Black women in the same age cohort (63 percent) (AAHF 1990). Sizable percentages of adult Samoan women in Hawaii and California have hypertension as well. Using the systolic criterion, 13 percent are hypertensive, while 18 percent are hypertensive by the diastolic criterion (Bindon and Crews 1990). In Hawaii, Native Hawaiians and Japanese Americans report high rates of hypertension, with a higher incidence among Native Hawaiian women than any other ethnic group in the state (Alu Like, Inc. 1985; Papa Ola Lokahi 1992).

HIV/AIDS

Although the reported patterns of transmission of the human immunodeficiency virus (HIV) that cause acquired immune deficiency syndrome (AIDS) vary by racial and ethnic group, all women of color have been affected by this disease. The number of cases reported among women of color who were 15 to 44 years old from 1981 to 1989 was greatest for Black non–Hispanic women and for Hispanic women (4,911 and 1,434 cases, respectively) with lesser incidence among Native American and Asian and Pacific Islander American women. The number of cases reported among all women age 15 to 44 over the 1981 to 1989 period was 8,556; the number of cases reported among all women of color over that period was 6,409 (Gayle, Selik, and Chu 1990).

As seen in Table 6, from 1981 to 1989 among women 15 to 44 years of age, Black non–Hispanic and Hispanic women were overrepresented in the proportion of reported HIV/AIDS cases when compared against their proportion in the total female population, while White, Native American, and Asian and Pacific Islander American women were underrepresented. Although Black non–Hispanic women comprised only 13.3 percent of all women, they accounted for nearly three-fifths of all HIV/AIDS cases among women. And while Hispanic women comprised only 7.9 percent of all women, they accounted for nearly 17 percent of all HIV/AIDS cases among women. According to Selik, Castro, and Pappaioanou (1988), AIDS is 13.2 times more common among Black non–Hispanic women and 8.1 times more common among Hispanic women than among White women.

Table 6 • DISTRIBUTION OF HIV/AIDS CASES AMONG WOMEN AGE 15 TO 44 BY RACE AND HISPANIC ORIGIN, 1981–1989

Race and Hispanic Origin	Percent Distribution of HIV/AIDS Cases	Percent Distribution of All Women Age 15–44
Non–Hispanic White	24.9	75.1
Non–Hispanic Black	57.6	13.3
Hispanic origin[1]	16.8	7.9
Asian and Pacific Islander	0.5	2.6
Native American	0.3	1.1
Total percent	100.0	100.0

[1]Persons of Hispanic origin may be of any race.
Source: Gayle, Selik, and Chu 1990.

When female AIDS cases reported through October 1991 were examined by methods of transmission, for almost all racial/ethnic groups the dominant mode of infection was intravenous drug use. The exception was among Asian and Pacific Islander women (see Table 7). Most of the HIV/AIDS cases among Hispanics are among Puerto Ricans, who are seven times more likely than non–Hispanic Whites to be diagnosed with HIV/AIDS.

Acculturation among Hispanics also seems to play a role in the transmission of HIV/AIDS, with intravenous drug use most prevalent among more acculturated Latinas. Less acculturated Latinas report a low perceived risk of

AIDS and less likelihood of using illegal drugs or engaging in sexual activity with multiple partners (Nyamathi et al. 1993).

Because it is difficult to conduct controlled experiments on intravenous drug users, this group of HIV/AIDS patients is less likely to be included in experimental protocols. This means that Black and Hispanic women may be less likely to receive antiviral medications in the future than other groups of HIV/AIDS patients, whose ranks are less dominated by intravenous drug users (Friedman et al. 1989).

Although heterosexual transmission is the second most frequently reported mode of AIDS infection for White, Black, Hispanic, and Native American women (and the dominant mode of transmission for Asian and Pacific Islander women), Black and Hispanic women may be more vulnerable than White women to heterosexual transmission of HIV/AIDS through sex with bisexual men. This is possible because, compared to White gay men, larger proportions of Black and Hispanic gay men report having sex with both men and women—30 percent for Black, 20 percent for Hispanic, and 13 percent for White gay men (Friedman et al. 1989).

Although only 22 cases of HIV/AIDS were reported among Native American women over the 1981 to 1989 period, this figure is probably an

Table 7 · SOURCES OF AIDS INFECTION AMONG WOMEN BY RACE AND HISPANIC ORIGIN, THROUGH OCTOBER 1991 (percent distribution)

Race and Hispanic Origin	Intra-venous Drug Use	Hetero-sexual Contact	Blood Trans-fusion	Other/ Undeter-mined	Total Percent[1]
Non-Hispanic Black	56	34	3	7	100
Non-Hispanic White	42	31	20	7	100
Hispanic origin[2]	50	38	5	7	100
Native American	55	21	12	12	100
Asian and Pacific Islander	16	35	31	17	99

[1]Totals may not add up to 100 percent due to rounding.
[2]Persons of Hispanic origin may be of any race.
Source: Asian American Health Forum, Inc. 1992.

underestimate, due to the difficulty in counting and tracking health conditions among Native Americans, some of whom are very mobile (Gayle, Selik, and Chu 1990). Men who have sex with men account for over half of all Native American cases, and Alaskan Native communities have been the hardest hit so far (HRSA 1992a). Between February 1991 and September 1992, the total number of cases reported among Native Americans increased from 244 to 416 (IHS 1991a; American Indian Health Care Association 1992).

Among women with HIV/AIDS, others in their households—lovers, spouses and/or children—are also likely to have the disease. Women with AIDS who must also fulfill their traditional roles as caregivers are likely to live shorter periods of time than women who do not have the added stress of providing care to others. In addition, women with AIDS often leave behind orphans with HIV/AIDS, many of whom subsequently are raised by their grandmothers, a fact that increases the stresses in the lives of these older women.

Access to Health Insurance and Health Care Services

Access to health care includes both access to health insurance coverage and access to providers and facilities that render services. Adequate access to providers and facilities encompasses the existence of conveniently located services and the availability of child care (to enable mothers to seek medical attention), transportation, and health care providers capable of giving sensitive and competent care.

Obtaining Health Insurance

Although wives are often insured as dependents of their husbands, estimates show that between 13 and 14 percent of all women, or 16 to 17 million women, lack insurance (Horton 1992). Just as people of color make up a sizable proportion of the uninsured—39 percent of the uninsured while they comprise only 24 percent of the total population—women of color make up a sizable proportion of all uninsured women.

Lack of health insurance varies markedly by race and ethnicity, with Hispanics and Asians 2.5 times and Blacks 1.8 times as likely to be uninsured as Whites (Horton 1992; AAPCHO n.d.). In 1990, over 6.9 million Hispanics (or 32.4 percent of the entire Hispanic population), nearly 6.1 million Blacks (or about 20 percent of all Blacks), and 26.9 million Whites (or 12.9 percent of the entire White population) were uninsured (Bastida 1992; National Council of La Raza 1992). For certain racial and ethnic groups, as for the entire population, the proportions uninsured are slightly higher for persons under age 65 (because of the existence of Medicare for the elderly)—35 percent of Hispanics, 25 percent of Blacks, and 15 percent of Whites (Short, Cornelius, and Goldstone 1990). As one representative group of Asian and Pacific Islander Americans, half of Koreans under age 65 are estimated to lack health insurance (Han 1990).

Blacks and Hispanics are also considerably less likely to have private health insurance (and the additional options and greater coverage it often affords) and are more likely to have public insurance than are Whites. In 1987, while 80 percent of Whites had private health insurance, less than half (49 percent and 46 percent, respectively) of Blacks and Hispanics did (Short, Cornelius, and Goldstone 1990).

Among subpopulations of Hispanics, health insurance coverage also varied considerably. In 1989, over half of Cuban Americans (56 percent) had private health insurance, while only 44 percent of both Mexican Americans and Puerto Ricans had private coverage. On the other hand, a third of Puerto Ricans (all of whom are citizens) received Medicaid—health insurance for lower-income persons funded partly by the federal government and partly by the states, and administered by the states—while only 14 percent and 12 percent, respectively, of Mexican Americans and Cuban Americans were enrolled in the Medicaid program. This difference reflects in part lower proportions of legal residents among Mexican Americans and Cuban Americans than among Puerto Ricans.

In addition, between February 1987 and May 1989, 46 percent of Hispanics, 40 percent of Blacks, and 24 percent of Whites were without health insurance coverage for at least a month. Women were slightly less likely than men (25 percent versus 28 percent) to have had gaps in coverage for two reasons. First, it was more common for women to live in families with incomes below the poverty level and, therefore, to be eligible for and to be enrolled in Medicaid. Second, a higher percentage of women than men were over 65 years of age and were likely to be enrolled in Medicare (Bureau of the Census 1992c).

Blacks also heavily use public insurance (Medicaid, Medicare, and public coverage through the Department of Veterans Affairs and the military). Twenty-six percent of Blacks under 65 years of age had public insurance in 1987 and Blacks are roughly 40 percent of all Medicaid enrollees (Rice and Winn 1991; Short, Cornelius, and Goldstone 1990). However, many Blacks reside in southern states where Medicaid is the least generous. Although all states place constraints on enrollment and limits on health services, the southern states impose the most severe ones (Leffall 1990). Many health care providers refuse to accept Medicaid reimbursement because it falls too far short of the actual costs incurred to provide services. Thus, Blacks who receive coverage through Medicaid might more properly be called underinsured and be added to the estimated one to two million Black Americans whose health insurance coverage is inadequate for their needs (Jaynes and Williams 1989).

Obtaining Health Care Services
One step beyond health insurance coverage is making contact with physicians or other providers. In the 1977 National Medical Care Expenditure Survey, the percentages of Whites, Blacks, and Hispanics who stated that a physician's office was their usual source of care were 70 percent, 46 percent, and 54 percent, respectively (Delgado and Trevino 1985). In contrast, in 1990, 48 percent of Blacks and 62 percent of Whites reported the physician's office as the usual place of contact for care.

Among Hispanics, substantially higher percentages of Puerto Ricans (than Mexican Americans and Cuban Americans) report hospital outpatient clinics and emergency rooms to be their usual source of care (Solis et al. 1990). Double the percentage of Blacks than of Whites (24 percent versus 12 percent) report that the hospital outpatient department (including hospital outpatient clinic, emergency room, and other hospital contacts) is their usual place of physician contact.

Among Asian and Pacific Islander Americans, 22 percent of Korean households in Southern California report that at one time or another since coming to the United States a family member has failed to get appropriate care. Although the most common barrier is financial, an additional 18 percent of Koreans reported not knowing where to go for care at some time since immigrating to the United States (Han 1990).

Native American Health Care System
The issues related to insurance coverage and access to care for Native Americans differ from those of other people of color because of the system for delivering care to them, which includes:

- Indian Health Service (IHS) clinics and hospitals;
- tribal clinics and hospitals;
- urban Indian clinics;
- local referral hospitals;
- tertiary medical centers (i.e., specialized facilities treating burns, trauma, etc.);
- Indian and non-Indian substance abuse treatment centers; and
- traditional Indian healers.

IHS hospitals and clinics are available only for use by Native Americans living on or near reservations—approximately 38 percent of all Native Americans in 1990. Because of geographic definitions, some Native Americans in urban areas are covered (Scott and Suagee 1992).

Government health care services for Native Americans in urban and nonreservation rural areas often are very limited and uncoordinated. For example, Native Americans living in urban areas can get treatment at IHS direct care facilities, but they are not eligible for the more specialized services that may be provided elsewhere (i.e., "contract care" services). By contrast, Native Americans on or near reservations—who are therefore eligible for the full range of IHS services—have access to both routine care and to the more specialized contract care services. Because of their eligibility for IHS services, nearly 55 percent of the eligible IHS population has neither private health insurance nor public coverage (other than IHS) (Beauregard, Cunningham, and Cornelius 1991).

Native Americans who do have private insurance (less than one-third of the Indian population in 1987), in fact, have a choice that most other Americans don't have—whether to get free health care where the choice of providers and services is limited, or whether to obtain private care elsewhere. The options for both private care and treatment at IHS facilities are limited by the distances that must be traveled to get to either. However, because the waiting times reported for treatment at IHS facilities exceed waiting times reported for services with other providers, Native Americans with private insurance often prefer to seek private care (Beauregard, Cunningham, and Cornelius 1991).

MORTALITY

The mortality (or death) rate in a specific population—determined by the quality of available medical care, income, nutritional status, environmental quality, and cultural habits—is a basic measure of the standard of living (Ewbank 1989). *Infant* mortality reflects not only the standard of living of a population but also mirrors the health of the mother. As seen in Table 8, among all women of color from 1984 to 1986, infant mortality rates were highest for the babies of Black women—at 18.3 deaths per 1,000 live births, more than double the 8.8 rate for White mothers and significantly greater than the rate for all mothers of 10.3 deaths per 1,000 live births.

Although associated with the high percentage of low weight infants born to Black women, the high Black infant mortality rate is also related to the intergenerational effects of socioeconomic conditions on the growth and development of a mother from prebirth to childhood, which may influence the intrauterine growth of her child (Schoendorf et al. 1992). Since many middle-class Blacks are the first generation in their families to achieve that status, a Black middle-class mother may be giving birth to an infant whose health is markedly determined by maternal childhood poverty (Jaynes and Williams 1989).

Table 8 • INFANT, NEONATAL, AND POSTNEONATAL MORTALITY RATES BY MOTHER'S RACE AND HISPANIC ORIGIN, FOR BIRTH COHORTS 1984–1986 (in numbers)[1]

Race and Hispanic Origin	Total Infant Deaths[2]	Neonatal Deaths[2]	Postneonatal Deaths[2]
Total	10.3	6.7	3.6
RACE			
White	8.8	5.7	3.1
Black	18.3	12.0	6.3
Native American	13.5	6.2	7.3
Total Asian and Pacific Islander	8.1	5.1	3.0
Chinese American	6.3	3.6	2.7
Japanese American	6.5	3.8	2.7
Filipino American	7.8	5.1	2.7
Other Asian and Pacific Islander[3]	8.9	5.7	3.2
HISPANIC ORIGIN			
Total Hispanic origin[4]	8.8	5.8	3.1
Mexican American	8.5	5.4	3.0
Puerto Rican	11.9	7.9	4.0
Cuban American	8.0	5.9	2.1
Central and South American	8.0	5.5	2.5
Other and unknown	9.4	6.0	3.4
Non-Hispanic White[5]	8.6	5.6	3.0
Non-Hispanic Black[5]	18.2	11.7	6.5

[1]Mortality rates are the number of deaths per 1,000 live births.
[2]Infant deaths are the sum of neonatal and postneonatal deaths; neonatal deaths occur within the first 28 days of life; and postneonatal deaths occur after the 28th day but before the 365th day of life.
[3]Includes Native Hawaiians.
[4]Persons of Hispanic origin may be of any race.
[5]These data apply only to births in those states that specify Hispanic origin as well as race on birth certificates. In the period from 1984 to 1986, 23 states and the District of Columbia did so.
Source: National Center for Health Statistics 1992a.

As Table 8 reveals, most infant deaths between 1984 and 1986 were neonatal for all groups except Native American infants. Of the 13.5 deaths of Native American infants (per 1,000 live births), 7.3—or 54 percent—occurred in the postneonatal period, often as the result of accidents or environmental hazards.

Native Americans had the second highest total infant mortality rate, followed by Puerto Ricans with 11.9 infant deaths per 1,000 live births. All the Asian and Pacific Islander American groups (for which data were reported) had infant mortality rates close to or lower than the infant mortality rates for Whites.

Mortality for women of color results from a variety of differing causes, although heart disease and cancer are the leading killers. For all women 15 to 44 years of age, death rates from AIDS have increased steadily since 1985, with the majority of deaths occurring in women age 25 to 34. As Table 9 demonstrates, the rates for Black women of all ages are at least seven times greater than the rates for White women.

Table 9 · MORTALITY RATES FROM AIDS FOR BLACK AND WHITE WOMEN BY AGE, 1990 AND 1991[1]

	1990	*1991*
Black women		
All ages	10.6	12.2
Under age 15	—	—
15–24	4.4	—
25–34	23.3	29.0
35–44	28.2	25.9
45–54	—	17.9
55 and over	—	—
Age-adjusted rate	10.2	12.0
White women		
All ages	1.1	1.5
Under age 15	—	—
15–24	—	—
25–34	3.0	3.4
35–44	2.0	3.2
45–54	1.1	1.6
55 and over	0.6	0.8
Age-adjusted rate	1.1	1.5

[1]Mortality rates are per 100,000 population.
Source: National Center for Health Statistics 1992b.

In 1988, 11 percent of all deaths of Black non-Hispanic women age 25 to 34 and three percent of all deaths of White women of the same age were AIDS-related. In New York and New Jersey, among Black women 15 to 44 years of age, AIDS inched ahead of cancer and heart disease to become the leading cause of death in 1987 (Chu, Buehler, and Berkelman 1990).

Six major health and mortality problems have been noted for Hispanic women and men: cancer, cardiovascular disease and stroke, chemical dependency (reflected partially in cirrhosis deaths), diabetes, homicides and accidents (unintentional injuries), and infant mortality (Delgado and Trevino 1985). For a few diseases, Mexican Americans exhibit higher death rates than for other Hispanics and for non-Hispanic Whites. While for most conditions Mexican Americans have death rates comparable to or lower than non-Hispanic Whites, the health status (and death rates) for Puerto Ricans is comparable to that of Blacks (Amaro 1992).

Among Chinese Americans, the top four causes of death are the same as among other racial and ethnic subpopulations—heart disease, cancer, cardiovascular disease, and accidents. For Chinese Americans of all ages (and both sexes), cancer accounts for over one-fourth (27.4 percent) of all deaths. The risk of death from many of the major causes also has been observed to be greater for foreign-born than for U.S.-born Asians (Yu 1986).

In the Pacific Islander population the leading causes of death for both women and men are heart disease, infections, accidents, and alcohol and substance abuse. Although underreported, infant mortality rates also are high, ranging from 9.2 per 1,000 live births for the population of the Hawaiian Islands to 14 per 1,000 live births in Guam, and 31 per 1,000 live births in the Marshall Islands, both U.S. territories (Hirota 1988). Average annual age-adjusted mortality rates from breast cancer, for example, also span a considerable range for Pacific Islanders—from eight per 100,000 population among Filipinos to 33 per 100,000 for Native Hawaiians, exceeding the rates for both Blacks and Whites (Leung and Lu 1990).

Among Native American women on reservations, the leading causes of death in the 1985 to 1987 period were heart disease, cancer, accidents, cerebrovascular disease, diabetes, and chronic liver disease and cirrhosis (IHS 1991b). Among urban Native American women, the leading causes of death were heart disease, cancer, cirrhosis, accidents, and homicides (O'Brien, Vanek, and Welper 1991).

There is enormous variability among tribes in alcohol-related deaths. However, among Native American women age 25 to 45 in 1988, the death rate from alcoholism was 10 times higher than for all other women in the U.S. population. The death rate from liver disease and cirrhosis was five times that of other women, and the death rate from homicide was three times that of other women. Native American women often cope with prior victimization (from incest, rape, and other forms of sexual assault) by escaping into alcohol and drugs; doing so, though, contributes to higher mortality rates (Horton 1992).

The overall rate of cancer mortality among Native American women is lower than for the general population. However, aggregate data from all the IHS regions masks the fact that several areas—Alaska; Aberdeen, South Dakota; Bimidji, Minnesota; and Billings, Montana—have higher cancer mortality rates among Native American women than among the general population of women (Scott and Suagee 1992).

A dramatic increase in mortality from lung cancer has also occurred among Native American women. In three regions—Alaska, North Dakota/South Dakota/Montana, and Michigan/Minnesota/Wisconsin—lung cancer mortality rates for Native American women have risen from rates lower than the national average to rates 2.5, 1.5, and 1.5 times the U.S. rates, respectively. Rates for Arizona and New Mexico have remained relatively flat, at less than one-third the national rate. For Alaska and the southwest region jointly, however, excess gallbladder cancer mortality is found among Native American women. All the IHS areas had cervical cancer mortality rates higher than the U.S. average. In the Billings, Montana IHS area, the death rate is over five times the national rate (IHS n.d.). The death rate for Native American women from cervical cancer is high because they are often diagnosed later and have a poorer survival rate than other women (IHS 1991b).

ISSUES RELATED TO IMPROVING THE HEALTH OF WOMEN OF COLOR

DATA COLLECTION PROBLEMS

Many subpopulations of women of color are only known by the absence of data on them. Because Native Americans, Hispanics, and Asian and Pacific Islander Americans are not broadly distributed across the United States, large national surveys do not sample these groups sufficiently to collect reliable data. Mortality data, for example, are collected in only 30 states for Hispanics, and poor reporting practices minimize the usefulness of the statistics that are available (GAO 1992).

In addition, aggregating data for these racial/ethnic groups often obscures the more meaningful differences among their subpopulations. For example, the mortality rate for Puerto Rican infants is higher than for Mexican American infants, while Chinese and Japanese Americans have infant mortality rates lower than other Asian and Pacific Islander American groups. Small populations without great geographic dispersion and with great cultural diversity within them create a challenging research setting. It is difficult to collect readily generalizable data that can be applied to the development of universally applied treatment responses (Levy 1992).

Two solutions are commonly employed to collect high quality data for small population subgroups not broadly distributed. First, one can use national sample survey techniques and oversample in areas with sizable populations of the minority groups of interest. To do so requires the use of many racial and ethnic identifiers and is likely to increase both the size of the sample and the cost of the survey.

Another approach is to survey the major racial/ethnic population subgroups in the areas where they dominate. This technique was employed in the Hispanic Health and Nutrition Evaluation Survey, which covered approximately 76 percent of the 1980 Hispanic-origin population in the United States, by surveying the three major subgroups in selected areas. Mexican Americans were surveyed in Arizona, California, Colorado, New Mexico, and Texas; Puerto Ricans were surveyed in the New York City metropolitan area (New York, New Jersey, and Connecticut); and Cuban Americans were surveyed in Dade County, Florida (Delgado et al. 1990).

Because over 70 percent of the Asian and Pacific Islander Americans are clustered in California, Hawaii, Illinois, New Jersey, New York, Texas, and Washington, this group might be amenable to a nationally representative analysis done in these seven states.

California, the state with the largest number of Asian and Pacific Islander Americans (2.8 million), currently collects data for 14 different Asian and Pacific Islander groups (Filipino, Chinese, Vietnamese, Japanese, Korean, Asian Indian, Khmer [Cambodian], Thai, Laotian, Samoan, Native Hawaiian, Tongan, Guamanian, and other Pacific Islanders). But in published reports, it lumps these groups into the category of "Asian and Other," a category that also includes Native Americans (American Indians, Eskimos, and Alaskan Aleuts). Reporting data in this manner obscures important differences among these groups and negates the possible benefit from the use of multiple ethnic identifiers during data collection (Ponce 1990).

When the relevant populations are surveyed, data on the degree of acculturation and immigration history need to be collected. For example, if survey respondents are overwhelmingly the more assimilated and American-born Asians, then their health profiles may obscure the morbidity and behavioral risk-factor patterns of newly arrived immigrants from the same place (Ponce 1990). For Native Americans, a problem arises in gathering accurate demographic data because of the cycles of urban-rural-reservation migration by individuals in various tribes. This migration can cause problems related to overcounting and undercounting, and in treating infectious conditions such as HIV/AIDS (HRSA 1992a).

Language familiarity, another aspect of acculturation, is also a factor in collecting reliable data. If concepts are indiscriminately transferred from one language or culture to another, misinformation may be collected from the survey population. In addition, if questions are posed as double negatives, as are some of the questions on the National Medical Expenditure Survey, they will be especially hard to understand by those for whom English is a second language (Scott and Suagee 1992).

What types of errors have been found in data collected on people of color? Indians and other minorities in urban areas are routinely undercounted. This leads to an overestimation of mortality rates for these groups because the population base (or denominator) used to calculate these rates is smaller than it really is (Scott and Suagee 1992). Undercounting of minorities can also result in overstating the cumulative incidence of AIDS, for example, since the base against which this condition is reported has been underenumerated (Friedman et al. 1989).

Furthermore, urban Indians are often misidentified by service providers, an occurrence that can result in underestimation of mortality rates, because the numerator in the fraction used to compute these rates is too small (Hahn, Mulinare, and Teutsch 1992; Sorlie, Rogot, and Johnson 1992). In Oklahoma, infants born to Native Americans have a 28 percent chance of being misclassified as another race on death certificates. After adjusting for this underreporting, the infant mortality among Native Americans in Oklahoma almost doubled from the 5.8 per 1,000 live births reported for 1987 to 1988 to an estimated rate of 10.4 per 1,000 live births over the same period (Scott and Suagee 1992). The degree of misclassification probably varies by location. Steps need to be taken to refine and improve the quality of the data collected on people of color.

A "chicken-and-egg" situation involving data can exist that may continue the status quo with regard to the health status of people of color. The data problems associated with Asian and Pacific Islander Americans illustrate this (Yu 1991). Health problems of Asian and Pacific Islander Americans are ignored because no population-based data documents the problems; yet existing, population-based data and research leave out Asian and Pacific Islander Americans because their health problems are not acknowledged.

RESEARCH AND TREATMENT NEEDS

Even medical officialdom has begun to acknowledge its lack of attention to the health needs of women in the formulation of research designs and treatment protocols (NIH 1991). For women of color, the issue is even more dramatic: including White women in an experimental group may yield knowledge and results relevant to treating White women, but not for treating women of color. For example, how frequently should women be screened for breast cancer? Although in dispute, current guidelines suggest mammograms every other year for women 40 to 49 years of age and annually for women 50 and older. Because sizable numbers of Black women younger than 40 are diagnosed with and die from breast cancer, should different guidelines be established for Black women? What guidelines should be set to screen Native American women for whom diabetes, tuberculosis, and liver disease are more common than among the general population (Lefkowitz and Underwood 1991)? Why is hypertension a problem among Native Hawaiian women beginning very early in life, and what is the best way to control it? Questions such as these cannot be addressed without integrating knowledge of the needs of racial/ethnic minority women into research and treatment evaluations.

The issues of alcohol and substance abuse, and HIV/AIDS also highlight the need for research and treatment oriented to the female client population. Addiction treatment alone for Native American women suffering from alcoholism is not enough. The cultural and social experiences of Native American women must be incorporated into the treatment setting in order to adequately answer the question, "What is the pain she is trying to numb?" (IHS 1991b: 8).

FACILITIES TO SERVE PEOPLE OF COLOR

In what settings are research and treatment being applied to meet the needs of women of color? The policy of targeting resources and facilities to people of color has encountered snags throughout history. The provision of hospitals for Blacks, the designation of service areas for Native Americans, and the targeting of health care services for Native Hawaiians all illustrate these problems.

The closing of hospitals serving predominantly Black communities is controversial and often has been found to be driven more by the racial composition of the hospitals' neighborhoods than by economic conditions (Rice and Payne 1981). The concept of these hospitals dates from an era when racial/ethnic minority populations were more highly segregated in

America's cities than many of them are today. As newer waves of immigrants have come to America who are able to choose increasingly not to live in racial/ethnic ghettos, it has become harder to define territorial "communities" for specific racial/ethnic groups and to meet their needs by placing facilities in these areas.

For example, the IHS regional designations reflect the population distribution of Native Americans in 1955 and are outdated today, when only 22 percent of Native Americans live on reservations and 67 percent live elsewhere, with a growing share in cities (Bureau of the Census 1992f). For Alaskan Natives who derive their livelihoods from seasonal employment such as fishing, it is difficult to get care during fishing season if the IHS facility is several hundred miles and several days journey from home. In most of Alaska, transportation poses a nearly insurmountable barrier to care, since there are only three urban IHS clinics to serve all the eligible people in the state. Many Alaskan Natives need temporary housing when they seek care at IHS medical facilities, since they are unable to return home the same day (HRSA 1992a).

Native Hawaiians must solve problems similar to those faced by American Indians. Although recognized as a high-risk group and in need of targeted health care services, because the living patterns on the Hawaiian Islands are racially/ethnically mixed, it is unrealistic to locate facilities to serve Native Hawaiians alone. On islands other than Oahu (the island on which Honolulu is located), Native Hawaiians are more likely to postpone care until they perceive a crisis in order to avoid travel problems.

Community-based, consumer-friendly facilities are often at a disadvantage when competing against larger organizations for resources to serve their clients. For instance, when seeking funds under the Ryan White Comprehensive Resources Emergency (CARE) Act of 1990, many smaller community groups oriented to serving women with HIV/AIDS complain of losing out to hospitals and larger organizations. In addition, the "AIDS establishment" of service organizations often fails to recognize local targeted groups serving women of color with AIDS, making case referrals difficult (HRSA 1991; HRSA 1992b). Programs developed by organizations such as the National Black Women's Health Project and the National Latina Health Network seek to bridge this gap in health care funding and services for their constituents.

The "one-stop shopping" model to provide health services for women has not caught on. Such centers would provide child care along with comprehensive services for the needs of women including reproductive, internal medicine, mental health, substance abuse, and HIV/AIDS care (HRSA 1992a).

NEED FOR MINORITY PHYSICIANS AND PROVIDERS

The federal government has designated several racial/ethnic groups as underrepresented in the population of physicians (and other health care providers) and has offered incentives to change this, based on the dual beliefs that minority doctors tend to locate in underserved areas and that they tend to care for more minority patients. In 1980, although Black Americans were three percent of all physicians (as opposed to nearly 12 percent of the general population), their share of the physician population had increased very little since 1950. Similarly, Mexican Americans and Puerto Ricans were only four percent of physicians in 1980, although they were then 5.5 percent of the total U.S. population; and Native Americans were only 0.1 percent of all physicians, while they comprised 0.6 percent of the population. Asian and Pacific Islander Americans, however, were 10 percent of all physicians, but only 1.6 percent of the U.S. population (Hanft and White 1989).

The belief that increasing minority representation among doctors will increase access of minorities to health care is supported by data on Black physicians. Although more than 80 percent of Blacks report having a White physician as their primary provider, 80 percent of the patients of Black physicians are Black (Jaynes and Williams 1989). The regional distribution of Black and Native American physicians, in particular, seems to be influenced by the location of substantial numbers of like minorities. It is estimated that 60 to 80 percent of the underrepresented students trained in the health professions voluntarily practice in or close to designated shortage areas with overwhelming minority populations (Scott and Suagee 1992). Although research on matching providers and patients on the basis of race or ethnicity is generally inconclusive, there seems to be consensus that the effectiveness of treatment (especially for substance abuse) is enhanced when the provider is culturally knowledgeable.

Although the federal government considers Asian and Pacific Islander Americans to be overrepresented among physicians, this assessment rests in part on the belief that all Asian and Pacific Islander American groups can be served by "generic" Asian and Pacific Islander health professionals. Gains in the number of health care workers among Asian and Pacific Islander Americans have occurred primarily among second and third generation Asian Americans, specifically Japanese and Chinese Americans. However, in the Pacific Trust territories, " . . . no single jurisdiction comes close to its marginally adequate level of health manpower." In the Republic of the Marshall Islands, for example, the minimum required number of physicians is 40, but only 14 are available (Forman 1990). Among psychiatrists, Asians were 8.6 percent of the total in the United States in 1984. Half of these (51 percent) were Asian Indians, however, and only 23 percent were of either Chinese or Japanese ancestry. This mix of providers differs markedly from the representation of Asian and Pacific Islander Americans in the United States.

The unmet demand for multicultural and multilingual health professionals needs to be addressed. However, discrimination in residency placement and licensure limits the ability of foreign-trained medical professionals to serve in the United States and help meet this need (Leung and Lu 1990). In addition, although the failure of facilities supported by federal funds to have medically trained translators to meet the needs of patients whose primary language is not English violates civil rights statutes, this is the status quo at many American health care centers. Continued failure to support the development of multicultural and multilingual health professionals discounts the degree to which language and culture influence access to and utilization of services, and can contribute to continued unnecessary disease and death.

CONCLUSION

Women of color are members of extremely heterogeneous groups. For example, Hispanic women include both Puerto Rican women, born with citizenship but also having a high incidence of AIDS and higher than average infant mortality rates, and Mexican American women, many of whom are foreign-born and who have lower infant mortality rates. Asian and Pacific Islander American women, in another example, include Native Hawaiian women with high rates of obesity, hypertension, and infant mortality—as well as Japanese American women, 86 percent of whom get prenatal care in the first trimester of pregnancy and whose low infant mortality rates may reflect this. In addition, Native American women in the Southwest have low cancer rates while their sisters in the Plains states and Alaska have extremely high rates. Finally, babies born to Black immigrant couples are of low weight less often than babies born to Black native couples.

Generalizations that create health profiles for these groups of women are dangerous because exceptions to the rules are numerous. The challenge instead is to refine the knowledge and understanding about these groups to the point that individualized care can be provided to each and every woman of color, regardless of race or ethnicity and health problem.

During the 1960s and much of the 1970s, increasing access was a major health policy objective. Since the 1980s, the emphasis has shifted to cost containment, and this focus may ultimately reduce access to care for women of color. If, under the guise of cost containment, renewed emphasis is placed on changing individuals' behavior, it would be all too easy to cross the line to "victim blaming."

Structural problems—such as limited employment opportunities, the lack of resources beyond those to meet basic needs, and the lack of public transportation—all contribute adversely to an individual's ability to change high-risk health behaviors. Programs designed to respect cultural norms and values that are cognizant of structural limits will be the most effective means to enhance the health of women of color.

THREE

★

Securing American Women's Reproductive Health

Rachel Benson Gold and Cory L. Richards

HIGHLIGHTS

REPRODUCTIVE HEALTH SERVICES ARE CRUCIAL to the lives and well-being of women and their families. These services have implications for women's ability not only to maintain overall health, but to choose whether or not to become pregnant; to decide the timing of births; and to prepare for pregnancy by identifying preexisting medical conditions or hazardous behaviors that may have an adverse impact on their own health and that of their infants. A woman's "reproductive years," which span on average half of her lifetime, encompass several stages during which, as her reproductive goals change, so do her reproductive health care needs.

The following points highlight some of the important dimensions of women's reproductive health status:

- Half of all American women of reproductive age—30.5 million women—are at risk of unintended pregnancy. The typical American woman spends 90 percent of her reproductive life seeking to avoid pregnancy.
- Ninety percent of women at risk of unintended pregnancy use some form of contraception to avoid pregnancy.
- Each year, 6.4 million women in the United States become pregnant. Of these pregnancies, 2.8 million are intended, but 3.6 million—56 percent—are unintended, the result of either failure to use contraceptives or contraceptives that do not work.
- Approximately four million women in the United States give birth annually. Although pregnancy and childbirth are relatively safe, six in 10 women experience some health problems during pregnancy or delivery; half of these problems are major.

- One-quarter of all women who gave birth in 1990 had no prenatal care in the first three months of pregnancy. Compared to women who obtain adequate prenatal care, women who lack it are twice as likely to have low birth weight or premature babies.
- Each year nearly 1.6 million American women terminate their pregnancies by abortion. Forty-seven percent of U.S. women will have had an abortion by the time they reach the age of 45.
- Overall, 7.5 million American women—13 percent of women of reproductive age—are either infertile or have an impaired ability to have children. Sexually transmitted diseases are a leading cause of infertility in the United States.

INTRODUCTION

In 1988, our colleague at the Alan Guttmacher Institute (AGI), Jacqueline Darroch Forrest, developed a useful construct for looking at a woman's changing health care needs over the course of her reproductive life (Forrest 1988). After first computing the median age of key events in the typical American woman's reproductive life, Forrest then divided the time span into several stages.

The first stage begins with the onset of menstruation, or menarche, on average at age 12.5, and ends with the beginning of sexual activity, at about age 17.4, as shown in Figure 1. During this period—approximately 14 percent of her reproductive life—a young woman is capable of becoming pregnant but is not yet sexually active. During these years, she needs education and information to prepare her for becoming sexually active—including knowledge about how to avoid pregnancy and how to preserve her fertility so that she can become pregnant when she wants to do so.

Figure 1 • STAGES OF A TYPICAL WOMAN'S REPRODUCTIVE LIFE

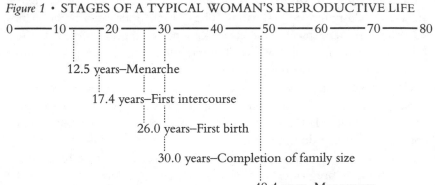

Source: Forrest 1988 updated in Forrest 1993.

During the second stage of a typical American woman's reproductive life, she is sexually active but seeking to postpone childbearing. This stage, which begins when she first has sexual intercourse, generally continues for 8.6 years until shortly before age 26, the typical age at which a woman has her first child. At this stage, a woman's reproductive needs are varied and include:

- the knowledge required to plan and prepare for a pregnancy that may occur in the future;
- contraceptive services to avoid unintended pregnancy;
- recourse to abortion if she becomes pregnant unintentionally; and
- information and services to preserve her fertility and prevent diseases, including sexually transmitted diseases (STDs) that threaten her health in general and her reproductive capacity in particular.

The third stage in a woman's reproductive life is her childbearing period, which runs on average from the birth of her first child until she is 30 years old, the age at which a typical American woman completes her family. Although this time period varies widely, and may not even be a continuous period for many women (as a result of life changes such as divorce and remarriage), for the average woman in the United States the years of actual childbearing account for only 11 percent of her entire reproductive life. During this stage, a woman requires

- education and preparation for childbirth;
- the full range of maternity and newborn services;
- recourse to abortion services if needed; and
- contraceptive services to allow her to space her pregnancies.

At this time an increasing number of women also need infertility services to assist them in becoming pregnant when they choose to do so (U.S. Congress 1988).

The final stage in a woman's reproductive life begins with the birth of her last child and ends with the completion of the transition to menopause, a period that, for the average American woman, comprises 51 percent of her reproductive years—from age 30 to age 48.4. During this period, a woman needs access to contraceptives (and especially sterilization services), recourse to abortion procedures if she becomes pregnant unintentionally, and services to avoid and treat STDs to preserve her health.

Forrest's construct makes a fundamental point: a woman's "reproductive years," which span half of her lifetime, are not a static period. Rather, those years encompass several stages during which, as her reproductive goals change, so does her requirement for specific reproductive health services.[1] Admittedly, not all women move through all of these stages, or do so at the same pace or in the same progression. Still, most American women will pass through these stages and, in consequence, have a wide range of health care needs over the course of their reproductive lives. For this reason, comprehensively addressing "women's reproductive health" is as complex as it is critical.

STATUS OF REPRODUCTIVE HEALTH CARE

In the United States in 1990, there were 61.8 million women age 13 to 44 (Henshaw and Forrest 1993). In 1990, half of all women of reproductive age—30.5 million women—were at risk of unintended pregnancy; that is, they were sexually active, they were fertile, and they did not want to become pregnant.

Of the women at risk of unintended pregnancy in 1990, 4.9 million had family incomes below the federal poverty level, 4.3 million had incomes between 100 and 185 percent of the poverty level, and 21.3 million were in families with incomes at or above 185 percent of the poverty level. Teenagers accounted for 4.6 million of the women at risk (Henshaw and Forrest 1993). Some 15.1 million of the women at risk of unintended pregnancy had incomes of less than 250 percent of the poverty standard or were teenagers and, therefore, may have needed subsidized or organized contraceptive services. African Americans comprised 2.9 million of the women at risk; and two million of the women at risk were Hispanic (Henshaw and Forrest 1993).

CONTRACEPTIVE USE

Ninety percent of sexually active women in 1988 used some form of contraception to avoid pregnancy. Contraceptive use increased as women aged, with teenagers much less likely than older women in 1988 to use a contraceptive method, as shown in Table 1 (Forrest and Singh 1990).

[1]For the purposes of this chapter, reproductive health services include preconceptional risk assessment and care; contraceptive services and supplies; abortion; voluntary contraceptive sterilization; screening for sexually transmitted diseases and cancers of the reproductive system; basic infertility services; and maternity care, including prenatal, delivery, and postnatal care. General gynecological care throughout a woman's life is not discussed.

Table 1 • WOMEN AT RISK OF UNINTENDED PREGNANCY BY
SELECTED CONTRACEPTIVE TYPE AND AGE, 1988[1] (percent
distribution)

Contraceptive Status		Age Groups					
	Total	15–19	20–24	25–29	30–34	35–39	40–44
Female sterilization	24.8	1.2	4.1	15.2	30.1	42.1	47.1
Male sterilization	10.5	0.2	1.6	5.4	13.0	18.4	20.5
Reversible methods[2]	54.8	77.5	82.0	68.9	49.6	33.3	24.6
No method	9.9	21.2	12.3	10.5	7.3	6.2	7.7
Total	100.0	100.0	100.0	100.0	100.0	100.0	100.0

[1]Women at risk of unintended pregnancy are sexually active, fertile, and do not want to
become pregnant.
[2]Reversible methods include spermicides, sponges, cervical caps, diaphragms, condoms,
oral contraceptives, and intrauterine devices.
Source: Forrest and Singh 1990.

As women's reproductive goals change over the course of their reproductive lives, the types of contraception they choose also change. Overall,
sterilization (both female and male) was the most common form of birth
control in 1988, followed by oral contraceptives. Other methods—including barrier methods (such as condoms and diaphragms) and intrauterine
devices (IUDs)—were used by fewer women, as shown in Table 2 (Mosher
1990).

Female sterilization is more commonly relied upon by previously married
women, by African American and Hispanic women, and by the least well-
educated and lowest-income women (Mosher 1990). Currently married
women and white women are more likely to depend on the vasectomies of
their sexual partners for contraception. Most likely to use IUDs are women
who intend to have no more children (Mosher 1990).

Oral contraceptives are utilized most often by women under age 25, by
unmarried women, and by those who intend to have children. Condoms
are used primarily by the sexual partners of teenage girls and unmarried
women. Diaphragms are used most often by white, college-educated, or
never-married women who intend to have children in the future (Mosher
1990). To this list of contraceptive types must be added two new methods:
Norplant, a long-lasting contraceptive implant, and Depo Provera, a long-
term injectable contraceptive. Both have entered the U.S. market too recently to be included in available statistics about contraceptive use.

Table 2 · CONTRACEPTIVE USERS AGE 15 TO 44 WHO RELY ON VARIOUS METHODS BY AGE, 1988

| Age | Number (in thousands) | Contraceptive Methods (in percentages) | | | | | |
		Female Sterilization	Male Sterilization	Pill	Intrauterine Device	Diaphragm	Condom
15–19	2,950	2	0	59	0	1	33
20–24	5,550	5	2	68	0	4	15
25–29	6,967	17	6	45	1	6	16
30–34	7,437	33	14	22	3	9	12
35–39	6,726	45	20	5	3	8	12
40–44	5,282	51	22	3	4	4	11
Total	34,912	28	12	31	2	6	15

Source: Mosher 1990.

SEXUALLY TRANSMITTED DISEASES AND INFERTILITY

Although the majority of women try to avoid pregnancy for most of their reproductive years, many women who seek to become pregnant are unable to do so. The incidence of infertility—generally defined as the inability of a couple to conceive after 12 months of intercourse without contraception (U.S. Congress 1988)—has remained relatively constant between 1982, when the data was first collected, and 1988. But while the proportion of the population that is infertile has not changed, the number of infertile couples has increased because the number of women of childbearing age has increased. The number of childless women 35 to 44 years of age with an impaired ability to have children increased by 37 percent between 1982 and 1988, from 454,000 to 620,000 (RESOLVE, Inc. and American Fertility Society 1993).

Rates of infertility increase with age. Few women under age 30 are infertile; however, one in 17 women age 30 to 34, one in nine women age 35 to 39, and one in five women age 40 to 44 are infertile. Overall, 7.5 million women, or 13 percent of women of reproductive age, are either infertile or have an impaired ability to get pregnant (AGI 1993b).

Sexually transmitted diseases are a leading cause of infertility in the United States. Each year, an estimated 100,000 to 150,000 women become infertile as a result of an STD that develops into pelvic inflammatory disease (PID); one in seven women becomes infertile after a single episode of PID. Between 15 and 30 percent of U.S. couples who are infertile may be unable to conceive as a result of an STD (Donovan 1993).

Twelve million sexually transmitted infections occur every year in the United States. At current rates, at least one in four Americans will contract an STD at some point in their lives. Women are hardest hit by STDs because they are more susceptible to infections and less likely to experience symptoms than men; as a result, detection is more difficult until serious problems develop (Donovan 1993).

In addition, complications of undiagnosed STD infections are far more common and severe in women. For example, one million women contract pelvic infections each year as a result of an undetected STD; many of these women become infertile as a result (Donovan 1993).

Teenagers account for 25 percent of all cases of STDs. STDs are likely to have a greater long-term impact on teenagers than on older women, particularly on their prospects for childbearing later in life. Yet, only one-third of sexually active teenage girls are screened for STDs each year (Donovan 1993).

PREGNANCY

Every year, 6.4 million women in the United States become pregnant. Of these pregnancies, 2.8 million—44 percent—are intended, but 3.6 million of them—56 percent—are unintended, resulting either from a failure to use contraceptives or from contraceptives that don't work (Harlap, Kost, and Forrest 1991). The likelihood of unintended pregnancy varies greatly with age, due to the interrelated factors of contraceptive use and the changing goals of women at different stages of their reproductive lives. Eighty percent of pregnancies among both teenagers and women 40 and older are unintended, compared with 60 percent of pregnancies among women age 20 to 24, and 50 percent among women age 25 to 29 (Harlap, Kost, and Forrest 1991).

Because the likelihood of becoming pregnant is so high for women who do not utilize contraception, the 10 percent of women at risk who use no contraceptive method account for 53 percent of all unintended pregnancies in the United States, or 1.9 million unintended pregnancies each year. The 90 percent who are contraceptive users comprise the remaining 47 percent of unintended pregnancies, mainly because of inconsistent or incorrect use (Harlap, Kost, and Forrest 1991).

The effectiveness of short-term contraceptive methods varied more by age, marital status, and poverty status than by method in 1988, as shown in Table 3, suggesting that failure more often resulted from improper and irregular use than from a method's inherent limitations.

Table 3 • WOMEN EXPERIENCING TYPES OF CONTRACEPTIVE
FAILURE DURING THE FIRST 12 MONTHS OF USE BY MARITAL
STATUS, POVERTY STATUS, AND AGE, 1988[1] (in percentages)

| Marital Status, Poverty Status, and Age | Contraceptive Failure Using | | | | | |
	Pill	Condom	Diaphragm	Periodic Abstinence	Spermicide	Other
NEVER MARRIED						
Under 200 percent of poverty						
Under age 20	12.9	27.3	37.3	51.7	49.8	43.7
20–24	15.0	31.1	42.1	57.3	55.4	49.1
25–29	12.8	27.0	36.9	—[2]	49.4	43.5
30 and over	9.6	20.8	—[2]	—[2]	39.6	—[2]
200 percent of poverty and over						
Under age 20	5.9	13.2	—[2]	27.5	26.3	22.5
20–24	6.9	15.2	21.4	31.4	30.0	25.8
25–29	5.9	13.0	18.4	27.2	26.0	22.3
30 and over	4.4	9.8	14.0	—[2]	—[2]	—[2]
EVER MARRIED						
Under 200 percent of poverty						
Under age 20	26.8	51.3	—[2]	—[2]	—[2]	—[2]
20–24	14.0	29.3	39.8	54.7	52.8	46.6
25–29	8.8	19.0	26.6	38.3	36.7	31.8
30 and over	6.2	13.8	19.5	28.7	27.5	23.6
200 percent of poverty and over						
Under age 20	12.9	—[2]	—[2]	—[2]	—[2]	—[2]
20–24	6.4	14.2	20.1	29.5	28.2	24.2
25–29	4.0	8.9	12.8	19.2	18.3	15.5
30 and over	2.8	6.4	9.1	13.9	13.2	11.2

[1]Percentages are adjusted for underreporting of abortion.
[2]Indicates subgroups represented in the *National Survey of Family Growth* by fewer than five intervals of contraceptive use. Note: The hazard model analysis of method-use failure rates includes duration of use, method, age, marital status, and poverty status, as well as the interactions of duration and poverty status, and of age and marital status.
Source: Jones and Forrest 1992.

Male and female sterilization, as well as the injectable contraceptive Depo Provera, and the implant Norplant, have the smallest likelihood of failure; less than one percent of women who utilize these methods become pregnant in the first year. On average, six percent of oral contraceptive users become pregnant within that time frame. At the other end of the spectrum, almost one-third of all spermicide users become pregnant in the first year, and 85 percent of sexually active women who utilize no contraceptive method at all can expect to become pregnant in the first year (Jones and Forrest 1992).

BIRTH

As shown in Table 4, sixty-two percent of pregnancies in the United States resulted in births in 1988 (National Center for Health Statistics [NCHS] 1992). Each year, approximately four million (seven percent) U.S. women age 15 to 44 give birth (AGI 1993c). Although pregnancy and childbirth are relatively safe, six in 10 women experience some health problems during pregnancy or delivery; half of these are major. Nearly one in seven pregnant women have complications during pregnancy; about nine in 10 of these are major.

Table 4 • PREGNANCY OUTCOME BY AGE OF WOMAN, 1988 (percent distribution)[1]

| Age of Woman | Pregnancy Outcome | | |
	Birth	Abortion	Miscarriage
Under 15	39.2	50.5	10.3
15–19	48.4	39.7	11.9
20–24	60.2	29.3	10.6
25–29	68.1	19.1	12.9
30–34	67.2	15.5	16.2
35–39	59.1	21.0	19.9
40 and over	51.6	30.9	17.4
Total	61.7	25.1	13.3

[1]Percentages are estimates.
Source: National Center for Health Statistics 1992.

Some of the more common major difficulties are conditions that may result in the early onset of labor, conditions that can cause fetal distress, and infections of the genito-urinary tract. Overall, the most common health problems—experienced by three in 10 women—are complications that occur during labor or delivery. They include

- umbilical cord complications;
- obstructed labor;
- breech (feet-first) presentation of the baby;
- severe lacerations of the perineal muscle, cervix, or vagina; and
- severe postpartum hemorrhage.

About two out of every 10 women deliver their babies by cesarean section, and almost half of these procedures are performed because of serious pregnancy complications, not including previous cesarean delivery (AGI 1987).

Whether a pregnancy is planned is crucial to a woman's ability to obtain preconception care that can help her to stop smoking, consuming alcohol, or using drugs—steps that will promote a healthy baby.

Further, a woman with an intended pregnancy is more likely to have early prenatal care, a vital step to avoid having a low birth weight baby that is significantly more likely to die within a year of its birth (Institute of Medicine 1985). Women who do not obtain adequate prenatal care are twice as likely as those who do to have low birth weight or premature babies. Of babies born in 1990, seven percent were of low birth weight (less than 5.5 pounds) and 11 percent were born prematurely (before 37 weeks of gestation) (NCHS 1993b). The incidence of prematurity and low birth weight follows the same pattern as the incidence of inadequate prenatal care—both problems are more common among Native American, African American, and Hispanic women than among white or Asian women (Singh, Forrest, and Torres 1989).

Only three-fourths of all women who gave birth in 1990 obtained prenatal care in the first three months of pregnancy, as shown in Table 5 (NCHS 1993b). Of all women giving birth, 16 percent receive inadequate prenatal care—either they do not begin care until at least the fifth month of pregnancy or they begin care earlier but have less than half of the 13 prenatal visits recommended by the American College of Obstetricians and Gynecologists (ACOG) (ACOG 1989; Singh, Forrest, and Torres 1989). One-third of teenagers giving birth receive inadequate prenatal care, as do 32 percent of Native American women, 27 percent of African American women, and 30 percent of Hispanic women. The comparable proportion of white and Asian women is 13 percent (Singh, Forrest, and Torres 1989).

Table 5 · LIVE BIRTHS BY MONTH PRENATAL CARE BEGAN AND AGE OF MOTHER, 1990 (percent distribution)

	Month Prenatal Care Began				
Age of Mother	*1–2 Months*	*3 Months*	*4–6 Months*	*7–9 Months*	*No Prenatal Care*
Under 15	19.9	16.5	40.2	13.3	6.3
15–19	31.6	22.1	32.2	8.0	3.5
20–24	45.7	21.6	22.5	5.3	2.5
25–29	60.1	20.0	13.6	2.9	1.5
30–34	64.4	19.2	11.8	2.2	1.2
35–39	63.2	19.2	11.1	2.4	1.4
40 and over	56.5	20.0	15.4	3.6	1.9
Total	53.7	20.4	17.7	4.0	1.9

Source: National Center for Health Statistics 1993b.

In 1989, 19 countries had lower rates of infant mortality (death before one year of age) than did the United States, partially because of America's relatively high rates of inadequate prenatal care and low birth weight babies (Children's Defense Fund 1991). Despite the fact that the U.S. infant mortality rate (infant deaths per 1,000 births) has fallen by half since 1970—from 20 in 1970 to 9.2 in 1990—almost one percent of all infants born in the United States die before their first birthdays (NCHS 1993a).

The infant mortality rate among African Americans (18 per 1,000 births) is more than twice that of whites (7.6 per 1,000 births). Similarly, the maternal mortality rate among African American women (22.4 deaths per 100,000 live births) is more than four times that of white women (5.4 deaths per 100,000 live births) (NCHS 1993a).

ABORTION

Although a small percentage of abortions involve women who become pregnant intentionally but whose life or medical circumstances change drastically, or who discover that their fetuses are afflicted with severe medical conditions, the vast majority of abortions in the United States are to women who become pregnant unintentionally. Forty-four percent of unintended pregnancies end in abortion, 43 percent result in birth, and 13 percent end in miscarriage (Harlap, Kost, and Forrest 1991).

Each year, nearly 1.6 million (three percent) American women of reproductive age terminate their pregnancies by abortion (Henshaw and Van

Vort 1990). By age 45, 47 percent of American women will have had an abortion (Gold 1990). Half of all women having an abortion used a contraceptive method in the month in which they conceived; only nine percent of women having an abortion have never used birth control (Henshaw and Silverman 1988).

As women's reproductive goals and the incidence of unintended pregnancy vary with the stages of their reproductive lives, so does the incidence of abortion. The majority of women obtaining abortions are young: 58 percent are under age 25 (including approximately 26 percent who are under age 19); only 20 percent are 30 or older (Henshaw, Koonin, and Smith 1991). Women age 18 and 19 have the highest abortion rate—64 abortions for every 1,000 women—of any age group (Henshaw, Koonin, and Smith 1991).

Most abortions are done early in pregnancy when the procedure is the safest for the woman. Eighty-nine percent of all abortions performed annually in the United States take place in the first trimester, with half taking place at eight weeks or less from the time the woman had her last menstrual period. Over 99 percent of all abortions in this country are performed before 21 weeks, as shown in Table 6. Only 0.01 percent occur after 24 weeks of pregnancy (Henshaw, Koonin, and Smith 1991).

The decision to have an abortion is a complex one for most women. Ninety-three percent of women who have had abortions say that more than one factor influenced their decision; on average, they cite four different reasons. The reasons given most frequently reflect the fact that many women having abortions are young, have never been married, and feel

Table 6 • ABORTIONS BY WEEK OF GESTATION, 1988 (in numbers and percent distribution)

Week of Gestation[1]	Number	Percent
8 weeks	800,480	50.3
9–10 weeks	424,270	26.7
11–12 weeks	198,320	12.4
13–15 weeks	96,620	60.1
16–20 weeks	60,400	3.8
21 weeks or more	10,660	0.7
Total	1,590,750	100.0

[1]Week of gestation is calculated from last menstrual period.
Source: Alan Guttmacher Institute 1992.

unprepared to begin families. Three in four women having abortions say that they are not ready for the changes a baby could bring to their lives. These women most frequently say that having a baby would interfere with work, school, or other responsibilities. Two-thirds of all women having abortions say that they cannot afford a baby at this point in their lives; half say either that they do not want to be single parents or that they are having problems in their relationships with husbands or partners (Torres and Forrest 1988).

Further reflecting the youth of many abortion patients, as many as three in 10 women having abortions say that they are not ready for the responsibility of a child, are not mature enough to be a parent, or are too young to have a child. Of those women under age 18 who are having abortions, eight in 10 say that they are not mature enough for parenthood, and four in 10 say that they do not want others to know that they have had sex or are pregnant (Torres and Forrest 1988).

ISSUES IN REPRODUCTIVE HEALTH CARE

Because women have reproductive health goals, and hence reproductive health care needs that change over the course of their lifetimes, they require access to various reproductive health care services at different points in their lives. Ensuring that the full range of reproductive needs are met for all women—regardless of age, race, marital status, or income—raises an array of important issues and public policy challenges.

FINANCIAL ACCESS—INSURANCE COVERAGE

Because health care in American society is not a right but rather a commodity that must be purchased, financial access to care is an omnipresent, and paramount, issue. Like their male counterparts, most American women of reproductive age—73 percent in 1985—relied on some form of private health insurance (AGI 1987). And although comprehensive data are not available, it is clear that private health insurance, as currently offered by insurers and purchased by employers for their workers, is not an adequate funding mechanism for the full range of reproductive health care services.

Many insurance policies do not cover contraceptive services. In 1986 less than 20 percent of insurance policies covered routine examinations such as family planning visits and screening for STDs, although some components of family planning visits were probably covered under the rubric of physician services (Health Insurance Association of America [HIAA] 1986b).

And while most policies cover prescription drugs (Bureau of Labor Statistics 1990), many may nonetheless exclude coverage of oral contraceptives because they are not considered therapeutic.

Abortion and Infertility Coverage
No reliable recent data exists on insurance coverage of abortion and infertility services. Although private insurance was listed as the expected source of payment for 62 percent of abortions performed in those hospitals reporting in 1985 to the Commission for Professional Hospital Activities, this finding cannot be extrapolated to all abortions, since 90 percent of abortions take place in freestanding clinics or private physicians' offices. Moreover, four states—Idaho, Kentucky, Missouri, and North Dakota—have enacted laws prohibiting insurance companies from covering abortion services, except in cases of life endangerment, unless the employee pays for a separate rider (AGI 1992b).

Because many policies traditionally excluded coverage for infertility treatment, five states—California, Connecticut, Illinois, New York, and Rhode Island—have passed laws requiring insurance policies in those states to cover infertility services, and six states—Arkansas, Connecticut, Hawaii, Illinois, Maryland, and Texas—require at least some insurance coverage of in vitro fertilization (AGI 1992b).

Maternity Coverage
Although private-sector insurance coverage for maternity care is more comprehensive than coverage for other reproductive services, it too has serious limitations. The federal Pregnancy Discrimination Act (PDA) of 1978 requires employer-provided insurance policies to treat maternity services as they do all other covered health care services (AGI 1987). This law has greatly increased the number of workers who have policies that cover maternity care—from 41 percent of employees in groups over 25 in 1978 to 99 percent in 1986 (HIAA n.d.; HIAA 1986a).

Nevertheless, the PDA has several loopholes that have left millions of American women without coverage. First, the law only applies to insurance policies purchased by employers for their workers; policies bought by individuals outside of employment are not required to cover maternity care. Second, the PDA mandates that policies include maternity coverage only for the employee and his or her spouse; it does not specify such coverage for nonspouse dependents such as the teenage daughter of the policyholder. As a result of this loophole, only 25 percent of typical insurance policies cover both a policyholder's pregnant daughter and the daughter's newborn child. Third, the PDA applies only to employers of 15 or more workers, leaving the millions of women employed by small businesses without any legal protection (AGI 1987).[2] Largely as a result of these loopholes, an estimated five million American women have private insurance coverage that does not include maternity care (AGI 1987).

Medicaid

Medicaid, a government-sponsored insurance program, provides health coverage for many low-income women. However, because it is generally open only to women whose income and family characteristics qualify them for welfare, Medicaid offers no assistance to women who are privately insured but whose coverage does not include a particular service, such as maternity care. Medicaid is a joint federal-state program, and Medicaid benefits differ from state to state.

Family planning—including contraceptive services and supplies, sterilization, and infertility services—is covered by Medicaid in all 50 states and the District of Columbia. Payment for abortion services is severely limited by Congress as a result of the Hyde amendment, which since 1981 has prohibited the use of federal funds to pay for abortions except when the life of the woman would be endangered if the pregnancy were carried to term. However, 13 states continue to use their own funds to pay for all or most medically necessary abortions for Medicaid recipients (Gold and Daley 1991).

As part of a major public policy effort to lower the rate of infant mortality in the United States, Medicaid coverage for prenatal care has expanded greatly over the past decade, in terms of both liberalized eligibility requirements for pregnant women and infants and the greater breadth of services that are included.

Beginning in 1985, Congress broke the historic link between welfare and Medicaid eligibility—at least where pregnant women and infants were concerned—by allowing pregnant women to qualify for Medicaid solely on the basis of their income regardless of whether they met the other criteria for welfare. Since April 1990, states have been required to cover all pregnant women with family incomes up to 133 percent of the federal poverty line, and they are permitted to cover women up to 185 percent of poverty. By 1992, all states had met the 133 percent floor, and 24 had exercised the option to offer Medicaid coverage to women with incomes above 133 percent of poverty (National Governors Association [NGA] 1992).

[2]Unfortunately, existing data concern only employees in groups of over 25; data do not exist on the policies of businesses with fewer than 15 workers (who are not covered by the PDA), or of employers with between 15 and 25 employees (who are covered by the PDA).

Further, Congress permitted states to take some steps, and required them to take others, to facilitate Medicaid enrollment by pregnant women. For example, Congress allowed states to establish so-called presumptive eligibility programs, in which a health care provider can grant immediate conditional Medicaid eligibility to a pregnant woman, thereby allowing her to obtain services while a final ruling on her application is pending. In addition, since 1985 Congress has allowed states to offer an enhanced benefit package for pregnant women that includes coverage for such important services as nutritional counseling and case management (NGA 1992).

These Medicaid expansions, like all Medicaid coverage for reproductive health care services, provide vital assistance to low-income women who meet the requirements for Medicaid eligibility (criteria that vary from state to state). In 1985, before the Medicaid expansions began, 4.2 million women—seven percent of women of reproductive age—had Medicaid coverage to finance their health care needs (AGI 1987). Since that time, Medicaid coverage for pregnant women has increased dramatically. While this is likely to mean a significant improvement for pregnant women and new infants, the effect of the Medicaid expansions on other women has been less significant. Under the terms of the Medicaid expansions, a woman remains eligible for Medicaid for only 60 days after the birth of her child (NGA 1992) unless she meets her state's basic welfare-connected eligibility criteria for Medicaid. If she does not, her coverage for other services (such as family planning) ends after that brief period. Sixty days may be enough time for a woman to obtain a sterilization or a long-lasting form of contraception such as the recently approved Norplant, but its utility in helping a woman afford oral contraceptives is clearly limited.

Uninsured Women

Many women fall into the gap between private insurance and Medicaid and are completely uninsured. In 1985, for example, 9.5 million women of reproductive age were uninsured, and another five million women had some form of private insurance that did not cover maternity care (AGI 1987). An even larger number of women have private health insurance that does not cover other vital reproductive health care needs such as contraceptive services and supplies, sterilization, or treatment for infertility.

Women in these circumstances must either pay for care completely out-of-pocket or seek the limited services available from other public sources such as the Title X Family Planning program, the Maternal and Child Health block grant, or the Community and Migrant Health Center program. Until there is a system in the United States that provides universal health care coverage, and that includes the full range of reproductive health care services, this patchwork system will remain a significant barrier.

ACCESS TO SERVICES—SOURCES OF CARE

Ensuring financial access to care, however critical, is not enough; women seeking reproductive health care services must also be able to find sources for that care. For two-thirds of the women in the United States who use a contraceptive method, that source of care is a physician's office or a health maintenance organization. For the remaining one-third, however, that source of care, most often, is a clinic, usually one supported in whole or in part with government funds. Some women—especially teenagers, African Americans, and those with low incomes—are more likely to seek care in clinics. Sixty percent of low-income women (with incomes below 250 percent of poverty), compared to 30 percent of more affluent women, obtain their family planning care from clinics. For many poor women clinics may be the only option; only half of obstetrician-gynecologists and family practitioners in private practice accept Medicaid patients for contraceptive care (AGI 1993a).

Another problem is that not all providers are willing to offer contraceptive, sterilization, or abortion services—or to do so confidentially without the consent or notification of a parent or a spouse. For these reasons, managed care arrangements that require women to use specific providers are problematic. The right of individuals or even institutions to decline on moral or religious grounds to provide certain reproductive services must be balanced against the right of individual patients to receive these services. Women must be allowed to seek (and be reimbursed for) contraceptive, sterilization, and abortion services outside any managed care network in which they might be enrolled.

Contraceptives

In addition to finding places and providers for care, women should have access to all the contraceptive methods that are legally available in the United States. Here again, financing is a major issue. While drug manufacturers have historically offered special low prices to family planning clinics, their willingness to do so in the future is uncertain. A provision of the Omnibus Budget Reconciliation Act of 1990 that requires pharmaceutical manufacturers to give state Medicaid programs access to these discounts has caused some manufacturers to raise their prices to providers such as family planning clinics. Faced with decreasing government funds, family planning clinics may not be able to subsidize the costs of certain contraceptives enough to make them affordable for clients.

Norplant, a newly approved long-lasting contraceptive implant, is the starkest example of this problem. Wyeth-Ayerst, Norplant's manufacturer, has so far refused to give discounts to any providers, leaving many clinics unable to offer this new method except to full-fee patients at one end of the income scale or Medicaid-enrolled patients at the other. (All 50 state Medicaid programs do reimburse clinics for Norplant.) It is women of modest means for whom cost is likely to be the greatest barrier. Unfortunately, some of the most effective and long-lasting contraceptive methods also have the highest up-front costs—compared, for example, with oral contraceptives, that allow the costs to be spread out over time.

Maternity

Not only do women need access to all available methods of contraception, they also must be able to exercise all reproductive health care options. For example, a system that makes maternity care available, but not contraception and abortion, or that provides access to sterilization services but not to abortion, is inherently coercive.

Maternity care poses an additional array of access issues. Even affluent women living in some parts of the United States may have difficulty locating a prenatal care provider. Large numbers of physicians are curtailing their obstetric practices, or eliminating them altogether, primarily because of a fear of malpractice litigation.

For Medicaid patients, the problem is particularly acute: they face both the overall shortage of providers and the unwillingness of some providers to accept low-income patients, in part because the amount reimbursed to a physician by Medicaid is far below the amount usually paid by a private patient. At most, 5,400 clinics are involved in the delivery of prenatal care to poor women nationwide; no prenatal care clinics appear to exist in 799 counties, more than one-fourth of all counties in the United States (Singh, Forrest, and Torres 1989).

In addition to medical prenatal care, many pregnant women need access to such services as nutrition counseling and substance abuse treatment. Beginning in 1985, Congress gave states the option of covering many of these services in their Medicaid programs; by 1992, 39 states had included these so-called enhanced benefits (NGA 1992). Ironically, coverage under private insurance seems to lag far behind Medicaid in paying for services of this type.

Abortion

Access to providers is an acute problem for women seeking abortions. Ninety percent of all abortions in the United States take place not in hospitals but in clinics or in physicians' offices. The number of abortion providers declined by four percent between 1985 and 1988.

Moreover, the geographic distribution of abortion services is extremely uneven: 83 percent of all U.S. counties—whose residents included 31 percent of America's women of reproductive age—lacked an abortion provider in 1988. Eighty-three percent of American women who lived outside metropolitan areas lived in the 93 percent of nonmetropolitan counties without an abortion provider (Henshaw and Van Vort 1990). More than one-quarter (27 percent) of women who received abortions in 1988 had to travel at least 50 miles from home to do so; nine percent had to travel at least 100 miles. In 1987, six percent of women who got abortions had to cross state lines for that purpose, and 33 percent had to leave their county of residence (Henshaw 1991).

Continued harassment of abortion providers and their patients is a serious problem. While the point-blank murder in March 1993 of Dr. David Gunn, an abortion provider in Pensacola, Florida, was the most extreme example of anti-abortion harassment and violence the United States had ever witnessed, it was not an isolated incident. Fully 61 percent of nonhospital abortion providers (and 88 percent of those doing more than 400 abortions per year) report being the target of some form of harassment, including personal harassment of themselves and/or their families away from the abortion facility (Henshaw 1991).

In 1990, the National Abortion Federation and the American College of Obstetricians and Gynecologists convened a nationwide symposium to explore the shortage of physicians willing to provide abortions. The symposium concluded that obstetrical and gynecological residency programs fall far short of their responsibility to train physicians in abortion (and contraceptive) services. Other factors contributing to the dwindling supply of abortion doctors included " . . . anti-abortion harassment and violence, social stigma, professional isolation, peer pressure, the 'graying' of providers, inadequate economic and other incentives, and the perception of abortion as an unrewarding field of medicine" (National Abortion Federation [NAF] and ACOG 1990:1). The symposium made several recommendations to encourage more doctors to provide abortion services, but also concluded that " . . . appropriately trained mid-level clinicians, including physician assistants, nurse practitioners, and certified nurse midwives, offer considerable promise for expanding the pool of qualified abortion providers" (NAF and ACOG 1990:1).

Other barriers to abortion are being imposed legislatively. In 1992, ruling in *Planned Parenthood of Southeastern Pennsylvania* v. *Casey,* the U.S. Supreme Court reaffirmed "the essential holding" in *Roe* v. *Wade*—that American women have a constitutional right to choose abortion prior to fetal viability—and declared that legislative attempts by states to make early abortions illegal will not be permitted. At the same time, however, the Court said that states have broad authority to regulate abortion throughout pregnancy so long as any regulations they enact do not impose an "undue burden" on a woman's "effective right to elect the procedure." The Court defined an undue burden as one that places a "substantial obstacle in the path of a woman seeking an abortion."

The most serious and far-reaching restrictions likely to be considered by the state legislatures involve

- subjecting women to compulsory, state-scripted "counseling," often under the guise of obtaining their "informed consent," followed by mandatory waiting periods;
- requiring parental involvement before a minor can obtain an abortion; and
- denying funds for abortions sought by medically indigent women.

These restrictions, often portrayed as "minor," can have devastating consequences for women—especially those who are already disadvantaged by youth, poverty, or the fact that they live in rural areas. For many, if not most, of these women—assuming they are able to obtain an abortion at all—the abortion will be delayed until later in pregnancy. In 1992, the Council on Scientific Affairs of the American Medical Association (AMA) cautioned against reviving restrictive abortion policies, saying that any attempt to limit or delay abortion services could have serious health consequences for women seeking abortions (AMA 1992).

APPROPRIATENESS OF CARE

The reproductive services to which women need access also must be appropriate, in terms of both their content and delivery. The question of the appropriateness of services raises several issues.

Allied Health Providers/Practitioners

Care needs to be furnished by the right providers. For some services, the only appropriate provider is a physician. However, for much reproductive health care, an allied health provider/practitioner can be as good or better than a doctor. Some needs, such as prenatal care, can effectively be met by nurse midwives or nurse practitioners with physician backup.

This type of arrangement can have many advantages. Allied health professionals such as nurse practitioners, nurse midwives, and specially trained counselors often have more training than physicians in the extensive counseling and information that is integral to many reproductive health services.

Further, allied health providers/practitioners may be willing to spend extensive time with patients and in some cases may find it easier to establish rapport with patients. In addition, appropriate use of related health professionals can greatly increase access to services for patients when no doctors are available. Having care furnished by nonphysicians, where appropriate, is more cost efficient. Because of the difference in the cost of a physician's time versus the time of an allied health provider/practitioner, a longer visit with the latter can cost less than a shorter visit with a doctor providing the same services.

Information and Counseling Restrictions

While all medical care has information and counseling aspects, the importance of these services to reproductive health care cannot be overstated. Counseling and information can take many forms:

- helping a pregnant woman choose a course of action;
- assisting a sexually active woman in selecting and effectively using a method of contraception;
- discussing with a couple the range of infertility options; and
- counseling a pregnant woman on prenatal genetic screening.

Unfortunately, because the important role of information and counseling services has often gone unacknowledged, these services are frequently not reimbursed by public or private insurance. Therefore, providers have little incentive to offer these services. The most effective way to ensure that information and counseling will be furnished is for providers to be paid for delivering these services—just as they are paid for delivering medical care.

Moreover, a provider's ability to assist a woman in making decisions about her reproductive needs depends on the free flow of complete information between the provider and the patient. To restrict information about reproductive choices is antithetical to the principle of truly informed decisionmaking. Examples of efforts to restrict women's access to information include the "gag rule" (now rescinded) that prohibited providers from offering pregnant women information about abortion, and state requirements still in place that every abortion patient be given a litany of pre-scripted information, whether or not it is relevant to her particular situation. The gag rule was recently lifted by the Clinton administration.

Restrictions on Medical Technology and Research

The third component of appropriate care involves the role of technology. No medical technology is perfect; virtually any medical procedure can be improved. Unfortunately, and largely for political and not scientific reasons, technological progress in reproductive health care in the United States has slowed in recent years. Also (partly as a result of the lawsuits filed by women who developed health problems after using the Dalkon Shield IUD) fear of product liability litigation has impeded the development of new methods of contraception.

Women in the United States have fewer methods of contraception from which to choose than do women in other parts of the world. Moreover, progress on new methods of overcoming infertility has been stymied by bans on federal funding for research on certain techniques, such as in vitro fertilization. Not only are American women limited in their reproductive choices, but they are also restricted to choosing among procedures, methods, and courses of action that may be more risky than they could be.

The case of RU-486 is perhaps the most publicized example of this problem (Richards and Gold 1990). RU-486 is an antiprogestin that dislodges a fertilized egg from the endometrial lining. It is most effective if used within 12 weeks of a woman's last menstrual period. Although the drug was approved for use as an abortifacient in France in 1988, anti-abortion politics in the United States led to a ban on federal funding for research involving RU-486, and in 1989 the drug was placed on the Food and Drug Administration's (FDA) "import alert" list. This is a designation reserved for drugs that are considered so risky to human health that they should not be allowed to cross the U.S. border. The effect of this political move was not only to ban the importation of RU-486 for personal use but also to deter the drug's manufacturer, Roussel-Uclaf, from conducting research in this country on RU-486 and from applying to the FDA for approval. President Bill Clinton announced a review of the FDA policy within days of his inauguration in 1993, and the FDA has emerged as a major player in the effort to bring the drug to the United States. However, valuable time has been lost. It still may take several years before this safe and effective alternative to surgical abortion is widely available to American women.

Technology holds great promise for the improved safety and delivery of reproductive health care services, but it also poses a challenge. It is important that reproductive technologies not be used inappropriately. For example, "high tech" procedures such as in vitro fertilization in general should be provided only after more basic approaches to treating infertility have been tried. Similarly, cesarean sections should be performed, and fetal monitors used, only when there are medical reasons to do so, and not out of fear of malpractice litigation.

Inappropriate uses of reproductive technologies drive up the costs of care while often providing patients with few, if any, benefits—and subjecting them to unnecessary risks. Unfortunately, no consensus exists among medical professionals or consumers about when use of these technologies is appropriate, and further research on reproductive technologies is needed.

Finally, ongoing review of reproductive health care technologies and service delivery is crucial to demonstrate effectiveness, as well as to identify where innovations are needed. The challenge is to design evaluations that are sufficiently informative but not so extensive that they themselves greatly increase health care costs or impede service delivery.

LOOKING TOWARD THE FUTURE

Progress in providing reproductive health care will depend upon a societal commitment to its importance. Without this, both individuals and society will suffer.

Unfortunately, America's failure to make reproductive health care a priority has resulted in inadequate sex education of the young. Most schools do have some form of sex education. However, most sex education teachers believe that the material presented to students is not sufficiently comprehensive, that not enough time is given to the subject, and that sex education often begins too late, following the initiation of sexual activity (AGI 1989). The consequences of an inadequate U.S. sex education system are catastrophic, both for individuals and for society as a whole. The teenage pregnancy rate in America is higher than in other developed countries. Four out of five teenage pregnancies in the United States are unintended, leading to high rates of abortion and inadequate prenatal care among teenagers who carry their unintended pregnancies to term (which, in turn, results in poor birth outcomes). Inadequate sex education is also an important factor in the skyrocketing numbers of Acquired Immune Deficiency Syndrome (AIDS) cases and the high rates of sexually transmitted diseases among teenagers (which can lead to infertility later in life).

Changing these troubling patterns will require a revamping of society's attitude toward reproductive health care services. The first step is to provide better information on topics such as preventing unintended pregnancy and avoiding sexually transmitted diseases. The second step is to develop a comprehensive approach to reproductive health care that ensures that lack of income is not a barrier to service, that providers are available to offer care, and that effective technologies are developed. Together, these steps will enhance the lives of girls and women and permit them to be full participants in American society, while also improving the health of individuals, families, and communities.

HEALTH CARE REFORM

The debate over national health care reform offers the opportunity

- to secure reproductive health services for all American women of child-bearing years (and for men, as needed);
- to correct the "biases" in the current health care system that limit true freedom of choice for women and men in regard to childbearing; and
- to promote the health and well-being of infants and children (Rosoff 1993).

The entire range of reproductive health services (i.e., contraceptive services, sterilization, abortion, and maternity care) as well as all approved methods of contraception (such as oral contraceptives, Norplant, etc.) must be included—without deductibles or copayments—in any benefits package that is part of health care reform. This would correct some of the inequities in the current system.

It is also important that health care reform eliminate the biases in coverage that exist in the current system. For example, private insurance appears often to cover surgical sterilizations—regardless of whether the procedure is for therapeutic or "elective" contraceptive reasons—but excludes coverage for IUDs; Norplant; and other expensive, long-lasting (but not permanent) contraceptives. Moreover, coverage for diaphragms and oral contraceptive "drugs" (methods that are used by some 12 million women each year) are often excluded.

In designing a health benefits package, it is important that the contraceptive services used by men, such as condoms and vasectomies, also be covered so that the burden and responsibility for seeking care is not placed entirely on women. Reform of the health care system must also eliminate deductibles, copayments, and limitations on coverage of preexisting medical conditions in order to ensure universal access to these important preventive services.

Much of the debate over health care reform has focused on the potential for managed care networks (which limit women's choice of providers) to better coordinate the delivery of health care and control costs. However, several concerns arise regarding managed care and reproductive services, one of which is whether women will have access to the full range of reproductive health services.

This issue first arose in the early 1980s in connection with Medicaid-funded family planning services, as states began to enroll Medicaid recipients in managed care systems. Unfortunately, some women enrolled in

Medicaid managed care systems faced difficulties or delays in obtaining family planning services because primary care physicians—usually for religious or moral reasons—neither offered nor referred their patients for the full range of family planning services (including all contraceptive methods and sterilization). Congress amended the Medicaid statute in 1987 to ensure that women who enroll in managed care plans under Medicaid remain free to seek family planning services from the provider of their choice.

Managed care entities should be made responsible under health care reform for providing the full range of reproductive health services to their enrollees. To ensure that this obligation is met, several quality assurance features are essential. First, managed care plans should be required to inform enrollees that all services (including sterilization, abortion, and STD screening) are available on a confidential basis. Second, plans should have procedures so that members who encounter difficulties in obtaining covered services can get assistance. Third, data systems that track the provision of reproductive health services by managed care networks should be developed and made available to consumers. Even with the best of intentions, however, it is likely that some enrollees will not have unimpeded access to the full range of reproductive health services within their managed care plans—necessitating the retention of the provisions of the Medicaid statute that permits patients to receive services "out of plan."

Another concern is that the "gatekeeper" system that is so basic to the managed care approach may delay rather than facilitate prompt receipt of needed reproductive health services. This is, in fact, what has occurred in Great Britain. Under Britain's National Health Service (NHS), a woman seeking an abortion must first see her primary care physician to verify pregnancy, be referred to an obstetrician-gynecologist, and then to a clinic or hospital (Office of Population Censuses and Surveys 1988; Henshaw and Van Vort 1992). As a result, " . . . referral and assessment for abortion takes longer with the National Health Service than in the private and charitable sectors. The NHS carries out only 21 percent of its abortions before the ninth week, as against 44 percent in the private sector" ("Reducing Late Abortion" February 1989). To avoid such delays and the unnecessary costs that often accompany them, providers of reproductive health services should be either recognized as primary care providers or designated as "gatekeepers" for other health services needed by patients.

One broad concern with health care reform is the need to guarantee confidentiality. This is key to whether many, if not most, reproductive health services are really accessible to everyone who needs them. Some of the proposals for health care reform advocate that each family—as the "covered unit"—receive a health card that will allow family members to access services. Under this system, it would be impossible for a family member—particularly an adolescent—to obtain confidential services if she or he must first obtain the family's insurance card, knowing that the policyholder (usually a parent in the case of a teenager) will submit the claim. One solution is to base eligibility for services on the individual, rather than the family unit.

As this book goes to press, the climate for health care reform is more favorable than it has been in decades. Politicians of both parties, many business groups, labor unions, and consumers all agree that reform is needed to bring the uninsured into the system and skyrocketing health care costs under control. The challenge is to make certain that health care reform incorporates the full range of services needed by women and their families. Contraceptive services, sterilization, abortion, and maternity care must all be included in any benefits package that adequately fills women's needs.

The achievement of universal coverage for the full range of reproductive health services will be a major first step. Also crucial is the development of a health care delivery system that *provides* these services to women and their families. The reproductive health programs that have been serving women and their families for decades—such as the maternal and child health programs and the family planning clinics—must not be left out of this delivery system.

Other industrialized countries have found that in addition to universal insurance coverage, supplementary programs—especially clinics and special educational programs—are necessary to address the needs of specific populations that include youth, disadvantaged minorities, and immigrants. This international experience powerfully documents the need to maintain, and even enhance, the existing network of maternal and child health, family planning, and other government supported programs in the United States, even should the long sought after health care reform become a reality.

FOUR

★

WOMEN AND
LONG-TERM CARE

Marilyn Moon

HIGHLIGHTS

ALL AMERICANS HAVE A STAKE in long-term care issues, but there is no doubt that women have the largest stake. Women are more likely than men both to need long-term care themselves and to provide it to others. Supportive services provided in the community, in the home, or in institutions are not sufficiently available to meet the needs of persons with disabilities. Although no consensus exists on how to improve that situation, several approaches have been proposed. Some would make fairly sweeping changes in the way long-term care is financed in this country; others are more limited in scope. Here are some of the reasons why women are particularly vulnerable:

- Women are more likely than men to live to an advanced age, when the chance of needing long-term care is greatest. Moreover, at any age over 65, women are more likely than men to have functional limitations.
- Over half of all women over the age of 85 have problems in managing such basic daily activities as bathing or eating.
- Women are more likely than men to have caregiving responsibilities for impaired family members. Women are only a third as likely as men to have a spouse as a caregiver.
- The typical woman age 75 or above has an income of $9,170—less than one-third what it would cost her to stay in the average nursing home for a year.
- The women most in need of long-term care are also very likely to be poor. This is particularly true in the case of minority women.

- Women with low incomes are also likely to have few assets on which they can draw to pay for long-term care.
- Medicaid, a joint federal/state program, pays nursing home costs for many poor people and for those who have become poor from exhausting all their income and assets. About 44 percent of the nation's total costs for nursing home care are paid by Medicaid.
- Contrary to what many people believe, Medicare covers very little in the way of long-term care. Less than five percent of the country's total costs for nursing home care are paid by Medicare, which is mostly an acute care program covering hospital and physician bills.
- Fewer than two million persons now have private long-term care insurance policies. Further expansion is likely to be quite slow.
- The use of home- and community-based services has been expanding rapidly, while nursing home use has leveled off. Nonetheless, many older women do not receive any formal care at home or in a nursing home, despite having substantial disabilities.

INTRODUCTION

Despite the many aspects of American life that have improved for women in the twentieth century, a major unmet challenge remains: the need for long-term care services. Society has made enormous advances in meeting acute health care needs, but less has been done to creatively deal with disability. Chronic disease and traumatic injuries leave individuals with medical and supportive service needs. Treatment requires a labor-intensive effort, the burdens of which fall on families—often the wives and daughters—and some government-provided programs. Too often these services fall short of the need for care.

Yet as inadequate as these services are at present, the aging of the population will lead to even greater future demand for long-term care. While long-term care is a problem for young as well as older persons, its prevalence increases dramatically for those over age 80 or 85. And while women and men are both affected, particularly at the end of life, American women more often face the prospect of a loss of independence and a lower quality of life from the impact of chronic disease or disability. Unfortunately, the services and support needed to enhance the independence and dignity of older women are sorely lacking.

DEFINING LONG-TERM CARE

Problems of poor health, disability, or frailty give rise to the need for something often referred to as "long-term care." There is little concrete agreement on what constitutes long-term care; it is something that people know when they see it, but it is also difficult to succinctly define. The term refers to the extended nature of the care provided, but there is also no agreement on when acute (hospital and physician) services become long-term care. Moreover, there is enormous variation in the types of care needed and received. Some services are more medical in nature and include, for example, rehabilitation and monitoring of medications, but many of the needs are supportive, helping the individual meet daily personal needs that range from housework to such basics as eating or bathing.

Nor is there specific agreement on who should receive such services. Usually, recipients of care can trace their disabilities back to specific illnesses or medical problems, such as broken hips or strokes. Dementia, stemming from Alzheimer's disease or other causes, also contributes to the need for long-term care. In other cases, frailty results from the slow deterioration in functional status from minor chronic problems exacerbated by the aging process. The only common theme is that long-term care represents a critical area of concern for older women.

Given the variability in needs, it is difficult to define exactly what an ideal long-term care system should look like. Institutional (nursing home) care for those who cannot remain at home and community-based services (that offer a variety of options for persons who remain in their homes) are both crucial components of a long-term care system. Institutional care may be needed not just for the level of skill required, but also for the constancy of care, such as round-the-clock supervision for those with Alzheimer's disease or dementia. But long-term care is not just nursing home care. Community-based care includes skilled and unskilled services in the home and programs such as adult day care or congregate meals. Recipients of such personal services require flexibility and choice.

Whatever the specific setting, long-term care services are likely to represent relatively permanent arrangements, stretching over months if not years. Thus, they need to reflect quality of life concerns and the living environment of the disabled. In this way, long-term care differs substantially from the acute care setting, which is designed for the convenience of the providers and to which patients are only briefly exposed. Actually, this distinction is more of a wish than a reality, since too often nursing homes take on the air of sterility and discomfort rather than incorporating the housing, services, and other needs of residents into facility design (Institute of Medicine 1986).

An important part of any ideal long-term care setting should also be the presence of informal care provided by relatives and friends. Again, it is essential to distinguish between medical needs that require highly skilled personnel, and supportive services that are most effective if they are part of a normal routine involving other family members. Indeed, such informal support has always been a crucial element in helping persons with disabilities and frailties; model systems seek to find ways to supplement rather than replace the informal care offered. Nonetheless, informal support is not costless. It often takes a toll on the caregivers in terms of lost earnings, delayed careers, and emotional stress.

WHY IS LONG-TERM CARE IDENTIFIED WITH WOMEN?

The stereotypical image of someone in need of long-term care is an older women in a nursing home. Why is long-term care associated with older women? Basically there are two reasons. First, women live longer than men, on average, and persons (of either sex) who reach advanced age are more likely to require long-term care services for chronic problems. Second, women in any age group over 65 are more likely than men to have functional limitations, in part because of chronic disabling problems, such as arthritis or osteoporosis, that contribute to greater use of formal and informal services.

But this stresses only the need side of the equation. Women are also the major deliverers of long-term care, in both informal and formal settings. Women are more likely to be family caregivers who support spouses or parents in need of care. The irony is that many women provide care to spouses, but when they in turn need supportive services, no family member is available to provide that support. Consequently, women are more likely to end up in institutions as they outlive their support groups. This is the downside of women's longer life expectancy. Further, when middle-aged women care for elderly parents, they may give up career opportunities and lower their own economic well-being indefinitely.

The majority of formal workers in the long-term care field are also women, as nurses or lower-skilled workers. Employment in this area is growing rapidly, but the work is demanding and the pay often quite low. Thus, yet another women's issue is the compensation they receive for this important work.

THE NATURE OF THE PROBLEM

A number of factors must change before the situation of women and others in need of long-term care will improve. First, care needs to be made more affordable through either improved individual resources or improved public programs. Women lack the economic resources to afford the heavy expenses associated with long-term care. Care is expensive but, in addition, those who need it most generally have limited incomes and few assets.

In many ways, long-term care is a good candidate for a public program. Need for care is unpredictable and those who have the misfortune to need it can seldom bear the costs out of income and savings. If the risks are shared across the whole population, however, they become more affordable. This creates a classic opportunity for social insurance; if everyone contributes, the cost to any one individual will be quite small.[1] But the current public program that provides protection for long-term care, Medicaid, is flawed and unpopular. As a means-tested program, it only provides support after catastrophe has struck.

There is little solace even for those women who can afford to raise the money needed to obtain long-term care services. Partly because so many have difficulty in paying for care, there has been little investment in developing a supply of services in many areas of the country; therefore, availability of high quality services is spotty around the country. Persons living in rural areas must often enter institutions because good home care is simply not available at any reasonable price. And institutional care may be a depressing and dismal choice in many areas where the quality of facilities is lacking. Finally, for those who are not able to serve as their own advocates, mistreatment and even abuse are all too frequent possibilities. Older women are often correct to fear losing their independence and dignity in these situations.

Certainly the picture is not all bad, and indeed a number of interesting and important innovations have been occurring in the area of long-term care. Some public support and oversight will be needed but, with the commitment of resources, the problem of inadequate and unacceptable treatment of women with disabilities could be largely resolved. The stumbling block is the will to expend those resources on this endeavor.

---

[1]The most familiar examples of social insurance programs are Social Security and Medicare.

LONG-TERM CARE NEEDS

The need for long-term care depends upon an individual's health or functional status. And whether those needs will be reasonably met turns on the availability of informal support services, the person's ability to pay for additional care, and whether she or he is eligible to participate in a public program covering long-term care services.

HEALTH AND FUNCTIONAL STATUS

Health problems that lead to disability and functional impairment are not necessarily closely connected to overall health status or expenditures. Indeed, when examining reported health status or amounts spent on health care services for persons over the age of 65 by gender, men appear to have greater needs. Self-reported health status has generally been shown to correlate well with acute care needs.[2] It is not as well correlated with measures associated with needs for long-term care. These long-term care indicators, measures of the ability to respond to needs for daily living, demonstrate quite a different picture (see Table 1). Women have substantially greater problems with both activities of daily living (ADL) and instrumental activities of daily living (IADL) measures. ADL measures capture very basic functioning including bathing, dressing, eating, toileting, and transferring (being able to move from chair to bed). IADL measures capture day-to-day activities such as managing money, shopping, and using the telephone.

Health experts thus distinguish between limitations on functioning that lead to needs for supportive services or devices and health problems associated with the need for acute medical care—hospitalization or physician visits, for example. There is clearly a relationship, but not a one-to-one correspondence, between these two types of needs. As Table 1 indicates, men are more likely to report fair or poor health status at any age, but less likely to report functional limitations. Further, functional limitations increase more rapidly with age as compared to deterioration in overall self-reported health status. For both women and men, functional limitations are found in a smaller share of those at young ages than is poor health status, but those proportions reverse in prevalence above age 85. Over half of all women over the age of 85 report limitations on activities of daily living.

[2]Self-reported health status is thought to be a reasonable indicator of need for health services and is often used as a proxy for predicting the use of such services.

Table 1 · HEALTH AND FUNCTIONAL STATUS OF ELDERLY
WOMEN AND MEN BY AGE, 1984

	Percent In Fair or Poor Health	*Percent With Functional Limitations*		
		ADL[1] Limitations	*IADL[2] Limitations*	*Both ADL and IADL Limitations*
Women				
Age				
65–74	30.0	18.4	25.4	14.3
75–84	32.7	31.1	39.6	25.6
85 and over	36.6	52.9	60.6	46.9
Men				
Age				
65–74	32.6	15.4	14.2	8.7
75–84	33.0	22.4	22.2	14.5
85 and over	35.0	39.9	43.2	31.2
Total	32.0	22.7	26.9	17.0

[1]ADL refers to activities of daily living.
[2]IADL refers to instrumental activities of daily living.
Source: Unpublished table prepared by Diane Rowland from the National Health
Interview Survey Supplement on Aging 1984.

Basically, a major reason why women are more likely to need long-term care services is that they are also more likely to survive to that age.

In addition, within any given age group, older women are more likely than older men to have ADL limitations. Part of the reason for these ADL limitations is the high incidence of chronic conditions for women (see Table 2). They are much more likely than men to suffer from arthritis or osteoporosis, diseases that limit mobility (Collins 1988). More surprising is the extent to which women have a higher incidence of heart disease than do men. They are also more likely to suffer from diabetes. Any of these chronic conditions may contribute to a loss of functioning, particularly as women age. But, these estimates are not age adjusted so some of these differences reflect differences in longevity. Moreover, for some conditions that lead to functional limitations—paralysis and mental retardation, for example—men have greater prevalence.

Table 2 • PREVALENCE OF SELECTED CHRONIC CONDITIONS BY
SEX, 1985

Conditions	Rate per 1,000 Persons[1]	
	Women	Men
Heart disease	86.6	79.5
Cerebrovascular disease	10.2	11.7
Emphysema	5.2	13.1
Asthma	39.5	34.6
Mental retardation	3.2	6.3
Paralysis of extremities	5.3	7.3
Multiple sclerosis	0.9	0.4
Arthritis	164.3	95.2
Diabetes	28.7	22.3

[1]Rates are not age-adjusted so higher rates for women may reflect their higher longevity.
Source: Collins 1988.

AVAILABILITY OF INFORMAL CARE

Living longer means that women are more likely to live alone. Most
women outlive their husbands. At birth, women have life expectancies of
about seven years longer than those of men (Public Health Service 1991).
And many women marry men who are older. Thus, it should not be surprising that life expectancy for widowed women in the United States is
about 17 years beyond the death of their spouses—years in which increased
frailty or disability are generally endured alone.

One dramatic indication of this imbalance between women and men can
be seen in Figure 1, which shows the number of men per 100 women by
age group in 1990 (Bureau of the Census 1992d). These numbers decline
dramatically for each higher age group. Above age 85, there are fewer than
four men for every 10 women in the United States. Interestingly, the ratios
are worse for whites than for other ethnic groups. For example, over the age
of 85, there are 38 white men for every 100 white women, but 42 black
men for every 100 black women; the ratio for Hispanics is 55 men to 100
women.

This imbalance is a major contributing factor to the large number of
women who live alone in the United States. Table 3 shows the proportion
of women living alone, living with spouses, or living with others in 1992.

Figure 1 • NUMBER OF MEN PER 100 WOMEN BY AGE, 1990

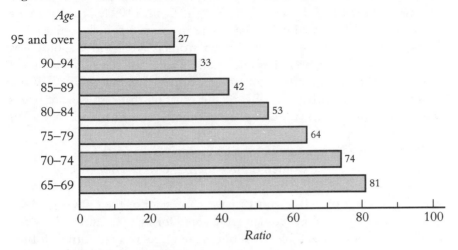

Source: Bureau of the Census 1992d.

Table 3 • LIVING ARRANGEMENTS OF WOMEN AGE 65 AND OVER
BY AGE, RACE, AND HISPANIC ORIGIN, 1992[1]

	Percent Distribution by Living Arrangement		
Women	*Living Alone*	*Living with Spouse*	*Living with Others*
Age 65–74			
All races	34.0	51.4	14.6
White	33.9	53.6	12.5
Black	38.6	32.1	29.4
Hispanic origin[2]	21.8	45.3	32.9
Age 75–84			
All races	50.9	28.6	20.5
White	51.7	29.7	18.6
Black	44.8	17.1	38.1
Hispanic origin	30.2	24.1	45.7
Age 85 and over			
All races	57.9	9.5	32.6
White	59.3	10.0	30.7
Black	37.8	4.7	57.5
Hispanic origin	30.2	2.3	67.5

[1]Includes only the noninstitutional population.
[2]Persons of Hispanic origin may be of any race.
Source: Bureau of the Census 1992c.

After age 85, fewer than one in 10 women lived with a spouse, and almost six out of every 10 lived alone (Bureau of the Census 1992c). And even for women 65 to 74, only a bit over half were in married-couple families. For black women, the proportion of all older women living with a spouse was much lower, but they were less likely to live alone after age 75. Extended families are more important for all minorities than for whites. White women are particularly vulnerable to the isolation that results from being widowed or divorced; many do not have a good support network to lean on for informal care.

Women are much more likely to be caregivers than to be the recipients of informal care. Since women outlive men, the wife is more likely to care for her husband during periods of disability. For example, 37 percent of men over the age of 65 receiving care were cared for by their wives in 1982, but only one-tenth of the women were cared for by their husbands (Manton and Liu 1984) (see Table 4). Women are more likely to turn to formal services to meet their needs. Overall, seven out of 10 caregivers are women; if not wives, they are usually daughters or daughters-in-law of those needing assistance (U.S. Congress 1987).

Table 4 • RELATIONSHIP OF CAREGIVERS TO ELDERLY WOMEN AND MEN RECEIVING CARE BY AGE OF CARE RECIPIENT, 1982

	Percent Cared For By		
Care Recipients	*Spouse*	*Relative*	*Formal Caregiver*
Women			
Age 65–74	18	62	20
Age 75–84	8	71	21
Age 85 and over	2	75	23
Total	10	69	21
Men			
Age 65–74	45	42	13
Age 75–84	35	48	17
Age 85 and over	20	61	19
Total	37	47	16

Source: Manton and Liu 1984.

The good news is that men's longevity is now increasing faster than that of women, meaning that the age differences by gender may lessen somewhat in the future (Bureau of the Census 1992d). But it will take a very long time for those changes to make a dent in the number of older women living alone. In the meantime, an imbalance in the availability and amount of informal services for American women is likely to persist.

THE ABILITY TO AFFORD CARE

For women who must turn to formal care, either at home or in an institutional setting, the question quickly arises as to whether there will be sufficient resources to meet the costs of such care. Even those with moderate levels of income may not be able to afford long-term care services, especially care in a nursing home. The costs of long-term care can quickly consume retirement incomes and then eliminate a lifetime of savings for most women. For example, a nursing home stay in 1988 cost about $22,000 per year—a figure now projected to be closer to $30,000 annually (Rivlin and Wiener 1988). In high cost areas, the annual charge for a nursing home stay can easily reach $45,000. Home care, if not round-the-clock or very intensive, is less costly. A visit can range from about $20 to $80 depending upon the services received. Data from 1987 found that the average cost of a visit was $49 and that a person with substantial disability (three or more ADLs) had, on average, annual charges over $4,000 (Altman and Walden 1993).

In general, women do not have substantial financial resources. Those with the highest incomes are women in married-couple families, who are also more likely to have access to informal support. Older women, particularly those living alone, have substantially fewer resources than do the elderly as a whole. For example, a typical woman living alone and over the age of 65 had an income of only $9,740 in 1991; this median income amount is about one-third of the cost of an average annual nursing home stay (Bureau of the Census 1992a). Actually, older men living alone also have relatively low incomes. Their median income is $12,257. A prototypical married couple age 65 or older has a median income of $25,512.

Further, the oldest old, who are most in need of expensive care, are the least able to pay for such services, since financial resources decline steadily by age. Women over the age of 75 who lived alone had median incomes of only $9,170 in 1991. Minority women also have substantially lower incomes. Black women age 75 and older had median incomes of $6,246 and women of Hispanic origin, $5,853.

Another way to look at economic resources is to focus on those who are most vulnerable. The poverty threshold in 1991 was set at $6,532 for single persons living alone over the age of 65.[3] Even at twice the poverty level ($13,064), most women would find it difficult to afford care. Black women over 75 had poverty rates of 40.8 percent, and 64.5 percent were below 1.5 times poverty. The corresponding figures for women of Hispanic origin over 75 were 27.4 percent and 50.2 percent (Bureau of the Census 1992b) (see Table 5). The numbers are even larger for "unrelated individuals living alone" over age 65—largely widows and divorced women living alone. Over one-fourth of all elderly women living alone were poor in 1991. That number jumped to four in 10 at just 1.25 times the poverty level and over two-thirds had incomes under twice the poverty level. And the picture was much worse for minority women; nearly nine out of every 10 black women living alone had incomes below two times the poverty threshold in 1991.

In considering prospects for the future, one should not assume a simple continuation of these income trends. Incomes of older women have grown in recent years, but this growth does not stem from just one component; rather, most sources of income for the elderly have grown substantially. For example, over the last 27 years, Social Security benefit increases have played an important role in income growth, although as a share of total income that role has grown little since 1975 (Yeas and Grad 1987; Social Security Administration 1990). The increase in Social Security benefits was due to a number of ad hoc policy expansions, and Social Security is not likely to be as strong a source of growth in the future.

The most dramatic growth for the last quarter century has occurred in pensions and asset incomes, reflecting savings and deferred consumption by persons at earlier points in their lives. These sources not only grew in absolute dollars, but they also constituted a considerably larger share of the pie over time. But again there is reason to expect a slowing over time. Coverage from private pensions, for example, has stopped expanding (Zedlewski et al. 1990). Consequently, average income growth from this source of income is also likely to slow in the future.

Another element of economic well-being, wealth, needs to be considered since women may spend down these resources to pay for care. The image of the elderly as "income poor but asset rich" is considerably exaggerated, however. Generally, those with the highest incomes also control the largest amounts of wealth. And older persons with modest means are

[3]This is lower than the poverty threshold for younger persons ($7,086). The reason is that the original poverty threshold measure was developed using only information on differences in food consumption. Most analysts believe that a lower poverty threshold for the elderly is no longer justified. Moreover, Ruggles (1990) has argued that the poverty thresholds are too low overall, meaning that they are particularly out of sync for the elderly. In fact, Ruggles favors using 1.25 times poverty as a better indicator of poverty among older persons.

Table 5 • ELDERLY WOMEN WITH INCOMES BELOW TWICE THE
POVERTY THRESHOLD BY AGE, RACE, AND HISPANIC ORIGIN,
1991

| | Race and Hispanic Origin | | | |
	All Races	White	Black	Hispanic Origin[1]
Women age 65 and over who live alone				
Percent with income				
Below poverty	26.6	23.6	57.8	50.3
Below 1.25 × poverty	40.8	37.6	74.9	76.7
Below 1.50 × poverty	50.8	48.3	79.2	84.5
Below 2.00 × poverty	66.6	64.7	85.7	89.6
All women age 75 and over[2]				
Percent with income				
Below poverty	18.9	17.0	40.8	27.4
Below 1.25 × poverty	29.6	27.7	54.0	43.7
Below 1.50 × poverty	39.8	37.8	64.5	50.2
Below 2.00 × poverty	54.9	53.0	76.7	65.8

[1]Persons of Hispanic origin may be of any race.
[2]Includes women in all living situations.
Source: Bureau of the Census 1992b.

likely to hold much of their wealth in housing—an asset that is difficult to
liquidate to meet short-term needs and that may carry substantial burdens in
the form of high taxes or maintenance costs as well. Financial assets, which
can be readily used to meet short-term needs, are very unequally distributed
across the elderly population. In 1985, the median value of financial assets
for the elderly in the top fifth as ranked by income was about $60,000; it was
only about $4,000 for the bottom fifth of the elderly (U.S. Congress 1989).
In fact, more than one-third of those over age 65 with incomes below the
poverty line reported total assets of less than $1,000 (Ruggles 1990).[4]

One detraction from the well-being of older Americans is the burden of
health care spending by individuals. Despite the presence of Medicare and
Medicaid, the percentage of income spent by individuals over age 65 on

[4]These figures are also interesting in the context of the claim that many older Americans are
divesting themselves of assets so they can qualify for Medicaid. While there are indeed cases
of such activity, there is little evidence that this is common; those most likely to need
institutional care simply have few resources to give away.

unreimbursed health care costs (out-of-pocket spending) and on premiums for Medicare or private insurance is at an all-time high and is projected to increase further (Moon 1993). Incomes have risen for this age group, but out-of-pocket health costs have simply risen faster.

Analyses of the acute care portion of these expenses reveal considerable burdens on those with low or moderate incomes. Feder, Moon, and Scanlon (1987) estimated that in 1986, elderly persons with a hospital stay and an income of less than $10,000 spent 18.3 percent of their income, on average, out of their own pockets for acute health care services (both for unreimbursed services and insurance premiums). And the burdens of these acute care expenses rise with age, so that the oldest old spend even more on acute health care services.

PUBLIC PROGRAMS FOR LONG-TERM CARE

The coverage offered by current public programs is generally agreed to be inadequate. Medicare, the universal program for the elderly and disabled, is an acute care program. It covers home health care and skilled nursing stays. But these benefits are really limited to post-acute care needs and are only available to persons who need skilled care, usually following a hospital stay. Especially for nursing home care, this is a very limited benefit.[5]

Individuals pay for nonskilled home care or nursing home care out of their own resources; when those resources are exhausted—or if they have none to begin with—women largely turn to the welfare-based Medicaid system for support. The sources of payment for formal long-term care services are shown in Figure 2.[6]

Unlike insurance, which protects people against financial catastrophe, the current U.S. system mainly provides protection after catastrophe occurs. Medicaid is thus not an insurance program; it is a welfare program for those who have impoverished themselves. To be eligible for Medicaid, individuals must either initially be poor or spend enough on acute or long-term health care so that their incomes minus health care spending are low enough to qualify. Further they must not have substantial assets.[7] Thus, although

[5]Home health care under Medicare is moving more in the direction of long-term care services, even though it is technically a skilled benefit. Moreover, since the size of the formal home care sector is relatively small, Medicare has played an important role thus far.
[6]In practice, some of the home care spending that goes on less formally—in terms of casual arrangements that involve hiring low-skilled helpers in the home—is not picked up.
[7]The requirements are much more stringent for single individuals—whose assets must generally be less than $2,000, for example. The Medicare Catastrophic Coverage Act relaxed the stringency of income and asset requirements for those with a spouse left in the community.

Figure 2 • SOURCES OF FUNDING FOR NURSING HOME CARE AND HOME HEALTH CARE[1] (percent distribution)

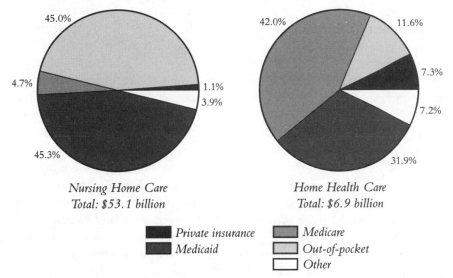

Nursing Home Care
Total: $53.1 billion

Home Health Care
Total: $6.9 billion

■ *Private insurance*   ▨ *Medicare*
■ *Medicaid*   ▨ *Out-of-pocket*
                         □ *Other*

[1]The home health care in this figure is what is reported as a part of health care spending. It consequently excludes informal services, such as help from families or relatives and some less formal paid care.
Source: Levit et al. 1991.

Medicaid does finance nursing home care, to obtain its benefits people give up all of their assets and almost all of their incomes—essentially impoverishing themselves before they can get assistance. This is referred to as "spending down." And even after becoming eligible, families must devote much of their incomes toward the cost of that care; that is, Medicaid only picks up the amounts not paid by the family or individual. In the case of a single person, this amounts to all income above a $30 per month personal needs allowance.

Medicaid is also a joint federal/state program. Although the federal government establishes many standards, it allows some discretion by states in both the breadth of care offered and the generosity of eligibility standards. Consequently, Medicaid is inadequate in another way. A major part of its expenditures are for nursing home care. Program rules encouraged this emphasis in the beginning and nursing home care is a required federal benefit. Although the federal government now allows greater flexibility in

---

In this case, the community dwelling spouse may retain an income of at least 150 percent of the poverty line and assets of up to $60,000.

the services that can be offered, states have been reluctant to also expand substantially into home- and community-based services. Such expansions would result in additional costs to Medicaid at a time when states are feeling considerable fiscal pressure. Thus, it is much easier to qualify for nursing home services than for home care, distorting individual choices.

Furthermore, it is not clear that states can continue to bear the costs of long-term care. In fiscal year 1992, Medicaid spent nearly $39 billion on long-term care (Burwell 1993). These figures represented a 14.3 percent increase in just one year, and long-term care now constitutes about 34 percent of all Medicaid spending. As the Medicaid program faces enormous cost pressures—not only from long-term care but also from its role as a health care safety net for the poor and uninsured—serious questions arise as to the adequacy and quality of the nursing home services Medicaid buys.

Other public programs offer much more modest coverage. Medicare, the acute care program for the aged and disabled, covers less than five percent of nursing home expenses. Indeed, many elderly persons are surprised to discover how little Medicare covers when they need long-term care. Skilled nursing facility benefits and home health care services are offered by Medicare, but are restricted to those with medical problems. At best Medicare provides for transition care for persons after acute episodes (see Figure 2).

Social Services block grants and elderly nutrition programs of the Administration on Aging also offer limited benefits. For example, these programs help fund case management programs and meals-on-wheels to some of those in need. But these are appropriated programs with set budgets each year. They are not very generously funded and have expanded little in the last decade. Moreover, the Social Services block grants cover a variety of services—and long-term care must compete for a share of the total dollars, which have been declining in real terms since 1980 (Pepper Commission 1990).

Private Insurance

Over the last decade, private insurance has emerged as a means for spreading the risk of long-term care. Today, fewer than two million Americans have private long-term care insurance policies.[8] However, if these policies promise adequate protection against likely costs (a standard many do not meet), they will probably not be affordable for the majority of senior citizens most in need of protection. The Health Insurance Association of America (1991)

[8]While two million policies have been sold, at least some of these policies are likely to have lapsed.

estimated the annual premium for such a policy at $1,400 for a 65-year-old in 1990; the average premium was over $4,000 for a 79-year-old. Moreover, these premium amounts would be even higher if they were available to everyone. One of the conditions for such insurance is a health screen; persons with heart conditions, diabetes, arthritis, and a long list of other conditions will likely be turned down for coverage.

A first step for making insurance a viable option would be to establish federal standards to protect consumers. These would include outlawing high pressure tactics in marketing, and requiring inflation protection so that the benefits would provide protection when the services were needed. If products are to be made attractive to younger persons, some type of nonforfeiture benefit is needed to guarantee that someone who pays in for 20 years but then lapses can withdraw some portion of the payments. (Insurance companies now price insurance premiums low for those in their forties, for example, precisely because they believe that many will fail to keep their premiums current until they need the care.) Americans thus far have shown a healthy skepticism about long-term care policies, and it is well-founded.

Estimates prepared for the Pepper Commission (1990) indicated that only six percent of today's elderly population could afford such a policy without spending more than five percent of their income—and even then, they would not be fully protected against the costs of care.[9] Many older Americans wishing to protect themselves from the costs of long-term care would have to lower their standards of living for many years in order to obtain partial protection. Rice, Thomas, and Weissert (1991) also found that the insurance policies they studied failed to provide much protection against the possibility of high out-of-pocket costs from long-term care expenses. High deductibles and relatively low daily payment rates may leave policyholders vulnerable to spending down their assets even if they have insurance, for example.

Thus, private insurance, with the addition of consumer protection standards, can provide a minority of Americans some security against the financial risks of long-term care. But for the vast majority of the elderly, anyone who already has a disabling condition, and the younger population with a small but real risk of long-term care needs, the emerging market provides little prospect of protection.

---

[9]Although five percent does not seem to be an exorbitant amount, it would be in addition to any insurance purchased for acute care. Moreover, since a premium must be consistently paid for many years, most analysts believe that the annual cost needs to be quite low.

PROSPECTS FOR THE FUTURE

If the current picture for long-term care financing looks bleak, the future looks even worse. Projections are that the elderly population will grow by 73 percent in the next 30 years (Bureau of the Census 1992d). The population over age 85, which is most likely to need long-term care, is expected to more than double in that period, growing by 115 percent. The hope is that with increased longevity, important advances against diseases of old age such as Alzheimer's will occur, thereby reducing disability at a particular age. Until recently, research seemed to show that longer lives had not translated into healthier lives, indicating a substantial increase in the need for long-term care (Guralnick 1991). But a study by Manton, Corder, and Stallard (1993) indicates that there may be some age-adjusted declines in disability. This would still mean that the incidence of disability would rise as the population ages, but not by as much as the simple aging of the population would indicate. As yet, it is not clear exactly what the trends will be in the future.

Private insurance coverage may continue to grow, as future older Americans with higher incomes are better able to afford its costs or to purchase it at younger ages. However, even optimistic projections of private insurance growth suggest that 30 years from now, no more than half the nation's senior citizens are likely to have long-term care protection (Rivlin and Wiener 1988). As a result, Rivlin and Wiener estimate that with no change in policy, the demands on the welfare-based Medicaid program will rise with the growth in the elderly population. Their projections indicate that even to keep pace with current levels of service—deemed inadequate by consumers, providers, and experts—expenditures on long-term care, net of inflation, would be triple today's levels.

THE AVAILABILITY AND USE OF SERVICES

As noted earlier, older women obtain long-term care in institutions and in their homes and communities. But the availability of services differs widely.

Care for the most disabled persons in American society has always been in institutions. Once a family can no longer care for the disabled relative, or when a person lives alone, a nursing home becomes the only viable option. In 1987, 59 percent of all residents of nursing homes had limitations in four or more ADLs, and the same percentage had some type of mental disorder (Agency for Health Care Policy and Research [AHCPR] July 1992; AHCPR August 1992). Moreover, women in these institutions were generally more impaired than men.

The 1990 Census found that 1.77 million persons were in nursing homes in 1989, and of that total 1.28 million were women (Bureau of the Census 1993). Women are also more likely to have stays of two years or longer—to be truly long-term residents of these facilities. While women make up 65.3 percent of nursing home admissions, they constitute 71.5 percent of those with long stays (Spence and Wiener 1990).

Two older surveys of nursing home residents offer a more disaggregated look at this population and how it has been changing over time (see Table 6). Overall, the proportion of the population age 55 and older in nursing homes declined between 1977 and 1985 (NCHS 1987). Exceptions were persons over the age of 85, which was dominated by a large increase in the proportion of black women over the age of 85.[10] The causes of this discrepancy are not known, although it may reflect a decline in discrimination, which traditionally limited minority admissions to such institutions.

Table 6 • NURSING HOME RESIDENTS OVER AGE 55 BY SEX, RACE, AND AGE, 1985 AND 1977

	Number of Residents *1985*	*Number of Residents per 1,000 Persons*	
		1985	*1977*
White women			
Age			
55–64	41,800	4.0	5.4
65–74	117,200	13.7	15.8
75–84	346,000	68.6	83.3
85 and over	458,900	258.0	264.6
Black women			
Age			
55–64	4,800	4.2	5.9
65–74	13,500	16.0	17.6
75–84	18,900	45.1	51.6
85 and over	22,800	162.7	125.2
Both sexes, all races			
Age			
55–64	91,800	4.1	4.9
65–74	212,100	12.5	14.5
75–84	509,000	57.7	68.0
85 and over	594,700	219.4	216.4

Source: National Center for Health Statistics 1987.

[10]A similar trend shows up for black men.

Today, many severely impaired individuals remain in their homes. Consequently, use of formal home- and community-based services has grown dramatically over time. Data from 1984 indicated that just 30 percent of all persons with one or more ADL limitations used home- and community-based services (Keenan 1988). By 1987, that figure had risen to 41 percent (AHCPR 1993).

Table 7 shows what types of home- and community-based services were used by women in 1987. Basic home care was by far the most important, followed by senior centers and home-delivered meals—both community-based services (AHCPR 1993). All of the groups in the table had at least one impairment, but other studies have demonstrated that older women are more likely to be severely impaired on average (see Table 1). Consequently, it is notable that use of services did not rise as dramatically by age as by level of impairment. Since impairment rises with age, these figures suggest that the oldest old are less likely to receive care for a given level of impairment. Why might this be so? The oldest old tend to be more isolated and suspicious of outsiders (Berkman 1988). Also as expected, persons who live alone are much more likely to receive formal care than those who live with others.

But equally important is the fact that many impaired women receive no formal home- or community-based services. Table 7 shows that only 41 percent of women with at least one impairment received any formal services. This means that 59 percent of all women with at least one impairment received no formal services at all. Of the severely impaired—women with three or more limitations in activities of daily living—46 percent received no formal services. Such women are generally considered sufficiently impaired to warrant being in nursing facilities. In 1987, this percentage translated into 320,000 women residing in communities with no formal care. Unmet need continues to be a major problem, due in part to lack of resources, but also to lack of a supply of services.

Even for women with sufficient resources to afford care or who qualify for eligibility through Medicare or Medicaid, services may fall short of what is desirable. In many parts of the country, a full range of options is simply not available.

Ideally, a full range of services should be available for persons in need, allowing the type of care received to be tailored to individuals' needs, not to a patchwork of what can be stitched together from what little is available. In some states, the supply of nursing home beds has been constrained in an effort to hold down the costs of providing care (Harrington et al. 1992). Fewer beds mean that even if many persons are eligible for Medicaid, only a limited number of beds are available at any point in time. Waiting lists for

Table 7 • USE OF FORMAL HOME- AND COMMUNITY-BASED SERVICES BY WOMEN AGE 65 AND OVER WHO HAVE FUNCTIONAL LIMITATIONS BY SELECTED CHARACTERISTICS, 1987

Women with Limitations	Number (in millions)	Any Service	Percent Receiving					
			Home Care	Senior Center	Group Meals	Home Meals	Phone Check	Transportation
Total	3.83	41.3	22.8	7.6	6.4	7.5	5.5	6.4
Age								
65–74	1.33	37.8	20.5	7.4	5.5	7.0	3.5	9.0
75–84	1.59	41.0	23.7	8.6	5.3	7.4	6.4	3.8
85 and over	.92	46.8	24.5	6.3	9.7	8.2	6.7	7.1
Functional status								
IADL only[1]	1.56	35.0	15.4	7.8	6.6	6.9	3.1	4.9
2 ADLs[2]	1.47	43.1	23.2	9.4	7.8	8.5	5.4	8.0
3 ADLs or more	.70	54.5	41.0	2.7	2.8	6.9	11.4	7.2
Live alone	1.91	52.5	29.7	8.7	10.1	11.4	7.2	9.1
Live with others	1.81	29.7	16.5	6.1	2.4	3.4	3.9	3.7

[1]IADL refers to instrumental activities of daily living.
[2]ADL refers to activities of daily living.
Source: Unpublished data, Agency for Health Care Policy and Research National Medical Expenditure Survey, 1993.

beds are not uncommon, particularly for those institutions that accept Medicaid patients. The national average of licensed nursing home beds per 1,000 persons age 85 and above—those most likely to use nursing homes—was 5.2 in 1989. But that ratio varied from a low of 0.3 in Alaska to a high of 24.0 in Iowa (Harrington et al. 1992).

Home care is scarce in rural areas, resulting in much greater reliance on nursing homes. While the number of home health agencies are nearly proportionate to the population in rural areas, they tend to be smaller than in urban settings. And when viewed in terms of personnel per square mile to be served, rural areas are much less well served than urban areas (Bishop and Kenney 1992).

Home care in rural areas is often not available because of the costs of sending teams into homes that are widely dispersed. Fewer persons can be served on any given day and, hence, it is not profitable to set up agencies to provide care in such areas. Similarly, in some urban high crime areas, it is difficult to recruit workers willing to make home visits. Both of these supply constraints mean that care is simply less likely to be available to a large proportion of older women.

Since services often follow reimbursement in American society, and since government programs to fund and facilitate long-term care services are not well coordinated and are often restricted, this sector of the economy has been slow to develop. Creative work in fashioning new living environments (such as life care communities) has led to some expansion in services and new exciting programs, but these tend to be limited to the small proportion of the elderly population who can afford to pay for them fully out-of-pocket or to those states that are making more creative use of their long-term care resources. For example, several big corporations, including Marriott and Hyatt, have moved into this market.

OPTIONS FOR REFORM

The current long-term care system creates a number of enormous gaps, resulting in much unmet need. Too little home care is offered for anyone. The need to rely on informal care places undue burdens on women who serve as caregivers. But the most challenging problem is the failure to protect those "in the middle." Very low-income women usually have access to Medicaid and the very well off can afford to pay for care. The biggest coverage gap is for moderate-income persons who must face the loss of their financial independence as well as their physical independence if they wish to have access to care.

While there is widespread agreement that long-term care should be covered by some form of insurance and that government must play a role in the development of that insurance, there is disagreement as to the roles the public and private sectors should play. As in acute care, options range from strategies that would promote private insurance as the most appropriate strategy for the majority of Americans—limiting the public sector to the role of safety net for the poor—to strategies for developing a universal social insurance system to protect all Americans, regardless of income, for long-term care needs. In between are strategies that would provide limited social insurance—combining social insurance for some benefits with a public/ private partnership for others.

PRIVATE INSURANCE/MEDICAID EXPANSION

Some argue that government can most efficiently promote long-term care services by facilitating the expansion of private long-term care insurance. Some advocates of this approach also would add subsidies for private insurance, through tax credits or the provision of enhanced public protections for those who buy insurance, to promote its purchase by moderate-income families. These subsidies would help to lower the costs of insurance. The expansion of private insurance, proponents argue, would minimize the need for government-financed care, although it might be accompanied by some improvements in Medicaid protection of income and assets.

A few states are now experimenting with promoting private insurance by expediting Medicaid eligibility for those who purchase such policies. The private policies are kept more affordable by covering only a limited time period. After that period, individuals could become eligible for Medicaid without spending down all of their assets. This preferential public coverage, added at the "back end" of a stay, would mean that for purchase of more modest insurance, individuals would get full protection for a long nursing home stay. Variations of this approach are being tried in several states, particularly New York and Connecticut (Mahoney 1990). Proponents argue that in the long run this should save Medicaid costs as people will remain off the rolls for longer. Detractors worry that this approach is more likely to appeal to those with higher incomes and still remain unaffordable for women with more modest resources.

Public education could also be expected to facilitate growth in the number of people purchasing long-term care insurance. Furthermore, public standards and oversight to ensure adequate value for the dollar and other consumer protections in the developing marketplace could reduce some of the fears about abuses. Finally, some enhancement of Medicaid benefits—to cover more care at home and to raise the low levels of income and assets nursing home residents are allowed to retain—could improve upon the current system and enhance the quality of life for the impaired population.

However, such a strategy also poses many problems. Even with subsidies, private insurance would remain too expensive for most elderly persons to purchase without substantial financial sacrifice. Subsidies could therefore disproportionately benefit the better off relative to the moderate-income elderly. Even more important, such a strategy would be inadequate to achieve universal protection against long-term care risks—unless the subsidies and Medicaid expansion were much greater than what is usually proposed. As indicated above, even optimistic projections indicate that it would be decades before significant numbers of the elderly had the resources to purchase private long-term care insurance. Moderate-income persons would be the ones who remained outside this system—unless they spent inordinately for insurance protection. In the meantime, inadequacies and impoverishment would persist. And even 40 years from now, long-term care insurance would remain too expensive for more than half of the elderly to purchase at a price less than five percent of income (Pepper Commission 1990).[11]

Pursuing such a strategy would seem ironic, indeed, given public outrage at today's combination of Medicaid and private insurance for the population under age 65. To repeat the nation's experience in health insurance—to intentionally build a system that would inevitably leave out vast numbers of Americans, entail innumerable inefficiencies, and produce uncontrolled increases in health care costs—would be a tragic and avoidable mistake. Much of the debate on health care reform focuses on the inability of low- and moderate-income persons to obtain coverage. The gaps that this mixed private and Medicaid system create for the under 65 acute care insurance environment are analogous to what could develop in long-term care. And just as the acute care environment is being heavily criticized for gaps in coverage, a mixed private-public approach to long-term care could fail to protect the most vulnerable group—women and men of moderate incomes.

---

[11]Early purchase of insurance makes it more affordable, but it also increases the risk of lapsing and receiving no benefits.

SOCIAL INSURANCE

The lack of a large private system of long-term care insurance in the current environment provides policymakers with an opportunity. Rather than struggling to mitigate the inefficiencies and inequities developed over the years, it is possible to build from scratch an efficient, effective system for financing and delivering long-term care.

A social insurance system—defined as one that would offer benefits to all disabled Americans, regardless of income, and that is financed by broad-based taxes—has considerable advantages. It could cover everyone in need and spread costs equitably and progressively across the full population, limiting burdens relative to the ability to pay. Evidence from state experience indicates that government can manage such a system—in ways that support, rather than replace, family-provided care—and contain the growth in service costs.

Despite these advantages, even advocates of this approach question the wisdom of embarking on an extensive public commitment at a time when the nation faces limited fiscal resources and so many worthy claims upon those resources. A full public insurance approach could cost as much as $60 billion annually in new government expenditures. Most particularly, people question the appropriateness of using public resources to provide unlimited protection of the assets or estates for older Americans when the standard of living for so many younger and more vulnerable Americans is in jeopardy. Social insurance ensures coverage to all—including both those with substantial resources and those with little or nothing.

LIMITED SOCIAL INSURANCE

Most people needing long-term care are not seeking to protect their estates. They are at home, struggling to obtain care and maintain their standard of living (Moon 1993). Even many nursing home residents return home after their stays. Evidence indicates that as many as half of nursing home residents stay in the institution less than six months and that half of these "short-stayers" are able to return home (Pepper Commission 1990).[12]

Thus, a third approach to solving the problem builds on the more critical needs of preserving standards of living for those who will remain or return to the community. Home care would be provided as a social insurance benefit. Most users of such care have relatively low incomes and few assets. Moreover, they need to retain a considerable share of their incomes and

---

[12]The others die or are transferred to other facilities.

assets since they remain at home and must continue to be able to afford the routine costs of living. Since home care is considerably less expensive than nursing home care, its expansion would be affordable.[13]

Nursing home care would rely on a more complicated system that would seek to balance needs for help in affording care and asset protection. Such a system would have three parts: social insurance, without regard to income, for people able to return home after short nursing home stays; a floor of asset protection to prevent impoverishment in the case of long nursing home stays; and, for the better off who have additional assets to protect (or who want additional benefits), promotion of private health insurance that satisfies standards for consumer protection—especially nonforfeiture requirements and inflation protection. The social insurance for "front end" protection would ensure that those who could return home would not have spent down their incomes and assets and hence be unable to afford to return to the community. After that initial period, persons would be expected to contribute more to the costs of their care, thus reducing costs over a full social insurance program. This latter part of the program would be similar to the current Medicaid system, but with more generous limits on assets and income.

This approach, which is similar to that recommended by the Pepper Commission (1990), provides the potential to achieve the risk-spreading and public support associated with universal entitlement, while targeting public resources to the low- and moderate-income populations. It also leaves a role for private insurance to serve those with substantial resources who desire further protection.

OTHER POSSIBLE EXPANSIONS

The above options focus on the broadest long-term care issues of financing and access. But there are also a number of other problem areas that policy changes might address, some of them relatively limited in scope.

First, a few expansions in Medicaid could help in the interim while broader changes in policy for long-term care are debated. Asset limits for eligibility could be expanded. And the personal needs allowance (the amount of income left to residents after they make their required contribution to the costs of their care) ought to be raised to at least $100 per month. It is closer to $30 per month now and has not changed for some time in

[13]Home care would be less expensive largely because it would be reserved for those more effectively served at home. For persons with very severe disabilities, comprehensive home care is actually more expensive than nursing home care.

most states. Medicaid should also be expanded to ensure the availability of more home- and community-based services in every state.

In addition, since long-term care insurance is now being offered and sold to Americans, new regulations are needed to protect purchasers and to guarantee that benefits will actually be delivered when needed. This should be federal legislation since many individuals will move across state lines between the initial purchase of policies and claiming benefits.

Some additional support for caregivers might help extend their ability to offer services. The recently passed Family and Medical Leave Act, which ensures that workers can care for sick relatives without jeopardizing their jobs, represents an area where support for caregivers has been increased; by itself, however, the act does not relieve all the burdens facing caregivers. Respite care—that is, giving relatives a chance to themselves recuperate by providing alternative care for periods of a week or two—is often cited by caregivers as an important benefit. This could be added to Medicare or some other existing program. Others have suggested financial support for caregivers in the form of tax credits. This approach would be aimed at compensating those who provide care, often at the expense of reduced family incomes.

Another area for expansion would focus on the supply of services. Coordination of housing, income support, and long-term care services could help stretch even existing public services. At the federal level, such programs are administered by different bureaucracies, creating conflicting rules and unnecessary stumbling blocks. Similarly, modest expansion of Social Services block grants to help facilitate the development of infrastructure—such as care coordination services and development of home modification programs—would be useful.

Finally, it is important to keep pushing for research that may prevent future disability. Some of this requires sophisticated research on the causes of Alzheimer's disease, arthritis, and other medical sources of disability. But research is also needed on ways to prevent falls, to improve nutritional standards, and to understand more about how to help older women remain independent for as long as possible.

CONCLUSION

Too often, long-term care is a subject that gets relegated to the category of "for future consideration." The challenges of meeting needs for disabled persons are formidable and it is not surprising that many policymakers are reluctant to take on this issue. Much of the problem centers on resources—

who will pay for the needs of America's disabled population. Polls indicate strong interest, but too little willingness to pay.

Nonetheless, this is not a problem likely to solve itself. The aging of the population implies increased demands for such services. The larger share of women working outside the home portends a diminished supply of informal caregivers. Prospects for breakthroughs in preventing disabling conditions or improving treatment of disabilities are not very promising.

In this period of national debate on health care reform, if long-term care needs are ignored, American women will be disproportionately disadvantaged. Resources may not be available for a full social insurance program, but this period should offer an opportunity for at least modest expansions to meet the enormous problems faced by the disabled—a group dominated by older women.

AMERICAN WOMEN TODAY: A STATISTICAL PORTRAIT

SECTION 1:

DEMOGRAPHICS[1]

This section profiles the U.S. population and looks at some of the demographic trends that shape—and are shaped by—the lives of individual
women and their families. The continued increase in the proportion of
American families that are headed by women is reflected in the substantial
percentage of children who live with only one of their parents, usually their
mothers. Also striking is the number of elderly women who live alone.

- The majority of Americans are female. Only in the age groups under 30
  do males outnumber females (see Figure 1-1).
- After dropping steeply for decades, fertility rates edged up slightly between 1980 and 1990 (see Figure 1-3).
- Age at first marriage has continued to rise for both women and men. The
  typical first-time bride in 1992 was three and one-half years older than her
  counterpart in 1970 (see Figure 1-5).
- Women and men living together but not married to each other accounted
  for more than three million American households in 1992. Another one-
  and-one-half million households were same sex partnerships (see Table
  1-4).
- Families headed by women have accounted for a growing proportion of
  American families over the last two decades. The proportion headed by
  men, although it remained very small, grew slightly. Still, married couples
  continued to predominate except among black families (see Table 1-3).

[1]The editors are deeply indebted to Bridget Rice for identifying and gathering the necessary
materials as well as for preparing tables and figures for this and the other statistical sections of
The American Woman 1994–95.

- The divorce rate—the number of divorces in a given year per 1,000 persons in the population—has declined slightly in recent years (see Figure 1-6). Even so, the ratio of currently divorced Americans to currently married Americans is at an all-time high (see Table 1-5).
- In 1992, one in five white children and nearly three in five black children lived with a single parent, usually the mother (see Table 1-6).
- In 1992, there were 7.6 million American women age 75 and over. More than half of them lived alone (see Figure 1-8).

Table 1-1 • POPULATION OF THE UNITED STATES IN 1990 BY RACE AND SEX, ACCORDING TO THE DECENNIAL CENSUS OF 1990

The 1990 Census counted more females than males in every racial group except "other."

Race and Sex	Population
Whites	
Females	102,210,190
Males	97,475,880
Blacks	
Females	15,815,909
Males	14,170,151
American Indians, Eskimos, and Aleuts	
Females	992,048
Males	967,186
Asians and Pacific Islanders	
Females	3,715,624
Males	3,558,038
Others[1]	
Females	4,736,684
Males	5,068,163

[1]"Others" are persons who did not classify themselves as one of the identified races.
Source: Bureau of the Census, *1990 Census of Population: General Population Characteristics, United States*, 1992, Table 16.

Figure 1-1 • POPULATION OF THE UNITED STATES BY AGE AND SEX, 1992[1]

Only in the age groups under 30 do males outnumber females.

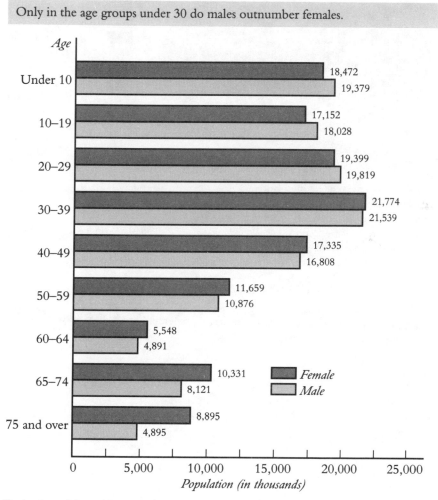

¹Projection of the resident population.

Source: Bureau of the Census, *Population Projections of the United States by Age, Sex, Race, and Hispanic Origin 1992–2050*, 1992, Table 2.

Figure 1-2 • POPULATION OF THE UNITED STATES BY SEX, RACE, AND HISPANIC ORIGIN, 1992[1] (percent distribution)

The proportion of non-Hispanic blacks is slightly larger among females than among males and the proportion of Hispanics is slightly larger among males than among females. In other respects, the distributions of the two sexes are nearly identical.

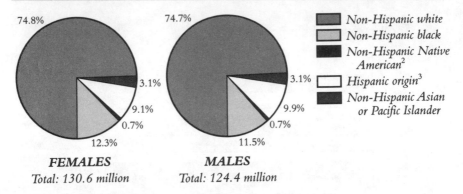

| Non-Hispanic white |
| Non-Hispanic black |
| Non-Hispanic Native American[2] |
| Hispanic origin[3] |
| Non-Hispanic Asian or Pacific Islander |

FEMALES
Total: 130.6 million

MALES
Total: 124.4 million

[1]Projection of the resident population.
[2]Includes non-Hispanic American Indians, Eskimos, and Aleuts.
[3]Persons of Hispanic origin may be of any race.
Source: Bureau of the Census, *Population Projections of the United States by Age, Sex, Race, and Hispanic Origin 1992–2050*, 1992, Table 2.

Figure 1-3 • U.S. FERTILITY RATES BY RACE, 1960–1990[1]

After dropping steeply for decades, fertility rates edged up slightly between 1980 and 1990.

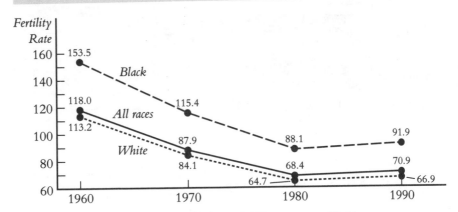

[1]Fertility rates are the number of live births per 1,000 women age 15–44.
Source: National Center for Health Statistics, "Advance Report of Final Natality Statistics, 1990," *Monthly Vital Statistics Report*, February 1993, Table 1.

Table 1-2 • MARITAL STATUS BY SEX, RACE, AND HISPANIC ORIGIN, MARCH 1992[1] (percent distribution)

A larger proportion of men than of women are either currently married and living with their spouses or have never married. This is because the formerly married account for a larger proportion of the women than of the men: in 1992, more than one-fifth of women overall were either widowed or currently divorced, compared to about 11 percent of men.

Marital Status	All Races		White		Black		Hispanic Origin[2]	
	Women	*Men*	*Women*	*Men*	*Women*	*Men*	*Women*	*Men*
Married, spouse present	55.3	60.3	58.6	63.1	31.4	39.1	53.3	53.7
Married, spouse absent	3.8	3.0	3.0	2.4	9.2	6.9	7.4	6.3
Widowed	11.7	2.9	11.8	2.7	12.3	4.5	7.2	1.7
Divorced	9.9	7.6	9.6	7.6	12.2	9.1	8.7	5.9
Never married	19.2	26.2	16.9	24.2	35.0	40.4	23.5	32.4
Total percent	100.0	100.0	100.0	100.0	100.0	100.0	100.0	100.0
Total number (in thousands)	96,599	88,663	81,628	75,970	11,505	9,457	7,249	7,171

[1]Persons age 18 and over.

[2]Persons of Hispanic origin may be of any race.

Source: Bureau of the Census, *Marital Status and Living Arrangements: March 1992*, 1992, Table 1.

Figure 1-4 • CURRENTLY MARRIED AND NEVER MARRIED ADULTS BY SEX, RACE, AND HISPANIC ORIGIN, MARCH 1992[1] (in percentages)

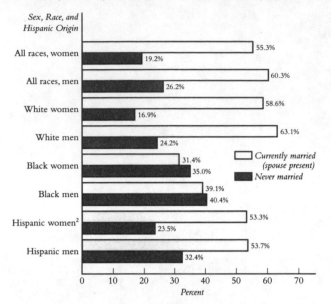

¹Persons age 18 and over.
²Persons of Hispanic origin may be of any race.
Source: Bureau of the Census, *Marital Status and Living Arrangements: March 1992,* 1992, Table 1.

Figure 1-5 • MEDIAN AGE AT FIRST MARRIAGE BY SEX, 1970–1992

Age at first marriage has continued to rise for both women and men. The typical first-time bride in 1992 was three and one-half years older than her counterpart in 1970.

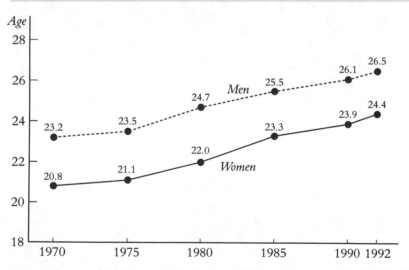

Source: Bureau of the Census, *Marital Status and Living Arrangements: March 1992,* 1992, Table B.

Table 1-3 • FAMILIES BY FAMILY TYPE, RACE, AND HISPANIC
ORIGIN, 1970, 1980, 1990, AND 1991 (percent distribution)

> Families headed by women have accounted for a growing proportion of American families over the last two decades. The proportion headed by men, although it remained very small, grew slightly—it was 4.5 percent in 1991. Still, although married couples account for a smaller proportion of families than they used to, they predominate except among black families.

Family Type	1970	1980	1990	1991
ALL RACES				
Married-couple	86.7	81.7	78.6	78.1
Wife in paid labor force	—	41.0	45.7	46.0
Wife not in paid labor force	—	40.7	32.9	32.1
Male-headed, no spouse present	2.4	3.2	4.4	4.5
Female-headed, no spouse present	10.9	15.1	17.0	17.4
Total percent	100.0	100.0	100.0	100.0
Total number (in thousands)	51,237	60,309	66,322	67,173
WHITE				
Married-couple	88.6	85.1	82.8	82.4
Wife in paid labor force	—	42.0	47.5	48.0
Wife not in paid labor force	—	43.1	35.2	34.4
Male-headed, no spouse present	2.2	3.0	4.0	4.1
Female-headed, no spouse present	9.1	11.9	13.2	13.5
Total percent	100.0	100.0	100.0	100.0
Total number (in thousands)	46,022	52,710	56,803	57,224
BLACK				
Married-couple	68.0	53.7	47.8	47.1
Wife in paid labor force	—	32.0	31.4	31.4
Wife not in paid labor force	—	21.7	16.3	15.7
Male-headed, no spouse present	3.7	4.6	6.3	6.5
Female-headed, no spouse present	28.2	41.7	45.9	46.4
Total percent	100.0	100.0	100.0	100.0
Total number (in thousands)	4,774	6,317	7,471	7,716

(continued)

Table 1-3 (continued)

Family Type	1970	1980	1990	1991
HISPANIC ORIGIN[1]				
Married-couple	—	73.1	69.3	68.2
Wife in paid labor force	—	33.8	35.2	35.6
Wife not in paid labor force	—	39.4	34.2	32.6
Male-headed, no spouse present	—	5.1	6.9	7.4
Female-headed, no spouse present	—	21.8	23.8	24.4
Total percent	—	100.0	100.0	100.0
Total number (in thousands)	—	3,235	4,981	5,177

[1]Persons of Hispanic origin may be of any race.
Source: Bureau of the Census, *Household and Family Characteristics: 1970,* 1971, Table 6; *Money Income and Poverty Status of Families in the United States: 1980,* 1981, Table 1; *Money Income of Households, Families and Persons in the United States: 1990,* 1991, Table 13 and *1991,* 1992, Table 13.

Table 1-4 • HOUSEHOLDS WITH UNRELATED PARTNERS BY SEX OF PARTNERS AND PRESENCE OF CHILDREN, 1992[1] (numbers in thousands)

In 1992, nearly five million households were composed of two adults living together as partners. About one-third of the households where the partners were of the opposite sex contained children, as did about one-sixth of those with two female partners. Children were rarely present in households where both partners were male.

Household Type	Number of Households	With Children	
		Number	Percent
Partners of opposite sex	3,308	1,121	33.9
Female householder, male partner	1,427	530	37.1
Male householder, female partner	1,881	591	31.4
Partners of same sex	1,564	130	8.3
Both partners female	660	110	16.7
Both partners male	904	20	2.2
Total	4,872	1,251	25.7

[1]Partners over age 18; children under age 15.
Source: Bureau of the Census, *Marital Status and Living Arrangements: March 1992,* 1992, Table 8.

Figure 1-6 • THE DIVORCE RATE, 1970, 1980, 1990, AND 1992[1]

The divorce rate—the number of divorces in a given year per 1,000 persons in the population—has declined slightly in recent years.

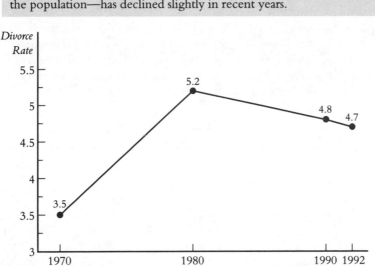

[1]The rate for 1992 is for the 12 months ending with September 1992.
Source: Bureau of the Census, *Statistical Abstract of the United States 1990,* 1990, Table 126 and *1992,* 1992, Table 134; and National Center for Health Statistics, *Monthly Vital Statistics Report,* February 16, 1993.

Table 1-5 • DIVORCE RATIOS BY SEX, RACE, AND HISPANIC ORIGIN, 1970, 1980, 1990, AND 1992[1]

Even though the divorce *rate* has declined recently (as shown in Figure 1-6), the divorce *ratio* has been rising because the number of currently divorced persons has continued to increase faster than the number of currently married persons. A relatively low proportion of currently married persons (as in the case of blacks— see Figure 1-4) helps produce a relatively higher divorce ratio.

	1970		1980		1990		1992	
	Women	*Men*	*Women*	*Men*	*Women*	*Men*	*Women*	*Men*
All races	60	35	120	79	166	118	179	126
White	56	32	110	74	153	112	164	120
Black	104	62	258	149	358	208	391	232
Hispanic origin[2]	81	40	132	64	155	103	161	110

[1]The divorce ratio is the number of divorced persons per 1,000 married persons with spouses present.
[2]Persons of Hispanic origin may be of any race.
Source: Bureau of the Census, *Marital Status and Living Arrangements: March 1990,* 1991, Table C and *Marital Status and Living Arrangements, March 1992,* 1992, Table D.

Table 1-6 • CHILDREN'S LIVING ARRANGEMENTS BY RACE AND HISPANIC ORIGIN, 1970, 1980, AND 1992[1] (percent distribution)

In 1992, one in five white children (21 percent) and nearly three in five black children (57 percent) lived with a single parent, usually the mother. The proportion was nearly one in three for Hispanic children (32 percent). Although the percentages of children living in single-father families increased between 1970 and 1992, they remained very small.

	1970	*1980*	*1992*
ALL RACES			
Living with two parents	85.2	76.7	70.7
Living with mother only	10.8	18.0	23.3
Living with father only	1.1	1.7	3.3
Other[2]	2.9	3.7	2.6
Total percent	100.0	100.0	100.0
Total number (in thousands)	69,162	63,427	65,965
WHITE			
Living with two parents	89.5	82.7	77.4
Living with mother only	7.8	13.5	17.6
Living with father only	0.9	1.6	3.3
Other	1.8	2.2	1.7
Total percent	100.0	100.0	100.0
Total number (in thousands)	58,790	52,242	52,493
BLACK			
Living with two parents	58.5	42.2	35.6
Living with mother only	29.5	43.9	53.8
Living with father only	2.3	1.9	3.1
Other	9.7	12.0	7.5
Total percent	100.0	100.0	100.0
Total number (in thousands)	9,422	9,375	10,427

(continued)

Table 1-6 (continued)

	1970	1980	1992
HISPANIC ORIGIN[3]			
Living with two parents	77.7	75.4	64.8
Living with mother only	—	19.6	28.5
Living with father only	—	1.5	3.7
Other	—	3.5	3.1
Total percent	—	100.0	100.0
Total number (in thousands)	4,006	5,459	7,619

[1]Children under age 18.
[2]Living with relatives other than parents or with nonrelatives.
[3]Persons of Hispanic origin may be of any race.
Source: Bureau of the Census, *Marital Status and Living Arrangements: March 1992,* 1992, Table G.

Figure 1-7 • HOUSEHOLDS WITH FEMALE HOUSEHOLDERS BY TENURE, TYPE, AND PRESENCE OF CHILDREN, MARCH 1991[1] (percent distribution)

Women who head families with children account for a much higher percentage of female householders who rent than of those who own. Most of the latter are women who live alone, who in 1991 accounted for 58 percent of female homeowners.

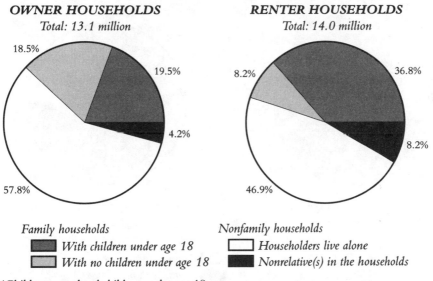

OWNER HOUSEHOLDS
Total: 13.1 million

18.5%
19.5%
4.2%
57.8%

RENTER HOUSEHOLDS
Total: 14.0 million

8.2%
36.8%
8.2%
46.9%

Family households
■ *With children under age 18*
▨ *With no children under age 18*

Nonfamily households
☐ *Householders live alone*
■ *Nonrelative(s) in the households*

[1]Children are related children under age 18.
Source: Bureau of the Census, *Household and Family Characteristics: March 1991,* 1992, Table 6.

Figure 1-8 • LIVING ARRANGEMENTS OF PERSONS AGE 65 AND OVER BY SEX, MARCH 1991 (percent distribution)

This figure illustrates the long-term consequences of women's longer life expectancy combined with their propensity to marry older men—women are likely to wind up living alone. In 1992, 34 percent of women age 65–74 lived alone; the comparable proportion of men was 13 percent. Of the women age 75 and over, over half lived alone and less than a quarter lived with a spouse.

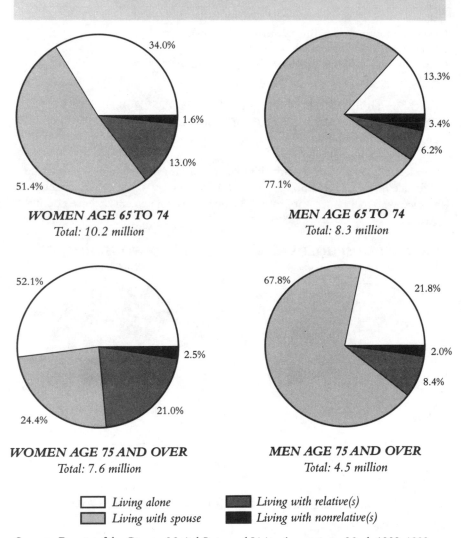

WOMEN AGE 65 TO 74
Total: 10.2 million

MEN AGE 65 TO 74
Total: 8.3 million

WOMEN AGE 75 AND OVER
Total: 7.6 million

MEN AGE 75 AND OVER
Total: 4.5 million

☐ *Living alone*   ▨ *Living with relative(s)*
▨ *Living with spouse*   ■ *Living with nonrelative(s)*

Source: Bureau of the Census, *Marital Status and Living Arrangements: March 1992*, 1992, Table J.

SECTION 2:

EDUCATION

The percentage of American women age 25 and over who have at least a high school education increased substantially between 1970 and 1990, particularly among black women. However, the trend with respect to college enrollment by blacks is not encouraging and the lack of secondary education is a major problem among foreign-born Hispanic women. At the post-secondary level, women have made notable gains: their share of college degrees awarded in science and math has grown and their presence among the graduates of dental, medical, and law schools has continued to increase.

- As of 1991, about two in five American women age 25 and over were high school graduates who had not gone on to college. Another 18.9 percent—nearly one in five—had finished at least four years of college (see Table 2-1).
- Although white women are still the most likely to have had 12 or more years of schooling, it was among black women that the proportion with at least 12 years of schooling increased most dramatically between 1970 and 1991 (see Figure 2-1).
- Whether U.S.-born or not, U.S. women of Asian descent are more likely than other U.S. women age 25 to 54 to have had four or more years of college (see Table 2-2).
- Lack of education is a particular problem among foreign-born women of Hispanic origin. As of 1989, over 40 percent of those age 25 to 54 had no more than eight years of schooling (see Table 2-2).
- Between 1976 and 1990, non-Hispanic whites' predominance among college students declined a few percentage points as the Hispanic and Asian/Pacific Islander proportions increased. The trend with respect to black enrollment was not encouraging (see Table 2-3).

- Of all women students in institutions of higher learning in 1990, one-third were at least 30 years old—double the comparable proportion in 1970 (see Figure 2-2).
- Women outnumbered men among the recipients of postsecondary degrees in 1989/90 at every level except the doctoral level (see Figure 2-4).
- The presence of women in America's medical schools has steadily increased, although it was among dentistry graduates that the presence of women increased most sharply between 1976/77 and 1989/90 (see Figure 2-6 and Table 2-7).
- In 1990/91, as in 1980/81, most of the men on the faculties of four-year colleges and universities had tenure and most of their female counterparts did not (see Figure 2-7).

Table 2-1 · EDUCATIONAL ATTAINMENT BY SEX, RACE, AND HISPANIC ORIGIN, 1991[1]

As of 1991, about two in five (41.3 percent) American women age 25 and over were high school graduates who had not gone on to college. Another 18.9 percent—nearly one in five—had finished at least four years of college. Educational attainment was typically lower among Hispanics of both sexes than among blacks or whites.

| | Number (in thousands) | Percent Distribution | | | | |
| | | −High School− | | | —College— | |
		0–8 Years	1–3 Years	4 Years	1–3 Years	4 Years or More
All races						
Women	82,635	9.6	11.5	41.3	18.7	18.9
Men	74,937	10.4	10.5	36.3	18.3	24.5
White						
Women	70,528	9.1	10.5	42.1	18.9	19.4
Men	65,003	9.8	9.9	36.3	18.5	25.5
Black						
Women	9,397	13.2	19.6	37.5	18.1	11.7
Men	7,518	15.8	16.6	38.9	17.2	11.6
Hispanic origin[2]						
Women	5,469	30.5	16.2	31.4	12.2	9.8
Men	5,315	31.4	15.3	29.5	13.4	10.4

[1]Persons age 25 and over.

[2]Persons of Hispanic origin may be of any race.

Source: Bureau of the Census, *Educational Attainment in the United States: March 1991 and 1990,* 1992, Table 1.

Figure 2-1 • WHITE, BLACK, AND HISPANIC WOMEN AGE 25 AND OVER WITH 12 OR MORE YEARS OF EDUCATION, 1970, 1980, AND 1991

Although as of 1991 white women remained the most likely to have had 12 or more years of schooling, it was among black women that the proportion with at least 12 years of education increased most dramatically between 1970 and 1991.

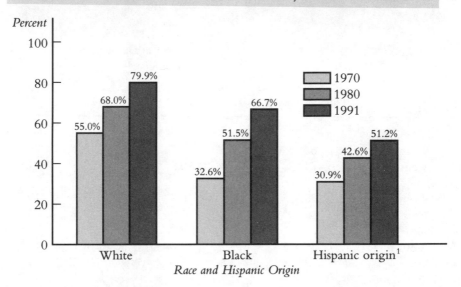

[1]Persons of Hispanic origin may be of any race.

Source: Bureau of the Census, *Statistical Abstract of the United States 1990,* 1990, Table 216 and *Statistical Abstract of the United States 1992,* 1992, Table 220.

Table 2-2 • EDUCATIONAL ATTAINMENT OF U.S.- AND
FOREIGN-BORN WOMEN AGE 25 TO 54 BY RACE AND HISPANIC
ORIGIN, 1989[1]

Whether born in this country or not, women of Asian descent are more likely
than other women between the ages of 25 and 54 to have had four or more years
of college. Lack of education is a particular problem among foreign-born
women of Hispanic origin. As of 1989, over 40 percent had had no more than
eight years of schooling.

	Number (in thousands)	Percent Distribution				
		—High School—			—College—	
		0–8 Years	*1–3 Years*	*4 Years*	*1–3 Years*	*4 Years or More*
Non-Hispanic white						
U.S.-born	37,928	2.2	7.6	43.4	22.3	24.6
Foreign-born	1,224	9.9	4.4	37.8	19.8	28.1
Non-Hispanic black						
U.S.-born	5,821	5.1	16.8	44.0	20.8	13.3
Foreign-born	314	11.7	6.7	46.6	20.3	14.8
Non-Hispanic Asian						
U.S.-born	312	1.0	1.3	33.5	26.5	37.7
Foreign-born	1,150	13.3	5.5	22.4	16.6	42.2
Hispanic origin[2]						
U.S.-born	2,125	15.1	15.9	42.4	17.2	9.5
Foreign-born	1,848	43.9	12.2	25.6	9.5	8.9

[1]Civilian noninstitutional population.
[2]Persons of Hispanic origin may be of any race.
Source: Bureau of Labor Statistics, "How Do Immigrants Fare in the U.S. Labor Market?"
Monthly Labor Review, December 1992, Table 5.

Table 2-3 · COLLEGE ENROLLMENT BY SEX, RACE, AND HISPANIC
ORIGIN, 1976, 1984, AND 1990[1] (percent distribution)

Between 1976 and 1990, non-Hispanic whites continued to predominate heavily among college students of both sexes, although their proportion declined a few percentage points as the Hispanic and Asian/Pacific Islander proportions increased. The trends with respect to black and Native American enrollment were not encouraging.

	Women			Men		
	1976	1984	1990[2]	1976	1984	1990[2]
Non-Hispanic white	82.4	80.9	78.8	84.4	82.4	80.0
Non-Hispanic black	11.5	10.7	10.6	9.0	8.3	8.4
Hispanic origin[3]	3.6	4.7	6.0	4.0	4.8	6.1
Asian/Pacific Islander	1.8	2.9	3.7	1.9	3.7	4.7
Native American	0.8	0.8	0.9	0.7	0.7	0.8
Total percent	100.0	100.0	100.0	100.0	100.0	100.0
Total number (in thousands)	4,475	5,535	6,427	4,801	4,860	5,210

[1]Table excludes nonresident alien students.
[2]Data for 1990 are preliminary.
[3]Persons of Hispanic origin may be of any race.
Source: National Center for Education Statistics, Digest of Education Statistics 1992, 1992, Table 194.

Figure 2-2 • WOMEN ENROLLED IN COLLEGES AND UNIVERSITIES BY AGE, 1970, 1980, AND 1990[1] (percent distribution)

One-third of all women students enrolled in institutions of higher learning in 1990 were at least 30 years old—double the comparable proportion in 1970.

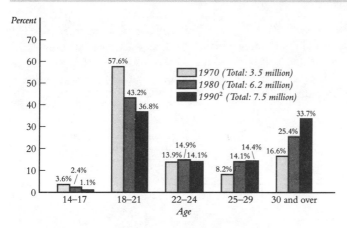

[1]Includes undergraduates, students in graduate programs, and students seeking first professional degrees (i.e., in law, medicine, etc.).
[2]Estimated.
Source: National Center for Education Statistics, *Digest of Education Statistics 1992,* 1992, Table 162.

Figure 2-3 • STUDENTS ENROLLED IN COLLEGES AND UNIVERSITIES BY SEX AND FULL- OR PART-TIME STATUS, 1970, 1980, AND 1990[1]

In 1990, nearly four million women were enrolled as full-time students in institutions of higher learning, up from about 2.3 million in 1970. The number of men enrolled full time increased by less than 300,000 over that period. The number of part-time students of both sexes increased, but much more dramatically for women.

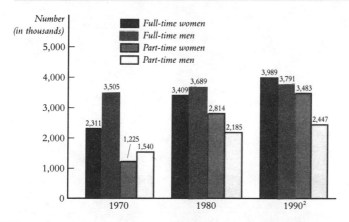

[1]Fall enrollments. Includes undergraduates, students in graduate programs, and students seeking first professional degrees (i.e., in law, medicine, etc.).
[2]Estimated.
Source: National Center for Education Statistics, *Digest of Education Statistics 1992,* 1992, Table 162.

Table 2-4 · WOMEN AWARDED UNDERGRADUATE DEGREES IN
SELECTED FIELDS, 1959/60–1989/90 (in percentages)

Between 1959/60 and 1989/90, women's share of all bachelor's degrees awarded
in biology doubled, and their share of business degrees sextupled. Women also
made gains in engineering and mathematics. Nevertheless, an English major
graduating from college in 1989/90 was even more likely to be a woman than
had been the case 30 years earlier.

| Field | Degrees Awarded to Women as a Percentage of All Degrees Awarded | | | |
	1959/60	1969/70	1979/80	1989/90
Biological sciences	25.2	27.8	42.1	50.7
Business	7.4	8.7	33.7	46.7
Computer and information sciences[1]	—	13.6	30.2	30.1
Education	71.1	75.0	73.8	78.1
Engineering	0.4	0.8	9.3	13.8
English	62.3	66.9	66.1	67.9
Health professions[1]	—	77.1	82.2	84.3
Mathematics	27.2	37.4	42.3	46.5
Physical sciences	12.5	13.6	23.7	31.2
Psychology	40.8	43.3	63.3	71.5
Social sciences[1]	—	36.8	43.6	44.2
Visual and performing arts[1]	—	59.7	63.2	61.4

[1]Data are for 1970/71 rather than 1969/70.
Source: National Center for Education Statistics, *Digest of Education Statistics 1992*, 1992,
Tables 263, 265, 266, 267, 269, 272, 273, 275, 276, 278, 280, and 282.

Table 2-5 • TEN MOST POPULAR MAJORS AMONG BACHELOR'S DEGREE RECIPIENTS BY SEX, AND BY RACE AND HISPANIC ORIGIN FOR WOMEN, 1989/90 (in rank order)[1]

Overall, women and men had seven favorite fields in common, although the rankings differed except for business and management. Asian/Pacific Islander women were the only women students for whom engineering ranked among the top 10.

Major Field	Men Total	Women Total	Non-Hispanic Women White	Black	Asian/Pac. Islander	Native American	Hispanic Women
Business and management[2]	1	1	1	1	1	2	1
Education	4	2	2	4	10	1	2
Social sciences	2	3	4	2	2	3	3
Health sciences	—	4	3	3	4	4	5
Psychology	10	5	5	5	6	5	4
Letters	9	6	7	8	9	6	7
Communications	5	7	6	6	—	9	6
Visual and performing arts[3]	—	8	8	—	7	10	—
Life sciences	6	9	9	9	3	—	10
Liberal/general studies	—	10	10	—	—	8	9
Public affairs[4]	—	—	—	7	—	7	—
Engineering	3	—	—	—	5	—	—
Foreign languages	—	—	—	—	—	—	8
Computer/information sciences	7	—	—	10	8	—	—
Engineering technologies	8	—	—	—	—	—	—
Percentage of all degree recipients accounted for by top 10 majors	77%	83%	83%	81%	80%	83%	81%

[1]Preliminary data. Nonresident aliens are excluded.

[2]Includes business and management, business and office, marketing and distribution, and consumer and personal services.

[3]Includes visual and performing arts and precision production.

[4]Includes public affairs and transportion and material moving.

Source: National Center for Education Statistics, *Digest of Education Statistics 1992,* 1992, Table 250.

Table 2-6 • WOMEN GRADUATES OF U.S. SERVICE ACADEMIES, 1980, 1990, AND 1993

The classes of 1980 were the first to include women. The increase in the percentage of women in the service academies since then has been modest.

| Service Academy | Women as a Percentage of Graduates | | | Number of Women in Class of 1993 |
	Class of 1980	*Class of 1990*	*Class of 1993*	
Air Force	10.9	10.4	10.9	105
Coast Guard	9.2	12.6	14.0	25
Military (West Point)	6.8	9.8	9.7	98
Naval	5.8	9.7	8.5	89

Source: Unpublished data provided by each service academy, June 1993.

Figure 2-4 • RECIPIENTS OF POSTSECONDARY DEGREES BY SEX, 1959/60–1989/90

In 1989/90, women outnumbered men among recipients of postsecondary degrees at every level except the doctoral level.

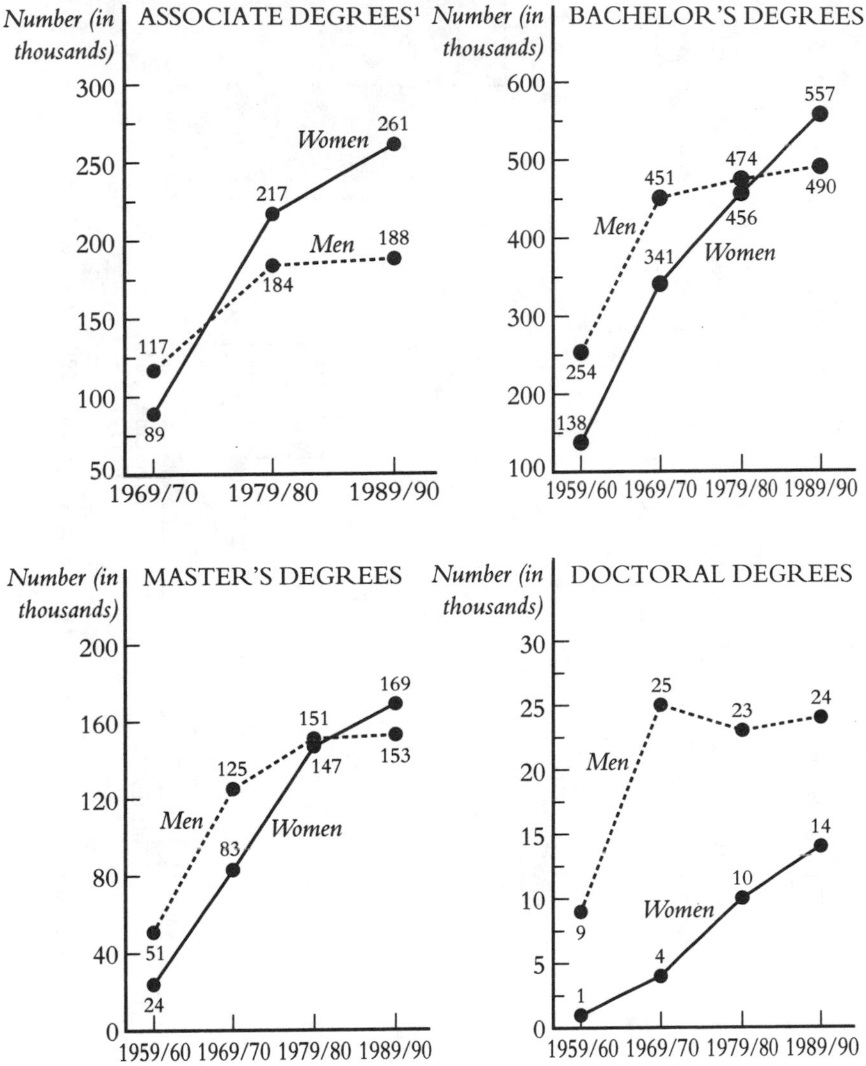

Number (in thousands) ASSOCIATE DEGREES[1]

Women 261
217
Men 188
184
117
89

1969/70   1979/80   1989/90

Number (in thousands) BACHELOR'S DEGREES

557
451   474
490
Men 456
341   *Women*
254
138

1959/60 1969/70 1979/80 1989/90

Number (in thousands) MASTER'S DEGREES

169
151
125   147   153
Men   *Women*
83
51
24

1959/60 1969/70 1979/80 1989/90

Number (in thousands) DOCTORAL DEGREES

25   24
23
Men
14
10
Women
9
4
1

1959/60 1969/70 1979/80 1989/90

[1]1959/60 data not available for associate degrees.
Source: National Center for Education Statistics, *Digest of Education Statistics 1992*, 1992, Tables 246, 249, 252, and 255.

Figure 2-5 • FIRST PROFESSIONAL DEGREES AWARDED IN SELECTED FIELDS BY SEX OF RECIPIENTS, 1989/90

Men predominated among those awarded their first professional degrees in dentistry, medicine, and law in 1989/90. However, as Table 2-7 below shows, this figure represents a good deal of progress for women in these fields.

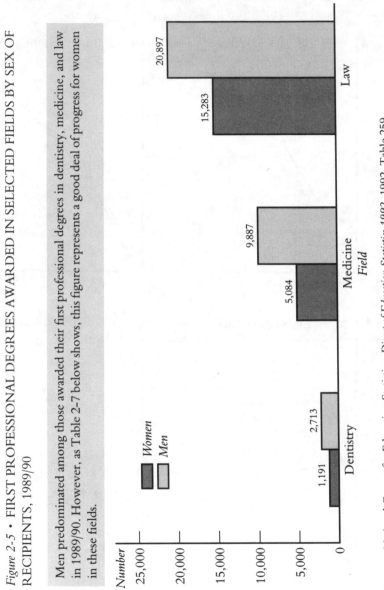

Source: National Center for Education Statistics, *Digest of Education Statistics 1992*, 1992, Table 259.

Table 2-7 • WOMEN AWARDED FIRST PROFESSIONAL DEGREES IN SELECTED FIELDS BY RACE AND HISPANIC ORIGIN, 1976/77 AND 1989/90[1] (percent distribution)

By 1989/90, the number of women who received dentistry degrees had tripled from 1976/77. Women's presence in the graduating classes of medical and law schools also increased, but not so sharply. Minority representation was highest among the recipients of dentistry degrees and lowest among law degree recipients.

	Dentistry		Medicine		Law	
	1976/77	1989/90	1976/77	1989/90	1976/77	1989/90
Total number of degrees awarded to women	367	1,191	2,543	5,084	7,630	15,283
Non-Hispanic white	82.8	68.1	86.7	77.1	90.5	86.9
Non-Hispanic black	12.0	7.2	9.5	9.1	5.8	6.3
Hispanic origin[2]	1.6	8.1	1.7	3.9	1.6	3.7
Asian/Pacific Islander	3.0	16.1	1.9	9.5	1.7	2.7
Native American	0.5	0.5	0.2	0.4	0.4	0.5
Total percent	100.0	100.0	100.0	100.0	100.0	100.0
Degrees awarded to women as a percentage of all degrees	7.3	29.1	19.1	33.6	22.5	41.9

[1]Data exclude nonresident aliens. Data for 1989/90 are preliminary.
[2]Persons of Hispanic origin may be of any race.
Source: U.S. Department of Health, Education, and Welfare, Office for Civil Rights, *Data on Earned Degrees Conferred by Institutions of Higher Education by Race, Ethnicity and Sex, Academic Year 1976–77* and National Center for Education Statistics, *Digest of Education Statistics 1992*, 1992, Table 259.

Table 2-8 · NEW ENTRANTS TO AND GRADUATES FROM U.S. MEDICAL SCHOOLS BY SEX, 1986–1992

	New Entrants		Graduates	
Year	Women	Men	Women	Men
1986	5,576	10,529	4,957	11,160
1987	5,767	10,160	5,107	10,723
1988	5,878	10,091	5,215	10,704
1989	6,025	9,842	5,221	10,409
1990	6,153	9,845	5,231	10,167
1991	6,433	9,778	5,553	9,874
1992	6,772	9,517	5,550	9,815

Source: Association of American Medical Colleges, *Facts: Applicants, Matriculants and Graduates 1986 to 1992,* October 20, 1992.

Figure 2-6 · GRADUATES FROM U.S. MEDICAL SCHOOLS BY SEX, 1986–1992

The number and proportion of women among the graduates of America's medical schools has been increasing. Judging by Table 2-8 above, which shows that women's presence has also been steadily increasing among those entering medical schools, it seems safe to assume that women's share of medical degrees will continue to increase.

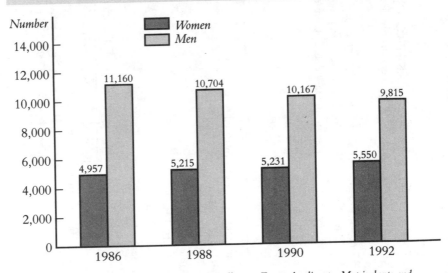

Source: Association of American Medical Colleges, *Facts: Applicants, Matriculants and Graduates 1986 to 1992,* October 20, 1992.

Figure 2-7 · FACULTY WITH TENURE BY SEX AND TYPE OF
INSTITUTION, 1980/81 AND 1990/91

In 1990/91, as in 1980/81, the majority of men on the faculties of four-year
colleges and universities had tenure and the majority of their female counterparts
did not—in fact, the tenured proportions hardly changed for either sex between
1980/81 and 1990/91.

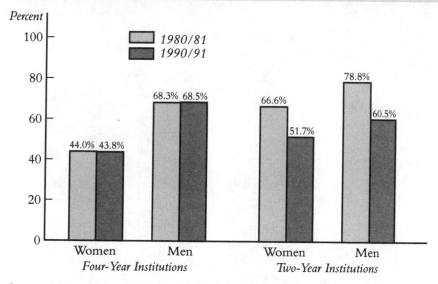

Source: National Center for Education Statistics, *Digest of Education Statistics 1992*, 1992,
Table 224.

Figure 2-8 • WOMEN HEADS OF PUBLIC AND PRIVATE COLLEGES
AND UNIVERSITIES, SELECTED YEARS, 1975–1992[1]

In 1992, 164 public colleges and universities had women CEOs, up from only
16 in 1975. The number of private institutions headed by women has consistently been higher. (However, according to the American Council on Education, in 1992 women constituted only about 12 percent of CEOs at all regionally
accredited institutions.)

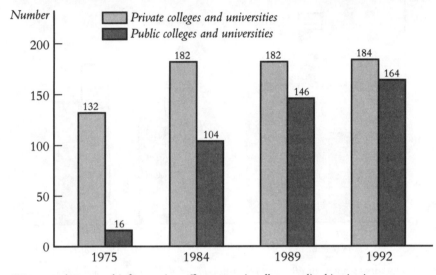

[1]Women who were chief executive officers at regionally accredited institutions.
Source: American Council on Education, Office of Women in Higher Education, *Women
Chief Executive Officers in U.S. Colleges and Universities, Table XIII, April 15, 1992,* 1992.

EMPLOYMENT

As women's labor force participation has grown steadily during the past several decades, the number of women who work full time has grown even faster. This trend is particularly striking in the case of working mothers, the majority of whom are employed full time. Women have significantly increased their presence in certain once heavily male-dominated professions—such as medicine and the law—but women's presence in skilled blue-collar jobs continues to be minute. In general, women workers—and especially black and Hispanic women—still tend to be more heavily concentrated than men in a few industries and occupations.

- Between 1960 and 1992, the female labor force participation rate rose from 38 percent to 58 percent and the female proportion of the U.S. labor force grew from 33 percent to 45 percent (see Figure 3-1 and Table 3-1).
- Between 1971 and 1991, while the total number of employed women increased by 60 percent, the number who were employed full time, year round doubled. Over half of all women employed in 1991 were full-time year-round workers, up from 42 percent two decades earlier (see Figure 3-5).
- Most working mothers work full-time, even if their children are toddlers. In 1992, nearly 70 percent of employed mothers with children under three worked full time, up from 64 percent in 1982 (see Table 3-16).
- Through the 1980s and into the early 1990s, the unemployment rate for black women was more than twice that for white women (see Figure 3-3).
- Well over three million women were working more than one job in 1991—double the comparable number in 1980 (see Figure 3-6).
- The percentage of workers of both sexes who are represented by labor

unions has been shrinking. Among women, it dropped from 17 percent to 15 percent between 1984 and 1992 (see Figure 3-8).

- Together, just two industries—services and trade—employed 68 percent of all female workers in 1992, compared to less than half of all male workers (see Figure 3-9).

- Women workers are concentrated in a narrower range of occupations than men. Administrative support jobs, professional specialty occupations, and service occupations accounted for 59 percent of all employed women in 1992 (see Figure 3-10).

- Black and Hispanic women workers are more concentrated in service occupations than white women. However, one in four black and Hispanic women workers is in an administrative support job—a proportion close to that of white women (see Figure 3-11).

- Women's presence has increased noticeably in once overwhelmingly male professions such as medicine and the law, but not in traditionally male skilled blue-collar trades (see Table 3-10).

- For families with working mothers, the single most common child care arrangement is care in another person's home, typically by a relative in the case of black children and by a nonrelative in the case of white children (see Table 3-17).

- Child care expenses consume about a fifth of the budgets of low-income families that pay for child care (Table 3-18).

Figure 3-1 • WOMEN IN THE LABOR FORCE, 1960–1992

The female labor force participation rate rose from 38 percent to 58 percent.

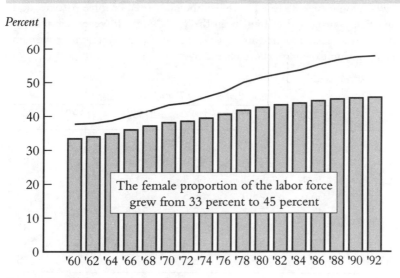

Source: See Table 3-1.

Table 3-1 • WOMEN'S LABOR FORCE PARTICIPATION RATE AND WOMEN AS A PERCENTAGE OF THE LABOR FORCE, 1960–1992[1]

Year	Women's Labor Force Partici- pation Rate[2]	Women as Percentage of Total Labor Force	Year	Women's Labor Force Partici- pation Rate[2]	Women as Percentage of Total Labor Force
1960	37.7	33.4	1978	50.0	41.7
1962	37.9	34.0	1980	51.5	42.6
1964	38.7	34.8	1982	52.6	43.3
1966	40.3	36.0	1984	53.6	43.8
1968	41.6	37.1	1986	55.3	44.5
1970	43.3	38.1	1988	56.6	45.0
1972	43.9	38.5	1990	57.5	45.3
1974	45.7	39.4	1992	57.8	45.5
1976	47.3	40.5			

[1]Civilians age 16 and over.
[2]Labor force participants as a percentage of all civilian women age 16 and over.
Source: Bureau of Labor Statistics, *Employment and Earnings,* January 1993, Table 2.

Table 3-2 • WOMEN'S LABOR FORCE PARTICIPATION RATES BY
AGE, 1960–1992 AND PROJECTED 2005[1]

Since 1990, women age 35 to 44 have had the highest labor force participation
rates, and that is projected to be true in the year 2005. However, labor force
participation is projected to increase by several percentage points among women
in every age group except for those 65 and over.

Age	*Labor Force Participation Rates*[2]					
	1960	*1970*	*1980*	*1990*	*1992*	*2005*[3]
Total	37.7	43.3	51.5	57.5	57.8	63.0
16–19	39.3	44.0	52.9	51.8	49.2	54.3
20–24	46.1	57.7	68.9	71.6	71.2	75.3
25–34	36.0	45.0	65.5	73.6	74.7	79.7
35–44	43.4	51.1	65.5	76.5	76.8	85.3
45–54	49.9	54.4	59.9	71.2	72.7	81.5
55–64	37.2	43.0	41.3	45.3	46.6	54.3
65 and over	10.8	9.7	8.1	8.7	8.3	8.8

[1]Civilian women age 16 and over.
[2]Labor force participants as a percentage of all women in age group.
[3]Using moderate growth projections.
Source: Bureau of Labor Statistics, *Handbook of Labor Statistics*, 1989, Table 5; "Labor
Force Projections: The Baby Boom Moves On," *Monthly Labor Review*, November 1991,
Table 3; and *Employment and Earnings*, January 1992, Table 3.

Table 3-3 • LABOR FORCE PARTICIPATION RATES BY SEX, RACE, AND HISPANIC ORIGIN, 1975, 1990, 1992, AND PROJECTED 2005[1]

Although white women have historically had lower labor force participation rates than women of other races, they had virtually caught up by 1992, and are projected to have the highest rate (among women) by 2005.

Sex, Race, and Hispanic Origin	Labor Force Participation Rates			
	1975	1990	1992	2005[2]
Women				
All races	46.3	57.5	57.8	63.0
White	45.9	57.5	57.8	63.5
Black	48.9	57.8	58.0	61.7
Asian and other[3]	51.3	56.7	57.5	58.9
Hispanic origin[4]	—	53.0	52.6	58.0
Men				
All races	77.9	76.1	75.6	75.4
White	78.7	76.9	76.4	76.2
Black	71.0	70.1	69.7	70.2
Asian and other	74.8	74.2	74.6	75.0
Hispanic origin	—	81.2	80.5	81.6

[1]Civilian labor force age 16 and over.
[2]Using moderate growth projections.
[3]Includes Asians, Pacific Islanders, American Indians, and Alaskan Natives.
[4]Persons of Hispanic origin may be of any race. Data for 1975 were not available.
Source: Bureau of Labor Statistics (BLS), "Labor Force Projections: The Baby Boom Moves On," *Monthly Labor Review,* November 1991, Table 3 and BLS, *Employment and Earnings,* January 1993, Table 39.

Table 3-4 • LABOR FORCE PARTICIPATION AND UNEMPLOYMENT RATES OF PERSONS OF HISPANIC ORIGIN BY SEX AND ORIGIN, 1992[1]

Among both women and men of Hispanic origin, Puerto Ricans have the lowest labor force participation rate and the highest unemployment rate.

	Origin			
	Mexican	*Puerto Rican*	*Cuban*	*Other*[2]
Women				
Total number (in thousands)	4,563	898	459	1,754
Labor force participation rate	52.1	47.1	50.3	57.4
Unemployment rate	11.7	12.3	8.9	10.5
Men				
Total number (in thousands)	4,806	730	408	1,625
Labor force participation rate	82.0	69.9	73.2	82.5
Unemployment rate	11.7	15.6	7.1	10.5

[1]Civilian labor force age 16 and over.

[2]"Other," which was derived by subtracting persons of Mexican, Puerto Rican, and Cuban origin from the totals of Hispanic origin, includes persons of Central and South American origin.

Source: Bureau of Labor Statistics, *Employment and Earnings,* January 1993, Table 40.

Figure 3-2 • THE HISPANIC LABOR FORCE BY SEX AND ORIGIN, 1992[1] (percent distribution)

Persons of Mexican origin account for by far the largest proportion of the Hispanic workforce in the United States, although that proportion is smaller among women than among men.

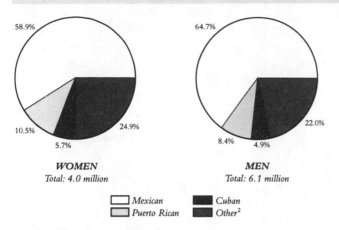

WOMEN
Total: 4.0 million

MEN
Total: 6.1 million

☐ *Mexican*   ■ *Cuban*
▨ *Puerto Rican*   ■ *Other*[2]

[1]Civilian labor force age 16 and over.
[2]"Other," which was derived by subtracting persons of Mexican, Puerto Rican, and Cuban origin from the totals of Hispanic origin, includes persons of Central and South American origin.
Source: Bureau of Labor Statistics, *Employment and Earnings,* January 1993, Table 40.

Table 3-5 • LABOR FORCE PARTICIPATION AND UNEMPLOYMENT RATES OF FOREIGN-BORN WOMEN, BY LANGUAGE SPOKEN AT HOME AND ENGLISH FLUENCY, NOVEMBER 1989[1]

Labor force participation is very high, and unemployment low, among foreign-born women who speak English well, whether or not they are native English speakers. Labor force participation is below average for foreign-born women whose English is poor or nonexistent.

English Fluency	Number in Labor Force (in thousands)	Labor Force Participation Rate	Unemployment Rate
Only English spoken at home	773	76.9	4.5
Other language spoken at home Workers speak English			
Very well or well	1,455	72.6	4.6
Not well or not at all	696	45.7	7.5

[1]Civilian women age 16 and over.
Source: Bureau of Labor Statistics, "How Do Immigrants Fare in the U.S. Labor Market?" *Monthly Labor Review,* December 1992, Table 8.

Table 3-6 • UNEMPLOYMENT RATES BY SEX, RACE, AND HISPANIC ORIGIN, 1980–1992[1]

Unemployment rates were lowest for whites and highest for blacks. Among blacks the rates for men exceeded those for women (except in 1988); the reverse was true among Hispanics (except in 1992).

Year	All Races		White		Black		Hispanic Origin[2]	
	Women	*Men*	*Women*	*Men*	*Women*	*Men*	*Women*	*Men*
1980	7.4	6.9	6.5	6.1	14.0	14.5	10.7	9.7
1982	9.4	9.9	8.3	8.8	17.6	20.1	14.1	13.6
1984	7.6	7.4	6.5	6.4	15.4	16.4	11.1	10.5
1986	7.1	6.9	6.1	6.0	14.2	14.8	10.8	10.5
1988	5.6	5.5	4.7	4.7	11.7	11.7	8.3	8.1
1990	5.4	5.6	4.6	4.8	10.8	11.8	8.3	7.8
1992	6.9	7.8	6.0	6.9	13.0	15.2	11.3	11.5

[1]Civilian labor force age 16 and over.
[2]Persons of Hispanic origin may be of any race.
Source: Bureau of Labor Statistics (BLS), *Handbook of Labor Statistics*, 1989, Table 28; and BLS, *Employment and Earnings*, January 1991, Table 39 and January 1993, Table 39.

Figure 3-3 · WOMEN'S UNEMPLOYMENT RATES BY RACE AND HISPANIC ORIGIN, 1980–1992[1]

Through the 1980s and into the early 1990s, the unemployment rate for black women was more than twice that for white women. The rate increased between 1990 and 1992 for women in every group, but the increase was sharpest for Hispanic women.

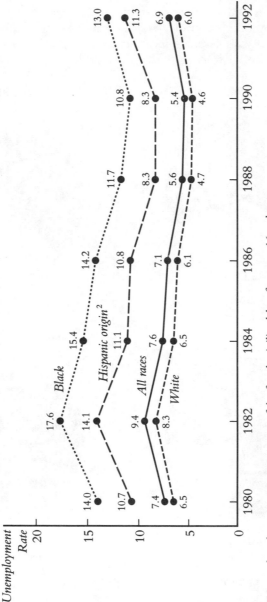

[1]Unemployed women as a percentage of the female civilian labor force age 16 and over.
[2]Persons of Hispanic origin may be of any race.

Source: Bureau of Labor Statistics (BLS), *Handbook of Labor Statistics*, 1989, Table 28; and BLS, *Employment and Earnings*, January 1991, Tables 3 and 44 and January 1993, Tables 3 and 44.

Figure 3-4 • UNEMPLOYED WORKERS AGE 20 AND OVER BY SEX AND REASON FOR UNEMPLOYMENT, 1990 AND 1992 (percent distribution)

In 1992, job losers on layoff—workers who expected to be called back to work—were a smaller proportion of the unemployed of both sexes than was the case in 1990. The proportion of other job losers—those with no expectation of getting their old jobs back—increased for both sexes, and accounted for over half of unemployed men in 1992.

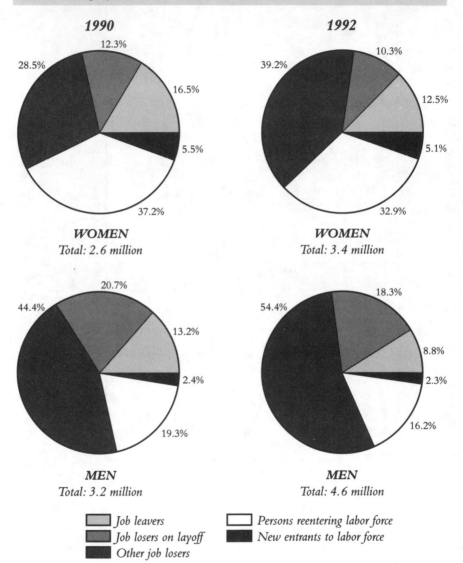

1990

12.3%
28.5%
16.5%
5.5%
37.2%

WOMEN
Total: 2.6 million

1992

10.3%
39.2%
12.5%
5.1%
32.9%

WOMEN
Total: 3.4 million

20.7%
44.4%
13.2%
2.4%
19.3%

MEN
Total: 3.2 million

18.3%
54.4%
8.8%
2.3%
16.2%

MEN
Total: 4.6 million

☐ *Job leavers*   ☐ *Persons reentering labor force*
☐ *Job losers on layoff* ■ *New entrants to labor force*
■ *Other job losers*

Source: Bureau of Labor Statistics, *Employment and Earnings,* January 1991, Table 12 and January 1993, Table 12.

Figure 3-5 • EMPLOYED WOMEN, 1971–1991

Between 1971 and 1991, the total number of employed women rose by 60 percent, and the number employed full time, year-round doubled. Over half of all women employed in 1991 were full-time, year-round workers.

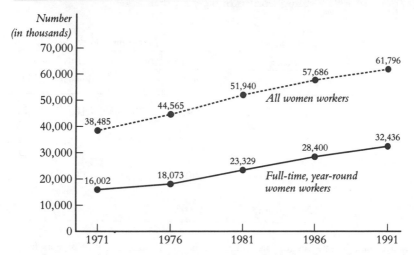

Source: Bureau of the Census, *Money Income of Households, Families, and Persons in the United States: 1991*, 1992, Table B-16.

Table 3-7 • WORKERS BY FULL- OR PART-TIME STATUS, SEX, AND RACE, 1992[1] (percent distribution)

Women in general are more likely than men to work part time. White women are considerably more likely than black women to do so (26.5 percent vs. 18.4 percent in 1992), and to do so voluntarily (22.1 percent vs. 12.2 percent).

Work Status	All Races		White		Black	
	Women	*Men*	*Women*	*Men*	*Women*	*Men*
Full time[2]	74.6	89.2	73.5	89.4	81.6	87.1
Part time	25.4	10.8	26.5	10.6	18.4	12.9
Voluntary	20.8	7.9	22.1	7.9	12.2	7.7
Involuntary	4.6	2.9	4.4	2.7	6.2	5.2
Total percent	100.0	100.0	100.0	100.0	100.0	100.0
Total number (in thousands)	53,793	63,805	45,770	55,709	6,087	5,846

[1]Civilians age 16 and over.
[2]Included in the full-time category are a small number of workers who usually work full time but who were on involuntary part-time schedules when surveyed.
Source: Bureau of Labor Statistics, *Employment and Earnings*, January 1993, Table 7.

Table 3-8 • FULL- AND PART-TIME WORKERS BY SEX AND AGE, 1992[1] (percent distribution)

The majority of women who work part time—whether voluntarily or not—are in their prime working years. Among men who are on voluntary part time, the larger proportions are young workers or older workers.

| | Full-Time Workers[2] | | Part-Time Workers | | | |
| | | | Voluntary | | Involuntary | |
Age	Women	Men	Women	Men	Women	Men
16–19	1.8	1.8	14.7	29.8	10.0	14.2
20–24	9.9	8.7	12.6	20.3	16.5	20.4
25–54	78.0	77.6	55.2	22.7	61.9	55.3
55 and over	10.3	11.9	17.5	27.2	11.6	10.1
Total percent	100.0	100.0	100.0	100.0	100.0	100.0
Total number (in thousands)	40,129	56,897	11,182	5,031	2,483	1,876

[1]Civilians age 16 and over.
[2]Included in the full-time category are a small number of workers who usually work full time but who were on involuntary part-time schedules when surveyed.
Source: Bureau of Labor Statistics, *Employment and Earnings,* January 1993, Table 7.

Figure 3-6 • WORKERS HOLDING MULTIPLE JOBS BY SEX, 1970, 1980, AND 1991[1]

In 1970, for every woman who worked multiple jobs, there were more than five men who did. By 1991, the situation had changed dramatically: there were three "moonlighting" women for every four moonlighting men.

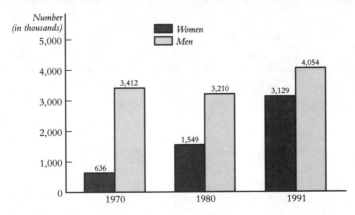

[1]Civilian workers age 16 and over.
Source: Bureau of Labor Statistics, "Multiple Jobholding Up Sharply in the 1980's," *Monthly Labor Review,* July 1990, Table 1 and Bureau of the Census, *Statistical Abstract of the United States 1992,* 1992, Table 628.

Figure 3-7 • WORKERS ON GOODS-PRODUCING AND
SERVICE-PRODUCING NONFARM PAYROLLS BY SEX, 1970–1992

Of the almost 26 million women's jobs added to nonfarm payrolls between 1970
and 1990, only 1.3 million—five percent—were in the goods-producing sector.
The net increase in men's jobs over the two decades was 13 million, less than
one percent of them in the goods-producing sector. Only female jobs in the
service-producing sector increased in number between 1990 and 1992.

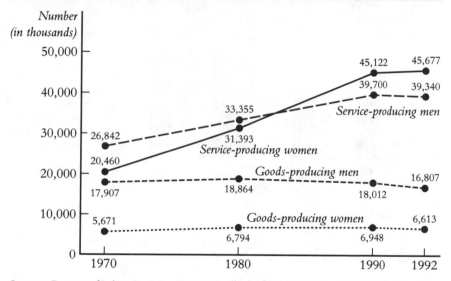

Source: Bureau of Labor Statistics (BLS), *Handbook of Labor Statistics,* 1989, Table 68 and
Table 73 (as corrected in BLS Bulletin 2340, March 1990); and BLS unpublished data,
1992.

Figure 3-8 • WORKERS WITH UNION AFFILIATION BY SEX, 1984 AND 1992[1]

As Figure 3-7 shows, goods-producing employees—the workers most likely to belong to unions—represent a much smaller proportion of American workers than they used to. This situation is reflected in the shrinking percentage of workers of both sexes who belong to or are represented by unions. As Table 3-9 below shows, black workers are the most likely to have union affiliation.

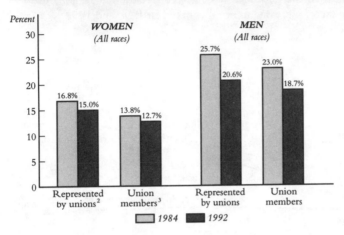

Footnotes and source: See Table 3-9.

Table 3-9 • WHITE, BLACK, AND HISPANIC WORKERS WITH UNION AFFILIATION BY SEX, 1984 AND 1992 (in percentages)[1]

	White		Black		Hispanic Origin[4]	
	Women	*Men*	*Women*	*Men*	*Women*	*Men*
1984						
Represented by unions[2]	15.6	24.9	25.7	33.4	18.4	26.2
Union members[3]	12.7	22.3	21.7	30.2	15.6	23.6
Total employed (in thousands)	36,139	43,932	4,880	4,819	2,204	3,067
1992						
Represented by unions	13.8	20.0	22.1	26.4	14.5	18.7
Union members	11.7	18.2	19.0	23.9	12.1	16.8
Total employed (in thousands)	41,892	46,732	5,936	5,480	3,386	4,954

[1]Employed wage and salary workers age 16 and over.
[2]Includes union or employee association members plus workers who reported no union affiliation but whose jobs were covered by employee association or union contracts.
[3]Members of labor unions or employee associations similar to unions.
[4]Persons of Hispanic origin may be of any race.
Source: Bureau of Labor Statistics, *Employment and Earnings,* January 1985, Table 52 and January 1993, Table 57.

Figure 3-9 • EMPLOYED WOMEN AND MEN BY INDUSTRY, 1992[1]
(percent distribution)

The service-producing sector comprises a number of industries. One is the services industry, which of all industries employs the largest percentage of workers of both sexes. Wholesale and retail trade, employing similar proportions of women and men, ranks second for both sexes. However, these two industries together employed 68 percent of all working women in 1992, compared to less than half of the men.

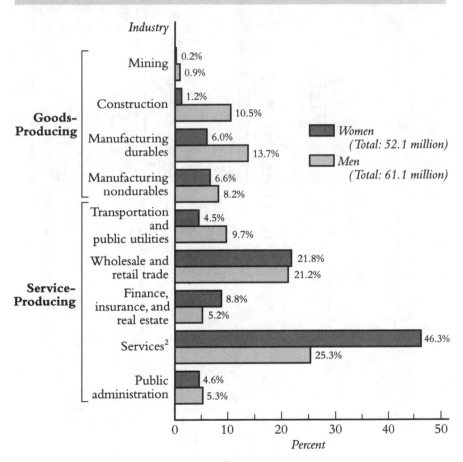

[1]Civilians age 16 and over employed in nonfarm industries.
[2]Excludes private households.
Source: Bureau of Labor Statistics, *Employment and Earnings,* January 1993, Table 27.

Figure 3-10 • EMPLOYED WOMEN AND MEN BY OCCUPATION, 1992[1] (percent distribution)

Women workers are concentrated in a narrower range of occupations than men. Administrative support jobs, accounting for more than one in four (27.5 percent) women workers in 1992, lead the list for women. Professional specialty occupations and service occupations (excluding private household and protective) tie for second place. Taken together, these three occupations accounted for 59 percent of all employed women in 1992.

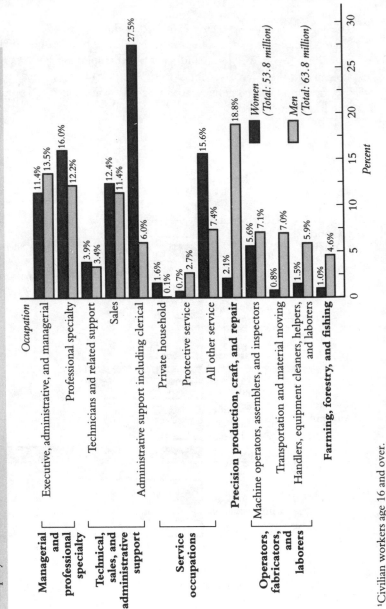

[1]Civilian workers age 16 and over.

Source: Bureau of Labor Statistics, *Employment and Earnings*, January 1993, Table 21.

Figure 3-11 • EMPLOYED WHITE, BLACK, AND HISPANIC WOMEN BY OCCUPATION, 1992[1] (percent distribution)

Black and Hispanic women workers are more concentrated in service occupations than are white women. However, one in four of all black and Hispanic women workers is in an administrative support job—a proportion close to that for white women.

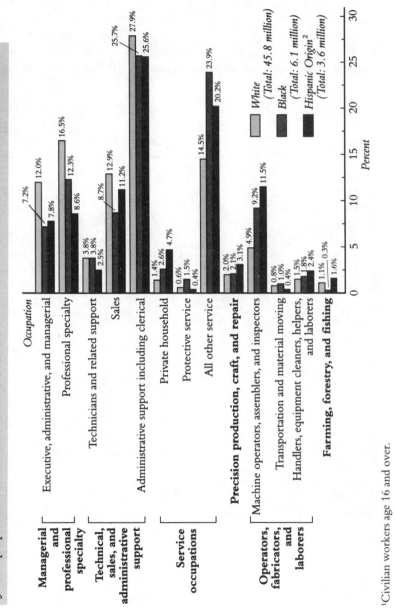

[1]Civilian workers age 16 and over.

[2]Persons of Hispanic origin may be of any race.

Source: Bureau of Labor Statistics (BLS), *Employment and Earnings*, January 1993, Table 21 and BLS, unpublished tabulations from the Current Population Survey, 1992 Annual Averages.

Table 3-10 · WOMEN AS A PERCENTAGE OF WORKERS IN
SELECTED OCCUPATIONS, 1975, 1984, AND 1992[1]

Are women moving into "nontraditional jobs" in a significant way? It depends
on the type of job. Between 1975 and 1992, women's presence increased noticeably in professional occupations (e.g., architect, physician), but in skilled
blue-collar trades (e.g., carpenter, welder), it was a different story. The proportions of women in these occupations, minute in 1975, were minute in 1992.

	Women as a Percentage of Total Employed		
Occupations	*1975*	*1984*	*1992*
Airplane pilots and navigators	—	2.1	2.3
Architects	4.3	10.8	15.3
Auto mechanics	0.5	0.8	0.8
Bus drivers	37.7	44.3	41.7
Carpenters	0.6	1.3	1.0
Child care workers in private households[2]	98.4	97.4	97.1
Computer programmers	25.6	35.4	33.0
Data entry keyers	92.8	91.3	84.9
Data processing equipment repairers	1.8	9.4	10.4
Dental assistants	100.0	98.2	98.6
Dentists	1.8	6.2	8.5
Economists	13.1	39.6	43.3
Editors and reporters	44.6	46.2	49.7
Lawyers and judges	7.1	16.2	21.4
Librarians	81.1	85.9	87.6
Mail carriers	8.7	17.1	27.8
Physicians	13.0	16.0	20.4
Registered nurses	97.0	96.0	94.3
Social workers	60.8	64.1	68.9
Teachers, college and university	31.1	36.6	40.9
Teachers, elementary school	85.4	84.6	85.4
Telephone installers and repairers	4.8	8.2	10.4
Waiters and waitresses	91.1	86.3	79.6
Welders	4.4	4.7	4.2

[1]Employed civilians age 16 and over.
[2]*Employment and Earnings,* January 1993 lists two additional classifications of child care
workers: "family child care providers" (98.7 percent female), and "early childhood
teachers' assistants" (95.9 percent female).
Source: Bureau of Labor Statistics (BLS), *Handbook of Labor Statistics,* 1989, Table 18; and
BLS, *Employment and Earnings,* January 1976, Table 2 and January 1993, Table 22.

Table 3-11 • WOMEN EMPLOYED IN SELECTED HEALTH CARE
INDUSTRIES, 1982 AND 1992[1]

The number of women working in hospitals, doctors' offices, nursing homes,
and other health facilities increased by two million (one-third) between 1982
and 1992. (Not all of the workers in health care "industries" are in health care
occupations—consider bookkeepers, janitors, etc.—just as not all workers in
health care occupations are employed in health care industries—consider, for
example, school nurses.)

Industry	Number of Women (in thousands)		Women as a Percentage of Total Employed	
	1982	1992	1982	1992
Hospitals	3,310	3,770	76.2	76.7
Offices and clinics of health practitioners	990	1,675	68.5	72.3
Nursing and personal care facilities[2]	1,060	1,510	87.1	86.3
Other health services	615	1,021	71.9	79.3

[1]Civilian workers age 16 and over.
[2]"Convalescent institutions" in 1982.
Source: Bureau of Labor Statistics (BLS), *Employment and Earnings,* January 1993, Table 22
and BLS, unpublished tabulations from the Current Population Survey, Annual Averages
1992.

Table 3-12 • WOMEN EMPLOYED IN SELECTED HEALTH CARE
INDUSTRIES BY RACE AND HISPANIC ORIGIN, 1992[1]

Black women are underrepresented among women workers in health practitioners' offices and clinics and overrepresented among those in the other settings, especially nursing and personal care facilities.

Industry	Total All Races (in thousands)	Percent		
		White	Black	Hispanic Origin[2]
Hospitals	3,770	79.7	15.7	4.8
Offices and clinics of health practitioners	1,675	93.1	3.5	6.6
Nursing and personal care facilities	1,510	74.6	22.2	4.4
Other health services	1,021	80.2	16.8	6.5

[1]Civilian workers age 16 and over.
[2]Persons of Hispanic origin may be of any race.
Source: Bureau of Labor Statistics, unpublished tabulations from the Current Population
Survey, Annual Averages 1992.

Table 3-13 · WOMEN EMPLOYED IN SELECTED HEALTH CARE
OCCUPATIONS BY RACE AND HISPANIC ORIGIN, 1992[1]

In 1992, one in five physicians was a woman, but the percentage of women was
considerably greater in most of the other occupations shown on this table. It was
highest—99 percent—among dental assistants. Black women were overrepresented in all the health service occupations shown here except dental assistant, in
which women of Hispanic origin were overrepresented.

Occupation	Number of Women (in thousands)	Women as Percentage of Total Employed	Percent of Women Who Are		
			White	Black	Hispanic[2]
All health diagnosing	168	18.3	81.5	3.6	4.8
Physicians	125	20.4	80.8	3.2	4.8
Dentists	14	8.6	78.6	7.1	7.1
All health assessment and treating	2,186	86.8	86.4	8.4	3.2
Registered nurses	1,702	94.3	86.3	8.3	2.8
Pharmacists	75	37.9	84.0	5.3	4.0
Therapists	303	79.5	91.7	5.6	3.6
Physicians assistants	25	55.6	80.0	16.0	4.0
All health technologists and technicians	1,240	81.8	84.2	11.8	4.5
Clinical lab technicians and technologists	233	77.4	80.3	11.6	5.1
Licensed practical nurses	429	94.7	80.4	17.0	3.0
All health service	1,869	88.7	68.8	27.9	7.0
Dental assistants	167	98.8	93.4	3.6	10.2
Health aides, except nursing	295	81.3	73.2	23.0	5.4
Nursing aides, orderlies, and attendants	1,407	89.4	64.9	31.8	6.8
Other					
Managers, medicine and health	239	65.7	88.7	9.2	2.1
Medical scientists	27	40.9	88.9	3.7	—

[1]Civilian workers age 16 and over.
[2]Persons of Hispanic origin may be of any race.
Source: Bureau of Labor Statistics, unpublished tabulations from the Current Population
Survey, Annual Averages 1992.

Table 3-14 • U.S. ACTIVE DUTY SERVICEWOMEN BY BRANCH OF
SERVICE, RANK, RACE, AND HISPANIC ORIGIN, FISCAL YEAR 1992[1]

The Air Force has the highest percentage of women of any service, the Marine
Corps the lowest. The Army has by far the largest proportions of black
women—they accounted for nearly half of the Army's enlisted women and
one-fifth of its female officers in fiscal year 1992.

Service and Rank[2]	Number of Women	Women as a Percentage of Total Personnel	Percent Distribution of Women			
			White	Black	Hispanic	Other
Army						
Enlisted	61,211	12.0	42.6	48.7	3.5	5.2
Officers	11,734	12.3	72.3	20.2	2.5	5.0
Navy						
Enlisted	47,688	10.2	61.2	26.8	8.3	3.7
Officers	8,304	12.0	84.8	8.1	2.7	4.4
Marine Corps						
Enlisted	7,704	4.7	58.7	28.6	8.4	4.4
Officers	653	3.4	85.8	8.0	3.7	2.6
Air Force						
Enlisted	55,598	14.8	69.3	23.7	3.5	3.5
Officers	12,683	14.0	82.5	11.0	2.2	4.3
Coast Guard						
Enlisted	2,803	8.5	73.9	16.0	4.7	5.4
Officers	425	5.7	90.1	3.1	2.1	4.7

[1]Coast Guard is as of March 1993.
[2]Officers include warrant officers.
Source: U.S. Department of Defense, Defense Manpower Data Center, unpublished data,
September 30, 1992 and U.S. Coast Guard, Enlisted Personnel Division, unpublished data,
March 1, 1993.

Figure 3-12 • WIVES IN THE PAID LABOR FORCE BY RACE AND
HISPANIC ORIGIN, 1981–1991 (in percentages)

Black wives have always been more likely than their white counterparts to be in
the paid labor force, and that continued to be the case over the 1981–1991
period. By 1991, two-thirds of all black wives and 58 percent of all white wives
were in the workforce.

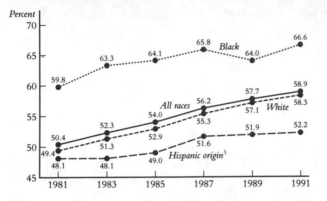

¹Persons of Hispanic origin may be of any race.
Source: Bureau of the Census, *Money Income of Households, Families, and Persons in the
United States: 1981*, 1982, Table 13; *1983*, 1984, Table 13; *1985*, 1986, Table 9; *1987*,
1988, Table 9; *1988 and 1989*, 1991, Table 13; and *1991*, 1992, Table 13.

Figure 3-13 • LABOR FORCE PARTICIPATION OF MOTHERS WITH
YOUNG CHILDREN BY MARITAL STATUS, 1980–1992¹ (in percentages)

The labor force participation rate for never-married mothers with young children was unstable between 1980 and 1992, winding up only slightly higher than
the rate at the beginning of the period. In contrast, labor force participation
increased steadily among married mothers with young children.

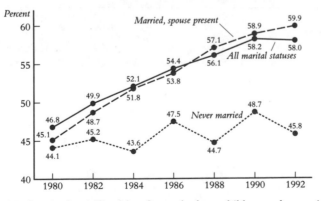

¹Mothers in the civilian labor force who have children under age six.
Source: Bureau of Labor Statistics (BLS), *Handbook of Labor Statistics*, 1989, Tables 56 and
57; and BLS, unpublished 1990 and 1992 data from the Current Population Survey.

Figure 3-14 • CHILDREN WITH MOTHERS IN THE WORKFORCE BY AGE OF CHILDREN, 1972–1992[1]

In 1972, less than 30 percent of children under six had working mothers; by 1987, more than half did. The proportion of school-age children with working mothers continued to grow between 1987 and 1992, but the comparable proportion of preschoolers changed very little.

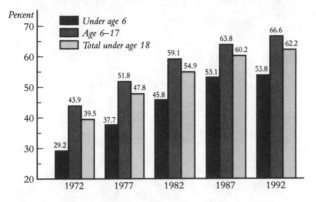

[1]Mothers in the civilian labor force.
Source: Bureau of Labor Statistics (BLS), *Handbook of Labor Statistics,* 1989, Table 59 and BLS, unpublished 1992 data from the Current Population Survey.

Table 3-15 • CHILDREN UNDER AGE 18 WITH WORKING PARENTS BY LIVING ARRANGEMENTS AND AGE OF CHILDREN, 1992[1]
(numbers in thousands)

Working parents are the norm for American children over age six, whether they live with both parents or with one.

Children's Living Arrangements	Total	Age of Children		
		Under 6	6–11	12–17
Live with both parents	46,638	16,685	15,864	14,089
Both parents employed				
Number	25,692	7,941	8,924	8,827
Percent	55.1	47.6	56.3	62.7
Live with mother only	15,396	5,481	5,263	4,652
Mother employed				
Number	8,009	2,188	2,871	2,950
Percent	52.0	39.9	54.6	63.4
Live with father only	2,182	773	674	736
Father employed				
Number	1,711	579	519	613
Percent	78.4	74.9	77.0	83.3

[1]Does not include children who live with neither parent.
Source: Bureau of the Census, *Marital Status and Living Arrangements: March 1992,* 1992, Table 6.

Table 3-16 • EMPLOYED MOTHERS BY FULL-TIME WORK STATUS
AND AGE OF CHILDREN, 1982 AND 1992[1]

Most employed mothers work full time, and the proportion who do has increased even among women with toddlers. In 1992, nearly 70 percent of employed mothers who had children under three worked full time, up from 64
percent in 1982.

| | Employed Mothers (numbers in thousands) | |
Age of Children	1982	1992
Under 3		
Total employed	3,542	4,776
Percentage working full time	64.0	69.4
Under 6		
Total employed	6,414	8,662
Percentage working full time	65.4	70.2
6–17[2]		
Total employed	10,440	12,390
Percentage working full time	71.2	76.3

[1]Women 16 and over.
[2]Women had no children younger than six.
Source: Bureau of Labor Statistics (BLS), *Handbook of Labor Statistics,* 1989, Table 56; and
BLS, unpublished tabulations from the March 1992 Current Population Survey.

Table 3-17 • CHILD CARE ARRANGEMENTS FOR THE YOUNG
CHILDREN OF WORKING MOTHERS BY RACE AND HISPANIC
ORIGIN, 1988[1] (percent distribution)

The single most common type of arrangement is for the child to be cared for in
another person's home (36.8 percent in 1988); except in the case of blacks, the
caretaker is more likely to be a nonrelative than a relative. Reliance on care in a
nonrelative's home—generally known as "family day care"—is especially strong
among Hispanic mothers (27.4 percent).

Arrangements	All Races	White	Black	Hispanic Origin[2]
Care in child's home	28.3	28.7	23.1	26.5
by father	15.1	16.5	6.8	11.4
by grandparent	5.7	5.1	7.8	7.8
by other relative	2.2	1.5	5.7	3.0
by nonrelative	5.3	5.6	2.8	4.3
Care in another home	36.8	36.5	40.2	41.0
by grandparent	8.2	7.4	12.0	9.2
by other relative	5.0	4.1	10.8	4.5
by nonrelative	23.6	24.9	17.4	27.4
Day/group care center	16.6	15.8	21.8	12.7
Nursery/preschool	9.2	9.3	9.8	10.4
Kindergarten or grade school-based	1.4	1.2	2.2	1.2
Child cares for self	0.1	0.1	0.0	0.0
Mother cares for child	7.6	8.3	3.0	8.3
Total percent	100.0	100.0	100.0	100.0
Total number (in thousands)	9,438	7,919	1,270	808

[1]Primary care arrangements for children under age five.
[2]Persons of Hispanic origin may be of any race.
Source: Bureau of the Census, *Who's Minding the Kids? Fall 1988*, 1992, Table 2.

Table 3-18 • CHILD CARE EXPENDITURES OF FAMILIES WITH
WORKING MOTHERS BY INCOME AND POVERTY STATUS, 1988

Not surprisingly, the cost of child care is most burdensome for low-income
families, even though they typically pay less for it than better-off families.

Family Income Level and Poverty Status	Number of Families Paying for Child Care (in thousands)	Mean Monthly Child Care Expenses (in dollars)	Percent of Family Income Spent on Child Care
Monthly income			
Less than $1,500	1,136	181	18.3
$1,500–2,999	2,654	201	8.7
$3,000–4,499	2,175	235	6.4
$4,500 and over	1,554	327	4.7
Poverty status			
Below poverty level	474	183	20.8
Above poverty level	7,046	237	6.5

Source: Bureau of the Census, *Who's Minding the Kids? Fall 1988,* 1992, Table 6.

Figure 3-15 • VOLUNTEER WORKERS BY SEX AND TYPE OF
ORGANIZATION THEY SERVE, 1989[1] (percent distribution)

Beyond church work—the single most popular activity for volunteers of both
sexes—the patterns of women and men diverge. For example, women are a
good deal less likely than men to give time to civic or political organizations.

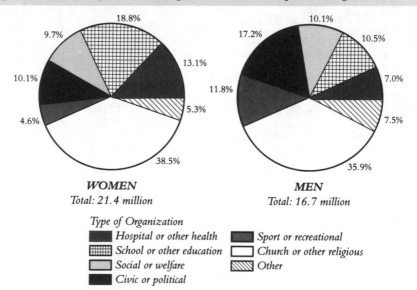

WOMEN
Total: 21.4 million

MEN
Total: 16.7 million

Type of Organization
- Hospital or other health
- School or other education
- Social or welfare
- Civic or political
- Sport or recreational
- Church or other religious
- Other

[1]Persons who performed unpaid volunteer work at some time during the year ending May
1989.
Source: Bureau of Labor Statistics, "Volunteers in the U.S.: Who Donates the Time?"
Monthly Labor Review, February 1991, Table 3.

SECTION 4:

EARNINGS AND BENEFITS

Whether measured by the median weekly earnings of full-time workers or by the median annual earnings of full-time, year-round workers, women's earnings have been increasing in recent years and men's earnings have been dropping. Both of these trends have contributed to a narrowing of the wage gap. Earnings gains for women have not been consistent across racial and ethnic groups (progress has been steady for white and black women but not for Hispanic women); earnings losses for men have been particularly heavy among Hispanics. Hispanic workers of both sexes are also less likely than other workers to have employer-provided health insurance and pension coverage.

In the population overall, men are more likely than women to lack health insurance. This is due to the fact that more women than men have Medicaid coverage—the proportions covered by private insurance are identical. Still, lack of health insurance is a major problem among women, many of whom are uninsured during their prime reproductive years.

- Between 1976 and 1991, the real (i.e., inflation-adjusted) earnings increased by 11 percent for female full-time, year-round workers overall, but the gain for Hispanic women was only one percent (see Figure 4-4).
- Between 1984 and 1992, men's earnings declined in five of the six broad occupational groups; only for men in managerial and professional occupations did median earnings increase. In three occupational groups women's earnings also declined, but usually not as much as men's (see Figures 4-2 and 4-3).
- The narrowing of the wage gap is a product of the overall decline in men's earnings as well as the overall increase in women's earnings (see Figure

4-1). In 1992, women overall earned 75.4 percent of what men earned, although the ratio was much narrower for black and Hispanic women (see Table 4-1).

• A larger proportion of males than of females lacked health insurance of any kind in 1991. A larger proportion of females than of males had Medicaid coverage. The proportions covered by private insurance were identical (see Figure 4-10).

• In 1991, about 60 percent of all uninsured men between the ages of 18 and 64 were under age 35. The comparable proportion of women was smaller; still, over half of all uninsured women were in their prime reproductive years (see Figure 4-12).

• Hispanic workers of both sexes are the least likely of all full-time, year-round workers to have health insurance. White men are the most likely to have insurance coverage through their own jobs (see Table 4-9).

• Most people of working age who have no health insurance do work and substantial proportions of them work full time, year round (see Figure 4-13).

• Many of the women who don't have coverage through their own jobs may be covered through their husbands' jobs. More than one in three of the women covered by private health insurance in 1991 had coverage through a family member's job (see Figures 4-7 and 4-8).

• More than a fifth of uninsured Americans are children under age 18. Another 16 percent are children over 18 who live with their parents (see Table 4-10).

• State and local governments are the employers most likely, and small private firms the least likely, to have unpaid maternity and paternity leave for full-time employees. Few employers provide paid parental leave (see Table 4-5).

Figure 4-1 • MEDIAN WEEKLY EARNINGS BY SEX, 1980–1992 (in constant 1992 dollars)[1]

The earnings gap has narrowed partly because women's earnings have been rising and partly because men's earnings have been falling.

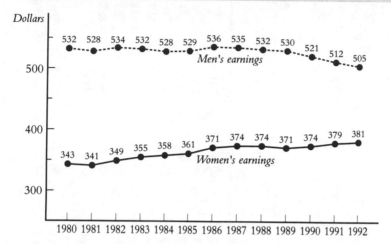

[1]Earnings of full-time civilian wage and salary workers age 16 and over. The CPI-U-X1 inflator was used.
Source: Bureau of Labor Statistics (BLS), *Handbook of Labor Statistics,* 1989, Table 43 and BLS, *Employment and Earnings,* January 1990, Table 56; January 1991, Table 56; January 1992, Table 56; and January 1993, Table 56.

Table 4-1 • FEMALE-TO-MALE EARNINGS RATIOS BY RACE AND HISPANIC ORIGIN, 1980–1992[1]

The typical American woman who worked full time in 1992 earned a little over 75 cents for every dollar her male counterpart earned. The earnings gap has been consistently wider for whites than for blacks and Hispanics, but it has been narrowing for all.

Race and Hispanic Origin	Ratio of Women's Earnings to Men's Earnings				
	1980	1983	1986	1989	1992
All races	64.4	66.7	69.2	70.1	75.4
White	63.3	65.6	67.9	69.3	74.9
Black	75.8	78.8	82.7	86.5	88.4
Hispanic origin[2]	—[3]	—[3]	—[3]	85.4	87.8

[1]Based on median weekly earnings of full-time wage and salary workers age 16 and over.
[2]Persons of Hispanic origin may be of any race.
[3]Data on median weekly earnings of Hispanic workers by sex were not available.
Source: Bureau of Labor Statistics (BLS), *Handbook of Labor Statistics,* August 1989, Table 41; and BLS, *Employment and Earnings,* January 1991, Table 54 and January 1993, Table 54.

Table 4-2 · MEDIAN WEEKLY EARNINGS BY SEX AND FEMALE-TO-MALE EARNINGS RATIOS BY OCCUPATION, 1984 AND 1992[1] (earnings in constant 1992 dollars)

Between 1984 and 1992, the earnings gap narrowed in all the occupations shown here except farming, forestry, and fishing. However, in 1992 as in 1984, the gap was considerably wider in some occupations than in others. Female full-time salesworkers, for example, earned less than 60 cents in 1992 for every dollar their male counterparts earned. At the other end of the scale were female mechanics/repairers, for whom the earnings gap had more than closed—in 1992 they were earning $1.05 for every dollar their male counterparts earned.

Occupation	1984			1992		
	Earnings		Earnings Ratio[2]	Earnings		Earnings Ratio
	Female	Male		Female	Male	
All occupations	358	528	67.8	381	505	75.4
Managerial and professional specialty	512	745	68.7	562	777	72.3
Executive, administrative, and managerial	491	770	63.9	519	784	66.2
Professional specialty	523	720	72.6	587	770	76.2
Technical, sales, and administrative support	350	541	64.6	365	519	70.3
Technicians and related support	423	605	69.9	436	591	73.8
Sales occupations	293	541	54.1	313	523	59.8
Administrative support, including clerical	351	510	68.8	364	482	75.5
Service occupations	243	358	67.9	248	330	75.2
Private household	180	—[3]	—	177	—[3]	—
Protective service	392	509	76.9	399	501	79.6
All other service occupations	247	302	81.7	248	283	87.6

Precision production, craft, and repair	346	532	65.0	336	503	66.8
Mechanics and repairers	444	526	84.4	523	496	105.4
Construction trades	—[3]	518	—	—[3]	495	—
Precision production occupations	331	547	60.5	316	520	60.8
Operators, fabricators, and laborers	286	428	66.9	279	393	71.0
Machine operators, assemblers, and inspectors	285	444	64.1	275	406	67.7
Transportation and material moving occupations	347	472	73.4	329	436	75.5
Handlers, equipment cleaners, helpers, laborers	282	352	80.1	279	314	88.9
Farming, forestry, and fishing	238	280	85.0	223	269	82.9

[1]Earnings of full-time wage and salary workers age 16 and over. The CPI-U-X1 inflator was used to calculate the 1992 equivalent of 1984 earnings.

[2]The 1984 earnings ratio was calculated on the basis of current 1984 dollars.

[3]The Bureau of Labor Statistics does not publish median earnings data when the base is less than 50,000 workers.

Source: Bureau of Labor Statistics (BLS), *Handbook of Labor Statistics*, August 1989, Table 43 and BLS, *Employment and Earnings*, January 1993, Table 56.

Figure 4-2 • PERCENT CHANGE IN REAL EARNINGS BY SEX AND OCCUPATIONAL GROUP, 1984–1992[1]

This figure illustrates why the earnings gap narrowed in every major occupational group but one—farming, forestry, and fishing—between 1984 and 1992 (see Table 4-2). Men's earnings declined in every category but managerial and professional; there, the earnings gap narrowed because while both sexes gained, the women gained more than the men.

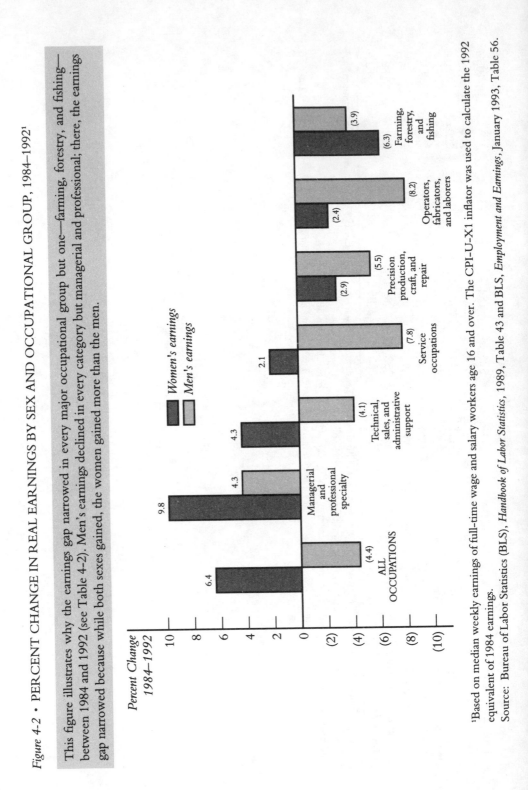

[1]Based on median weekly earnings of full-time wage and salary workers age 16 and over. The CPI-U-X1 inflator was used to calculate the 1992 equivalent of 1984 earnings.

Source: Bureau of Labor Statistics (BLS), *Handbook of Labor Statistics*, 1989, Table 43 and BLS, *Employment and Earnings*, January 1993, Table 56.

Figure 4-3 • MEDIAN ANNUAL EARNINGS BY SEX AND RACE, 1971–1991 (in constant 1991 dollars)[1]

In this 20-year perspective on the earnings of full-time, year-round workers, white men continued to have by far the highest earnings of all, with black men a distant second. But men's earnings declined toward the end of the second decade while women's continued to rise.

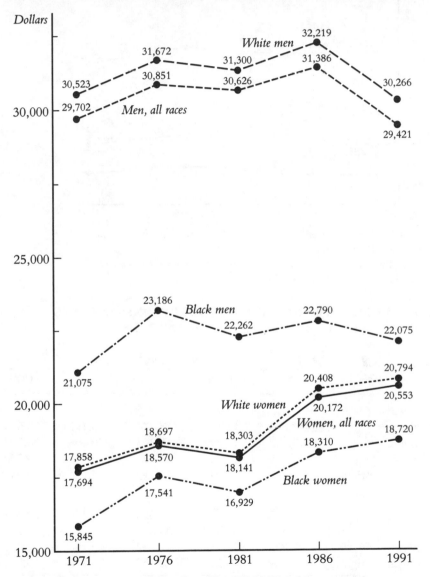

[1]Earnings of full-time, year-round workers. The CPI-U-X1 inflator was used.
Source: Bureau of the Census, *Money Income of Households, Families, and Persons in the United States: 1991,* 1992, Table B–16.

Figure 4-4 • MEDIAN ANNUAL EARNINGS BY SEX AND HISPANIC ORIGIN, 1976–1991 (in constant 1991 dollars)[1]

In 1991, Hispanic women who worked full time, year round earned only about one percent more than their counterparts in 1976. Hispanic men in 1991 earned 16 percent less than their counterparts in 1976.

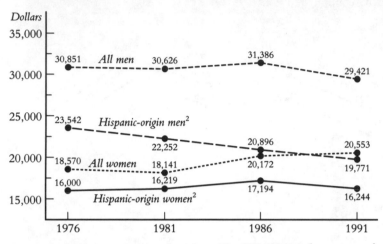

[1]Earnings of full-time, year-round workers. The CPI-U-X1 inflator was used.
[2]Persons of Hispanic origin may be of any race.
Source: Bureau of the Census, *Money Income of Households, Families, and Persons in the United States: 1991*, 1992, Table B-17.

Table 4-3 • MEDIAN ANNUAL EARNINGS BY SEX, RACE, AND HISPANIC ORIGIN, 1971–1991 (in constant 1991 dollars)[1]

Sex, Race, and Hispanic Origin	Median Annual Earnings				
	1971	*1976*	*1981*	*1986*	*1991*
Women					
All races	17,674	18,570	18,141	20,172	20,553
White	17,858	18,697	18,303	20,408	20,794
Black	15,845	17,541	16,929	18,310	18,720
Hispanic origin[2]	—[3]	16,000	16,219	17,194	16,244
Men					
All races	29,702	30,851	30,626	31,386	29,421
White	30,523	31,672	31,300	32,219	30,266
Black	21,075	23,186	22,262	22,790	22,075
Hispanic origin	—	23,542	22,252	20,896	19,771

[1]Earnings of full-time, year-round workers. The CPI-U-X1 inflator was used.
[2]Persons of Hispanic origin may be of any race.
[3]Earnings data for 1971 were not available by Hispanic origin of workers.
Source: Bureau of the Census, *Money Income of Households, Families, and Persons in the United States: 1991*, 1992, Table B-17.

Table 4-4 · MEDIAN WEEKLY EARNINGS BY SEX AND FEMALE-
TO-MALE EARNINGS RATIOS IN SELECTED HEALTH CARE
OCCUPATIONS, 1992[1]

The earnings range is narrower for women in health care occupations than for
men. In 1992, a salaried female physician typically made three times what a
female nursing aide made; a salaried male physician made four times what a male
nursing aide made. The female-to-male earnings ratio for physicians was wider
than for other health care workers (and than for workers overall—see Table
4-2).

Occupation	Median Weekly Earnings (in dollars)		Earnings Ratio
	Women	Men	
All health diagnosing occupations[2]	749	1,029	72.8
Physicians	859	1,190	72.2
All health assessment and treating occupations	658	737	89.3
Registered nurses	663	633	104.7
Pharmacists	808	897	90.1
Therapists	639	667	95.8
All health technologists and technicians	415	501	82.8
Clinical lab technologists and technicians	493	577	85.4
Licensed practical nurses	411	—[3]	—
All health service occupations	276	292	94.5
Dental assistants	333	—[3]	—
Health aides, except nursing	303	—[3]	—
Nursing aides, orderlies, and attendants	265	276	96.0

[1]Earnings of full-time wage and salary workers.
[2]Full-time wage and salary workers accounted for a minority (less than 40 percent) of
persons employed in health diagnosing occupations overall in 1992, judging by a
comparison with data on the total number of persons employed in these occupations in that
year. Presumably, the majority were self-employed. However, 62 percent of women
physicians *were* full-time wage and salary workers. In the other overall occupational groups
shown in this table, full-time wage and salary workers accounted for between 69 and 74
percent of total workers.
[3]The Bureau of Labor Statistics does not publish earnings data when the base is less than
50,000 workers.
Source: Bureau of Labor Statistics, *Employment and Earnings,* January 1993, Table 56.

Figure 4-5 • MEDIAN WEEKLY EARNINGS OF FEMALE REGISTERED NURSES AND LICENSED PRACTICAL NURSES, 1983–1992 (in constant 1992 dollars)[1]

Median weekly earnings increased by 19 percent for RNs between 1983 and 1992. The gain for LPNs was modest—about five percent.

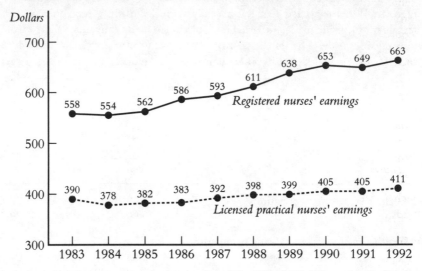

[1]Includes only full-time wage and salary workers. The CPI-U-X1 inflator was used.
Source: Bureau of Labor Statistics (BLS), *Handbook of Labor Statistics,* 1989, Table 43; and BLS, *Employment and Earnings,* January 1990, Table 56; January 1991, Table 56; January 1992, Table 56; and January 1993, Table 56.

Table 4-5 • AVAILABILITY OF PARENTAL LEAVE TO FULL-TIME EMPLOYEES BY SIZE AND TYPE OF EMPLOYER, 1989 AND 1990[1]

State and local governments are the employers most likely, and small private firms the least likely, to have unpaid maternity and paternity leave.

| | *Percentage Offering Employees* | | | |
| | *Maternity Leave* | | *Paternity Leave* | |
Employer Size and Type	*Paid*	*Unpaid*	*Paid*	*Unpaid*
Firms with fewer than 100 employees	2	17	—[2]	8
Firms with more than 100 employees	3	37	1	18
State and local governments	1	51	1	33

[1]Firms with more than 100 employees ("medium and large private establishments") were surveyed in 1989, small private establishments and state and local governments in 1990.
[2]Less than 0.5 percent.
Source: Bureau of Labor Statistics, "Benefits in State and Local Governments Address Family Concerns," *Monthly Labor Review,* March 1992, Table A-1.

Table 4-6 · WORKERS ON FLEXIBLE WORK SCHEDULES BY
OCCUPATION AND SEX, 1991[1]

Men who work full time as managers or professionals are more likely than their
female counterparts to be on flexible work schedules. However, managers and
professionals of both sexes are more likely to be on flexible schedules than their
counterparts in other occupations.

Occupation	Women		Men	
	Number of Workers (in thousands)	*Percent on Flexible Schedules*	*Number of Workers (in thousands)*	*Percent on Flexible Schedules*
Managerial and professional specialty	10,953	18.3	12,037	25.4
Technical, sales, and administrative support	15,206	15.0	8,910	22.3
Service occupations	4,060	11.1	4,329	10.0
Precision production, craft, and repair	807	8.6	9,464	8.1
Operators, fabricators, and laborers	3,303	6.0	10,211	7.7
Farming, forestry, and fishing	177	12.4	1,355	11.1

[1]Wage and salary workers age 16 and over who are usually full time on their principal jobs.
Source: Bureau of Labor Statistics, unpublished data from the May 1991 Current
Population Survey.

Table 4-7 • PENSION PLAN COVERAGE OF WORKERS BY SEX, AND
OF WOMEN WORKERS BY RACE AND HISPANIC ORIGIN, 1991[1]

Among full-time, year-round workers overall, a larger proportion of women
than of men have a pension plan offered at work, but the women are less likely
than the men to be in the plan.

	Number of Workers (in thousands)	Percentage	
		With Pension Plan Offered at Work	Worker Included in Plan
Worked in 1991			
Men, all races	72,064	52.0	42.7
Women			
All races	61,959	50.9	37.4
White	52,631	50.8	37.3
Black	7,145	53.8	40.0
Other	2,183	44.8	30.9
Hispanic origin[2]	4,172	37.4	26.2
Worked full time, year round in 1991			
Men, all races	47,897	61.7	55.3
Women			
All races	32,491	64.0	54.4
White	27,318	63.9	54.3
Black	4,008	67.5	57.6
Other	1,165	54.8	45.4
Hispanic origin	2,122	48.4	40.2

[1]"Pension plan" refers to an employer- or union-provided pension or retirement plan.
[2]Persons of Hispanic origin may be of any race.
Source: Bureau of the Census, unpublished data from the March 1992 Current Population
Survey.

Table 4-8 • ALL WORKERS AND WORKERS WITH PENSION PLAN
COVERAGE BY SEX AND EMPLOYER SIZE, 1991[1] (percent distribution)

About 58 percent of both women and men who are in pension plans through
their jobs work for the biggest employers—those with 1,000 employees or
more—although firms of this size employ less than 40 percent of workers.

Employer Size (number of employees)	All Workers		Pension Plan Offered and Worker Included in Plan	
	Women	Men	Women	Men
Under 25	28.4	31.6	8.0	10.0
25–99	12.3	13.4	8.8	10.3
100–499	14.5	13.4	16.7	15.1
500–999	6.2	4.8	8.5	6.7
1,000 or more	38.7	36.7	58.0	57.8
Total percent	100.0	100.0	100.0	100.0
Total number of workers (in thousands)	61,959	72,064	23,162	30,751

[1]"Pension plan" refers to an employer- or union-provided pension or retirement plan.
Source: Bureau of the Census, unpublished data from the March 1992 Current Population
Survey.

Figure 4-6 • WORKERS WITH HEALTH INSURANCE THROUGH THEIR OWN JOBS BY SEX AND EMPLOYER SIZE, 1991[1] (percent distribution)

Half of the female workers—and nearly half of the male workers—who have health insurance through their own jobs work for employers with 1,000 or more employees, although, as shown in Table 4-8, less than 40 percent of all workers are employed by the largest firms.

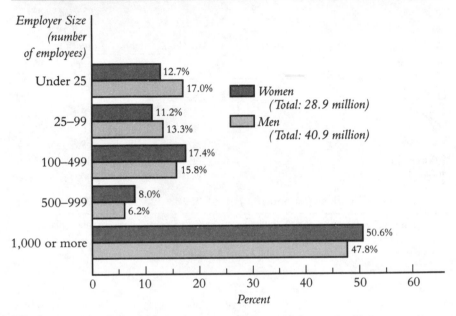

[1]Workers age 15 and over with employer- or union-provided group health insurance in their own names.
Source: Bureau of the Census, unpublished data from the March 1992 Current Population Survey.

Table 4-9 • FULL-TIME, YEAR-ROUND WORKERS WITH AND WITHOUT HEALTH INSURANCE THROUGH THEIR OWN JOBS BY SEX, RACE, AND HISPANIC ORIGIN, 1991[1] (numbers in thousands)

Hispanics of both sexes are the least likely of all full-time, year-round workers to have health insurance through their jobs. White men are the most likely to have coverage. (Many of the women who don't have coverage through their own jobs may be insured through their husbands' jobs; see Figure 4-8.)

Sex, Race, and Hispanic Origin	*Number of Workers*	*With Health Insurance Through Own Jobs[2]*	
		Number	*Percent*
All races			
Women	32,491	22,030	67.8
Men	47,897	33,907	70.8
White			
Women	27,318	18,560	67.9
Men	42,072	20,091	71.5
Black			
Women	4,008	2,711	67.7
Men	4,159	2,705	65.0
Other			
Women	1,165	759	65.2
Men	1,666	1,111	66.7
Hispanic origin[3]			
Women	2,122	1,226	57.8
Men	3,753	2,148	57.2

[1]Workers age 15 and over.
[2]With employer- or union-provided group health insurance in their own names.
[3]Persons of Hispanic origin may be of any race.
Source: Bureau of the Census, unpublished data from the March 1992 Current Population Survey.

Figure 4-7 • WOMEN WORKERS WITH AND WITHOUT HEALTH INSURANCE THROUGH THEIR OWN JOBS BY EMPLOYER SIZE, 1991[1] (percent distribution)

More than 40 percent of women workers who are not covered by health insurance through their own jobs work for employers with fewer than 25 employees.

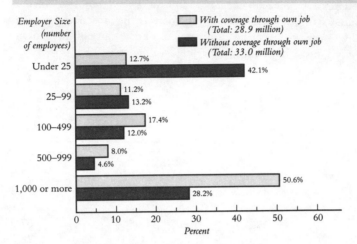

[1]Workers age 15 and over with and without employer- or union-provided group health insurance in their own names.
Source: Bureau of the Census, unpublished data from the March 1992 Current Population Survey.

Figure 4-8 • PERSONS AGE 18 TO 64 WITH PRIVATE HEALTH INSURANCE BY SEX AND SOURCE OF COVERAGE, 1991[1] (percent distribution)

Only half of all women with private health insurance in 1991 were covered through their own jobs, compared to nearly three-fourths of privately insured men.

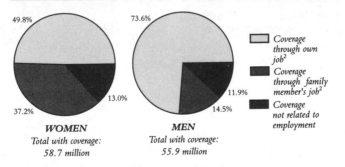

[1]Persons with coverage for all or part of the year.
[2]Coverage related to current or past employment.
Source: Bureau of the Census, *Poverty in the United States: 1991,* 1992, Table 24.

Figure 4-9 • WOMEN AGE 18 TO 64 WITH PRIVATE HEALTH INSURANCE BY AGE AND SOURCE OF COVERAGE, 1991[1] (in percentages)

Fully one-fourth of all insured women in their early sixties, and nearly a fourth of those between the ages of 18 and 24, have coverage that is unrelated to employment, which almost certainly means that they have purchased individual health insurance policies. Individual policies are typically far more expensive than employer-provided group policies, and often offer fewer benefits.

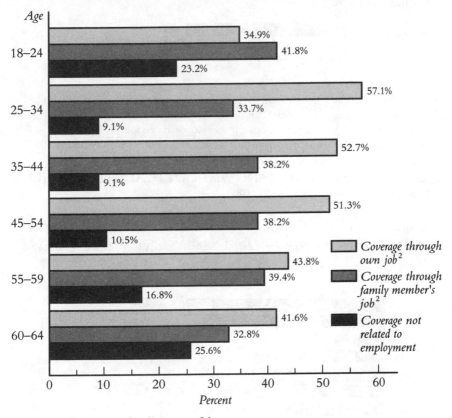

[1]Women with coverage for all or part of the year.
[2]Coverage related to current or past employment.
Source: Bureau of the Census, *Poverty in the United States: 1991,* 1992, Table 24.

A larger proportion of males than of females lacked health insurance of any kind in 1991. A larger proportion of females than of males had Medicaid coverage.

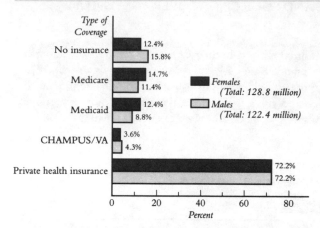

[1]Persons of all ages. The "insured" had coverage for all or part of 1991; the uninsured had no coverage at any time during 1991. Percentages for each sex sum to more than 100 percent because some insured had coverage from more than one source.
Source: Bureau of the Census, *Poverty in the United States: 1991,* 1992, Table 24.

Figure 4-11 • PERSONS WITH AND WITHOUT HEALTH INSURANCE COVERAGE BY SEX AND AGE, 1991

The majority of people of all ages are covered by some form of health insurance, but coverage varies by both sex and age. For example, in 1991, of the roughly 32 million females under 18, four million—12 percent—had no coverage.

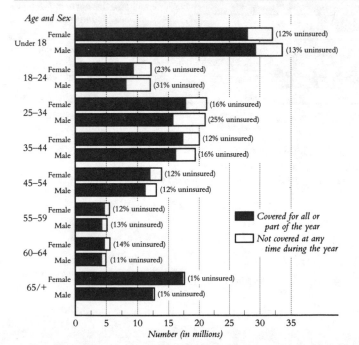

Source: Bureau of the Census, *Poverty in the United States: 1991,* 1992, Table 24.

Figure 4-12 • PERSONS AGE 18 TO 64 WITH NO HEALTH INSURANCE
COVERAGE BY SEX AND AGE, 1991[1] (percent distribution)

In 1991, about 60 percent of all uninsured men between the ages of 18 to 64
were under age 35. The comparable proportion of women was smaller (52
percent); still, over half of all uninsured women were in their prime reproductive years.

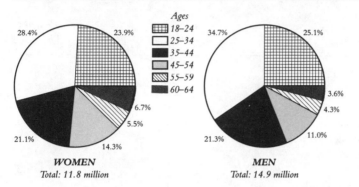

WOMEN
Total: 11.8 million

MEN
Total: 14.9 million

[1]Persons who had no coverage at any time during the year.
Source: Bureau of the Census, *Poverty in the United States: 1991,* 1992, Table 24.

Figure 4-13 • PERSONS AGE 16 TO 64 WITH NO HEALTH INSURANCE
COVERAGE BY SEX AND WORK EXPERIENCE, 1991[1] (percent
distribution)

Most people of working age who have no health insurance do work, and in
1991, one-fourth of uninsured women, and well over one-third of uninsured
men, worked full time, year round.

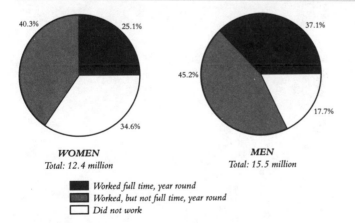

WOMEN
Total: 12.4 million

MEN
Total: 15.5 million

■ *Worked full time, year round*
▨ *Worked, but not full time, year round*
□ *Did not work*

[1]Persons with no coverage at any time during the year.
Source: Bureau of the Census, *Poverty in the United States: 1991,* 1992, Table 24.

326 / The American Woman 1994-95

Table 4-10 • PERSONS WITH NO HEALTH INSURANCE COVERAGE
BY FAMILY RELATIONSHIP, 1991[1] (percent distribution)

More than a fifth of Americans with no health insurance coverage are children
under 18; another 16 percent are children *over* 18 who live with their parents.

Relationship	Percent of Uninsured
Persons living in families	
Wives	13.4
Husbands	13.2
Female householders	5.3
Children under age 18	22.5
Children over age 18	15.9
Other[2]	9.5
Persons not living in families	
Unrelated females	6.9
Unrelated males	11.9
In unrelated subfamilies	1.3
Total percent	100.0
Total number (in thousands)	35,358

[1]Persons who had no health insurance coverage at any time during the year.
[2]Could include male householders with no spouse present, as well as other relatives.
Source: Bureau of the Census, *Poverty in the United States: 1991,* 1992, Table 24.

SECTION 5:

ECONOMIC SECURITY [1]

The real median income of married couples with working wives increased between 1971 and 1991. Families of other types were typically less well off in 1991 than their counterparts in 1971. Median income of families headed by persons under age 25 declined fairly steeply; the median for elderly families increased. Although as a rule poverty rates are low for married couples, nearly one-quarter of Hispanic couples with children were poor in 1991. The poverty rate for female-headed families with children was nearly 50 percent.

- The net increase in family incomes between 1971 and 1991 was driven almost entirely by the gains for married couples with working wives, the only family type for which real income increased both significantly and steadily over the period (see Figure 5-1).
- Between 1981 and 1991, real income increased for black families of every type, although only marginally for female-headed families. Median income dropped for Hispanic families of every type except female-headed (see Table 5-1).
- Families with a head of household over age 35 were typically doing better in 1991 than their counterparts in 1971, but those with a head of household under age 35 were not doing as well. The decline in the income of the youngest families was striking (see Figure 5-2).

[1]Health insurance coverage and assets are important factors in determining Americans' economic security. Statistics on health insurance coverage can be found in Section 4 (Earnings and Benefits) of this book. Regarding assets other than homeownership, the data published in *The American Woman 1992–93* remain the most recent available as *1994–95* goes to press and those data have not been repeated in this new edition.

- A family headed by a woman is more likely to be poor than a married couple family or one headed by a man. A family with children is more likely to be poor than its counterpart without children (see Figure 5-4).
- When a family with children is headed by a woman, the odds that it is in poverty approach one in two (see Figure 5-4).
- In 1991, 23.5 percent of Hispanic couples with children were poor—a poverty rate far higher than those of their black and white counterparts (see Table 5-6).
- Black women are only half as likely as white women to be awarded child support. Poverty rates are very high among mothers who have not been awarded child support (see Tables 5-4 and 5-5).
- Poverty rates are higher at every age for women who live alone or with nonrelatives than for their male counterparts. The disparities are widest after age 55 (see Table 5-8).
- Less than six percent of nonelderly women had income from self-employment in 1991. The average for those who did was about $9,400 (see Table 5-2).
- Men age 65 and over received an average of $20,381 in 1991, about 80 percent more than women in that age group averaged. The women were less than half as likely as the men to be getting a pension (see Table 5-9).
- The percentage of American households that owned their homes declined between 1981 and 1991 in every age group except those 65 and over. The drops are most noticeable in the age groups under age 45 (see Figure 5-5).

Figure 5-1 • MEDIAN FAMILY INCOME BY FAMILY TYPE, 1971–1991 (in constant 1991 dollars)[1]

The net increase in family income between 1971 and 1991 was driven almost entirely by the gains for married couples with working wives, the only family type for which real income increased both significantly and steadily over the period.

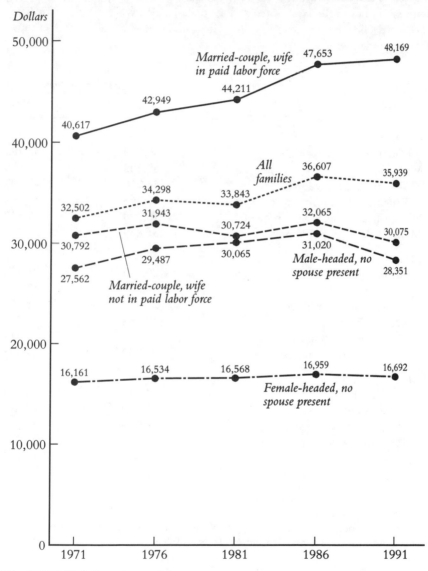

[1]The CPI-U–X1 inflator was used.

Source: Bureau of the Census, *Money Income of Households, Families, and Persons in the United States: 1991,* 1992, Tables B-6 and B-11.

Table 5-1 • MEDIAN INCOME OF WHITE, BLACK, AND HISPANIC
FAMILIES BY FAMILY TYPE, 1981 AND 1991 (in constant 1991 dollars)[1]

Between 1981 and 1991, real income increased for black families of every type,
with the largest gain for couples with working wives. White couples with working wives also saw a healthy increase, but income declined for white couples
with wives not in the labor force and for male-headed white families. Median
income declined over the decade for Hispanic families of every type except
female-headed.

| Race, Hispanic Origin, | Median Income | |
and Family Type	1981	1991
WHITE		
All family types	35,550	37,783
Married-couple	38,508	41,506
Wife in paid labor force	44,916	48,802
Wife not in paid labor force	31,563	30,792
Female-headed, no spouse present	18,908	19,547
Male-headed, no spouse present	30,869	28,924
BLACK		
All family types	20,055	21,548
Married-couple	29,665	33,307
Wife in paid labor force	37,852	41,353
Wife not in paid labor force	18,655	20,288
Female-headed, no spouse present	11,346	11,414
Male-headed, no spouse present	21,902	24,508
HISPANIC[2]		
All family types	24,794	23,895
Married-couple	29,219	28,594
Wife in paid labor force	35,737	35,655
Wife not in paid labor force	23,508	21,923
Female-headed, no spouse present	11,467	12,132
Male-headed, no spouse present	22,362	21,759

[1]The CPI-U-X1 inflator was used.
[2]Persons of Hispanic origin may be of any race.
Source: Bureau of the Census, *Money Income of Households, Families, and Persons in the
United States: 1981,* 1983, Table 13 and *1991,* 1992, Table 13.

Figure 5-2 • MEDIAN FAMILY INCOME BY AGE OF HOUSEHOLDER, 1971–1991 (in constant 1991 dollars)[1]

Families in all the age groups over 35 were typically doing better in 1991 than their counterparts in 1971, but those under age 35 were not doing as well. The decline in the income of the youngest families is striking; it was probably partly accounted for by a growing proportion of female-headed families. (However, just between 1981 and 1991, the median income of married couples in the youngest age group dropped by eight percent.)

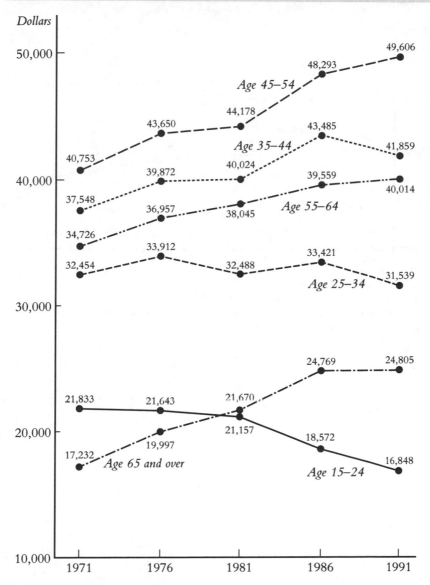

[1]The CPI-U-X1 inflator was used.

Source: Bureau of the Census, *Money Income of Households, Families, and Persons in the United States: 1991,* 1992, Table B-10.

Figure 5-3 • MEDIAN INCOME OF FAMILIES WITH CHILDREN BY FAMILY TYPE, 1976–1991 (in constant 1991 dollars)[1]

The typical married couple with children had a higher real income in 1991 than its counterpart in 1976. This was not true of single-parent families with children whose purchasing power was lower at the end of the period than at the beginning—by some four percent for the families headed by women, by nearly 20 percent for those headed by men.

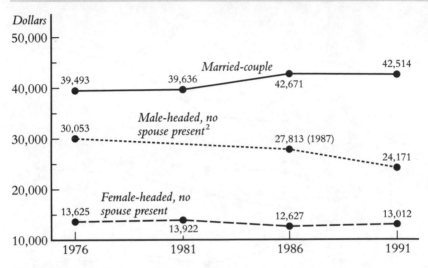

[1]The CPI-U-X1 inflator was used.
[2]1981 and 1986 data were not available for male-headed families.
Source: Bureau of the Census, *Money Income of Households, Families, and Persons in the United States: 1991,* 1992, Table B-12.

Table 5-2 • SOURCES OF INCOME FOR WOMEN AGE 15 TO 64 BY RACE AND HISPANIC ORIGIN, 1991

A woman may have personal income from more than one source, but wages or salaries are by far the most common source of income for nonelderly women and, on average, produce by far the largest amount of income. In 1991, among women of all races who were age 15 to 64 and had income, 76 percent had wage and salary income; the average amount was $16,260. Income from self-employment ran second in terms of amount ($9,392), but the proportion of women who had self-employment income was very small—5.5 percent overall in 1991.

Source of Income	With Income From Source		Mean Income From Source (in dollars)
	Number (in thousands)	Percent	
Total[1]			
All races	75,030	100.0	15,179
White	63,033	100.0	15,412
Black	9,222	100.0	13,449
Hispanic origin[2]	5,454	100.0	11,392
Wage and salary			
All races	57,060	76.0	16,260
White	48,235	76.5	16,371
Black	6,849	74.3	15,034
Hispanic origin	3,961	72.6	12,896
Self-employment[3]			
All races	4,128	5.5	9,392
White	3,755	6.0	9,268
Black	205	2.2	8,532
Hispanic origin	186	3.4	9,293
Unemployment compensation			
All races	3,183	4.2	1,945
White	2,635	4.2	1,938
Black	445	4.8	1,970
Hispanic origin	286	5.2	1,623

[1]Totals comprise women who had income from any source in 1991. However, not every source of income is detailed in this table.
[2]Persons of Hispanic origin may be of any race.
[3]Excludes farm self-employment, from which 262,000 women had income in 1991.

(continued)

Table 5-2 (continued)

| Source of Income | With Income From Source | | Mean Income From Source (in dollars) |
	Number (in thousands)	Percent	
AFDC[4]			
All races	3,666	4.9	3,643
White	2,111	3.3	3,716
Black	1,418	15.4	3,443
Hispanic origin	561	10.3	4,640
Interest			
All races	44,348	59.1	992
White	40,029	63.5	1,027
Black	2,687	29.1	538
Hispanic origin	1,935	35.5	494
Child support			
All races	3,995	5.3	3,134
White	3,363	5.3	3,303
Black	542	5.9	2,065
Hispanic origin	246	4.5	2,294

[4]Excludes women who had income from other forms of public assistance as well as from Aid to Families with Dependent Children (AFDC).

Source: Bureau of the Census, unpublished data from the March 1992 Current Population Survey.

• The proportion of women who were supposed to receive child support but actually received none declined a bit between 1978 and 1989. The proportion receiving the full amount increased a bit. • Black women are only half as likely as white women to be awarded child support. • Poverty rates are very high among mothers who have not been awarded child support.

Table 5-3 • RECEIPT OF CHILD SUPPORT PAYMENTS BY MOTHERS AWARDED SUPPORT, 1978 AND 1989

| | *Percent Distribution* | |
Mother Received	*In 1978*	*In 1989*
Full award amount	48.9	51.4
Partial amount	22.8	23.8
No payments	28.3	24.8
Total percent	100.0	100.0
Total number of women who should have received payments (in thousands)	3,424	4,953

Table 5-4 • WOMEN WITH CHILD SUPPORT AWARDS BY RACE AND HISPANIC ORIGIN, 1989

	Women Eligible for Child Support[1] (numbers in thousands)	*Percent Awarded Child Support*
All races	9,955	57.7
White	6,905	67.5
Black	2,770	34.5
Hispanic origin[2]	1,112	40.6

Table 5-5 • WOMEN ELIGIBLE FOR CHILD SUPPORT BY POVERTY STATUS, RACE, AND HISPANIC ORIGIN, 1989

	Number Awarded Child Support (in thousands)	*Percent in Poverty*	*Number Not Awarded Child Support (in thousands)*	*Percent in Poverty*
All races	5,748	24.1	4,207	43.2
White	4,661	20.6	2,244	35.7
Black	955	40.2	1,815	51.2
Hispanic origin[2]	452	39.2	660	54.4

[1]Women age 15 and over with children under age 21 whose fathers are absent.
[2]Persons of Hispanic origin may be of any race.
Source: Bureau of the Census, *Child Support and Alimony 1987,* 1990, Table B (for 5-3); *Statistical Abstract of the United States 1992,* 1992, Tables 596 and 597 (for 5-3, 5-4, and 5-5).

Figure 5-4 • POVERTY RATES OF FAMILIES BY FAMILY TYPE AND PRESENCE OF CHILDREN, 1991¹

When a family with children is headed by a woman, the odds that it is in poverty approach one in two: 47 percent of female-headed families with children were poor in 1991.

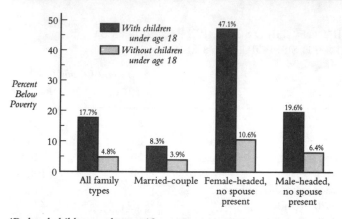

¹Related children under age 18.
Source: Bureau of the Census, *Poverty in the United States: 1991,* 1992, Table 4.

Figure 5-5 • HOMEOWNERSHIP BY AGE OF HOUSEHOLDER, 1981 AND 1991¹

In 1991, householders in every age group under 65 were less likely to own their own homes than their counterparts in 1981. The differences are most noticeable for the groups under age 45.

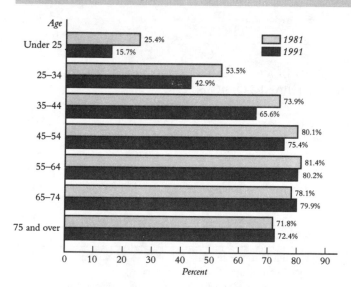

¹March 1981 and March 1991.
Source: Bureau of the Census, *Household and Family Characteristics: March 1981,* 1982, Table 24 and *March 1991,* 1992, Table 16.

Table 5-6 • POVERTY RATES OF WHITE, BLACK, AND HISPANIC
FAMILIES BY FAMILY TYPE AND PRESENCE OF CHILDREN, 1991[1]

Although married-couple families with children are more likely to be poor than
couples without children, they are less likely to be poor than other types of
families with children. This holds true for Hispanic families, but it is notable that
in 1991, 23.5 percent of Hispanic couples with children were poor—a poverty
rate far higher than those of their black and white counterparts.

| | | | *Percent in Poverty* | |
| | | | *Families with* | |
Race and Hispanic Origin and Presence of Children	*All Family Types*	*Married-Couple Families*	*Female Head[2]*	*Male Head[2]*
WHITE				
All families	8.8	5.5	28.4	10.8
Families with children	13.7	7.7	39.6	16.5
Families without children	4.0	3.4	8.1	5.1
BLACK				
All families	30.4	11.0	51.2	21.9
Families with children	39.2	12.4	60.5	31.7
Families without children	12.7	9.1	19.5	12.7
HISPANIC[3]				
All families	26.5	19.1	49.7	18.5
Families with children	33.7	23.5	60.1	29.4
Families without children	9.8	9.1	14.9	6.1

[1]Related children under age 18.
[2]With no spouse present.
[3]Persons of Hispanic origin may be of any race.
Source: Bureau of the Census, *Poverty in the United States: 1991,* 1992, Table 4.

Table 5-7 • LABOR MARKET PROBLEMS AMONG WOMEN
WORKERS WHO MAINTAIN FAMILIES BY POVERTY STATUS, 1990[1]
(in percentages)

Poor women workers who maintain families are much more likely than their
nonpoor counterparts to have low earnings, spells of unemployment, and having
to settle for part-time work when they want to work full time.

| | Percentage Having Problem | |
| | Women At or Above Poverty | Women Below Poverty |
Labor Market Problem		
Low earnings	8.5	73.9
Unemployment	9.0	43.3
Involuntary part-time work	5.3	25.0

[1]Women who maintained families and who were in the labor force for more than half the
year as full-time wage and salary workers.
Source: Bureau of Labor Statistics, "Working and Poor in 1990," *Monthly Labor Review,*
December 1992, Table 5.

Table 5-8 • POVERTY RATES OF UNRELATED INDIVIDUALS BY SEX
AND AGE, 1991[1]

Poverty rates are higher at every age for women who live alone or with nonrelatives than for their male counterparts. The disparities are widest after age 54.

| | Women | | Men | |
| | Number (in thousands) | Percent in Poverty | Number (in thousands) | Percent in Poverty |
Age				
Under 18	113	97.0	71	—[2]
18–24	2,067	34.2	2,296	29.4
25–34	3,282	15.8	5,507	12.2
35–44	2,073	15.6	3,533	14.5
45–54	1,985	20.0	2,065	17.9
55–59	936	26.6	744	17.2
60–64	1,205	29.9	723	18.3
65 and over	7,784	27.0	2,455	18.5
Total	19,445	24.5	17,395	17.3

[1]Persons who live alone or with nonrelatives.
[2]Not published because base is less than 75,000.
Source: Bureau of the Census, *Poverty in the United States: 1991,* 1992, Table 5.

Table 5-9 · SOURCES OF INCOME FOR PERSONS AGE 65 AND OVER
BY SEX, 1991

In 1991, average income for men age 65 and over was $20,381, about 80 percent
more than the average for women. The most common sources of income for
both sexes were Social Security (received by over 92 percent of the women and
about 90 percent of the men) and interest.

| Source of Income | Persons With Income From Source | | Mean Income From Source (in dollars) |
	Number (in thousands)	Percent	
Total[1]			
Women	17,539	100.0	11,323
Men	12,717	100.0	20,381
Earnings			
Women	1,951	11.1	9,039
Men	2,780	29.9	18,979
Social Security			
Women	16,202	92.4	5,637
Men	11,396	89.6	7,643
Supplemental Security Income (SSI)			
Women	1,314	7.5	2,498
Men	408	3.2	2,580
Survivors' benefits			
Women	1,719	9.8	6,045
Men	277	2.2	8,216
Pensions			
Women	3,818	21.8	5,186
Men	6,176	48.6	9,855
Interest			
Women	11,788	67.2	3,229
Men	8,924	70.2	3,624
Dividends			
Women	2,747	15.7	3,428
Men	2,550	20.1	3,715
Rents and royalties			
Women	1,415	8.1	3,968
Men	1,372	10.8	4,395

[1]Totals comprise persons who had income from any source in 1991. However, not every
source of income is detailed in this table.
Source: Bureau of the Census, unpublished data from the March 1992 Current Population
Survey.

Table 5-10 · SOURCES OF INCOME FOR WHITE, BLACK, AND
HISPANIC WOMEN AGE 65 AND OVER, 1991

As a rule, elderly white women are more likely than their black and Hispanic
counterparts to have income from any given source other than SSI, and their
income from most sources is higher. However, elderly black women are slightly
more likely than their white counterparts to have earnings, and black women
who have pensions receive, on average, a larger dollar amount than their white
counterparts.

| | With Income From Source | | Mean Income |
| | Number | | From Source |
Source of Income	(in thousands)	Percent	(in dollars)
Total[1]			
White	15,688	100.0	11,701
Black	1,504	100.0	7,754
Hispanic origin[2]	630	100.0	7,640
Earnings			
White	1,715	10.9	9,239
Black	180	12.0	7,089
Hispanic origin	55	—[3]	—[3]
Social Security			
White	14,602	93.1	5,714
Black	1,330	88.4	4,903
Hispanic origin	501	79.5	4,607
Supplemental Security Income (SSI)			
White	826	5.3	2,411
Black	409	27.2	2,363
Hispanic origin	188	29.8	3,264
Survivors' benefits			
White	1,631	10.4	6,109
Black	78	5.2	4,619
Hispanic origin	37	—[3]	—[3]
Pensions			
White	3,556	22.7	5,112
Black	217	14.4	6,333
Hispanic origin	52	—[3]	—[3]

[1]Totals comprise women who had income from any source in 1991. However, not every
source of income is detailed in this table.
[2]Persons of Hispanic origin may be of any race.
[3]Not published because base is less than 75,000.

(continued)

Table 5-10 (continued)

Source of Income	With Income From Source		Mean Income From Source (in dollars)
	Number (in thousands)	Percent	
Interest			
White	11,212	71.5	3,297
Black	396	26.3	1,415
Hispanic origin	207	32.9	2,393
Dividends			
White	2,706	17.3	3,443
Black	14	—[3]	—[3]
Hispanic origin	13	—[3]	—[3]
Rents and royalties			
White	1,329	8.5	3,980
Black	67	—[3]	—[3]
Hispanic origin	19	—[3]	—[3]

[3]Not published because base is less than 75,000.

Source: Bureau of the Census, unpublished data from the March 1992 Current Population Survey.

Figure 5-6 • HOMEOWNERSHIP BY FAMILY TYPE, PRESENCE OF
CHILDREN, RACE, AND HISPANIC ORIGIN, MARCH 1991[1] (in
percentages)

Whether it is white, black, or Hispanic, a female-headed family with children is
less likely to own its home than any other type of family of the same race or
ethnicity. However, a white family of any given type is more likely to own its
home than a black or Hispanic family of the same type. As a rule, homeownership rates are lower for families of any particular type if they have children
(male-headed Hispanic families are the exception).

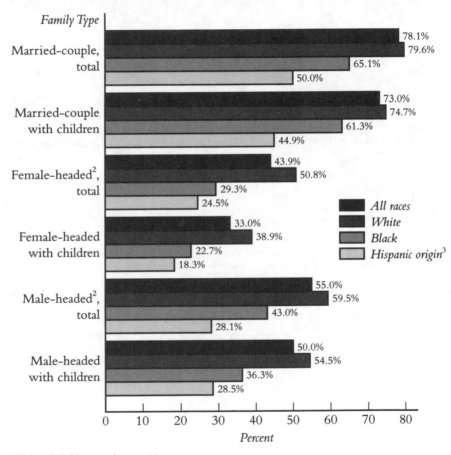

[1]Related children under age 18.
[2]With no spouse present.
[3]Persons of Hispanic origin may be of any race.
Source: Bureau of the Census, *Household and Family Characteristics: March 1991*, 1992,
Table 16.

Table 5-11 • THE HOUSING COST BURDEN BY HOUSEHOLD TYPE
AND TENURE, SELECTED AGE GROUPS, 1989[1]

The housing cost burden is the ratio of a household's housing costs to its income.
The federal government considers that paying up to 30 percent of income is
affordable, but many renters pay far more than that. Elderly women who rent
typically have the highest burdens.

Household Type	Housing Costs as a Percentage of Income	
	Owners	Renters
Two-or-more-person households		
Married couples, all ages	13.7	21.7
Age 25–29	19.8	21.0
Age 30–34	18.8	20.5
Age 35–44	16.3	20.8
Age 65 and over	13.4	32.4
Female householders, all ages	17.7	40.1
Age 65 and over	14.0	44.9
Male householders, all ages	16.9	28.7
Age 65 and over	12.6	33.6
One-person households		
Female householders, all ages	22.2	38.8
Age 65 and over	24.2	44.5
Male householders, all ages	15.3	24.5
Age 65 and over	19.5	38.7

[1]The age group refers to the age of the person identified as the householder. In the case of
married couples, this is usually—but not necessarily—the husband.
Source: Bureau of the Census and Department of Housing and Urban Development,
American Housing Survey for the United States in 1989, 1991, Tables 3-20, 3-21, 4-20, and
4-21.

SECTION 6:

Elections and
Officials

The election of 1992 was a watershed event for American women in politics, tripling the number of elected women in the U.S. Senate and nearly doubling the number of women in the House of Representatives. As has been true in every national election beginning with 1980, not only did more women than men go to the polls on November 3, 1992 but a larger percentage of women than of men voted.

Women's increased political participation has been reflected in a larger percentage of women among high-level federal appointments. One-fifth of President Bush's appointees to positions requiring Senate confirmation were women—a considerably better record in this regard than previous administrations. As this book goes to press, President Clinton's appointments are far from complete, but he has made a promising beginning. If, as is anticipated, Ruth Bader Ginsburg is confirmed to the U.S. Supreme Court in the summer of 1993, there will be now two women serving on the Court.

- White, black, and Hispanic women were more likely than their male counterparts to vote in the 1992 election. However, voter participation was lower among black women and men than among their white counterparts, and very low among women and men of Hispanic origin (see Figure 6-1).
- Voter participation has consistently been low in the age group just old enough to vote, but women age 18 and 19 have been consistently more likely to vote than their male peers (see Table 6-2).
- In the age groups over 55, turnout has tended to be relatively high for both sexes, but higher for men than for women. Nevertheless, voter

participation has been generally increasing among older women (see Table 6-2).

- The election of 1992 brought a significant increase in the number and percentage of elected women in the U.S. Congress. The election of Kay Bailey Hutchison (R-TX) to the Senate in a special election in June 1993 brought to seven the number of women in the U.S. Senate, where there were only two elected women in 1991 (see Table 6-3).

- American women's increased participation in the political process is reflected in the growing presence of women in high-level federal appointed jobs. Twenty percent of President Bush's appointments to Senate-confirmed positions were women, a notably higher percentage than in previous administrations. President Clinton seems likely to achieve an even higher percentage (see Table 6-5).

Figure 6-1 • VOTER PARTICIPATION IN THE 1992 NATIONAL ELECTION BY SEX, RACE, AND HISPANIC ORIGIN[1] (in percentages)

A higher percentage of women than of men voted in the 1992 national election. This was true across the board. However, voter participation was lower among blacks of both sexes than among their white counterparts, and very low among men and women of Hispanic origin.

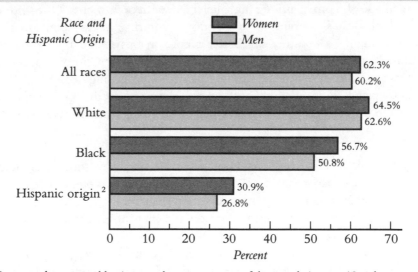

[1]Persons who reported having voted as a percentage of the population age 18 and over.
[2]Persons of Hispanic origin may be of any race.
Source: Bureau of the Census, *Voting and Registration in the Election of November 1992,* 1993, Table 2.

Table 6-1 • VOTER PARTICIPATION IN NATIONAL ELECTIONS BY SEX, RACE, AND HISPANIC ORIGIN, 1976–1992[1] (in percentages)

A greater proportion of white women and men turned out for the 1992 election than for any of the previous four national elections. However, for black and Hispanic voters of both sexes, the 1984 election was the recent high-water mark of voter participation.

Year	All Races		White		Black		Hispanic Origin[2]	
	Women	Men	Women	Men	Women	Men	Women	Men
1976	58.8	59.6	60.5	61.5	49.9	47.2	30.1	33.9
1980	59.4	59.1	60.9	60.9	52.8	47.5	30.4	29.2
1984	60.8	59.0	62.0	60.8	59.2	51.7	33.1	32.1
1988	58.3	56.4	59.8	58.3	54.2	48.2	30.1	27.4
1992	62.3	60.2	64.5	62.6	56.7	50.8	30.9	26.8

[1] Persons who reported having voted as a percentage of the population age 18 and over.
[2] Persons of Hispanic origin may be of any race.

Source: Bureau of the Census, *Voting and Registration in the Election of November 1976*, 1978, Table 2; *Voting and Registration in the Election of November 1980*, 1982, Table 2; *Voting and Registration in the Election of November 1984*, 1986, Table 2; *Voting and Registration in the Election of November 1988*, 1989, Table 2; and *Voting and Registration in the Election of November 1992*, 1993, Table 2.

Figure 6-2 • VOTERS IN THE 1992 NATIONAL ELECTION BY SEX AND AGE[1]

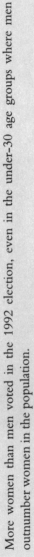

More women than men voted in the 1992 election, even in the under-30 age groups where men outnumber women in the population.

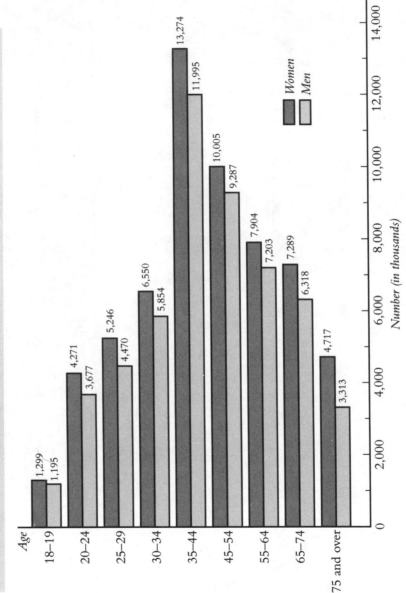

[1]Persons who reported having voted.

Source: Bureau of the Census, *Voting and Registration in the Election of November 1992*, 1993, Table 1.

Table 6-2 • VOTER PARTICIPATION IN NATIONAL ELECTIONS BY SEX AND AGE, 1976–1992[1] (in percentages)

Voter participation has consistently been low in the age group just old enough to vote, but women age 18 and 19 have been consistently more likely to vote than their male peers. In the age groups over 55, by contrast, turnout has tended to be relatively high for both sexes, but higher for men than for women. Nevertheless, the general trend has been one of increasing participation among the older women voters.

Age	1976		1980		1984		1988		1992	
	Women	Men	Women	Men	Women	Men	Women	Men	Women	Men
18–19	38.8	34.6	34.5	33.9	37.6	32.5	34.4	29.9	39.5	36.2
20–24	45.3	43.7	43.9	40.4	44.6	41.0	39.7	35.8	47.2	42.1
25–29	53.9	51.6	52.4	50.0	53.3	48.2	46.0	41.2	52.8	46.8
30–34	58.9	58.2	59.6	56.7	61.1	56.1	54.1	50.2	58.5	53.6
35–44	64.1	62.5	66.0	62.7	64.9	62.0	63.3	59.1	65.7	61.5
45–54	67.9	67.9	67.6	67.3	68.0	67.0	66.6	66.6	69.2	68.2
55–64	67.9	71.8	70.2	72.6	71.5	72.7	68.9	69.8	71.4	71.9
65–74	63.0	70.9	66.7	72.7	70.2	73.9	71.5	75.0	71.8	76.2
75 and over	50.1	62.9	52.9	65.7	57.2	68.3	57.5	70.2	60.8	71.4
Total	58.8	59.6	59.4	59.1	60.8	59.0	58.3	56.4	62.3	60.2

[1]Persons who reported having voted as a percentage of the population age 18 and over.

Source: Bureau of the Census, *Voting and Registration in the Election of November 1976*, 1978, Table 1; *Voting and Registration in the Election of November 1980*, 1982, Table 1; *Voting and Registration in the Election of November 1984*, 1986, Table 1; *Voting and Registration in the Election of November 1988*, 1989, Table 1; and *Voting and Registration in the Election of November 1992*, 1993, Table 1.

Table 6-3 • WOMEN IN ELECTIVE OFFICE, SELECTED YEARS, 1975–1993

The elections of 1992 brought a real increase in the number and percentage of women in the U.S. Congress. The election of Kay Bailey Hutchison (R-TX) to the Senate in a special election in June 1993 brought to seven the number of elected women in the U.S. Senate, where there had never before been more than two.

Elected Officeholders	Percent Women					Number of Women 1993
	1975	*1981*	*1987*	*1991*	*1993*	
Members of Congress	4	4	5	6	10	55[1]
Statewide elected officials[2]	10	11	14	18	22	72
State legislators	8	12	16	18	20	1,517
Mayors[3]	5	8	11	17	18	176

[1]As of June 30, 1993. Includes 48 women in the House of Representatives (one of whom is the nonvoting delegate from the District of Columbia) and seven women in the Senate.
[2]Does not include officials in appointive state cabinet-level positions, officials elected to executive posts by state legislatures, members of the judicial branch, or elected members of university boards of trustees or boards of education.
[3]Mayors of cities with populations over 30,000.
Source: Center for the American Woman and Politics, *Women in Elective Office 1991 Fact Sheet*, 1991; *Women in the U.S. Congress 1993 Fact Sheet*, 1993; *Statewide Elective Executive Women 1993 Fact Sheet*, 1993; *Women in State Legislatures 1993 Fact Sheet*, 1993; and National Women's Political Caucus, *Factsheet on Women's Political Progress*, June 1993.

Table 6-4 • WOMEN ON THE FEDERAL BENCH[1]

| | *Women Judges* | |
	Number	*As a Percentage of All Judges*
Supreme Court justices	2	22.2
Circuit court judges[2]	19	12.2
District court judges[3]	54	9.7
Bankruptcy court judges	39	13.3
U.S. magistrates (full-time)	59	18.2

[1]Supreme Court as of August 3, 1993 when the U.S. Senate confirmed Ruth Bader Ginsburg's appointment to the Court; other courts as of September 30, 1991.
[2]Includes judges on the Temporary Emergency Court of Appeals.
[3]Includes Territorial Courts, Claims Court, Court of International Trade, Special Court–Regional Rail Reorganization Act of 1973, and Judicial Panel on Multidistrict Litigation.
Source: Administrative Office of the United States Courts, *Annual Report on the Judiciary Equal Employment Opportunity Program for the Twelve-Month Period Ended September 30, 1991,* 1992, Table 1 and U.S. Supreme Court 1993.

Table 6-5 • WOMEN PRESIDENTIAL APPOINTEES TO SENATE-CONFIRMED POSITIONS, 1977–MAY 1993[1]

Twenty percent of President Bush's appointments to Senate-confirmed positions were women, a notably higher percentage than in previous administrations. President Clinton seems likely to achieve an even higher percentage.

President	*Total Number of Appointments*	*Number of Women Appointed*	*Percent Women*
Jimmy Carter (1977–81)	919	124	13.5
Ronald Reagan (1981–89)	2,349	277	12.0
George Bush (1989–92)	1,079	215	19.9
Bill Clinton (January–May 1993)	456	169	37.1

[1]Figures for the Clinton administration reflect the first five months only and are not really comparable to data for earlier administrations. Included in the Clinton data are some positions not counted for earlier administrations and vice versa.
Source: National Women's Political Caucus, *Factsheet on Women's Appointments,* 1993.

WOMEN IN THE 103RD CONGRESS

NINETEEN NINETY-TWO TURNED OUT to be a banner year for women. An unprecedented 48 women were elected to the House of Representatives (including Eleanor Holmes Norton for the District of Columbia), up from the 29 elected in 1990. Altogether, women now represent 27 states and the District of Columbia in the 103rd Congress, up from 20 in the 102nd Congress.

In the Senate women made major inroads as well. The election of five women (four newly elected and one incumbent) on November 8, 1992—and the subsequent election of Kay Bailey Hutchison in the Texas election to fill the unexpired term of Secretary of the Treasury Lloyd Benson—makes seven women in the Senate (the other incumbent woman Senator was not up for reelection), an increase from the two elected to the 102nd Congress.

The gains for women are dramatic. However, it is important to remember that women still make up only about 10 percent of Congress, even though they account for more than half the U.S. population.

WREI is pleased to include, in this fifth edition of *The American Woman*, brief biographies of the 55 women elected to serve in the 103rd Congress.

Representative Helen Delich Bentley *(Republican, 2nd District, Maryland)* was first elected to Congress in 1985. In the House, she serves on the Appropriations Committee.

Prior to her election to Congress, Rep. Bentley was chair of the Federal Maritime Commission. Rep. Bentley also spent many years as a journalist, specializing in maritime issues. Born in 1923 in Ruth, Nevada, Rep. Bentley is a graduate of the University of Missouri. She is married and has no children.

She has devoted her career in Congress to advocating on behalf of the shipping and maritime industries. She has earned a reputation as an expert on these issues, as well as on trade and defense.

Senator Barbara Boxer *(Democrat, California),* is in her first term as a member of the U.S. Senate, following 10 years as a member of the House of Representatives.

Senator Boxer sits on the Banking, Housing, and Urban Affairs Committee; the Environment and Public Works Committee; and the Committee on the Budget.

During her tenure in the House, then-Rep. Boxer led the fight for federal funding of abortions for women who are the victims of rape or incest. In the Senate, she has championed the Violence Against Women Act and legislation to make threatening or harassing behavior a federal crime.

Born in Brooklyn, New York in 1940, Senator Boxer has a B.A. degree in economics from Brooklyn College. She is married and the mother of two children. Prior to coming to Congress, she was a six-year member of the Marin County Board of Supervisors.

Representative Corrine Brown *(Democrat, 3rd District, Florida)* is serving her first term in the House of Representatives.

Rep. Brown holds B.S. and M.A. degrees from Florida A & M University and an education specialist degree from the University of Florida. She has served as a member of the faculty at Florida Community College of Jacksonville, as well as on the faculties of the University of Florida and Edward Waters College. Rep. Brown was born in 1946 in Jacksonville, where she still resides.

Prior to her election to Congress, Rep. Brown served for 10 years in the Florida House of Representatives, where she was the chair of the Prison Construction and Operations Subcommittee and vice chair of the Regulatory Subcommittee.

In Congress, Rep. Brown serves on the Public Works and Transportation Committee; the Committee on Veterans' Affairs; and the Committee on Government Operations. Her legislative priorities include education, aging, and economic development issues.

Representative Leslie Byrne *(Democrat, 11th District, Virginia)* was elected to Congress in November 1992. She is the first woman to serve in the House of Representatives from Virginia.

Prior to her election to Congress, Ms. Byrne served as a member of the Virginia House of Delegates for seven years. Her legislative priorities in Congress include consumer protection, economic growth, and protecting a woman's right to reproductive choice. Rep. Byrne is a member of the Committee on Public Works and Transportation and the Post Office and Civil Service Committee.

Congresswoman Byrne, who was born in 1946 in Salt Lake City, Utah, is married and has two children. She attended the University of Utah.

Representative Maria Cantwell *(Democrat, 1st District, Washington)* is presently serving her first term as a member of the House of Representatives. She sits on the Foreign Affairs Committee; the Public Works and Transportation Committee; and the Committee on Merchant Marine and Fisheries.

Prior to her election to the House, Rep. Cantwell was a member of the Washington state legislature, where she concentrated her energies on economic development and employment issues. In the Washington legislature, Ms. Cantwell chaired the Committee on Trade and Economic Development.

Rep. Cantwell was born in 1958 in Indianapolis, Indiana, and received her B.A. degree from Miami University in Ohio.

Representative Eva Clayton *(Democrat, 1st District, North Carolina)* is serving her first full term as a member of Congress. She was elected to the House in a combination general and special election in November 1992 to fill the seat left vacant by the death of her predecessor.

Rep. Clayton is not only the first woman elected to Congress from North Carolina, but also the first woman to be elected president of the Democratic freshman class. Rep. Clayton sits on the House Agriculture Committee and the Small Business Committee. Congresswoman Clayton was born in 1934 in Savannah, Georgia. She is married to Theaoseus Clayton, an attorney in Warrenton, North Carolina. She has four children and two grandchildren. Prior to her election to Congress, Rep. Clayton served as a member of the Warren County Board of Commissioners.

Congresswoman Clayton has been an active advocate for rural health care, housing assistance, and job training.

Representative Barbara-Rose Collins *(Democrat, 15th District, Michigan)* is serving her second term in the House of Representatives. She sits on the Post Office and Civil Service Committee, where she chairs the Subcommittee on Postal Operations and Services. She is also a member of the Public Works and Transportation Committee and the Government Operations Committee.

Ms. Collins was a member of the Detroit City Council from 1982 until her election to Congress. She also served in the Michigan House of Representatives for six years, where she chaired the Standing Committee on Urban Affairs. Born in 1939 in Detroit, Michigan, Rep. Collins attended Wayne State University. She has two children and four grandchildren.

Rep. Collins' legislative agenda includes providing a tax credit to employers who make mammography available for their employees.

Representative Cardiss Collins *(Democrat, 7th District, Illinois),* the longest-serving African American woman in Congress, was first elected to the House of Representatives in June 1973, in a special election to fill the seat of her late husband.

Rep. Collins sits on the Energy and Commerce Committee where she chairs the Subcommittee on Commerce, Consumer Protection, and Competitiveness. She is also a member of the Government Operations Committee. Rep. Collins has long been an advocate of universal health insurance, as well as a champion for increased funding for breast cancer research and screening.

Rep. Collins was born in 1931 in St. Louis, Missouri, and earned her B.A. degree at Northwestern University.

Representative Patricia Danner *(Democrat, 6th District, Missouri)* was elected to Congress in November 1992. She is a member of the House Committee on Public Works and Transportation and the Committee on Small Business.

Prior to her election to Congress, Ms. Danner served for 10 years as a member of the Missouri Senate, where she chaired the Transportation Committee. During her tenure in the state senate, Ms. Danner worked on legislation to enhance federally funded vocational technical programs by providing tuition waivers for displaced homemakers. She also authored Missouri's "Extended Day Child Care Act," which provided funds for after-school day care services.

Rep. Danner was born in 1934 in Louisville, Kentucky. She graduated with honors from Northeast Missouri State University where she earned her B.A. degree. She is married and has four children.

Representative Rosa DeLauro *(Democrat, 3rd District, Connecticut)* was first elected to Congress in 1990. She sits on the House Appropriations Committee.

Rep. DeLauro was born in New Haven, Connecticut in 1943, and has been in public service for much of her lifetime. She was the first woman to serve as executive assistant to the mayor of New Haven and was chief of staff to Connecticut Senator Christopher Dodd. Prior to her election, Ms. DeLauro was the executive director of EMILY's List, a national organization committed to increasing the number of women in elected office.

Congresswoman DeLauro has made improving the delivery of health care a priority of her tenure in Congress, sponsoring legislation to increase funding for medical research into women's health.

Rep. DeLauro received her B.A. degree from Marymount College and her M.A. degree in international politics from Columbia University. She is married to pollster Stanley Greenberg and has three grown children.

Representative Jennifer Dunn *(Republican, 8th District, Washington)* is one of two women elected to Congress from Washington state in the November 1992 election. In the House of Representatives, Rep. Dunn serves on the Public Works and Transportation Committee; the Committee on Science, Space, and Technology; and the House Administration Committee.

Prior to her election to Congress, Ms. Dunn was chairperson of the Washington state Republican Party, a position to which she was reelected five times. Rep. Dunn also served as a delegate to the thirtieth United Nations Commission on the Status of Women, which was held in Vienna, Austria in 1984. She also participated as a member of the Preparatory Commission for the 1985 World Conference on the Status of Women held in Nairobi, Kenya.

Congresswoman Dunn was born in Seattle, Washington in 1941, and holds a B.A. degree from Stanford University. She is the mother of two.

Representative Karan English *(Democrat, 6th District, Arizona)* was elected to her first congressional term in November 1992. Rep. English serves on the Committee on Natural Resources and the Committee on Education and Labor.

Prior to her election to Congress, Ms. English served for two terms in the Arizona House of Representatives from 1986 to 1990. Her legislative successes in the state house include passage of legislation earmarking funds for rural economic development for small businesses. She also served in the Arizona Senate, where she chaired the Environment Committee.

Born in Berkeley, California in 1949, Rep. English is a graduate of the University of Arizona. She resides in Flagstaff, Arizona with her husband, Rob Elliot, and their children.

Representative Anna Eshoo *(Democrat, 14th District, California)* was elected to her first term in Congress in 1992. Rep. Eshoo sits on the House Committees on Merchant Marine and Fisheries and Science, Space, and Technology.

As a 10-year member of the San Mateo County Board of Supervisors, Ms. Eshoo worked to expand perinatal services and reform Medicaid in the county. She also was responsible for securing funds for California's first freestanding nursing facility for AIDS patients.

Congresswoman Eshoo was born in New Britain, Connecticut in 1942. She is the mother of two children. She has her A.A. degree from Canada College in Redwood City, California.

Senator Dianne Feinstein *(Democrat, California)* was elected to the Senate in November 1992 to complete the unexpired term of Pete Wilson, who had been elected governor of California.

Ms. Feinstein served as mayor of San Francisco from 1978 to 1988. Prior to her election as mayor, she was a member of the San Francisco Board of Supervisors.

Senator Feinstein sits on the Appropriations and Judiciary Committees. She has focused her attention in the Senate on creating jobs in California.

A native of San Francisco, Senator Feinstein was born in 1933. She is married to Richard Blum and has one child and three stepchildren.

Representative Tillie Fowler *(Republican, 4th District, Florida)* is serving her first term as a member of the House of Representatives, where she sits on the Armed Services and Merchant Marine and Fisheries Committees.

Prior to her election to Congress, Ms. Fowler was a member of the Jacksonville City Council for seven years, and was the council president for two years. She began her career of public service on the staff of former Rep. Robert Stephens, Jr. (D-GA), and then served as general counsel in the White House Office of Consumer Affairs during the Nixon administration.

Rep. Fowler was elected to Congress on a platform that stressed both congressional and budget reform and term limits, pledging to stay in Congress for no more than eight years. She supports abortion rights for women.

Rep. Fowler was born in 1942 in Milledgeville, Georgia. She holds both a B.A. degree and a law degree from Emory University. She is married and has two daughters.

Representative Elizabeth Furse *(Democrat, 1st District, Oregon)* was elected in 1992 to her first term in Congress. She was born in Nairobi, Kenya in 1936 and was raised in South Africa. She came to the United States as a young woman and became an American citizen in 1972.

In the House, Rep. Furse sits on the Banking, Finance, and Urban Affairs Committee; the Environment and Natural Resources Committee; and the Committee on Education and Labor. During the 103rd Congress, Rep. Furse also is a temporary member of the Armed Services Committee.

A long-time community activist, Congresswoman Furse worked during the 1960s as a community organizer in Los Angeles, and on behalf of the northwest Indians during the 1970s. In 1986, she founded the Oregon Peace Institute, an organization whose goal is to resolve conflict through nonviolence.

She received her B.A. degree from Evergreen State College in Olympia, Washington. She is married and has two children.

Representative Jane Harman *(Democrat, 36th District, California)* comes to her first term in Congress with considerable Washington experience.

Ms. Harman worked in Washington during the 1970s as legislative director to then-Senator John Tunney (D-CA) and later as chief counsel and staff director of the Senate Judiciary Subcommittee on Constitutional Rights. She also served in the Carter administration as deputy secretary to the cabinet and eventually as special counsel to the Department of Defense. For the past 14 years, Rep. Harman has been a corporate lawyer with several firms.

Her seats on the House Armed Services Committee and the Science, Space, and Technology Committee will allow Rep. Harman to work to fulfill her commitment to retaining and building high-skill, high-wage jobs in the Los Angeles area.

Born in New York City in 1945, Rep. Harman is a graduate of Smith College and Harvard University Law School. She is married to Sidney Harman, chairman and chief executive officer of Harman International and the former undersecretary of commerce. The couple has four children.

Senator Kay Bailey Hutchison *(Republican, Texas)* was elected in June 1993 to fill the unexpired term of Secretary of the Treasury Lloyd Benson. She serves on the Foreign Relations Committee; the Small Business Committee; and the Commerce Committee.

Raised in La Marque, Texas, Ms. Hutchison is a graduate of the University of Texas at Austin and the University of Texas School of Law. She is married to Ray Hutchison, a Dallas attorney and former member of the Texas legislature.

Prior to her Senate position, Ms. Hutchison was elected Texas state treasurer, making her the first Republican woman elected to a statewide office. A former member of the Texas House of Representatives, she was appointed by then-president Ford to be vice chair of the National Transportation Safety Board.

Winner of numerous leadership awards, Senator Hutchison brings to her office various experiences, including banking and banking law, business enterprise, and work as a TV news correspondent.

Representative Eddie Bernice Johnson *(Democrat, 30th District, Texas)* is presently serving her first term as a member of the House of Representatives where she sits on the Committee on Public Works and Transportation and the Committee on Science, Space, and Technology.

Prior to her election to Congress, Ms. Johnson enjoyed a distinguished career as a business entrepreneur; professional nurse; health care administrator; and member of the Texas House of Representatives, where she was the first black woman since 1935 to be elected to public office in Texas. Rep. Johnson left the state legislature in 1977 to become the regional director of the then-Department of Health, Education, and Welfare during the Carter administration. In

1986, Ms. Johnson successfully sought a seat in the Texas Senate, which she held until her election to Congress.

Rep. Johnson is a graduate of Texas Christian University and earned her M.P.A. degree from Southern Methodist University. Rep. Johnson was born in 1935 in Waco, Texas and is the mother of one child.

Representative Nancy Johnson *(Republican, 6th District, Connecticut)* was first elected to Congress in 1983. In 1988, she became the first Republican woman to be named to the Ways and Means Committee, where she continues to serve. Since 1991, Rep. Johnson has also been a member of the Committee on Standards of Official Conduct.

Rep. Johnson was born in Chicago, Illinois in 1935. She received her B.A. degree from Radcliffe and served as a civic leader and adjunct professor before embarking on her political career. Prior to her election to Congress, Ms. Johnson served three terms in the Connecticut Senate. She is married to Dr. Theodore Johnson and has three children.

Rep. Johnson has spent much of her congressional career advocating for women in the areas of health care, child care, welfare reform, and reproductive rights.

Representative Marcy Kaptur *(Democrat, 9th District, Ohio)* has been in Congress since 1983. In addition to serving on the House Appropriations Committee, she is also treasurer of the Congressional Caucus for Women's Issues.

Rep. Kaptur was born in 1946 in Toledo, Ohio, and earned her B.A. degree from the University of Wisconsin and her M.A. degree in urban planning from the University of Michigan. She practiced as an urban planner for 15 years prior to seeking office and was a doctoral candidate at the Massachusetts Institute of Technology in urban studies. Rep. Kaptur also served as an urban advisor during the Carter administration and as the first deputy director of the National Cooperative Consumer Bank.

In the House, Rep. Kaptur has long advocated for tighter restrictions on trade and tougher lobbying restrictions on top-level federal officials.

Senator Nancy Landon Kassebaum *(Republican, Kansas)* was first elected to the United States Senate in 1978. She presently sits on the Labor and Human Resources Committee; the Committee on Foreign Relations; and the Select Committee on Indian Affairs. She also sits on the Joint Committee on the Organization of Congress.

Born in Topeka, Kansas in 1932, Senator Kassebaum is the daughter of Alfred M. Landon, former governor of Kansas and Republican presidential nominee. She earned her B.A. degree from the University of Kansas and her M.A. degree in diplomatic history from the University of Michigan. A former radio executive, Ms. Kassebaum entered politics as a member of the Maize, Kansas school board. She is the mother of four children.

From her position as the ranking Republican member on the Labor and Human Resources Committee, Senator Kassebaum has been able to play a leading role in education and children's issues. She also has led the fight on funding for international family planning programs and abortion rights.

Representative Barbara Kennelly *(Democrat, 1st District, Connecticut)* has served in Congress since 1982. She is one of two women who sit on the Ways and Means Committee. With her appointment as one of four Chief Deputy Majority Whips, Rep. Kennelly has become the highest ranking woman member in the history of the House of Representatives. She also served for six years as a member of the House Intelligence Committee, the first woman ever to sit on that committee.

Born in 1936 and raised in Hartford, Connecticut, Rep. Kennelly earned her B.A. degree from Trinity College in Washington, DC, and her M.A. degree from Trinity College in Hartford. She is married to James J. Kennelly, former Connecticut state representative and Speaker of the House, and has four children. Prior to her election to Congress, Ms. Kennelly served as secretary of state in Connecticut and as a member of the Hartford Court of Common Council.

During her tenure in Congress, Rep. Kennelly has championed welfare reform, tax policies that help families, and long-term care insurance. She served as a member of the U.S. Commission on Interstate Child Support and has recently introduced comprehensive child support enforcement legislation.

Representative Blanche Lambert *(Democrat, 1st District, Arkansas)* was elected to her first term in Congress in 1992. She is a member of the House Energy and Commerce Committee, the Committee on Agriculture, and the Merchant Marine and Fisheries Committee.

Congresswoman Lambert began her political career as an aide to Rep. Bill Alexander, whom she defeated in the 1992 primary. After she left her staff position on Capitol Hill, Ms. Lambert spent the next several years doing legislative research at law and governmental lobbying firms.

Born in 1960 in Helena, Arkansas, Rep. Lambert is a graduate of Randolph-Macon Women's College. She was elected to Congress on a platform that stressed job creation and development, agricultural incentives, and universal access to health care.

Representative Marilyn Lloyd *(Democrat, 3rd District, Tennessee)* became the first woman from Tennessee elected by popular vote to the House of Representatives in 1974. She is a member of the Committee on Science, Space, and Technology, where she chairs the Subcommittee on Energy. She also serves on the Armed Services Committee, and she was appointed to chair the Armed Services Committee Panel to the North Atlantic Assembly, the parliamentary body of the North Atlantic Treaty Organization (NATO).

Rep. Lloyd was born in Fort Smith, Arkansas in 1929, and is the mother of four children. Prior to her election to Congress, Ms. Lloyd was the owner and manager of a radio station.

Rep. Lloyd has championed improved screening and detection of breast cancer, as well as legislation to establish mammography quality standards.

Representative Jill Long *(Democrat, 4th District, Indiana)* was first elected to Congress in a special election in 1989. She serves on the Agriculture Committee and the Committee on Veterans' Affairs.

Rep. Long was born in Warsaw, Indiana in 1952. She was first elected to public office in 1983, when she won a seat on the Valparaiso City Council. Prior to entering politics, she was an assistant professor of business administration at Valparaiso University, where she earned her B.A. degree, and an adjunct professor of marketing at Indiana University, where she earned both her M.B.A. degree and her Ph.D.

Rep. Long has been a leading advocate for comprehensive health care services for women veterans, including counseling for women who were sexually harassed or assaulted while in military service.

Representative Nita Lowey *(Democrat, 18th District, New York)* was first elected to the House of Representatives in 1988. She is a member of the Appropriations Committee.

Rep. Lowey was born in Bronx, New York in 1937, and received her B.A. degree from Mount Holyoke College. She served in the New York Department of State for 12 years and was one of the founders of the New York State Association of Women Office Holders. She is married and has three children.

Rep. Lowey's legislative efforts include improving federal research into women's health concerns such as breast and cervical cancer, and expanding the availability of quality child care services. Rep. Lowey is also a leader in the fight to guarantee and protect a woman's right to reproductive choice.

Representative Carolyn Maloney *(Democrat, 14th District, New York)* was elected in November 1992 to her first term in the House of Representatives. She is a member of the Banking, Finance, and Urban Affairs Committee and the Committee on Government Operations.

Rep. Maloney brings to Congress a strong interest and commitment to women's and children's issues. During her 10 years on the New York City Council, she offered a comprehensive legislative package to increase the availability and affordability of child care services. She also led efforts to create the Joint Mayoral-Council Commission on Early Childhood Development Programs.

Rep. Maloney is a native of Greensboro, North Carolina, where she was born in 1948. She is a graduate of Greensboro College. She is married and has two daughters.

Representative Marjorie Margolies-Mezvinsky *(Democrat, 13th District, Pennsylvania)* was elected to her first term in the House of Representatives in 1992. She is the first woman ever elected in her own right to the House from Pennsylvania. Rep. Margolies-Mezvinsky is a member of the Energy and Commerce Committee; the Committee on Small Business; and the Government Operations Committee.

Prior to her election to Congress, Rep. Margolies-Mezvinsky was a reporter with NBC in both New York and Washington, DC. She won five Emmy Awards, as well as numerous other honors, for her reporting.

Shortly after her election to Congress, Rep. Margolies-Mezvinsky organized and led several bipartisan meetings with the 24 newly elected women members where they developed an agenda that included passing the Family and Medical Leave Act, addressing the issue of sexual harassment in Congress, and codifying *Roe v. Wade*.

Rep. Margolies-Mezvinsky was born in Philadelphia in 1942, and is married to former Rep. Edward Mezvinsky (D-Iowa). The two have 11 children.

Representative Cynthia McKinney *(Democrat, 11th District, Georgia),* currently serving her first term in Congress, is the first African American woman elected to the House of Representatives from Georgia. She sits on the Agriculture and the Foreign Affairs Committees.

Born in 1955 in Atlanta, Georgia, Rep. McKinney is a graduate of the University of Southern California. She is presently a Ph.D. candidate in international relations from Tufts University. Before her election to Congress, she was a professor of political science at Agnes Scott College in Decatur, Georgia.

Rep. McKinney has identified her legislative priorities as full funding for Head Start, universal immunization for children, and campaign finance reform.

Representative Carrie Meek *(Democrat, 17th District, Florida)* was elected in November 1992 to her first term in the House of Representatives. She is the only first-term Democratic member appointed to the Appropriations Committee.

Rep. Meek comes to Congress following a dozen years of service in the Florida legislature, where she served in both chambers. During her final term in the Florida Senate, Ms. Meek chaired the Appropriations Subcommittee on Education.

Rep. Meek was born in 1926 in Tallahassee, Florida. She is a graduate of Florida A & M University and holds an M.A. degree from the University of Michigan. She has three children.

Although it is early in her congressional career, Rep. Meek has become a leader in the effort to guarantee that domestic workers receive coverage under the Social Security system. She also is working to improve the access that low-income individuals have to government services such as housing and education.

Representative Jan Meyers *(Republican, 3rd District, Kansas)* was first elected to Congress in 1984. She is the ranking Republican on the Small Business Committee, as well as a member of the Foreign Affairs Committee.

Born in Lincoln, Nebraska in 1928, Rep. Meyers earned a B.A. degree in communications from the University of Nebraska. She served for five years on the Overland Park, Kansas City Council and for 12 years in the Kansas Senate prior to her election to Congress. She is married and has two children.

In the House, Rep. Meyers has given her attention to older women's issues, as well as women's health care.

Senator Barbara Mikulski *(Democrat, Maryland),* who was first elected to the Senate in 1986, is the first Democratic woman to hold a Senate seat not previously held by her husband, as well as the first Democratic woman to have served in both the House and the Senate.

Senator Mikulski came to Congress in 1976 as a member of the House of Representatives, where she distinguished herself as the first woman ever appointed to the Energy and Commerce Committee.

Ms. Mikulski began her career in public service as a social worker in Baltimore, Maryland, and entered politics with her election to the Baltimore City Council. Born in Baltimore in 1936, Senator Mikulski earned her B.A. degree from Mount Saint Agnes College in Baltimore and received her M.S.W. degree from the University of Maryland.

In the Senate, Ms. Mikulski has been a leader on women's health issues, winning enactment of legislation requiring licensing of clinical laboratories to ensure proper analysis of Pap smears.

Representative Patsy Mink *(Democrat, 2nd District, Hawaii)* was first elected to Congress in 1964 and served until 1977, then returned to the House in 1990 when she was elected to complete the unexpired term of Daniel Akaka, who was appointed to the Senate.

In the House, Rep. Mink sits on the Education and Labor Committee; the Natural Resources Committee; and the Committee on the Budget. She has been a leader on education issues, sponsoring legislation to eliminate restrictions that prevent nontraditional students from receiving financial assistance. She also has been an advocate for women's health issues, introducing the Ovarian Cancer Research Act.

Rep. Mink was born in 1927 in Paia, Hawaii, and has been in public service for more than 35 years. After earning a B.A. degree from the University of Hawaii and a Doctor of Law from the University of Chicago, Ms. Mink went on to serve in Hawaii's House of Representatives and later in the state senate. During the period between her congressional terms, Rep. Mink was appointed by President Carter to be assistant secretary of state for oceans and international, environmental, and scientific affairs. She also served on the Honolulu City Council, and as chair of the council for two years. She is married and has one daughter.

Representative Susan Molinari *(Republican, 13th District, New York)* came to Congress in a special 1990 election to fill the seat left vacant by the election of her father, Guy V. Molinari, as borough president of Staten Island. She serves on the Committee on Public Works and Transportation and the Education and Labor Committee.

Born on Staten Island, New York in 1958, Rep. Molinari earned both her B.A. and M.A. degrees from the State University of New York at Albany. She became the youngest person ever elected to the New York City Council in 1985, where she served before entering the House of Representatives.

Rep. Molinari is an advocate for women's rights, introducing and pushing through to passage the Glass Ceiling Initiative.

Representative Constance Morella *(Republican, 8th District, Maryland)* was first elected to the House in 1986. Her committee assignments are the Post Office and Civil Service Committee and the Committee on Science, Space, and Technology. Rep. Morella also chairs the Arms Control and Foreign Policy Caucus.

Ms. Morella was born in Somerville, Massachusetts in 1931. Rep. Morella received her A.B. degree from Boston University and her M.A. degree from the American University in Washington, DC. She served for eight years in the Maryland General Assembly. Prior to entering politics, Ms. Morella was a professor of English at Montgomery College. She is married and has raised nine children.

Rep. Morella has been a leader on women's issues, championing legislation to increase research and prevention of AIDS in women. She also has been a leader in the fight against domestic violence, winning enactment of several bills addressing this issue.

Senator Carol Moseley-Braun *(Democrat, Illinois)*, who is serving her first term, is the first African American woman to be elected to the Senate. She sits on the Judiciary Committee; the Banking, Housing, and Urban Affairs Committee; and the Committee on Small Business.

Senator Moseley-Braun is a graduate of the University of Illinois in Chicago and earned her law degree from the University of Chicago. Following law school she worked as a prosecutor in the U.S. Attorney's office.

In 1978, she was elected to the Illinois legislature, where she earned a reputation as a leader in the field of education. In 1987, Ms. Moseley-Braun was elected Cook County Recorder of Deeds. Senator Moseley-Braun was born in 1947 in Chicago. She is the mother of one child.

Senator Patty Murray *(Democrat, Washington)* was elected to the Senate in 1992, where she sits on the Appropriations Committee; the Committee on Banking, Housing, and Urban Affairs; and the Committee on the Budget.

Prior to her election to Congress, Ms. Murray served in the Washington state senate, where she championed legislation to provide family leave to parents of terminally ill children. Senator Murray earned notoriety during her U.S. Senate campaign when she ran as a "mom in tennis shoes." She built her campaign around the issues of families and children, supporting family and medical leave, abortion rights, and tax relief for the middle class.

Born in 1950, Senator Murray is a native of Seattle. She is married and has two children. She earned her B.A. degree from Washington State University.

Representative Eleanor Holmes Norton *(Democrat, District of Columbia Delegate)* was elected to Congress in 1990 as the nonvoting delegate from the District of Columbia. She is the first woman elected to represent the District in the House.

Rep. Norton serves on the Post Office and Civil Service Committee, where she chairs the Subcommittee on Compensation and Employee Benefits; the Committee on Public Works and Transportation; and the District of Columbia Committee, as the chair of the Subcommittee on Judiciary and Education.

Born in the District of Columbia in 1937, Rep. Norton is a graduate of Antioch College. She holds both her M.A. and law degrees from Yale University. Prior to her election to Congress, Ms. Norton was a professor of law at Georgetown University. She was the chair of the Equal Employment Opportunity Commission under President Carter.

In the House, Rep. Norton has been a champion for civil rights issues and for the economic and political independence of the District of Columbia.

Representative Nancy Pelosi *(Democrat, 8th District, California)* was elected to Congress in 1987. She sits on the House Appropriations Committee and the Committee on Standards of Official Conduct.

Born in 1940 in Baltimore, Maryland, Ms. Pelosi comes from a family with a tradition of public service. Her father, Thomas D'Alesandro, Jr., represented Baltimore in Congress for 10 years, and then went on to be mayor of the city. Her brother also served as mayor of Baltimore. Rep. Pelosi earned her B.A. degree from Trinity College in Washington, DC, and later served as the state chair of the California Democratic Party. She and her husband have five children.

In the House, Rep. Pelosi has focused much of her attention on funding for AIDS research and prevention, and on increasing perinatal care for low-income families. She is also responsible for the enactment of legislation to alleviate homelessness among individuals with AIDS.

Representative Deborah Pryce *(Republican, 15th District, Ohio)* is serving her first term as a member of the House of Representatives. She sits on the Committee on Banking, Finance, and Urban Affairs and the Government Operations Committee.

Prior to her election to Congress, Rep. Pryce served as a judge on the Franklin County Municipal Court. She is a graduate of Ohio State University and holds a law degree from Capital University in Columbus, Ohio. She was born in 1952 in Warren, Ohio, is married to Randy Walker, and has two children.

Rep. Pryce came to Congress on a platform that stressed fiscal constraint and congressional reform. Rep. Pryce was elected by her freshman colleagues to serve as interim class president.

Representative Ileana Ros-Lehtinen *(Republican, 18th District, Florida)* was elected to the House of Representatives in a special election in 1989. She is a member of the Committee on Foreign Affairs and the Government Operations Committee.

Ms. Ros-Lehtinen was a member of the Florida state legislature for seven years, serving for three years in the house and four years in the senate.

Rep. Ros-Lehtinen was born in Havana, Cuba in 1952. She obtained her A.A. degree from Miami-Dade Community College and her B.A. and M.S. degrees from Florida International University. She is married and has two daughters.

Representative Marge Roukema *(Republican, 5th District, New Jersey)* was first elected to Congress in 1980. She sits on the Banking, Finance, and Urban Affairs Committee and the Committee on Education and Labor.

Rep. Roukema was born in 1929 in Newark, New Jersey. She has her B.A. degree from Montclair State College in New Jersey. Prior to her election to Congress, Ms. Roukema was a secondary school teacher. She is married and has two children.

Rep. Roukema has been active on a variety of women's issues, including family and medical leave, welfare reform, and child support enforcement. She served on the U.S. Interstate Commission on Child Support.

Representative Lucille Roybal-Allard *(Democrat, 33rd District, California)* is the first Mexican American woman elected to the House of Representatives. Presently serving her first term as a member of Congress, Rep. Roybal-Allard was elected to fill the seat vacated by the retirement of her father, Edward Roybal.

Congresswoman Roybal-Allard sits on the House Banking, Finance, and Urban Affairs Committee and the Small Business Committee. Prior to her election to Congress, Ms. Roybal-Allard served in the California State Assembly. At the state level, she was active on women's issues, authoring and winning passage of legislation requiring the courts to take an individual's history of domestic violence into consideration during child custody hearings. She also won passage of the nation's first statute to establish licensure discipline for sexual misconduct by attorneys.

Rep. Roybal-Allard was born in Los Angeles, California in 1941. She has her B.A. degree from California State University at Los Angeles. She is married to Edward Allard, III, and has two children.

Representative Lynn Schenk *(Democrat, 49th District, California)* is serving her first term as a member of Congress. In the House, Rep. Schenk is a member of the Energy and Commerce Committee and the Merchant Marine and Fisheries Committee.

Ms. Schenk's career in public service includes having served as the secretary of business, transportation, and housing for the state of California. She also is a past commissioner and vice chair of the San Diego Unified Port District.

Rep. Schenk has a B.A. degree from the University of California at Los Angeles and a law degree from the University of San Diego. She was born in New York City in 1945, is married, and has three stepchildren and four step-grandchildren.

Representative Patricia Schroeder *(Democrat, 1st District, Colorado)* has served in the House of Representatives since 1972 and is the most senior woman in Congress.

As the third-ranking Democrat on the House Armed Services Committee, Rep. Schroeder chairs the Subcommittee on Research and Technology. She also sits on the Judiciary Committee and the Committee on Post Office and Civil Service. She is the cochair of the Congressional Caucus for Women's Issues.

Rep. Schroeder was born in Portland, Oregon in 1940. She earned her B.A. degree from the University of Minnesota and her J.D. from Harvard University. Before her election to Congress, Ms. Schroeder practiced law. She is married and has two grown children.

In the House, Rep. Schroeder has been a leader on women's issues, focusing on family issues, women's health, and civil and constitutional rights. She is the original author of the Family and Medical Leave Act.

Representative Karen Shepherd *(Democrat, 2nd District, Utah)* was elected in 1992 to her first term as a member of Congress.

Rep. Shepherd has her B.A. degree from the University of Utah and an M.A. degree in British literature from Brigham Young University. She began her career as a high school and college English teacher. She then went on to be the director of social services for Salt Lake County. In 1990, Ms. Shepherd was elected to the Utah Senate.

In the House, Rep. Shepherd sits on the Natural Resources Committee and the Committee on Public Works and Transportation. During her campaign, Rep. Shepherd stressed such issues as child support enforcement and full funding of the Head Start program.

Born in Silver City, New Mexico in 1940, Rep. Shepherd is married and has two children.

Representative Louise Slaughter *(Democrat, 28th District, New York)* was elected to the House of Representatives in 1986. She is a member of the Rules Committee, as well as the Budget Committee.

Rep. Slaughter was born in Harlan County, Kentucky in 1929, and received both her B.S. and M.S. degrees from the University of Kentucky. She entered the Monroe County Legislature in New York in 1975 and went on to serve in the New York State Assembly before she ran successfully for Congress. She is married and the mother of three grown children.

In the House, Rep. Slaughter has been tireless in her efforts to provide educational opportunities for homeless children. She also has worked for increased funding for women's health research programs.

Representative Olympia Snowe *(Republican, 2nd District, Maine)* is serving her eighth term in the House of Representatives. She sits on the Committee on Foreign Affairs and the Budget Committee. She is cochair of the Congressional Caucus for Women's Issues.

Rep. Snowe was born in Augusta, Maine in 1947 and received her B.A. degree from the University of Maine. She began her political career in 1973 when Ms. Snowe was first elected to the Maine House of Representatives to fill the seat vacated by her late husband. She is married to Maine Governor John McKernan, Jr.

In the House, Rep. Snowe has focused her energies on ensuring that women are included in medical research by establishing an Office of Research on Women's Health at the National Institutes of Health. She also has been a leader on international family planning issues.

Representative Karen Thurman *(Democrat, 5th District, Florida)* was elected to her first term in the House of Representatives in November 1992. She sits on the Agriculture Committee and the Committee on Government Operations.

Born in Rapid City, South Dakota in 1951, Rep. Thurman is a graduate of the University of Florida. She is married and has two children.

Prior to her election to Congress, Ms. Thurman served on the Dunnellon, Florida City Council and was the city's mayor from 1979 to 1981. She also served in the Florida Senate for 10 years, where she chaired the Agriculture Committee.

Rep. Thurman is a supporter of abortion rights and is working to broaden traditional women's issues to areas beyond health care and jobs.

Representative Jolene Unsoeld *(Democrat, 3rd District, Washington)* was elected to the House in 1988. She is a member of the Education and Labor Committee and the Committee on Merchant Marine and Fisheries.

Born in Corvallis, Oregon in 1931, Rep. Unsoeld is a graduate of Oregon State University. Prior to her election to Congress, Ms. Unsoeld was member of the Washington state legislature. She is the first woman to have climbed the direct north face of the Grand Teton mountain. She is widowed and has three grown children.

Rep. Unsoeld has championed environmental issues during her tenure in Congress. She also has introduced legislation to prevent pregnant and parenting teens from dropping out of school.

Representative Nydia Velazquez *(Democrat, 12th District, New York),* who is serving her first term in Congress, is the first Puerto Rican woman elected to the House of Representatives.

Born in Puerto Rico in 1953, Rep. Velazquez received her B.A. degree from the University of Puerto Rico. She also has her M.A. degree in political science from New York University.

In the House, she sits on the Banking, Finance, and Urban Affairs Committee and the Committee on Small Business. As a member of Congress, she is continuing her work on women's and poverty issues.

Prior to her election to Congress, Ms. Velazquez worked as a liaison between the Puerto Rican government and the Puerto Rican community in New York, where she organized efforts to increase AIDS education and to register voters. Ms. Velazquez also was the first Hispanic woman to be elected to the New York City Council, on which she served from 1984 to 1986.

Representative Barbara Vucanovich *(Republican, 2nd District, Nevada)* is serving her sixth term in the House of Representatives, where she sits on the Appropriations Committee and the Committee on Natural Resources. She is the first woman to be elected to federal office in Nevada.

Prior to her election to Congress, Ms. Vucanovich was active in politics, managing several successful campaigns in Nevada. She served as district director for Senator Paul Laxalt from 1974 until she ran for Congress in 1982. Born at Camp Dix, New Jersey in 1921, Rep. Vucanovich is married and has five children, 15 grandchildren, and two great-grandchildren.

The issues of prevention and treatment of breast cancer are a top priority to Rep. Vucanovich. Bills introduced by her include a proposal to increase the availability of mammography and to require Medicaid coverage of mammography.

Representative Maxine Waters *(Democrat, 35th District, California)* was elected to the House in 1990. She sits on the Banking, Finance, and Urban Affairs Committee and the Committee on Small Business.

Ms. Waters served for 15 years in the California State Assembly, where she was the first woman in the state's history to be elected chair of the assembly's Democratic Caucus. Rep. Waters was born in St. Louis, Missouri in 1938, and has her B.A. degree from California State University at Los Angeles. She is married and has two children.

Rep. Waters has been a leader on the issue of AIDS in the African American community. She also has been a vocal advocate of increased investment in programs and services to the nation's urban areas.

Representative Lynn Woolsey *(Democrat, 6th District, California)*, who was elected in November 1992 to her first term in the House of Representatives, is the first former welfare mother ever elected to Congress.

A member of the Committee on Education and Labor and the Science, Space, and Technology Committee, Rep. Woolsey plans to continue her work on education and employment issues, as well as protecting the environment.

Before her election to Congress, Ms. Woolsey was a member of the Petaluma, California City Council, where she was the city's vice mayor. She was successful in her efforts to expand available low- and moderate-income housing and led the fight to build the first emergency family shelter for homeless families in Sonoma County.

Rep. Woolsey was born in Seattle, Washington in 1937 and has four children. She is a graduate of the University of San Francisco.

CONGRESSIONAL CAUCUS FOR WOMEN'S ISSUES [1]

Neil Abercrombie (D-HI)
Gary L. Ackerman (D-NY)
Michael A. Andrews (D-TX)
Robert Andrews (D-NJ)
Tom Andrews (D-ME)
Tom Barrett (D-WI)
Anthony C. Beilenson (D-CA)
Howard L. Berman (D-CA)
Lucien Blackwell (D-PA)
Sherwood Boehlert (R-NY)
David E. Bonior (D-MI)
Robert A. Borski (D-PA)
★Corrine Brown (D-FL)
George E. Brown, Jr. (D-CA)
John Bryant (D-TX)
★Leslie Byrne (D-VA)
Ben Nighthorse Campbell (D-CO)
★Maria Cantwell (D-WA)
Benjamin L. Cardin (D-MD)
William Clay (D-MO)
★Eva Clayton (D-NC)
Ronald D. Coleman (D-TX)
★Barbara-Rose Collins (D-MI)

★Cardiss Collins (D-IL)
Gary Condit (D-CA)
John Conyers, Jr. (D-MI)
Jerry F. Costello (D-IL)
Robert (Bud) Cramer, Jr.(D-AL)
★Pat Danner (D-MO)
Peter A. DeFazio (D-OR)
★Rosa DeLauro (D-CT)
Ronald V. Dellums (D-CA)
Norman D. Dicks (D-WA)
John D. Dingell (D-MI)
Julian C. Dixon (D-CA)
Calvin Dooley (D-CA)
Richard J. Durbin (D-IL)
Don Edwards (D-CA)
★Karan English (D-AZ)
★Anna Eshoo (D-CA)
Lane Evans (D-IL)
Sam Farr (D-CA)
Vic Fazio (D-CA)
Dianne Feinstein (Sen-D-CA)
Hamilton Fish, Jr. (R-NY)
Floyd Flake (D-NY)

[1]Because the caucus is a body of the House of Representatives, the congressional representatives on the list are members of the caucus. The senators are subscribers.

Thomas M. Foglietta (D-PA)
Thomas S. Foley, Speaker of the
  House (D-WA)
William Ford (D-MI)
*Tillie Fowler (R-FL)
Barney Frank (D-MA)
Martin Frost (D-TX)
*Elizabeth Furse (D-OR)
Sam Gejdenson (D-CT)
Richard A. Gephardt (D-MO)
Benjamin A. Gilman (R-NY)
*Jane Harman (D-CA)
Bill Hefner (D-NC)
George J. Hochbrueckner (D-NY)
Steny H. Hoyer (D-MD)
Daniel K. Inouye (D-HI)
William Jefferson (D-LA)
*Eddie Bernice Johnson (D-TX)
*Nancy L. Johnson (R-CT)
Harry Johnston (D-FL)
*Marcy Kaptur (D-OH)
Joseph P. Kennedy, II (D-MA)
*Barbara Kennelly (D-CT)
Dale E. Kildee (D-MI)
Gerald D. Kleczka (D-WI)
Herb Kohl (Sen-D-WI)
Mike Kopetski (D-OR)
John J. LaFalce (D-NY)
*Blanche Lambert (D-AR)
Tom Lantos (D-CA)
Larry LaRocco (D-ID)
Jim Leach (R-IA)
Richard Lehman (D-CA)
Sander Levin (D-MI)
John Lewis (D-GA)
William O. Lipinski (D-IL)
*Marilyn Lloyd (D-TN)
*Jill L. Long (D-IN)
*Nita Lowey (D-NY)
Ronald K. Machtley (R-RI)
*Carolyn Maloney (D-NY)

*Marjorie Margolies-Mezvinsky
  (D-PA)
Edward J. Markey (D-MA)
Matthew G. Martinez (D-CA)
Robert T. Matsui (D-CA)
Romano L. Mazzoli (D-KY)
Frank McCloskey (D-IN)
Jim McDermott (D-WA)
*Cynthia McKinney (D-GA)
Michael McNulty (D-NY)
Martin Meehan (D-MA)
*Carrie Meek (D-FL)
*Jan Meyers (R-KS)
Kweisi Mfume (D-MD)
Barbara Mikulski (Sen-D-MD)
George Miller (D-CA)
Norman Y. Mineta (D-CA)
*Patsy Mink (D-HI)
John Joseph Moakley (D-MA)
*Susan Molinari (R-NY)
James Moran (D-VA)
*Constance A. Morella (R-MD)
John Murtha (D-PA)
Jerrold Nadler (D-NY)
Richard E. Neal (D-MA)
Stephen L. Neal (D-NC)
*Eleanor Holmes Norton (Del-D-DC)
James L. Oberstar (D-MN)
Major R. Owens (D-NY)
Ed Pastor (D-AZ)
Donald M. Payne (D-NJ)
*Nancy Pelosi (D-CA)
Pete Peterson (D-FL)
Owen Pickett (D-VA)
Jim Ramstad (R-MN)
Charles B. Rangel (D-NY)
Jack F. Reed (D-RI)
Bill Richardson (D-NM)
Charles Robb (Sen-D-VA)
Charles Rose (D-NC)
*Marge Roukema (R-NJ)

*Lucille Roybal-Allard (D-CA)
Martin Olav Sabo (D-MN)
Bernard Sanders (I-VT)
George E. Sangmeister (D-IL)
Paul Sarbanes (Sen-D-MD)
Thomas C. Sawyer (D-OH)
*Lynn Schenk (D-CA)
*Patricia Schroeder (D-CO)
Charles Schumer (D-NY)
Jose E. Serrano (D-NY)
*Karen Shepherd (D-UT)
Paul Simon (Sen-D-IL)
David E. Skaggs (D-CO)
*Louise Slaughter (D-NY)
*Olympia J. Snowe (R-ME)
Pete Stark (D-CA)
Louis Stokes (D-OH)
Gerry E. Studds (D-MA)

Dick Swett (D-NH)
Al Swift (D-WA)
Mike Synar (D-OK)
*Karen Thurman (D-FL)
Edolphus Towns (D-NY)
Walter R. Tucker (D-CA)
*Jolene Unsoeld (D-WA)
*Nydia Velazquez (D-NY)
Bruce F. Vento (D-MN)
Peter J. Visclosky (D-IN)
Craig A. Washington (D-TX)
*Maxine Waters (D-CA)
Henry A. Waxman (D-CA)
Alan Wheat (D-MO)
Pat Williams (D-MT)
*Lynn Woolsey (D-CA)
Ron Wyden (D-OR)
Sidney R. Yates (D-IL)

*Executive committee member.

References

WOMEN AND HEALTH

ONE   ASSESSING AND IMPROVING WOMEN'S HEALTH

Adams, P.F., and V. Benson. "Current Estimates from the National Health Interview Survey." National Center for Health Statistics. *Vital and Health Statistics* 10, No. 181 (December 1991).

Agency for Health Care Policy and Research (AHCPR). *National Medical Expenditure Survey, 1987*. Washington, DC: AHCPR, 1987.

Althaus, Frances A. "Special Report: An Ounce of Prevention . . . STDs and Women's Health." *Family Planning Perspectives* 23, No. 4 (July 1991): 173–177.

Amaro, Hortensia. "In the Midst of Plenty: Reflections on the Economic and Health Status of Hispanic Families." Paper presented at the American Psychological Association Convention, Washington, DC, August 14–18, 1992.

American Cancer Society (ACS). *Cancer Facts and Figures—1992*. Atlanta, Georgia: ACS, 1992.

American College of Obstetricians and Gynecologists. "A Survey of State Medicaid Policies for Coverage of Screening Mammography and Pap Smear Services." *Legis-Letter* 10, No. 2 (Spring–Summer, 1991).

American Medical Association, Council on Scientific Affairs. "Violence Against Women: Relevance for Medical Practitioners." *Journal of the American Medical Association* 267, No. 23 (June 17, 1992): 3184–3189.

Anthony, James C., and Kenneth R. Petronis. "Suspected Risk Factors for Depression Among Adults 18–44 Years Old." *Epidemiology* 2, No. 2 (March 1991): 123–132.

Aronson, M.K., W.I. Ooi, H. Morgenstern, et al. "Women, Myocardial Infarction, and Dementia in the Very Old." *Neurology* 40 (1990): 1102–1106.

Becker, Richard C. "Introductory Article: Clinical Highlights and Future Directions. Cardiovascular Disease in Women." *Cardiology* 77, Suppl. 2 (1990): 1–5.

Berk, Marc L., and Amy K. Taylor. "Women and Divorce: Health Insurance Coverage, Utilization, and Health Care Expenditures." *American Journal of Public Health* 74, No. 11 (November 1984): 1276–1278.

Boring, Catherine C., Teresa S. Squires, and Tony Tong. "Cancer Statistics." *CA-A Cancer Journal for Clinicians* 42, No. 1 (January–February 1992): 19–38.

Brownson, Ross C., Jeannette Jackson-Thompson, Joan C. Wilkerson, et al. "Demographic Differences in Beliefs about the Health Effects of Smoking." *American Journal of Public Health* 82, No. 1 (January 1992): 99–103.

Bureau of the Census. Current Population Reports, Series P-60, No. 181. *Poverty in the United States: 1991.* Washington, DC: U.S. Government Printing Office, August 1992.

———. *Current Population Survey March 1991.* Washington, DC: Bureau of the Census, 1991.

Cates, Willard, and Judith N. Wasserheit. "Genital Chlamydial Infections: Epidemiology and Reproductive Sequelae." *American Journal of Obstetrics and Gynecology* 164, No. 6 (June 1991): 1771–1781.

Centers for Disease Control. "Use of Mammography—United States, 1990." *Morbidity and Mortality Weekly Report* 39, No. 36 (September 14, 1990a): 621–630.

———. "Regional Variation in Diabetes Mellitus Prevalence—United States, 1988 and 1989." *Morbidity and Mortality Weekly Report* 39, No. 45 (November 16, 1990b): 805–812.

———. "Trends in Lung Cancer Incidence and Mortality—United States, 1980–1987." *Morbidity and Mortality Weekly Report* 39, No. 48 (December 7, 1990c): 875–883.

———. "Smoking-Attributable Mortality and Years of Potential Years Lost—United States, 1988." *Morbidity and Mortality Weekly Report* 40, No. 4 (February 1, 1991a): 62–71.

———. "Cigarette Smoking Among Reproductive-Aged Women—Behavioral Risk Factor Surveillance System, 1989." *Morbidity and Mortality Weekly Report* 40, No. 42 (October 25, 1991b): 719–723.

———. Sexually Transmitted Disease Surveillance. Unpublished data, 1992a.

———. "Public Health Focus: Mammography." *Morbidity and Mortality Weekly Report* 41, No. 5 (June 26, 1992b): 454–459.

———. "Cerebrovascular Disease Mortality and Medicare Hospitalization—United States, 1980–1990." *Morbidity and Mortality Weekly Report* 41, No. 26 (July 3, 1992c): 477–480.

———. "Trends in Ischemic Heart Disease Mortality—United States, 1980–1988." *Morbidity and Mortality Weekly Report* 41, No. 30 (July 31, 1992d): 548–555.

———. "Increased HIV/AIDS Mortality Among Residents Aged 25–44 Years—Baltimore, Maryland, 1987–1989." *Morbidity and Mortality Weekly Report* 41, No. 38 (September 25, 1992e): 708–715.

Clancy, Carolyn, and Charlea T. Massion. "American Women's Health Care: A

Patchwork Quilt with Gaps." *Journal of the American Medical Association* 268, No. 14 (October 14, 1992): 1918–1920.

Clyne, Christopher A. "Antithrombotic Therapy in the Primary and Secondary Prevention of Coronary-Related Death and Infarction: Focus on Gender Differences." *Cardiology* 77, Suppl. 2 (1990): 99–109.

Condemi, John J. "The Autoimmune Diseases." *Journal of the American Medical Association* 268, No. 20 (November 25, 1992): 2882–2892.

Coryell, William, Jean Endicott, and Keller Martin. "Major Depression in a Non-clinical Sample: Demographic and Clinical Risk Factors for First Onset." *Archives of General Psychiatry* 49 (February 1992): 117–125.

Cummings, Steven R., and Dennis Black. "Should Perimenopausal Women be Screened for Osteoporosis?" *Annals of Internal Medicine* 104 (1986): 817–823.

DeLozier, J.E., and R.O. Gagnon. "1989 Summary: National Ambulatory Medical Care Survey." *Advance Data from Vital and Health Statistics,* No. 203. Hyattsville, MD: National Center for Health Statistics, 1991.

Donovan, Patricia. *Testing Positive: Sexually Transmitted Disease and the Public Health Response.* New York: Alan Guttmacher Institute, 1993.

Farmer, Mary E., Lon White, Jacob Brody, et al. "Race and Sex Differences in Hip Fracture Incidence." *American Journal of Public Health* 74, No. 12 (December 1984): 1374–1380.

Flegal, Kathleen M., Trena M. Ezzati, Maureen I. Harris, et al. "Prevalence of Diabetes in Mexican Americans, Cubans, and Puerto Ricans from the Hispanic Health and Nutrition Examination Survey, 1982–1984." *Diabetes Care* 14, No. 7 (July 1991): 628–638.

Giacoia, George P. "Transplacentally Transmitted Autoimmune Disorders of the Fetus and Newborn: Pathogenic Considerations." *Southern Medical Journal* 85, No. 2 (February 1992): 139–145.

Halbreich, Uriel, Jacques Vital-Herne, Susanne Goldstein, et al. "Differences in Biological Factors Putatively Related to Depression," *Journal of Affective Disorders* 7 (1989): 223–233.

Hankinson, Susan E., Graham A. Colditz, David J. Hunter, et al. "A Quantitative Assessment of Oral Contraceptive Use and Risk of Ovarian Cancer." *Obstetrics and Gynecology* 80, No. 4 (October 1992): 708–714.

Haywood, Rodney A., Martin F. Shapiro, Howard E. Freeman, et al. "Who Gets Screened for Cervical Cancer?" *Archives of Internal Medicine* 148 (May 1988): 1177–1181.

Hendel, Robert. "Myocardial Infarction in Women." *Cardiology* 77, Suppl. 2 (1990): 41–57.

Horton, Jacqueline A., editor. *The Women's Health Data Book: A Profile of Women's Health in the United States.* Washington DC: Jacobs Institute of Women's Health, 1992.

Kelsey, Jennifer. "Breast Reproduction Cancers: An Overview." Paper presented at the eleventh annual meeting of the American College of Epidemiology, Bethesda, MD, September 17–18, 1992.

Lefkowitz, D., and C. Underwood. *Personal Health Practices: Findings From the Sur-*

vey of American Indians and Alaska Natives. National Medical Expenditure Survey, Research Findings 10, Agency for Health Care Policy and Research. Pub. No. 91–0034. Rockville, MD: Public Health Service, July 1991.

Lerner, Debra J., and William B. Kannel. "Patterns of Coronary Heart Disease Morbidity and Mortality in the Sexes: A 26 Year Follow-Up of the Framingham Population." *American Heart Journal* 111, No. 2 (1986): 383–390.

Makuc, Diane M., Virginia M. Freid, and Joel C. Kleinman. "National Trends in the Use of Preventive Health Care by Women." *American Journal of Public Health* 79, No. 1 (January 1989): 21–26.

Manson, JoAnn E., Meir J. Stampfer, Graham A. Colditz, et al. "A Prospective Study of Aspirin Use and Primary Prevention of Cardiovascular Disease in Women." *Journal of the American Medical Association* 266, No. 4 (July 1991): 521–527.

Melton, L. Joseph, David M. Eddy, and C. Conrad Johnston, Jr. "Screening for Osteoporosis." *Annals of Internal Medicine* 112, No. 7 (April 1, 1990): 516–528.

Merlis, Mark. *Health Care Reform: Managed Competition.* Library of Congress, CRS Issue Brief. Washington, DC: Library of Congress, January 6, 1993.

Mettlin, Curtis. "Breast Cancer Risk Factors: Contributions to Planning Breast Cancer Control." *Cancer* 68, No. 7, Supplement (April 1, 1992): 1904–1910.

Miller, Anthony B., Cernelia J. Baines, Teresa To, et al. "Canadian National Breast Screening Study, 1. Breast Cancer Detection and Death Rates Among Women Aged 40 to 49 Years." *Canadian Medical Association Journal* 147, No. 10 (1992): 1459–1476.

Minkoff, Howard L., and Jack A. DeHovitz. "Care of Women Infected with the Human Immunodeficiency Virus." *Journal of the American Medical Association* 266, No. 16 (October 23/30, 1991): 2253–2258.

Mitchell, Janet B. "Physician Participation in Medicaid Revisited." *Medical Care* 29, No. 7 (July 1991): 645–653.

National Center for Health Statistics. "Births, Marriages, Divorces and Deaths for February 1991." *Monthly Vital Statistics Report,* Vol. 40, No. 2 (June 12, 1991).

———. "Births, Marriages, Divorces and Deaths for April 1991." *Monthly Vital Statistics Report,* Vol. 40, No. 4 (August 5, 1991).

———. *Health, United States, 1991 and Prevention Profile.* Hyattsville, MD: U.S. Department of Health and Human Services, 1992.

———. "Advance Report of Final Mortality Statistics, 1990." *Monthly Vital Statistics Report,* Vol. 41, No. 7. Hyattsville, MD: Public Health Service, 1993.

———. Unpublished cancer statistics, January 1993.

O'Conner, Gerald. "Differences in Care and Outcomes of Care for Cardiovascular Disease in Men and Women." Paper presented at the eleventh annual meeting of the American College of Epidemiology, Bethesda, MD, September 17–18, 1992.

Older Women's League (OWL). *Critical Condition: Midlife and Older Women in America's Health Care System.* Washington, DC: OWL, 1992.

Padian, Nancy. "Pelvic Inflammatory Disease and Progression to Infertility and

Ecoptic Pregnancy." Paper presented at the eleventh annual meeting of the American College of Epidemiology, Bethesda, MD, September 17–18, 1992.

Pettiti, Diana. "Hormone Replacement Therapy: Risks and Benefits." Paper presented at the eleventh annual meeting of the American College of Epidemiology, Bethesda, MD, September 17–18, 1992.

Pfeiffer, Naomi. "Highlights from the National Conference on Women and HIV Infection. Part One: Early Care and Policy Issues." *AIDS Patient Care* 5, No. 2 (April 1991): 67–69.

Piacentini, Joseph S., and Jill D. Foley. *EBRI Databook on Employee Benefits*. Second Edition. Washington DC: Employee Benefits Research Institute, 1992.

Piani, A., and C. Schoenborn. "Health Promotion and Disease Prevention." National Center for Health Statistics. *Vital and Health Statistics* 10, No. 185 (1993).

Pritchard, M.H. "An Examination of the Role of Female Hormones and Pregnancy as Risk Factors for Rheumatoid Arthritis, Using Male Population as Control Group." *British Journal of Rheumatology* 31, No. 6 (1992): 395–399.

Public Health Service Task Force on Women's Health Issues. "Women's Health: Report of the Public Health Service Task Force on Women's Health Issues." *Public Health Reports* 100, No. 1 (January–February 1985): 74–106.

Resnick, Neil M., and Susan L. Greenspan. "Panel Session: Management/Education. Osteoporosis in the Older Woman: A Reappraisal." *Public Health Reports* 104, Suppl. (September–October 1989): 80–83.

Schoenberg, Bruce S., Dallas Anderson, and Armin Haerer. "Severe Dementia: Prevalence and Clinical Features in a Biracial U.S. Population." *Archives of Neurology* 42 (August 1985): 740–743.

Schoenberg, Bruce S., Emre Kokmen, and Haruo Okazaki. "Alzheimer's Disease and Other Dementing Illnesses in a Defined United States Population: Incidence Rates and Clinical Features." *Annals of Neurology* 22, No. 6 (December 1987): 724–729.

Smith, Mark Scott. "Anorexia Nervosa and Bulimia." *Journal of Family Practice* 18, No. 5 (May 1984): 757–766.

Stampfer, Meir J., and Graham A. Colditz. "Estrogen Replacement Therapy and Coronary Heart Disease: A Quantitative Assessment of the Epidemiologic Evidence." *Preventive Medicine* 20 (1991): 47–63.

Sugg, Nancy K., and Thomas Inui. "Primary Care Physicians' Response to Domestic Violence: Opening Pandora's Box." *Journal of the American Medical Association* 267, No. 23 (July 17, 1992): 3157–3160.

Summer, Laura. *Limited Access: Health Care for the Rural Poor*. Washington, DC: Center on Budget and Policy Priorities, March 1991.

Treves, Therese A. "Epidemiology of Alzheimer's Disease." *Psychiatric Clinics of North America* 14, No. 2 (June 1991): 251–265.

U.S. Congress, House Committee on Ways and Means. *Overview of Entitlement Programs: 1992 Green Book*. Washington, DC: U.S. Government Printing Office, 1992.

U.S. Congress, House Committee on Ways and Means, Office of Technology Assessment. *Adolescent Health. Volume II: Background and the Effectiveness of Selected Prevention and Treatment Services*. Washington, DC: U.S. Government Printing Office, 1991.

————, Office of Technology Assessment. *Does Health Insurance Make a Difference?—A Background Paper*. Washington, DC: U.S. Government Printing Office, 1992.

U.S. Department of Health and Human Services. *Healthy People 2000*. Washington, DC: U.S. Government Printing Office, 1991a.

————. *Health Status of Minorities and Low-Income Groups: Third Edition*. Washington, DC: U.S. Government Printing Office, 1991b.

U.S. Preventive Services Task Force. *Guide to Clinical Preventive Services: An Assessment of the Effectiveness of 169 Interventions*. Baltimore: Williams and Wilkins, 1989.

Waldron, Ingrid. "Patterns and Causes of Gender Differences in Smoking." *Social Science and Medicine* 32, No. 9 (1991): 989–1005.

Weissman, Myrna M., Philip J. Leaf, Charles E. Holzer, et al. "The Epidemiology of Depression: An Update on Sex Differences in Rates." *Journal of Affective Disorders* 7 (1984): 179–188.

World Health Organization (WHO). *1991 World Health Statistics Annual*. Geneva, Switzerland: WHO, 1992.

TWO THE HEALTH STATUS OF WOMEN OF COLOR

Alston, Dana. "Transforming a Movement: People of Color Unite at Summit Against 'Environmental Racism.' " *Network News*. New York: National Network of Grantmakers, 1992.

Alu Like, Inc. (Native Hawaiian Health Research Consortium). *E Ola Mau: The Native Hawaiian Health Needs Study—Medical Task Force Report*. Honolulu: Alu Like, Inc., 1985.

Amaro, Hortensia. "In the Midst of Plenty: Reflections on the Economic and Health Status of Hispanic Families." Paper presented at the American Psychological Association Convention, Washington, DC, August 14–18, 1992.

Amaro, Hortensia, Rupert Whitaker, Gerald Coffman, and Timothy Heeren. "Acculturation and Marijuana and Cocaine Use: Findings from the Hispanic Health and Nutrition Evaluation Survey (HHANES), 1982–1984." *American Journal of Public Health* 80 (1990): 54–60.

American Indian Health Care Association (AIHCA). *Native Newsbriefs*. St. Paul: AIHCA, 1992.

Asian American Health Forum, Inc. (AAHF). *Fact Sheets*. San Francisco: AAHF, 1990.

————. "Asian and Pacific Islander Women: Setting an Agenda for Health." *Focus* 3 (1992): 1.

Association of Asian Pacific Community Health Organizations (AAPCHO). *Selected Health and Population Statistics for Asians and Pacific Islanders*. Oakland: AAPCHO, n.d.

Bastida, Elena. "Macro Structural Factors Impacting on Hispanic Health." Paper presented at the Conference on Behavioral and Sociocultural Perspectives on Ethnicity and Health, Chapel Hill, NC, September 1992.

Beauregard, Karen, Peter Cunningham, and Llewellyn Cornelius. *Access to Health Care: Findings from the Survey of American Indians and Alaska Natives.* National Medical Expenditure Survey, Research Findings 9, Agency for Health Care Policy and Research. Pub. No. 91-0028. Rockville, MD: Public Health Service, 1991.

Bell, Bella Zi, Eleanor C. Nordyke, and Patricia O'Hagan. "Fertility and Maternal and Child Health." *Social Progress in Hawaii* 32 (1989): 87–103.

Bindon, James R., and Douglas E. Crews. "Measures of Health and Morbidity in Samoans." Abstract of a paper presented at the Third Asian American Health Biennial Forum, entitled Asian and Pacific Islanders: Dispelling the Myth of a Healthy Minority, Bethesda, MD, November 1990.

Bureau of the Census. Current Population Reports, Series P-20, No. 455. *The Hispanic Population in the United States: March 1991.* Washington, DC: U.S. Government Printing Office, 1991.

———. Current Population Reports, Series P-20, No. 459. *The Asian and Pacific Islander Population in the United States: March 1991 and 1990.* Washington, DC: U.S. Government Printing Office, 1992a.

———. Current Population Reports, Series P-20, No. 464. *The Black Population in the United States: March 1991.* Washington, DC: U.S. Government Printing Office, 1992b.

———. *Health Insurance: Who Was Covered Between 1987 and 1990?* Statistical Brief SB/92-8. Washington, DC: U.S. Department of Commerce, 1992c.

———. *Statistical Abstract of the United States: 1992 (112th edition).* Washington, DC: U.S. Government Printing Office, 1992d.

———. *We Asked . . . You Told Us: Hispanic Origin.* Census Questionnaire Content, 1990 CQC-7. Washington, DC: U.S. Department of Commerce, 1992e.

———. *We Asked . . . You Told Us: Race.* Census Questionnaire Content, 1990 CQC-4. Washington, DC: U.S. Department of Commerce, 1992f.

Chu, Susan Y., James W. Buehler, and Ruth L. Berkelman. "Impact of the Human Immunodeficiency Virus Epidemic on Mortality in Women of Reproductive Age, United States." *Journal of the American Medical Association* 264 (1990): 225–229.

Communications Consortium Media Center (CCMC) and the National Council of Negro Women (NCNW). *The 1991–1992 Women of Color Reproductive Health Poll.* Washington, DC: CCMC and NCNW, n.d.

Delgado, Jane L., and Fernando M. Trevino. "The State of Hispanic Health in the United States." In *The State of Hispanic America Vol. II.* Oakland: National Hispanic Center for Advanced Studies and Policy Analysis, 1985.

Delgado, Jane L., Clifford L. Johnson, Ila Roy, and Fernando Trevino. "Hispanic Health and Nutrition Examination Survey: Methodological Considerations." *American Journal of Public Health* 80 (1990): 6–10.

Ewbank, Douglas C. "History of Black Mortality and Health Before 1940." In *Health Policies and Black Americans,* edited by David P. Willis. New Brunswick, NJ: Transaction Publishers, 1989.

Forman, Malaya. "The Development of Asian/Pacific Islander Health Professionals: The Myth of Overrepresentation." In *Policy Papers.* San Francisco: Asian American Health Forum, Inc., 1990.

Friedman, Samuel J., Jo L. Sotheran, Abu Abdul-Quader, Beny J. Primm, Don C. Des Jarlais, Paula Kleinman, Conrad Mauge, Douglas S. Goldsmith, Wafaa El-Sadr, and Robert Maslansky. "The AIDS Epidemic Among Blacks and Hispanics." In *Health Policies and Black Americans,* edited by David P. Willis. New Brunswick, NJ: Transaction Publishers, 1989.

Gayle, Jacob A., Richard M. Selik, and Susan Y. Chu. "Surveillance for AIDS and HIV Infection Among Black and Hispanic Children and Women of Childbearing Age, 1981–1989." *Morbidity and Mortality Weekly Report* 39 (July 1990): 1–6.

General Accounting Office. *Hispanic Access to Health Care: Significant Gaps Exist.* GAO/PEMD-92-6. Washington, DC: U.S. Government Printing Office, 1992.

Guendelman, Sylvia, Jeffrey B. Gould, Mark Hudes, and Brenda Eskenazi. "Generational Differences in Perinatal Health Among the Mexican American Population: Findings from HHANES, 1982–1984." *American Journal of Public Health* 80 (1990): 61–65.

Hahn, Robert A., Joseph Mulinare, and Steven M. Teutsch. "Inconsistencies in Coding of Race and Ethnicity Between Birth and Death in U.S. Infants." *Journal of the American Medical Association* 267 (1992): 259–263.

Han, Eugene. "Korean Health Survey in Southern California: A Preliminary Report on Health Status and Health Care Needs of Korean Immigrants." Abstract of a paper presented at the Third Asian American Health Biennial Forum, entitled Asian and Pacific Islanders: Dispelling the Myth of a Healthy Minority, Bethesda, MD, November 1990.

Hanft, Ruth S., and Catherine C. White. "Constraining the Supply of Physicians: Effects on Black Physicians." In *Health Policies and Black Americans,* edited by David P. Willis. New Brunswick, NJ: Transaction Publishers, 1989.

Haynes, Suzanne G., Clair Harvey, Henry Montes, Herbert Nickens, and Bernice Cohen. "Patterns of Cigarette Smoking Among Hispanics in the United States: Results from the HHANES, 1982–1984." *American Journal of Public Health* 80 (1990): 47–53.

Headen, Alvin E., Jr., and Sandra W. Headen. "General Health Conditions and Medical Insurance Issues Concerning Black Women." *Review of Black Political Economy* 14 (1985–86): 183–197.

Health Resources and Services Administration. *HIV/AIDS Workgroup on Health Care Access Issues for Hispanic Americans.* Washington, DC: U.S. Department of Health and Human Services, 1991.

———. *HIV/AIDS Workgroup on Health Care Access Issues for American Indians and*

Alaska Natives. Washington, DC: U.S. Department of Health and Human Services, 1992a.

Health Resources and Services Administration. *HIV/AIDS Workgroup on Health Care Access Issues for Women*. Washington, DC: U.S. Department of Health and Human Services, 1992b.

Higginbotham, John C., Fernando M. Trevino, and Laura A. Ray. "Utilization of Curanderos by Mexican Americans: Prevalence and Predictors—Findings from HHANES, 1982–1984." *American Journal of Public Health* 80 (1990): 32–35.

Hirota, Sherry. "Needs Assessment of Pacific Islander Americans." In *Summary of "Breaking the Barriers" Conference by Asian American Health Forum, Inc.* (AAHF). San Francisco: AAHF, April 1988.

Hogue, Carol J. Rowland, and Martha A. Hargraves. "Class, Race and Infant MortalityintheUnitedStates."*American Journal of Public Health*83(1993):9–12.

Horton, Jacqueline A., editor. *The Women's Health Data Book: A Profile of Women's Health in the United States*. Washington, DC: Jacobs Institute of Women's Health, 1992.

Hu-DeHart, Evelyn. "From Yellow Peril to Model Minority: The Columbus Legacy and Asians in America." In *The New World*. Washington, DC: Smithsonian Institution, 1992.

Indian Health Service. *Cancer Mortality Among Native Americans in the United States: Regional Differences in Indian Health, 1984–1988 & Trends Over Time, 1968–1987*. Washington, DC: Public Health Service, n.d.

———. *Disabilities and Their Effects on American Indian and Alaska Native Communities: Final Report*. Albuquerque: Public Health Service, 1991a.

———. *Indian Women's Health Issues: Final Report*. Tucson: Public Health Service, 1991b.

———. *Trends in Indian Health 1992*. Washington, DC: Public Health Service, 1992.

Jaynes, Gerald D., and Robin M. Williams. "Black Americans' Health." In *A Common Destiny: Blacks and American Society*, edited by Gerald D. Jaynes and Robin M. Williams. Washington, DC: National Academy Press, 1989.

Lee, Marion. "Breast and Cervical Cancer in Asian and Pacific Islander Women." *Focus* 3 (1992): 2.

Leffall, LaSalle D. "Health Status of Black Americans." In *The State of Black America 1990*. New York: National Urban League, Inc., 1990.

Lefkowitz, D., and C. Underwood. *Personal Health Practices: Findings from the Survey of American Indians and Alaska Natives*. National Medical Expenditure Survey, Research Findings 10, Agency for Health Care Policy and Research. Pub. No. 91-0034. Rockville, MD: Public Health Service, July 1991.

Leigh, Wilhelmina A. *A Health Assessment of Black Americans: A Fact Book*. Washington, DC: Joint Center for Political and Economic Studies, 1992.

Leung, Mingyew, and Michael C. Lu. "Ethnocultural Barriers to Care." In *Policy Papers*. San Francisco: Asian American Health Forum, Inc., 1990.

Levy, Jerrold E. "The Health of North American Indians." Paper presented at the American Psychological Association Convention, Washington, DC, August 14–18, 1992.

Liu, William T., and Elena S.H. Yu. "Ethnicity, Mental Health, and the Urban Delivery System." In *Urban Ethnicity in the United States,* edited by Lionel Maldonado and Joan Moore. Beverly Hills: Sage Publications, 1985.

Liu, William T., Elena S.H. Yu, Ching-Fu Chang, and Marilyn Fernandez. "The Mental Health of Asian American Teenagers: A Research Challenge." In *Ethnic Issues in Adolescent Mental Health,* edited by Arlene R. Stiffman and Larry E. Davis. New York: Sage Publications, 1990.

Manton, Kenneth G., Clifford H. Patrick, and Katrina W. Johnson. "Health Differentials Between Blacks and Whites: Recent Trends in Mortality and Morbidity." In *Health Policies and Black Americans,* edited by David P. Willis. New Brunswick, NJ: Transaction Publishers, 1989.

Markides, Kyriakos, Laura A. Ray, Christine A. Stroup-Benham, and Fernando Trevino. "Acculturation and Alcohol Consumption in the Mexican American Population of the Southwestern United States: Findings from HHANES, 1982–1984." *American Journal of Public Health* 80 (1990): 42–46.

Menendez, Barbara S. "AIDS Mortality Among Puerto Ricans and Other Hispanics in New York, 1981–1987." *Journal of Acquired Immune Deficiency Syndromes* 3 (1990): 644–648.

Miller, S.M. "Race in the Health of America." In *Health Policies and Black Americans,* edited by David P. Willis. New Brunswick, NJ: Transaction Publishers, 1989.

National Center for Health Statistics. *Health, United States, 1990.* Hyattsville, MD: Public Health Service, 1991.

———. *Health, United States, 1991.* Hyattsville, MD: Public Health Service, 1992a.

———. "Annual Summary of Births, Marriages, Divorces, and Deaths: United States, 1991." *Monthly Vital Statistics Report,* Vol. 40, No. 13. Hyattsville, MD: Public Health Service, 1992b.

National Council of La Raza. *Hispanics and Health Insurance—Volume 2: Analysis and Policy Implications.* Washington, DC: Labor Council for Latin American Advancement and National Council of La Raza, 1992.

National Institutes of Health (NIH). *Report of the National Institutes of Health: Opportunities for Research on Women's Health.* Hunt Valley, MD: Office of Research on Women's Health, NIH, 1991.

Nyamathi, Adeline, Crystal Bennett, Barbara Leake, Charles Lewis, and Jacquelyn Flaskerud. "AIDS-Related Knowledge, Perceptions, and Behaviors Among Impoverished Minority Women." *American Journal of Public Health* 83 (1993): 65–71.

O'Brien, Marilyn O., Jerome Vanek, and Leigh Welper. *Urban Indian Health Comparative Analysis Report.* St. Paul: American Indian Health Care Association, 1991.

Papa Ola Lokahi. *Native Hawaiian Health Data Book 1992*. Honolulu: Papa Ola Lokahi, 1992.

Petrakis, Nicholas. "Chinese and Breast Cancer." In *Summary of "Breaking the Barriers" Conference by Asian American Health Forum, Inc.* (AAHF). San Francisco: AAHF, April 1988.

Ponce, Ninez. "Asian and Pacific Islander Health Data: Quality Issues and Policy Recommendations." In *Policy Papers*. San Francisco: Asian American Health Forum, Inc., 1990.

Rice, Haynes, and LaRah D. Payne. "Health Issues for the Eighties." In *The State of Black America 1981*. New York: National Urban League, Inc., 1981.

Rice, Mitchell F., and Mylon Winn. "Black Health Care and the American Health System: A Political Perspective." In *Health Politics and Policy*, edited by Theodor J. Litman and Leonard S. Robins. New York: Delmar Publishers, 1991.

Rosenbach, Margo L., and Barbara Butrica. "Issues in Providing Drug Treatment Services to Racial and Ethnic Minorities." Paper prepared for the Second Annual Advisory Committee Meeting for the National Institutes of Health, National Institute on Drug Abuse, Center for Drug Abuse Services Research, Tyngsboro, MA, May 1991.

Schoendorf, Kenneth C., Carol J.R. Hogue, Joel C. Kleinman, and Diane Rowley. "Mortality Among Infants of Black as Compared with White College-Educated Parents." *New England Journal of Medicine* 326 (1992): 1522–1526.

Scott, Sheri. *Urban National Plan to Meet the Year 2000 Objectives*. St. Paul: American Indian Health Care Association, 1991.

Scott, Sheri, and Mary Suagee. *Enhancing Health Statistics for American Indian and Alaskan Native Communities: An Agenda for Action—A Report to the National Center for Health Statistics*. St. Paul: American Indian Health Care Association, 1992.

Scrimshaw, Susan C.M., Ruth Zambrana, and Christine Dunkel-Schetter. "Issues in Latino Women's Health: Myths and Challenges." In *Women's Health: The Dynamics of Diversity*, edited by S. Ruzek, V. Oleson, and A. Clarke. Philadelphia: Temple University Press, 1990.

Selik, Richard M., Kenneth G. Castro, and Marguerite Pappaioanou. "Racial/Ethnic Differences in the Risk of AIDS in the United States." *American Journal of Public Health* 78 (1988): 1539–1544.

Short, Pamela F., Llewellyn J. Cornelius, and Donald E. Goldstone. "Health Insurance of Minorities in the United States." *Journal of Health Care for the Poor and Underserved* 1 (1990): 9–24.

Smith, George D., and Matthias Egger. "Socioeconomic Differences in Mortality in Britain and the United States." *American Journal of Public Health* 82 (1992): 1079–1081.

Solis, Julia M., Gary Marks, Melinda Garcia, and David Shelton. "Acculturation, Access to Care, and Use of Preventive Services by Hispanics: Findings From HHANES, 1982–1984." *American Journal of Public Health* 80 (1990): 11–19.

Sorlie, Paul D., Eugene Rogot, and Norman J. Johnson. "Validity of Demographic

Characteristics on the Death Certificate." *Epidemiology* 3 (1992): 181–184.

U.S. Commission on Civil Rights. *Civil Rights Issues Facing Asian Americans in the 1990s*. Washington, DC: U.S. Commission on Civil Rights, 1992.

U.S. Department of Health and Human Services (DHHS). *Wellness for Women: Issues in Women's Health Care Today*. Washington, DC: U.S. DHHS, n.d.

Wilkinson, Doris Y., and Gary King. "Conceptual and Methodological Issues in the Use of Race as a Variable: Policy Implications." In *Health Policies and Black Americans,* edited by David P. Willis. New Brunswick, NJ: Transaction Publishers, 1989.

Yu, Elena S.H. "Problems in Pacific/Asian American Community Research." In *Methodological Problems in Minority Research,* edited by William T. Liu. Chicago: Pacific/Asian American Mental Health Research Center, 1982.

———. "Health of the Chinese Elderly." *Research on Aging* 8 (1986): 84–109.

———. "The Health Risks of Asian Americans." *American Journal of Public Health* 81 (1991): 1391–1393.

Yu, Elena S.H., and William T. Liu. "The Underutilization of Mental Health Services by Asian Americans: Implications for Manpower Training." In *The Pacific/Asian American Mental Health Research Center: A Decade Review,* edited by William T. Liu. Chicago: University of Illinois, 1987.

Zambrana, Ruth E. "The Relationship Between Use of Health Care Services and Health Status: Dilemmas in Measuring Medical Outcomes in Low-Income and Racial/Ethnic Populations." In *Medical Effectiveness Research Data Methods,* edited by M.L. Grady and H. Schwartz. Rockville, MD: U.S. Department of Health and Human Services, 1992.

**THREE   SECURING AMERICAN WOMEN'S
REPRODUCTIVE HEALTH**

Alan Guttmacher Institute (AGI). *Blessed Events and the Bottom Line: Financing Maternity Care in the United States*. New York: AGI, 1987.

———. *Risk and Responsibility: Teaching Sex Education in America's Schools Today*. New York: AGI, 1989.

———. *Abortion Factbook, 1992 Edition: Readings, Trends, and State and Local Data to 1988*. New York: AGI, 1992a.

———. *Coverage of Reproductive Health Care Services Under Private Health Insurance and Medicaid*. New York: AGI, 1992b.

———. *Facts in Brief: Contraceptive Services*. New York: AGI, 1993a.

———. *Facts in Brief: Contraceptive Use*. New York: AGI, 1993b.

———. *Facts in Brief: Pregnancy and Birth*. New York: AGI, 1993c.

American College of Obstetricians and Gynecologists (ACOG). *Standards for Obstetric-Gynecological Services, 7th ed.* Washington, DC: ACOG, 1989.

American Medical Association (AMA) Council on Scientific Affairs. *Induced Termination of Pregnancy Before and After Roe v. Wade: Trends in the Mortality and Morbidity of Women*. Chicago: AMA, 1992.

Bureau of Labor Statistics. *Employee Benefits in Medium and Large Firms, 1989.* Washington, DC: U.S. Government Printing Office, 1990.

Children's Defense Fund (CDF). *The State of America's Children, 1991.* Washington, DC: CDF, 1991.

Donovan, Patricia. *Testing Positive: Sexually Transmitted Disease and the Public Health Response.* New York: Alan Guttmacher Institute, 1993.

Forrest, Jacqueline D. "Contraceptive Needs Through Stages of Women's Reproductive Lives." *Contemporary Ob/Gyn* 12 (1988): 12–22, updated in Forrest, Jacqueline D., "Timing of Reproductive Life Stages." *Obstetrics and Gynecology* 82 (1993): in press.

Forrest, Jacqueline D., and Susheela Singh. "The Sexual and Reproductive Behavior of American Women, 1982–1988." *Family Planning Perspectives* 22 (1990): 206–215.

Gold, Rachel Benson. *Abortion and Women's Health.* New York: Alan Guttmacher Institute, 1990.

Gold, Rachel Benson, and Daniel Daley. "Public Funding of Contraceptive, Sterilization and Abortion Services, Fiscal Year 1990." *Family Planning Perspectives* 23 (1991): 204–212.

Harlap, Susan, Kathryn Kost, and Jacqueline D. Forrest. *Protecting Pregnancy, Protecting Health.* New York: Alan Guttmacher Institute, 1991.

Health Insurance Association of America (HIAA). *New Group Health Insurance Policies Issued in 1978.* Washington, DC: HIAA, n.d.

———. *New Group Insurance, 1986.* Washington, DC: HIAA, 1986a.

———. *A Profile of Group Major Medical Expense Insurance in the United States.* Washington, DC: HIAA, 1986b.

Henshaw, Stanley K. "The Accessibility of Abortion Services in the United States." *Family Planning Perspectives* 23 (1991): 246–253.

Henshaw, Stanley K., and Jacqueline D. Forrest. *Women at Risk of Unintended Pregnancy, 1990 Estimates.* New York: Alan Guttmacher Institute, 1993.

Henshaw, Stanley K., and Jane Silverman. "The Characteristics and Prior Contraceptive Use of U.S. Abortion Patients." *Family Planning Perspectives* 20 (1988): 158–168.

———. *Abortion Factbook, 1992 Edition: Readings, Trends, and State and Local Data to 1988.* New York: Alan Guttmacher Institute, 1992.

Henshaw, Stanley K., and Jennifer Van Vort. "Abortion Services in the United States, 1987 and 1988." *Family Planning Perspectives* 22 (1990): 102–109.

Henshaw, Stanley K., Lisa M. Koonin, and Jack C. Smith. "Characteristics of U.S. Women Having Abortions, 1987." *Family Planning Perspectives* 23 (1991): 75–81.

Institute of Medicine (IOM), Committee to Study the Prevention of Low Birthweight. *Preventing Low Birthweight.* Washington, DC: IOM, 1985.

Jones, Elise F., and Jacqueline D. Forrest. "Contraceptive Failure Rates Based on the 1988 National Survey of Family Growth." *Family Planning Perspectives* 24 (1992): 12–19.

Mosher, William D. "Contraceptive Practice in the United States, 1982–1990." *Family Planning Perspectives* 22 (1990): 198–205.

National Abortion Federation (NAF) and American College of Obstetricians and Gynecologists (ACOG). *Who Will Provide Abortions? Ensuring the Availability of Qualified Practitioners: Recommendations from a National Symposium.* Santa Barbara, CA: NAF and ACOG, 1990.

National Center for Health Statistics. *Monthly Vital Statistics Report,* Vol. 41, No. 6, Supplement. Hyattsville, MD: Public Health Service, 1992.

———. "Advance Report of Final Mortality Statistics, 1990." *Monthly Vital Statistics Report,* Vol. 41, No. 7, Supplement. Hyattsville, MD: Public Health Service, 1993a.

———. "Advance Report of Final Natality Statistics, 1990." *Monthly Vital Statistics Report,* Vol. 41, No. 9. Hyattsville, MD: U.S. Department of Health and Human Services, 1993b.

National Governors Association (NGA). *MCH Update: State Coverage of Pregnant Women and Children—July 1992.* Washington, DC: NGA, July 1992.

Office of Population Censuses and Surveys. *Abortion Statistics, 1988, England and Wales.* London, England: Her Majesty's Stationery Office, 1988.

"Reducing Late Abortion." British Journal of Obstetrics and Gynecology 96 (February 1989): 135–139.

RESOLVE, Inc. and American Fertility Society. *Infertility and National Health Care Reform: A Briefing Paper.* Washington, DC: RESOLVE, Inc., 1993.

Richards, Cory L., and Rachel Benson Gold. "RU 486: Medical Breakthrough Held Hostage." *Issues in Science and Technology,* Vol. 6, No. 4. (Summer 1990): 74–79.

Rosoff, Jeannine I. *Health Care Reform: A Unique Opportunity to Provide Balance and Equity to the Provision of Reproductive Health Services.* New York: Alan Guttmacher Institute, 1993.

Singh, Susheela, Jacqueline D. Forrest, and Aida Torres. *Prenatal Care in the United States: A State and County Inventory.* New York: Alan Guttmacher Institute, 1989.

Torres, Aida, and Jacqueline D. Forrest. "Why Do Women Have Abortions?" *Family Planning Perspectives* 20 (1988): 169–176.

U.S. Congress, Office of Technology Assessment. *Infertility: Medical and Social Choices.* Washington, DC: U.S. Government Printing Office, 1988.

FOUR WOMEN AND LONG-TERM CARE

Agency for Health Care Policy and Research (AHCPR). "Nursing Home Residents: Mental Health Status." *Highlights, NMES: National Medical Expenditure Survey,* No. 14. Rockville, MD: AHCPR, July 1992.

———. "Nursing Home Residents: Demographic Characteristics and Functional Status." *Highlights, NMES: National Medical Expenditure Survey,* No. 15. Rockville, MD: AHCPR, August 1992.

———. Unpublished data from the National Medical Expenditure Survey, U.S. Department of Health and Human Services, 1993.

Altman, Barbara, and Daniel Walden. *Home Health Care: Use, Expenditures and Source of Payment.* National Medical Expenditure Survey, Research Findings No. 15. Rockville, MD: Agency for Health Care Policy and Research, 1993.

Berkman, Lisa. "The Changing and Heterogeneous Nature of Aging and Longevity: A Social and Biomedical Perspective." In *Annual Review of Gerontology and Geriatrics,* edited by George Maddox and M. Powell Lawton, vol. 8. New York: Springer Publishing Co., 1988.

Bishop, Christine, and Genevieve Kenney. *Home Health Costs in Urban and Rural Areas.* Urban Institute Working Paper. Washington, DC: Urban Institute, 1992.

Bureau of the Census. Current Population Reports, Series P-60, No. 180. *Money Income of Households, Families, and Persons in the United States: 1991.* Washington, DC: U.S. Government Printing Office, 1992a.

————. Current Population Reports, Series P-60, No. 181. *Poverty in the United States: 1991.* Washington, DC: U.S. Government Printing Office, 1992b.

————. Current Population Reports, Series P-20, No. 468. *Marital Status and Living Arrangements: March 1992.* Washington, DC: U.S. Government Printing Office, 1992c.

————. Current Population Reports, Special Studies, P-23-178. *Sixty-Five Plus in America.* Washington, DC: U.S. Government Printing Office, 1992d.

————. Decennial Census, unpublished data. Washington, DC, 1993.

Burwell, Brian. "Medicaid Long Term Care Expenditures in FY1992." Unpublished memorandum, Lexington, MA: Systemetrics, February 1, 1993.

Collins, John. "Prevalence of Selected Chronic Conditions, United States, 1983–85." National Center for Health Statistics, *Advance Data,* No. 155. Hyattsville, MD: U.S. Department of Health and Human Services, May 24, 1988.

Feder, Judith, Marilyn Moon, and William Scanlon. "Medicare Reform: Nibbling at Catastrophic Costs." *Health Affairs* 6 (Winter 1987): 5–19.

Guralnick, Jack. "Prospects for the Compression of Morbidity: The Challenge Posed by Increasing Disability in the Years Prior to Death." *Journal of Aging and Health* 3 (May 1991): 138–154.

Harrington, Charlene, Steve Preston, Leslie Grant, and James H. Swan. "Revised Trends in States' Nursing Home Capacity." *Health Affairs* 11 (Summer 1992): 170–180.

Health Insurance Association of America (HIAA). *Long Term Care Insurance: A Market Update.* Research Bulletin. Washington, DC: HIAA, January 1991.

Institute of Medicine. *Improving the Quality of Care in Nursing Homes.* Washington, DC: National Academy Press, 1986.

Keenan, Marianne. *Changing Needs for Long Term Care: A Chartbook.* Washington, DC: American Association of Retired Persons, 1988.

Levit, Katherine, Helen Lazenby, Cathy Cowan, and Suzanne Letsch. "National Health Expenditures 1990." *Health Care Financing Review* 14 (Summer 1991): 29–54.

Mahoney, Kevin. "The Connecticut Partnership for Long-Term Care." *Generations* 14 (Spring 1990): 71–72.

Manton, Kenneth, and Korbin Liu. "The Future Growth of the Long-Term Care Population: Projections Based on the 1977 Nursing Population and the 1982 Long Term Care Survey." Unpublished mimeo. Washington, DC: Urban Institute, 1984.

Manton, Kenneth, Larry Corder, and Eric Stallard. "Estimates of Change in Chronic Disability and Institutional Incidence and Prevalence Rates in the U.S. Elderly Population from the 1982, 1984 and 1989 National Long Term Care Survey." *Journal of Gerontology* 48 (July 1993): S153–S166.

Moon, Marilyn. *Medicare Now and In the Future.* Washington, DC: Urban Institute Press, 1993.

National Center for Health Statistics. *Health Statistics on Older Persons: United States, 1986.* Series 3, No. 25. Hyattsville, MD: U.S. Government Printing Office, 1987.

Pepper Commission (U.S. Bipartisan Commission on Comprehensive Health Care Reform). *A Call For Action.* Final Report. Washington, DC: U.S. Government Printing Office, September 1990.

Public Health Service (PHS). *Health, United States, 1990.* Pub. No. PHS 91-1232. Hyattsville, MD: PHS, 1991.

Rice, Thomas, Kathleen Thomas, and William Weissert. "The Effect of Owning Private Long-Term Care Insurance Policies on Out-of-Pocket Costs." *Health Services Research* 25 (February 1991): 907–934.

Rivlin, Alice, and Joshua Wiener. *Caring for the Disabled Elderly.* Washington, DC: Brookings Institution, 1988.

Rowland, Diane. Unpublished table. National Health Interview Survey Supplement on Aging, 1984. Baltimore, MD: Johns Hopkins University.

Ruggles, Patricia. *Drawing the Line: Alternative Poverty Measures and Their Implications for Public Policy.* Washington, DC: Urban Institute Press, 1990.

Social Security Administration. *Income of the Population 55 or Older, 1988.* Washington, DC: U.S. Government Printing Office, June 1990.

Spence, Denise, and Joshua Wiener. "Nursing Home Length of Stay Patterns: Results from the 1985 National Nursing Home Survey." *Gerontologist* 30 (February 1990): 16–25.

U.S. Congress, Congressional Budget Office. *The Economic Status of the Elderly.* Washington, DC: U.S. Government Printing Office, May 1989.

U.S. Congress, House Select Committee on Aging. *Exploding the Myths: Caregiving in America.* Washington, DC: U.S. Government Printing Office, January 1987.

Yeas, Martynas, and Susan Grad. "Income of Retirement Aged Persons in the United States." *Social Security Bulletin* 50 (1987): 5–14.

Zedlewski, Sheila, Robert Barnes, Martha Burt, Timothy McBride, and Jack Meyer. *The Needs of the Elderly in the 21st Century.* Urban Institute Report 90-5. Washington, DC: Urban Institute, 1990.

AMERICAN WOMEN TODAY: A STATISTICAL PORTRAIT

SECTION 1: DEMOGRAPHICS

Bureau of the Census. Current Population Reports, Series P-20, No. 218. *Household and Family Characteristics: 1970.* Washington, DC: U.S. Government Printing Office, 1971.

——. Current Population Reports, Series P-20, No. 458. *Household and Family Characteristics: March 1991.* Washington, DC: U.S. Government Printing Office, 1992.

——. Current Population Reports, Series P-20, No. 450. *Marital Status and Living Arrangements: March 1990.* Washington, DC: U.S. Government Printing Office, May 1991.

——. Current Population Reports, Series P-20, No. 468. *Marital Status and Living Arrangements: March 1992.* Washington, DC: U.S. Government Printing Office, December 1992.

——. Current Population Reports, Series P-25-1092. *Population Projections of the United States, by Age, Sex, Race, and Hispanic Origin, 1992 to 2050.* Washington, DC: U.S. Government Printing Office, November 1992.

——. Current Population Reports, Series P-60, No. 127. *Money, Income and Poverty Status of Families, and Persons in the United States: 1980.* Washington, DC: U.S. Government Printing Office, 1981.

——. Current Population Reports, Series P-60, No. 174. *Money Income of Households, Families, and Persons in the United States: 1990.* Washington, DC: U.S. Government Printing Office, 1990.

——. Current Population Reports, Series P-60, No. 180. *Money Income of Households, Families, and Persons in the United States: 1991.* Washington, DC: U.S. Government Printing Office, August 1992.

——. *1990 Census of the Population: General Population Characteristics. United States 1990.* Washington, DC: U.S. Government Printing Office, 1992.

——. *Statistical Abstract of the United States 1990 (110th edition).* Washington, DC: U.S. Government Printing Office, 1990.

——. *Statistical Abstract of the United States 1992 (112th edition).* Washington, DC: U.S. Government Printing Office, 1992.

National Center for Health Statistics. "Births, Marriages, Divorces, and Deaths for September 1992." *Monthly Vital Statistics Report,* Vol. 41, No. 9. Hyattsville, MD: U.S. Department of Health and Human Services, February 16, 1993.

——. "Advance Report of Final Natality Statistics, 1990." *Monthly Vital Statistics Report,* Vol. 41, No. 9, Supplement. Hyattsville, MD: U.S. Department of Health and Human Services, February 25, 1993.

SECTION 2: EDUCATION

American Council on Education (ACE). Office of Women in Higher Education. *Women Chief Executive Officers in U.S. Colleges and Universities Table XII, April 15, 1992.* Washington, DC: ACE, June 1992.

Association of American Medical Colleges (AAMC). *Facts: Applicants, Matriculants and Graduates 1986–1992*. Washington, DC: AAMC, 1993.

Bureau of the Census. Current Population Reports, Series P-20, No. 462. *Educational Attainment in the United States: March 1991 and 1990*. Washington, DC: U.S. Government Printing Office, 1992.

———. *Statistical Abstract of the United States 1990 (110th edition)*. Washington, DC: U.S. Government Printing Office, 1990.

———. *Statistical Abstract of the United States 1992 (112th edition)*. Washington, DC: U.S. Government Printing Office, 1992.

Bureau of Labor Statistics. "How Do Immigrants Fare in the U.S. Labor Market?" *Monthly Labor Review* 115, No. 12 (December 1992): 3–19.

———. *Digest of Education Statistics 1992*. Washington, DC: U.S. Department of Education, 1992.

U.S. Department of Health, Education and Welfare. Office for Civil Rights. *Data on Earned Degrees Conferred by Institutions of Higher Education by Race, Ethnicity and Sex, Academic Year 1976–1977*. Photocopy, n.d.

SECTION 3: EMPLOYMENT

Bureau of the Census. Current Population Reports, Series P-20, No. 468. *Marital Status and Living Arrangements: March 1992*. Washington, DC: U.S. Government Printing Office, December 1992.

———. Current Population Reports, Series P-60, No. 127. *Money Income of Households, Families, and Persons in the United States: 1981*. Washington, DC: U.S. Government Printing Office, March 1983.

———. Current Population Reports, Series P-60, No. 146. *Money Income of Households, Families, and Persons in the United States: 1983*. Washington, DC: U.S. Government Printing Office, April 1985.

———. Current Population Reports, Series P-60, No. 156. *Money Income of Households, Families, and Persons in the United States: 1985*. Washington, DC: U.S. Government Printing Office, August 1987.

———. Current Population Reports, Series P-60, No. 162. *Money Income of Households, Families, and Persons in the United States: 1987*. Washington, DC: U.S. Government Printing Office, February 1989.

———. Current Population Reports, Series P-60, No. 172. *Money Income of Households, Families, and Persons in the United States (1988 and 1989)*. Washington, DC: U.S. Government Printing Office, July 1991.

———. Current Population Reports, Series P-60, No. 180. *Money Income of Households, Families, and Persons in the United States: 1991*. Washington, DC: U.S. Government Printing Office, August 1992.

———. Current Population Reports, Series P-70-30. *Who's Minding the Kids? Child Care Arrangements: Fall 1988*. Washington, DC: U.S. Government Printing Office, August 1992.

Bureau of Labor Statistics. *Employment and Earnings*. Washington, DC: U.S. Government Printing Office, January 1976.

Bureau of Labor Statistics. *Employment and Earnings*. Washington, DC: U.S. Government Printing Office, January 1985.

———. *Employment and Earnings*. Washington, DC: U.S. Government Printing Office, January 1991.

———. *Employment and Earnings*. Washington, DC: U.S. Government Printing Office, January 1992.

———. *Employment and Earnings*. Washington, DC: U.S. Government Printing Office, January 1993.

———. *Handbook of Labor Statistics*. Washington, DC: U.S. Government Printing Office, 1989.

———. "Multiple Jobholding Up Sharply in the 1980's," *Monthly Labor Review* 113, No. 7 (July 1990): 3–10.

———. Unpublished data, Washington, DC: 1990 and 1992.

———. "Volunteers in the United States: Who Donates the Time?" *Monthly Labor Review* 114, No. 2 (February 1991): 17–23.

———. "Outlook: 1990–2005: Labor Force Projections: The Baby Boom Moves On." *Monthly Labor Review* 114, No. 11 (November 1991): 31–44.

———. *Statistical Abstract of the United States, 1992 (112th edition)*. Washington, DC: U.S. Government Printing Office, 1992.

———. "How Do Immigrants Fare in the U.S. Labor Market?" *Monthly Labor Review* 115, No. 12 (December 1992): 20–28.

———. Current Population Survey 1992 Annual Averages. Unpublished tabulations, Washington, DC: 1993.

U.S. Coast Guard. Enlisted Personnel Division. Unpublished information, March 1, 1993.

U.S. Department of Defense, Defense Manpower Data Center. Unpublished information, September 30, 1992.

SECTION 4: EARNINGS AND BENEFITS

Bureau of the Census. Current Population Reports, Series P-60, No. 180. *Money Income of Households, Families, and Persons in the United States: 1991*. Washington, DC: U.S. Government Printing Office, August 1992.

———. Current Population Reports, Series P-60, No. 181. *Poverty in the United States: 1991*. Washington, DC: U.S. Government Printing Office, 1992.

———. Current Population Survey March 1992. Unpublished data, Washington, DC.

Bureau of Labor Statistics. *Handbook of Labor Statistics*. Washington, DC: U.S. Government Printing Office, August 1989.

———. *Employment and Earnings*. Washington, DC: U.S. Government Printing Office, January 1990.

———. *Employment and Earnings*. Washington, DC: U.S. Government Printing Office, January 1991.

———. *Employment and Earnings*. Washington, DC: U.S. Government Printing Office, January 1992.

Bureau of Labor Statistics. Current Population Survey March 1991. Unpublished data, Washington, DC.

———. "Benefits in State and Local Governments Address Family Concerns." *Monthly Labor Review* 115, No. 3 (March 1992): 32–37.

———. *Employment and Earnings.* Washington, DC: U.S. Government Printing Office, January 1993.

SECTION 5: ECONOMIC SECURITY

Bureau of the Census. Current Population Reports, Series P-20, No. 371. *Household and Family Characteristics: March 1981.* Washington, DC: U.S. Government Printing Office, May 1982.

———. Current Population Reports, Series P-23, No. 167. *Child Support and Alimony 1987.* Washington, DC: U.S. Government Printing Office, 1990.

———. Current Population Reports, Series P-60, No. 137. *Money Income of Households, Families, and Persons in the United States: 1981.* Washington, DC: U.S. Government Printing Office, March 1983.

———. Current Population Reports, Series P-60, No. 180. *Money Income of Households, Families, and Persons in the United States: 1991.* Washington, DC: U.S. Government Printing Office, August 1992.

———. Current Population Reports, Series P-60, No. 181. *Poverty in the United States: 1991.* Washington, DC: U.S. Government Printing Office, August 1992.

———. Current Population Reports, Series P-60, No. 458. *Household and Family Characteristics: March 1991.* Washington, DC: U.S. Government Printing Office, February 1992.

———. Current Population Survey March 1992. Unpublished data, Washington, DC.

———. *Statistical Abstract of the United States 1992 (112th edition).* Washington, DC: U.S. Government Printing Office, 1992.

Bureau of the Census and Department of Housing and Urban Development, *American Housing Survey for the United States in 1989.* Washington, DC: U.S. Government Printing Office, 1991.

Bureau of Labor Statistics. "Working and Poor in 1990." *Monthly Labor Review* 115, No. 12 (December 1992): 20–28.

SECTION 6: ELECTIONS AND OFFICIALS

Administrative Office of the United States Courts. *Annual Report on the Judiciary Equal Employment Opportunity Program for the Twelve-Month Period Ending September 30, 1991.* Washington, DC: Administrative Office of the United States Courts, 1992.

Bureau of the Census. Current Population Reports, Series P-20, No. 322. *Voter Participation in the Election of November 1976.* Washington, DC: U.S. Government Printing Office, 1978.

Bureau of the Census. Current Population Reports, Series P-20, No. 370. *Voting and Registration in the Election of November 1980*. Washington, DC: U.S. Government Printing Office, 1982.

————. Current Population Reports, Series P-20, No. 405. *Voting and Registration in the Election of November 1984*. Washington, DC: U.S. Government Printing Office, 1986.

————. Current Population Reports, Series P-20, No. 440. *Voting and Registration in the Election of November 1988*. Washington, DC: U.S. Government Printing Office, 1989.

————. Current Population Reports, Series P-20, No. 466. *Voting and Registration in the Election of November 1992*. Washington, DC: U.S. Government Printing Office, 1993.

Center for the American Woman and Politics. *Women in Elective Office 1991 Fact Sheet*, 1991; *Women in the U.S. Congress 1993 Fact Sheet*, 1993; *State Wide Elective Executive Women 1993 Fact Sheet*, 1993; and *Women in State Legislatures 1993 Fact Sheet*, 1993.

National Women's Political Caucus. *Factsheet on Women's Political Progress*, June 1993.

Notes on the Contributors

Elizabeth Chait is a research assistant with the Kaiser Commission on the Future of Medicaid. Her areas of interest are the health needs of underserved populations, women's health, and international health. She has completed internships with the Boston City Council and with Save the Children in Cameroon.

Karen Scott Collins, M.D., M.P.H., is the senior program officer for health at the Commonwealth Fund in New York, with program responsibilities in women's health, health care reform, and minority health. She was previously an instructor in health policy at The Johns Hopkins School of Hygiene and Public Health, and a principal policy analyst for the Kaiser Commission on the Future of Medicaid, where her work focused on the health status and delivery of health care to low-income populations. She was at Johns Hopkins at the time this chapter was prepared.

Betty Dooley has been executive director of the Women's Research and Education Institute since 1977. An early Texas feminist, she was active in state politics before moving to Washington, DC. In 1964, she was a candidate for the U.S. House of Representatives from the 16th congressional district of Texas. She served for several years as director of the Health Security Action Council, an advocacy organization that worked for comprehensive national health insurance.

Rachel Benson Gold, M.P.A., is senior public policy associate in the Washington office of the Alan Guttmacher Institute, where she monitors activities in Congress, the executive branch, and the states—and provides information and analysis on the role of the public and private sectors in promoting access to reproductive health care services. The author of numerous publications in the field of reproductive health, she serves on the advisory board of the Southern Regional Project on Infant Mortality and the advisory board of the National Abortion Federation.

Wilhelmina A. Leigh, Ph.D., is a senior research associate at the Joint Center for Political and Economic Studies, specializing in policy research in health and housing. Dr. Leigh was a principal analyst at the Congressional Budget Office for nearly a decade before coming to her present position in 1991. She also has taught at Harvard University and currently is an adjunct professor at Georgetown University. Her most recent publication (1992) is *A Health Assessment of Black Americans: A Fact Book.*

Marilyn Moon, Ph.D., is a senior research associate with the Health Policy Center of the Urban Institute. Prior to this position, she served as director of the Public Policy Institute of the American Association of Retired Persons. She has written extensively on health policy, policy for the elderly, and income distribution. Her current work focuses on health system reform and financing. She has recently completed a book entitled *Medicare Now and in the Future.*

Cory L. Richards is vice president for public policy and director of the Washington office of the Alan Guttmacher Institute. A long-time advocate of reproductive health and reproductive rights, he was appointed public member of the Reproductive Freedom Task Force, U.S. Commission on International Women's Year, 1976. Mr. Richards has also served on the boards of directors of the National Abortion Rights Action League, the National Abortion Federation, and the National Family Planning and Reproductive Health Association, as well as on the action board of the American Public Health Association. He is currently on the board of the Sex Information and Education Council of the United States.

Diane Rowland, Sc.D., is senior vice president of the Henry J. Kaiser Family Foundation. She also serves as executive director of the Kaiser Commission on the Future of Medicaid (which focuses on health care financing and delivery issues facing poor and disabled populations) and is an adjunct associate professor of health policy at The Johns Hopkins School of Hygiene and Public Health. She has served on the staff of the House Energy and Commerce Subcommittee on Health and the Environment and as a health policy consultant to the Clinton administration. Dr. Rowland has written and edited a number of books and articles on a wide range of health issues.

Alina Salganicoff is a principal policy analyst with the Kaiser Commission on the Future of Medicaid and serves as a research associate at The Johns Hopkins School of Hygiene and Public Health. Her work focuses on improving access to health care for low-income populations. She has also worked on the health program staff of the Pew Charitable Trusts and as a trainer and counselor at Choice, a Philadelphia-based reproductive health advocacy organization.

About the Women's Research and Education Institute

Betty Dooley, *Executive Director*
Cynthia Costello, Ph.D., *Research Director*
Patricia M. Gormley, *Director of Women in the Military Project*
Amanda Maisels, *Research Assistant*
Shari Miles, *Fellowship Program Director/Research Associate*
Bridget C. Rice, *Research Assistant*
Kathleen Stevenson-Pagano, *Office Manager/Development Assistant*
Anne J. Stone, *Senior Research Associate*

THE WOMEN'S RESEARCH AND EDUCATION INSTITUTE (WREI) is a nonprofit (501[c][3]) organization located in Washington, DC. Established in 1977, WREI provides information, research, and policy analysis to the members of Congress who support equity for women. Over the years, WREI's reputation as a source of reliable data and clear thinking about the status of American women has traveled far beyond the nation's Capitol.

- WREI's resources are among the nation's best, and include research and policy centers throughout the country where scholars are conducting cutting-edge research on a host of issues concerning women.
- WREI puts vital information on key issues affecting women into the hands of policymakers in the form of reports and fact sheets that are prepared by WREI staff or outside scholars.
- WREI urges researchers to consider the public policy implications of their work, and fosters the exchange of ideas and expertise between researchers and policymakers.
- WREI promotes the informed scrutiny of policies regarding their effect on women, and encourages the development of policy options that recognize the circumstances of today's women and their families.
- WREI identifies and trains new leaders through its Congressional Fellowships on

Women and Public Policy. Established in 1980, this program enhances the research capacity of congressional offices, especially with respect to legislative implications for women, and has given scores of promising women hands-on experience in the federal legislative process.

• WREI is a national information source and clearinghouse. Reporters, researchers, public officials, government agencies, advocacy organizations, and others contact WREI for information relating to women.

BOARD OF DIRECTORS

Index

Page numbers in *italics* denote illustrations.

abortion, 30, 31, 198, 207–9
  access to, 213–16
  by age, *table* 205, 208
  insurance coverage for, 210, 211
  for poor women, 61, 211
  reasons for, 30, 208–9
  teenage pregnancy and, 44, *table* 205, 208
  by week of gestation, 208, *table* 208
  see also RU-486
abortion rights, 30, 39, 51, 56, 59, 70, 75
  ABA and, 65
  Colorado's protection of, 82
  gag rule and, 55, 58, 72, 76, 217
  Hyde amendment and, 81, 88, 211
  political parties and, 59, 60, 66
  religion and, 60
  Reno and, 80, 85
  waiting period and, 65, 73, 81
  see also anti-abortion activity; Supreme Court, U.S., abortion rights and
abstinence, sexual, *table* 204
Abzug, Bella, 57
accidents, *table* 114, 188
Achtenberg, Roberta, 86
Action Plan for Women's Health (Public Health Service), 99
activities of daily living (ADL), limitations of, 228–29, *table* 229, 233, 240, 242, *table* 243

Adams, P. F., 142
Administration on Aging, 238
Aetna Life and Casualty, 49
African Americans, *see* black men; blacks; black women
age
  abortion and, *table* 205, 208
  contraception and, 200–202, *table* 201, *table* 202, 203–4, *table* 204
  economic security and, 327, *figure* 331, *table* 338
  employment and, *table* 284, *table* 292; children of working parents, *figure* 303, *table* 303, *table* 304
  at first marriage, by sex, 253, *figure* 258
  health and functional status of elderly women and men by, 228–29, *table* 229
  health insurance and, 144, *table* 145, 308, *figure* 324
  hospital discharge rates by sex and, 140, *figure* 141
  living arrangements of women age 65 and over by race, Hispanic origin and, 230–32, *table* 231
  number of men per 100 women by, 230, *figure* 231
  nursing home residents over age 55 by sex, race and, 241, *table* 241
  physician visits and usual source of care by sex and, 140, *table* 141

age (continued)
  population by sex and, 253, figure 255
  poverty status and, 142–43, table 143,
    234, table 235, table 338
  pregnancy outcome by, 204, table 205
  of preventive services' users, table 135,
    figure 136; mammography, 135–36,
    figure 137; Pap smear, table 135, figure
    136
  voter participation by, 345–46, figure
    348, table 349
  women enrolled in colleges and
    universities by, 266, figure 271
  women smokers by, 133, figure 133
  see also children; elderly; elderly men;
    elderly women; older women, health
    concerns of; teenage girls; younger
    women, health concerns of
Agency for Health Care Policy and
  Research (AHCPR), 143, 240, 242
aging studies, women excluded from, 25,
  95, 99
AIDS (Acquired Immune Deficiency
  Syndrome), 26, 52, 70, 117–19
  mortality rates for, 26, 117, 187, table 188
  research on, 98, 101, 102, 107
  spread of, 26, 52, 117–19, figure 117,
    figure 118, 219
  see also HIV/AIDS (human
    immunodeficiency virus/Acquired
    Immune Deficiency Syndrome)
Aid to Families with Dependent Children
  (AFDC) Program, 51, 77, 146, 147,
  table 334
Air Force, U.S., 50, table 274, table 301
Alan Guttmacher Institute (AGI), 198, 202,
  205, 206, 209–13, 219
Albright, Madeline, 77
alcohol, alcohol consumption, 41, 55, 116,
  174
  breast cancer and, 126
  of Hispanic women, 162, 174
alcoholism, 71, 107, 170
  Native American women and, 28, 159,
    188
allied health providers/practitioners, 216–17
Allstate Insurance, 68
Alston, Dana, 158

Althaus, Frances A., 115, 116
Altman, Barbara, 233
Alu Like, Inc., 168, 169, 179
Alzheimer's disease, 27, 110, 131, 225, 240,
  249
Amaro, Hortensia, 133, 154n, 161, 162,
  187
ambassadors, 77, 80
Amendment 1 (Iowa), 67
American Association of Retired Persons
  (AARP), 82
American Association of University
  Women, 52
American Association of University
  Women Foundation, 86
American Bar Association (ABA), 65
American Business Collaboration for
  Quality Dependent Care, 68
American Cancer Society, 124, 126, 135
American College of Cardiology, 80
American College of Obstetricians and
  Gynecologists (ACOG), 94, 135, 140,
  206, 215
American Express, 68
American Fertility Society, 202
American Indian Health Care Association,
  182
American Mathematical Society, 50
American Medical Association (AMA), 48,
  60–61, 121, 122
  Council on Scientific Affairs (ACS) of,
    126, 128, 136, 216
American Medical Women's Association,
  44–45
American Nurses Association, 94
American Psychiatric Association, 94
American Woman Award, 45, 68
Amoco, 68
Anderson, Dallas, 131
Andrews, Julie, 55
Angelou, Maya, 73
angina, 122, 123
anorexia nervosa, 120
Anthony, James C., 120
anti-abortion activity, 52, 71, 77, 79, 80,
  82, 215
  Operation Rescue and, 40, 41, 42, 44,
    58, 76

antistalking legislation, 80
Army, U.S., 59, 68, *table* 301
Army Research Institute, 68
Aronson, M. K., 131
arthritis, 121
  long-term care and, 31, 226, 229, *table*
    230, 249
Asian American Health Forum, Inc.
    (AAHF), 169, 179
Asian and Pacific Islander men,
    demographics on, *table* 254, *figure* 256
Asian and Pacific Islanders
  employment of, *table* 285
  mortality rates for, 188
  physicians and providers, 194–95
  use of term, 157*n*
Asian and Pacific Islander women, 44
  AIDS in, 179, *table* 180, 181, *table* 181
  alcohol and, 155, 174
  births of, 206
  cancer in, 29, 175, 177
  data collection problems for, 190–91
  demographics on, *table* 254, *figure* 256
  education of, 265, *table* 269, *table* 273,
    table 277; college enrollment, 265
  health status of, 28–29, 154, 157,
    167–84, 187–95
  hepatitis B of, 177
  hypertension in, 179
  life expectancy of, 155
  mortality rates for, 188; infant, neonatal
    and postneonatal, *table* 186, 188
  obesity of, 155, 169, 172
  prenatal care of, 176, *table* 176, 206
  preventive health measures of, 175, 176
  smoking by, 173, *table* 173
  uninsured, 28–29, 182, 183
Aspin, Les, 68, 84
aspirin study of heart attack, 25, 91, 95,
    138
assets, financial, long-term care and,
    234–37, 247–48
Association of Asian Pacific Community
    Health Organizations (AAPCHO),
    176, 178, 182
asthma, *table* 230
astronauts, 56, 68
AT&T, 68

AT&T Technologies, Inc., 41
autoimmune diseases, 121
automobile industry, 72

Baez, I. Evelyn, 154*n*
Baird, Zoe E., 76–79
Baltimore Longitudinal Study of Aging, 95,
    99
Bankers Trust, 81
basketball, 44, 52, 87
Bastida, Elena, 160, 182
Battle, Kathleen, 61
James Beard Awards, 58
Beauregard, Karen, 185
Becker, Richard C., 123
Bell, Bella Zi, 174
Bell, Derrick, 54, 63
Bellamy, Carol, 57
benefits, *see* earnings and benefits; health
    insurance; pensions
Benson, V., 142
Benten, Leona, 63, 64
Bentley, Helen Delich, 354, *354*
Bentsen, Lloyd, 86
Bergen, Candice, 59, 69
Bergman, Barbara, 70
Berk, Marc L., 146
Berkelman, Ruth L., 188
Berkman, Lisa, 242
Bianchi-Sand, Susan, 51
Bindon, James R., 179
birth, *see* childbirth
birth control, *see* contraception
birth control pills, 43, 57, 201, *table* 202,
    210, 214, 220
  cancer and, 126
  failure rate of, *table* 204, 205
birth defects, 47
Bishop, Christine, 244
bishops, female, 60
Black, Dennis, 139
black men, 160, 164, 230
  earnings and benefits of, *table* 309, *figure*
    313, *table* 314, *table* 321
  leading causes of mortality for, 114, *table*
    115
  life expectancy of, *table* 112, *table* 171
Blackmun, Harry A., 62

blacks
    demographics, 253, *table* 259; children's
        living arrangements, 254, *table* 262;
        divorce ratios, *table* 261; marital status,
        table 257, *figure* 258; population, *table*
        254, *figure* 256
    education of, 265, *table* 267, *table* 270
    employment of, 281, 282, *table* 285, *table*
        288, *figure* 289, *table* 291, *table* 294,
        figure 297, *table* 299, *table* 300, *table*
        301, *figure* 302, *table* 305
    families, 253, *table* 259; income, 327,
        table 330; poverty rates, *table* 337
    hospitals for, 192–93
    job training and, 40
    physicians, 194
    use of term, 157*n*
    voter participation of, 345, *figure* 346,
        table 347
black women, 51, 68, 71, 75, 85, 200, 213
    AIDS and, 26, 28, 110, 117–18, *figure*
        117, *figure* 118, 155, 160, 180, *table*
        180, 181, *table* 181; mortality rates,
        188, *table* 188
    alcohol use of, 174
    births of, 206
    cancer in, 123, *table* 123, 155, 188;
        breast, 123, *table* 123, 124, 126–27,
        figure 127, *figure* 128, 137, 177, 192;
        cervical, 29, 123, *table* 123, 125, *figure*
        126, 175; lung, 123, *table* 123, 124;
        ovarian, 123, *table* 123, 126
    cerebrovascular disease in, *table* 115,
        128–29
    child support and, 34
    contraception of, 201
    depression in, 119
    diabetes of, 28, *table* 115, 129, *figure* 129,
        154, 177–78
    drug use of, 174
    earnings and benefits, 32, 308, *table* 309,
        313, *table* 321; median annual, *figure*
        313, *table* 314
    economic security of, *table* 333–34, *table*
        335, *table* 340–41
    education of, 33, *table* 269; college, *table*
        273, *table* 277; 12 or more years, 265,
        figure 268

employment of, *table* 301, *figure* 302;
    child care, 282, *table* 305; health care,
    table 299, *table* 300; occupation, 282,
    figure 297, *table* 300; unemployment
    rate, 34, 281, *figure* 289
fertility of, *figure* 256
health care services used by, 184
health insurance of, 182–84; uninsured,
    29, 182
health status of, 28–29, 154, 155, 157,
    163–67, 171–88, 192–95
high cholesterol of, 173
hypertension, 28, 138–39, 164, 178, *table*
    179
infant mortality, 29, 165, 166, 185–86,
    table 186, 207
as law professors, 54
leading causes of mortality for, *table* 114,
    115
life expectancy of, 27, 28, *table* 112, 113,
    155, 171, *table* 171
literary figures, 63, 73, 85
living arrangements of, age 65 and over,
    table 231, 232
long-term care for, 231, *table* 231, 233,
    234, *table* 235, 241, *table* 241
obesity of, 155, 172, *table* 172
in politics, 55, 72
poverty status of, *table* 143, 144
prenatal care of, 176, *table* 176, 206
preventive services used by, *table* 135,
    175, 176
smoking by, 133, 173, *table* 173
STDs of, 116
blood pressure
    high, *see* hypertension
    measurement of, 132, *table* 132, *table* 135,
        138
blue-collar jobs, 34
Boggs, Lindy Claiborne, 42
Lindy Claiborne Boggs Reading Room
    (Room H-235), 42
Bolin, Jane, 85
Boring, Catherine C., 127
Boston Women's Health Book Collective, 70
Boxer, Barbara, 63, 354, *354*
Bray v. Alexandria Women's Health Clinic,
    76, 77

Breast and Cervical Cancer Mortality
  Prevention Act (1990), 104
breast cancer, 29, 155, 175, 177
  female mortality from, *figure* 124, 188
  incidence and death rates for, 123, *table*
    123, 126–27, *figure* 127
  lung cancer compared with, 26, 103,
    109, 124, *figure* 124
  politics of, 102–4
  research and studies on, 25, 56, 69, 98,
    101–4
  screening for, *see* mammography
  survival chances and, 50
  treatment for, 56, 93, 102
  white and black women with, percentage
    early diagnosis and five-year survival,
    figure 128
breast exam, clinical, *table* 132, *table* 135,
  136–37, 175
breast implants, 53, 56, 75
Brown, Corrine, 355, *355*
Brown, Jesse, 80
Browne, Le Lieu, 53
Browner, Carol M., 74, 76
Brownson, Ross C., 134
Buehler, James W., 188
bulimia nervosa, 120
Bureau of Labor Statistics, U.S., 48, 210
Burhansstipanov, Linda, 154*n*
Burt, John, 80
Burwell, Brian, 238
Bush, Barbara, 66, 67
Bush, George, 40, 42, 49, 50, 61, 64, 71,
  79, 98, 345, 346, *table* 351
  abortion rights and, 52, 66
  domestic violence and, 59–60
  Family and Medical Leave Act and, 46,
    49, 65, 68, 69, 70, 77
Bush administration, gag rule and, 55, 58,
  72
business, women-owned, 64
business schools, women in, 69–70
Butrica, Barbara, 162
Byrne, Leslie, 355, *355*
Byron, Beverly, 68

California, University of (Berkeley), Boalt
  Hall at, 62

California, University of (Los Angeles)
  (UCLA), 88
California, University of (San Francisco),
  77–78
Cambodian Women, 176
Cammermeyer, Margarethe, 59
Campaign for Women's Health, 105
Canada
  female life expectancy in, 113, *figure* 113
  health care in, 150–51
cancer, 27, 109, 123–28, 177, 188
  mortality rates for, 113, 114, *table* 114,
    123, *table* 123, 125–27, *figure* 127, 188,
    189
  screening for, 128, *see also*
    mammography; Pap smears
  selected, incidence and death rates for,
    123, *table* 123
  see also breast cancer; cervical cancer;
    endometrial (uterine) cancer;
    gallbladder cancer; lung cancer;
    ovarian cancer
Candace Awards, 61
Cantwell, Maria, 356, *356*
Capitol, U.S., Room H-235 in, 42
Cappai, Ronald, 46, 64
cardiovascular disease, *table* 132, 188
caregivers
  men compared with women as, 32, 61,
    223, 226, 232
  relationship of, to elderly women and
    men receiving care by age of recipient,
    232, *table* 232
Carter, Jimmy, 54, *table* 351
Castro, Kenneth G., 180
Catalyst, 54, 87
Cates, Willard, 116
Census Bureau, U.S., 53, 59, 74, 142–44,
  147, 149, 157, 160, 161, 163, 164,
  165, 167, 183, 193, 230, 231, 232,
  234, 240, 241
Center for Budget and Policy Priorities, 51
Center for the Study of the States, 51
Centers for Disease Control (CDC), 44, 55,
  104, 105, 116, 118, 125, 129, 133,
  134, 136
Central and South Americans, 160, 161
  women, *table* 176, *table* 186

cerebrovascular disease, 27, 128–29, 178
  men compared with women for, *table*
    115, *table* 230
  mortality rates for, *table* 115
  see also multi-infarct dementia; stroke
cervical cancer, 29, 155, 175, 177
  AIDS and, 118, 119
  incidence and death rates for, 123, *table*
    123, 125–26, *figure* 125
  research on, 101
  screening for, *see* Pap smears
cesarean sections, 106
Chafee, John, H., 47
Chait, Elizabeth, 26–28, 109–53
CHAMPUS/VA insurance, *figure* 323
Chandler, Christy, 39*n*
Chao, Elaine L., 44
Chase Manhattan Bank, 81
chefs, 58
Chicago, University of, 84
child abuse, 43–44
childbearing period, 198–99, *figure* 198
childbirth, 66, 205–7, *table* 205
  complications of, 197, 205–6
  hospital stays for, 140–42, *figure* 141
  by month prenatal care began and age of
    mother, 206, *table* 207
child care, 43, 48–49, 64, 68, 70, 81, 182
  expenditures for, 282, *table* 306
  teacher wages and, 83
  for working mothers by race and
    Hispanic origin, 282, *table* 305
  in workplace, 44, 45, 49, 81, 83–84
Child Care Employee Project, 83
children
  economic security and, 328, *table* 335,
    figure 336, *table* 337, *figure* 342
  households with female householders by
    tenure, type, and presence of, *figure*
    263
  households with unrelated partners by
    sex of partners and presence of, *table*
    260
  labor force participation of mothers with,
    figure 302
  living arrangements of, 254, *table*
    262–63, *table* 303
    with mothers in workforce by age of
      children, *figure* 303
    poor, 34, 63
    uninsured, 34, 308, *table* 326
Children's Defense Fund, 63, 207
child support, 34, 42, *table* 334, *table* 335
Chinese Americans, 168
  mortality rates for, 188
  as physicians and providers, 194, 195
Chinese American women, 174, 177, 178,
    table 186
  prenatal care of, *table* 176
chlamydia, 105, 115, 116
cholesterol
  HDL, 122–23
  high, 172–73
Christian Coalition, 67
Christopher, Warren, 87
chronic obstructive pulmonary disease, *table*
    114, 115
Chu, Susan Y., 154*n*, 179, 182, 188
cirrhosis, 28, *table* 114, 159, 187, 188–89
Citadel, 60, 67
Civil Rights Act (1991), 49
  1992 amendment of, 54
Clancy, Carolyn, 150
Clayton, Eva, 356, *356*
clinics, 213, 214
  family planning, 55, 58, 72, 76, 213–14
Clinton, Bill, 73–82, 86, 87, 88, 91, 218,
    345, 346, *table* 351
Clinton, Hillary Rodham, 39–40, 65, 77,
    79, 85, 107
Clutter, Mary E., 67
Clyne, Christopher A., 123
coaches, 44, 87
Coast Guard, U.S., *table* 274, *table* 301
cocaine, 47, 64–65
Colburn, Don, 50
Colditz, Graham A., 138
colleges and universities
  enrollment: by sex and full- or
    part-time status, *figure* 271; by sex,
    race, and Hispanic origin, 265, *table*
    270; women, by age, 266, *figure* 271
  faculty with tenure by sex and type of
    institution, 266, *figure* 279

first professional degrees awarded in selected fields by sex of recipient, *figure* 276

recipients of postsecondary degrees by sex, 266, *figure* 275

ten most popular majors among bachelor's degree recipients by sex and by race and Hispanic origin for women, *table* 273

women awarded first professional degrees in selected fields by race and Hispanic origin, 266, *table* 277

women awarded undergraduate degrees in selected fields, *table* 272

women heads of, *figure* 279

Collins, Barbara-Rose, 48, 357, *357*

Collins, Cardiss, 357, *357*

Collins, John, 229

Collins, Karen Scott, 26–28, 109–53

Colorado, abortion rights in, 82

combat training and roles, 50, 58, 66, 68, 71–72, 82, 84

Commission for Professional Hospital Activities, 210

Commission on Civil Rights, U.S., 170

Commodity Exchange of New York, 55

Commonwealth Fund, 61

Communications Consortium Media Center (CCMC), 175

Communications Workers of America, 56

Community and Migrant Health Center program, 212

composers, women, 67–68

Condemi, John J., 121

condoms, 55, 85, 163, 201, *table* 202

failure rate of, *table* 204

for women, 52, 84–85

Conference Board, 53

Congress, U.S., 49, 61, 84, 199, 202, 214, 232, 235

domestic violence and, 43–44

House of Representatives, 25, 58, 71, 72, 84, 88, 100, 103; Appropriations Committee of, 107; Armed Services Committee of, 68, 84; Energy and Commerce Subcommittee on Health and the Environment of, 95–96, 98,

105; Family and Medical Leave Act and, 49, 65, 70, 77; Government Operations Committee Subcommittee on Human Resources and Intergovernmental Relations, 75; Judiciary Committee of, 85–86; Ways and Means Committee of, 140; Ways and Means Subcommittee on Health of, 81; women in, 72, 106, 107, 345, 353–80, *354–80*

Joint Economic Committee of, 51

mammography and, 104–5

Management Foundation, 50

Medicaid eligibility and, 211–12

Medicare Catastrophic Coverage Act and, 102–3

NIH and, 97, 98, 100, 101

Office of Technology Assessment, 107, 120, 144, 147

Senate, 48, 52, 54, 58, 69, 71, 72, 80, 86, 88, 100; Armed Services Committee of, 60, 84; breast cancer and, 103–4; Ethics Committee of, 73, 78, 86; Family and Medical Leave Act and, 46, 65, 77; Judiciary Committee of, 45, 46, 47, 57, 65, 75, 80; Labor and Human Resources Committee of, 54, 85, 98; Rules Committee of, 74, 86; staff of, 50; women in, 55, 63, 72, 75–76, 86, 106, 345, 346, 353, 354, *354*, 360, *360*, 362, *362*, 364, *364*, 369, *369*, 371, *371*, 372, *372;* women presidential appointees confirmed by, 346, *table* 351; Women's Health and Equity Act and, 25, 98

sexual harassment and, 78–79

women in, 39, 48, 50, 55, 63, 72, 75–76, 86, 106, 107, 345, 346, *table* 350, 353–83, *354–80*

Congressional Caucus for Women's Issues, 42, 75, 79, 81

Economic Equity Act and, 46–47

members of, 381–83

politics of women's health and, 23–26, 91–108; breast cancer, 102–4; extended beyond research, 104–5; GAO report, 95–97; health agenda

Congressional Caucus (*continued*)
    expansion, 92–93; legislative strategy,
    101–2; reform principles, 105–6;
    research need identified, 93–94
Congresswomen's Caucus, *see*
    Congressional Caucus for Women's
    Issues
conjunctivitis, 116
contingent workers, 82
contraception, 142, 200–202
    access to, 213–14
    coverage of, 209–10, 220
    Depo Provera, 92, 201, 204
    failure of, by marital status, poverty
        status, and age, 203–4, *table* 204
    health care reform and, 220
    Norplant, 49, 70, 92, 201, 204, 212,
        213–14, 220
    research on, 25, 92–93, 98, 101, 102,
        218
    risk of unintended pregnancy by age and
        type of, 197, 200–201, *table* 201
    users age 15–44 who rely on various
        methods by age, 201–2, *table* 202
    see also birth control pills; condoms,
        diaphragms; intrauterine devices
        (IUDs); spermicide; sterilization
Convention on the Elimination of All
    Forms of Discrimination Against
    Women, 87
Cook County Hospital, 61
Corder, Larry, 240
Cornelius, Llewellyn J., 183, 185
Corning, 49
Cornum, Rhonda, 62
*Corporate Reference Guide to Work-Family
    Programs,* 49
Corporation Counsel, 85
Coryell, William, 119
Cosby, Camille, 61
Costello, Cynthia, 23–35
Coughlin, Paula, 44, 47, 48, 61, 63
Council of Economic Advisers, 74, 78
counseling, 110, 217
    nutritional, 212, 214
Court of Appeals, U.S., 42, 49, 79
court system
    sexual harassment in, 65

women in, *table* 351
see also Supreme Court, U.S.
Cowan, Alison Leigh, 69–70
Crews, Douglas E., 179
Crisp, Mary Dent, 59
Cubans, 160, 161, 190
    employment and, *table* 286, *figure* 287
    health insurance of, 183
Cuban women, 161, *table* 172, 174, 175,
        184, *table* 186
    diabetes in, *figure* 129
    high cholesterol of, 172
    hypertension in, 178, *table* 179
    prenatal care of, 28, 154, *table* 176
    smoking by, *table* 173
Cummings, Steven R., 139
Cunningham, Peter, 185
Cuomo, Mario, 79
Current Population Survey (1991), 143–44,
        146, 148, 149
Customs, U.S., 62–63

Dade County, Fla., family and medical
        leave law in, 55
Daley, Daniel, 211
Dalkon Shield IUD, 218
Danner, Patricia, 358, *358*
Danowitz, Jane, 48
Dash, Julie, 51, 61
data collection problems, 189–91
Daughters of the Dust (movie), 51
day care, *see* child care
Decade of the Executive Woman, 88
Defense Department, U.S., 61, 69, 71, 83,
        84, 107
    breast cancer research and, 103–4
DeHovitz, Jack A., 118, 119
DeLauro, Rosa, 358, *358*
Delgado, Jane L., 173, 177, 178, 184, 188,
        190
DeLozier, J. E., 142
Democrats, Democratic party, U.S., 46, 55,
        57, 60, 63, 67, 72, 80
    1992 Convention of, 63–64
demographics, 253–64
    children's living arrangements by race
        and Hispanic origin, 254, *table*
        262–63

currently married and never married adults by sex, race, and Hispanic origin, *figure* 258

divorce rate, 254, *figure* 261, *table* 261

families by family type, race, and Hispanic origin, 253, *table* 259–60

fertility rates by race, 253, *figure* 256

households with female householders by tenure, type, and presence of children, *figure* 263

households with unrelated partners by sex of partners and presence of children, 253, *table* 260

living arrangements of persons age 65 and over by sex, 254, *figure* 264

marital status by sex, race, and Hispanic origin, *table* 257

median age at first marriage by sex, 253, *figure* 258

see also population, U.S.

dentistry, education in, 266, *figure* 276, *table* 277

Depo Provera, 92, 201, 205

depression, 27, 50, 110, 119–20, 121

Detroit, Mich., public schools in, 43

De Varona, Donna, 68

diabetes, 27, 109, 122, 129–30, 177–78, 188, 229

  amputations and, 28, 154

  of black women, 28, *table* 114, 115, 129, *figure* 129, 154, 178

  mortality rates for, *table* 114, 115

  in Native American women, 154, 155, 178, 192

  risk factors for, 130

  among women age 45–74, selected races and Hispanic origins, 129, *figure* 129

diaphragms, 201, *table* 202, *table* 204, 220

diet, 29, 126, 130, 139, 178

disabled, 70, 102, 231, 234

  see also long-term care

discrimination, 70, 79, 154, 158, 162, 165–67

  based on race, 40, 42, 54

  based on sex, 40–41, 42, 46, 52–55, 57, 60, 61, 63, 64, 67, 70–74, 84, 86, 87

education and, 43, 49, 52–55, 60, 61, 67, 70, 86

job, 40–43, 49, 54, 57, 73–74, 84

displaced homemakers, health insurance of, 105

dividends, *table* 339, *table* 341

divorce, 44, 74, 120, 234, *table* 257

  rate, 254, *figure* 261

  ratios by sex, race, and Hispanic origin, 254, *table* 261

Dixon, Alan, 55

doctors, *see* physicians

Dole, Bob, 74

domestic violence, 48, 51, 82, 156, 159

  first national conference on, 80–81

  help for victims of, 59–60

  immigrant women and, 43–44

  incidence of, 26, 110

  physician responsibilities and, 60–61, 122

  pregnancy and, 26, 110, 121, 122

  against younger women, 121–22

Donovan, Patricia, 118, 202–3

Dooley, Betty, 23–35

Dove, Rita, 85

Downey, Thomas, 43

driving, 55, 64

drug use, 41, 55, 116, 159, 170, 174

  birth defects and, 47

  Hispanics and, 162, 163

  treatment for, 84

Duke University, 74

Dunkel-Schetter, Christine, 162

Dunleavy, Richard M., 58

Dunn, Jennifer, 359, *359*

earnings and benefits, 307–26, *table* 339, *table* 340

  family leave, 308, *table* 316

  female-to-male ratios: by occupation, *table* 310–11, *table* 315; by race and Hispanic origin, 308, *table* 309

  flexible schedules, *table* 317

  median annual, 307, *figure* 313, *figure* 314, *table* 314

  median weekly, *figure* 309, *table* 310–11, *table* 315; for health care occupations, *table* 315, *figure* 316

earnings and benefits (*continued*)
  real, by sex and occupational group,
    figure 312
  see also health insurance; pensions
Easterling, Barbara J., 56
Eastman Kodak, 68
eating disorders, 27, 120
Economic Equity Act (EEA), 46–47, 93
economic security, 327–43
  child support and, *table* 334, *table* 335
  homeownership and, 328, *figure* 342
  housing cost and, *table* 343
  income sources and, 328, *table* 333–34,
    table 339, *table* 340–41
  long-term care and, 234–37, 247–48
  median family income and, 327,
    figure 329, *table* 330, *figure* 331, *figure*
    332
  poverty status and rates and, 328, *table*
    335, *figure* 336, *table* 337, *table* 338
education, 52, 265–79
  AIDS, 55
  athletic, 54–55, 63, 78
  attainment: by sex, race, and Hispanic
    origin, 265, *table* 267; U.S.- and
    foreign-born women age 25–54 by
    race and Hispanic origin, 265, *table*
    269
  discrimination and, 43, 49, 52–55, 60,
    61, 67, 70, 86
  financial aid for, 64
  health care and, 26, 27
  job training and, 59
  math, 50
  military, 43, 49, 60, 67, 70, 86; women
    graduates of U.S. service academies,
    table 274
  of preventive services' users, *table* 135,
    figure 137
  remedial, 41
  Rhodes Scholars and, 73
  sex, 31, 198, 219
  sexual harassment and, 52, 53–54
  white, black, and Hispanic women age
    25 and over with 12 or more years of,
    265, *figure* 268
  see also colleges and universities; medical
    schools and education

Education Act (1972), Title IX of, 53–54,
    55, 61, 63, 78, 87
Education Department, U.S., 46, 48–49,
    54, 100, 107
Egger, Matthias, 165
elderly, 46, 53, 68, 226
  health and functional status of, by age,
    228–29, *table* 229
  health insurance of, 144, 147, 150;
    Medicare, 102–3, 147, *table* 148, 156;
    sex and income, *table* 148
  living arrangements of, by sex, 254, *figure*
    264
  see also long-term care
elderly men
  economic security of, 328, *table* 339
  relationship of caregivers to, by age of
    care recipients, 232–33, *table* 232
elderly women
  economic security of, 328, *table* 339, *table*
    340–41
  heart disease and, 80
  income of, 31–32, 234, *table* 235
  osteoporosis prevention in, 139
  relationship of caregivers to, by age of
    care recipients, 232–33, *table* 232
Elders, Joycelyn, 75
election of 1992, 63–64, 66, 72, 106, 345,
    346
  voter participation in, 345, *figure* 346,
    figure 348
elections, 345–51
  women, selected years, 346, *table* 350
  women on federal bench, *table* 351
  women presidential appointees to
    Senate-confirmed positions, 346, *table*
    351
  see also voter participation
*Emerging Role of the Work-Family Manager,
  The* (Conference Board), 53
EMILY's List, 72
emphysema, *table* 230
employer-mandate approach, 150–51
employment, 281–306
  discrimination and, 40–43, 49, 54, 57,
    73–74, 84
  glass ceiling and, 42, 43, 54, 65–66, 71,
    73–74

in long-term care, 226
U.S. servicewomen by branch, rank, race, and Hispanic origin, *table* 301
volunteer workers by sex and type of organization, *figure* 306
of women, 1971–1991, 281, *figure* 291
workers holding multiple jobs by sex, 281, *figure* 292
workers on goods-producing and service-producing nonfarm payrolls by sex, *figure* 293
see also full-time workers; industry(ies); labor force; labor force participation rates; labor unions; occupation(s); part-time workers; unemployment, unemployment rate; working mothers
Endicott, Jean, 119
endometrial (uterine) cancer, 128, 138
incidence and death rates for, 123, *table* 123, 128
Energy Department, U.S., 75, 76
English, Karan, 359, *359*
Environmental Protection Agency, 69, 74, 76
Equal Employment Opportunity Commission (EEOC), 41
Equal Rights Amendment (ERA), 92
Eshoo, Anna, 360, *360*
estrogen therapy, *see* hormone replacement therapy
Evangelical Lutheran Church, 60
Ewbank, Douglas C., 166, 185
executive-level jobs
female senior, 54, 88
glass ceiling and, 42, 43, 54, 65–66, 71, 73–74
Executive Recruiter News, 42
exercise, 27, 130, 139
Exxon, 68
eye disease, 116, 130

Families and Work Institute, 44, 49, 84
family
of Asians and Pacific Islanders, 170
black, 253, *table* 259, 327, *table* 330, *table* 337
extended, 231
by family type, race, and Hispanic origin, 253, *table* 259–60

female-headed, 34, 253, *table* 259–60; economic security, 327, 328, *figure* 329, *table* 330, *figure* 332, *figure* 336, *table* 337, *figure* 342, *table* 343
Hispanic, 161, 162, *table* 260, 327, 328, *table* 330, *table* 337
income, 34, 51; median, 327, *figure* 329, *table* 330, *figure* 331, *figure* 332
male-headed, *figure* 329, *table* 330, *figure* 332, *figure* 336, *table* 337, *figure* 342, *table* 343
poverty rates of, 328, *table* 337
welfare, 51–52
workplace changes and, 44, 45, 49, 53, 57, 81, 83–84
Family and Medical Leave Act (1991), 46, 49, 65, 68, 69, 70, 77, 78, 249
family leave, 44, 46, 53, 55
see also maternity leave; paternity leave
family planning
clinics: discounts to, 213–14; gag rule and, 55, 58, 72, 76
coverage for, 209, 211
family values, 66–67
Family Violence Prevention and Services Act (1992), 59–60
Family Violence Prevention Fund, 82
Farmer, Mary E., 130
fathers, 59, *table* 303
drug use of, 47
Fazio, Vic, 47
Feder, Judith, 236
federal government
glass ceiling in, 71
workplace changes in, 49, 57
see also specific branches, departments, and agencies
Federal Highway Administration, 64
fee-for-service insurance, *see* health insurance, private
Feinstein, Dianne, 63, 75, 360, *360*
Fel-Pro, Inc., 84
Feminist Empowerment Center, 46
Feminist Majority Foundation, 44–45, 46
Fenwick, Millicent, 69
Ferraro, Geraldine, 57, 67
fertility rates by race, 253, *figure* 256
fetal alcohol syndrome (FAS), 174

Filipino women, 174, 177, 178, *table* 186, 188
 prenatal care of, *table* 176
film, 51
financial assets, long-term care and, 234–37, 247–48
Fisher, Mary, 66
flextime, 44, 45, 53, 83–84, *table* 317
Florida Supreme Court, 64–65
Florio, Jim, 51
Foley, Jill D., 146, 149
Foley, Thomas, 42
Food and Drug Administration (FDA), 53, 56, 57, 75, 83, 84–85, 218
Forman, Malaya, 194
football, 52
Forrest, Jacqueline Darroch, 198–200, *figure* 198, 203, 205, 206, 207, 209, 214
Fortas, Abe, 87
Foundation for Prevention of Sexual Harassment and Workplace Discrimination, 85
Fowler, Tillie, 360–61, *360*
France
 female life expectancy in, 113, *figure* 113
 RU-486 in, 63, 218
Franklin, Barbara, 54
Franklin v. *Gwinnett County Public Schools,* 53–54
Freedom of Access to Clinic Entrances Act, 80, 85
Freedom of Choice Act, 86
Freid, Virginia M., 133, 134, 139
Friedheim Awards, 67–68
Friedman, Samuel J., 166, 181, 191
"From Welfare to Work" program, 41
full-time workers
 family leave of, 308, *table* 316
 with and without health insurance, 308, *table* 321
 mothers, by age of children, *table* 304
 by sex and age, *table* 292
 by sex and race, *table* 291
 women, 1971–1991, 281, *figure* 291
Fund for the Feminist Majority, 71
fundraising, 52
Furse, Elizabeth, 361, *361*

Gagnon, R. O., 142
gag rule, 55, 58, 72, 76, 217
gallbladder cancer, 189
Garrett, H. Lawrence, 48, 61–62
Gayle, Jacob A., 179, 182
"gender dynamics" seminars, 54
General Accounting Office (GAO), 40–41, 50, 56–57, 160, 189
 National Institutes of Health report of, 95–97, 100
genetics, 67, 71
Ghali, Boutros, 55
Giacoia, George P., 121
Ginsburg, Ruth Bader, 87, 345
Girls, Inc., 45
glass ceiling, 42, 43, 54, 65–66, 71, 73–74
glass walls, 54
Gold, Rachel Benson, 30–31, 197–222
Goldman, Sachs & Company, 81
Goldstone, Donald E., 183
gonorrhea, 115–16
Goodacre, Glenna, 49
"Good Guy" awards, 47
Goodman, Ellen, 60
goods-producing workers
 by industry, *figure* 295
 by sex, *figure* 293
Gore, Al, 54, 64
Grad, Susan, 234
Great Britain
 National Health Service (NHS) of, 221
 RU-486 in, 63
Greenberger, Marcia, 43
Greenspan, Susan L., 130
Greer, Frank, 47
Gridiron Club of Washington, 50
Griffin, Michael, 80
Gross National Product, 48
"Growing Presence of Women in Psychiatry" *(Washington Post),* 45
Guam, abortion in, 73
Guendelman, Sylvia, 162
Gueron, Judith, 41
Guerrero, Lena, 69
Gunn, David, 80, 215
Guralnick, Jack, 240
gynecologists, use of, 140–142, 150, 213

Haerer, Armin, 131
Hahn, Robert A., 191
Halbreich, Uriel, 119
Han, Eugene, 183, 184
Hanft, Ruth S., 194
Hankinson, Susan E., 126
Hargraves, Martha A., 165, 166
Harlap, Susan, 203, 207
Harman, Jane, 361–62, *361*
Harrell, Tylene, 154*n*
Harriman, Averell, 80
Harriman, Pamela, 80
Harrington, Charlene, 242, 244
Harris, Patricia R., 76*n*
Louis Harris & Associates, 86
Harris v. Forklift Systems, 79
Hartmann, Heidi, 70
Harvard Law School, 54, 63
Haynes, Suzanne G., 173
Haywood, Rodney A., 134
Headen, Alvin E., Jr., 165, 178
Headen, Sandra W., 165, 178
health and functional status of elderly
   women and men by age, 228–29, *table*
   229
Health and Human Services Department,
   U.S. (DHHS), 41, 48–49, 64, 74, 95,
   100, 107, 119, 120, 130, 174
health care, 70
   access to, 27, 28–29, 31, 152; delivery of
   services, 149–50; financial and
   structural barriers, 142–49;
   improvement, 140–51; people of
   color, 182–85; preventive services,
   139; reproductive, 213–16
   appropriateness of, 216–19
   Clinton task force on, 77, 79, 81
   utilization of, 140, *figure* 141, *table* 141,
   142
   Veterans Affairs Dept. and, 87
   see also specific topics
health care industries, women employed in,
   table 299
health care occupations
   median weekly earnings for, *table* 315,
   figure 316
   women employed in, by race and
   Hispanic origin, *table* 300

health care reform, 25–28, 110, 150–53
   eight principles of, 105–6
   employer-mandate approach, 151
   for long-term care, *see* long-term care,
   reform options for
   managed competition, 151–52
   reproductive health and, 31, 220–22
   single-payer plan, 150–51
health insurance, 28, 105, 144–49, 182–84
   cost of, 33
   coverage status of women and men age 18
   to 64 by age and income, 144, *table* 145
   depression and, 120
   inadequate, 27, 184
   job, 308, *figure* 322; sex, race, and
   Hispanic origin, 308, *table* 321; sex
   and employer size, *figure* 320
   lack of, *see* uninsured
   private (fee-for-service), 144–46, *table*
   145, 148, *table* 148, 183, 209, 210,
   211, 308, *figure* 323; long-term care,
   32–33, 224, *figure* 237, 238–39, 240,
   245–46; persons 18 to 64 by sex and
   source of coverage, *figure* 322; women
   18 to 64, by age and source of
   coverage, *figure* 323
   reproductive health and, 209–12
   by sex and type of insurance, 308, *figure*
   323
   social, 227, 245, 247; limited, 247–48; *see
   also* Medicaid; Medicare
Health Insurance Association of America
   (HIAA), 209, 210, 239
health maintenance organizations (HMOs),
   139–40, 213
Health Resources and Services
   Administration (HRSA), 158, 160,
   161, 162, 182, 193
health studies
   women excluded from, 25, 91, 95, 99
   Women's Health Initiative, 25, 70, 88,
   100
Healy, Bernadine, 25, 84, 88, 99–100
heart attack, aspirin study of, 25, 91, 95, 138
heart disease, 27, 42, 106, 122–23, 130, 178
   men compared with women for, 26, 42,
   80, 106, 109, *table* 114, 122–23, 229,
   table 230

heart disease (*continued*)
   menopause and, 26, 110, 122, 138
   mortality rates for, 114–15, *table* 114
   prevention of, 27, 138–39
   studies of, 25, 91, 95
   treatment of, 42, 80
Heckler, Margaret M., 76*n*
Hee, Wendy, 154*n*
Hendel, Robert, 123
Henshaw, Stanley K., 200, 207, 215, 221
hepatitis B, 176–77
herpes simplex 2 virus, 115, 116
Higginbotham, John C., 161
high density lipoprotein (HDL), 122–23
Higher Education Act (1992), 64
Hill, Anita, 46, 47–48, 57, 58, 65, 72, 75, 82
Hills, Carla, 54
hip fractures, 130, 139
Hirota, Sherry, 188
Hispanic Health and Nutrition Evaluation Survey, 190
Hispanic men, 230
   earning and benefits of, 308, *table* 309, *figure* 314, *table* 314, *table* 321
   life expectancy of, *table* 171
Hispanics
   demographics on, *figure* 256, *table* 257, *figure* 258, *table* 260, *table* 261, *table* 263
   employment of, 282, *table* 285, *figure* 287, *table* 299, *table* 300, *table* 301, *figure* 302, *table* 305; unemployment rates, *table* 288, *figure* 289; union affiliation, by sex, *table* 294
   education of, *table* 267; college enrollment, 265, *table* 270
   families, 161, 162, *table* 260, 327, 328, *table* 330, *table* 337
   health improvements for, 83
   mortality rates for, 188, 189–90
   poverty status of women and men, by age, race, and Hispanic origin, 142–43, *table* 143
   use of term, 157*n*
   voter participation of, 345, *figure* 346, *table* 347

Hispanic women, 69, 200
   AIDS and, *figure* 117, *figure* 118, 155, 162–63, 180–81, *table* 180, *table* 181
   alcohol use of, 162, 174
   births of, 206
   cancer of, 29, 175, 177, 188
   child support of, *table* 335
   contraception of, 201
   depression in, 119
   diabetes in, 129, *figure* 129, 187
   drug use of, 174
   earnings and benefits of, 307, 308, *table* 309, *table* 318, *table* 321; median annual, *figure* 314, *table* 314
   economic security of, *table* 333–34, *table* 335, *table* 340–41
   education of, 33, 265, *figure* 268, *table* 269, *table* 273, *table* 277
   elderly, with incomes below twice the poverty threshold, 234, *table* 235
   employment of, 34, *figure* 289, *table* 301, *figure* 302, *table* 305; health care, *table* 299, *table* 300; occupation, 282, *figure* 297, *table* 300
   health care services used by, *table* 135, 184
   health status of, 28–29, 154, 155, 157, 160–63, 171–75, 177–87, 189–90, 193–95
   hypertension in, 178–79, *table* 179
   infant, neonatal, and postneonatal mortality rates for, *table* 186, 187
   as judges, 70
   life expectancy of, 28, 155, 171, *table* 171
   living arrangements after age 65 of, 230–31, *table* 231
   long-term care for, 230–31, *table* 231, 233, 234
   obesity of, 172, *table* 172, 178
   poverty status of, *table* 143, 144
   prenatal care of, 176, *table* 176, 206
   smoking by, 173, *table* 173
   uninsured, 28–29, 149, 182–83
   see also specific ethnic groups
HIV/AIDS (human immunodeficiency virus/Acquired Immune Deficiency

Syndrome), 26, 52, 66, 70, 116–19, 155, 179–82, 191, 193, 219
black women and, 26, 28, 110, 117–18, *figure* 117, *figure* 118, 155, 160, 180, *table* 180, 181, *table* 181, 187, *table* 188
education about, 55
in females age 13 and over by race and Hispanic origin, 117–18, *figure* 117, *figure* 118
in men compared with women, 26, 110, 118
mortality rates and, 187, *table* 188
research on, 98, 101, 102, 107
sources of, among women by race and Hispanic origin, 180–81, *table* 181
teenagers and, 41
among women age 15–44 by race and Hispanic origin, 180, *table* 180
Hobby, Oveta Culp, 76*n*
Hogue, Carol J. Rowland, 165, 166
Holmes, Steven, 41–42
Holtzman, Elizabeth, 57, 67
homeownership, 328, *figure* 342
homicides, 188, 189
homosexuals, in military, 59–60, 84
Honda Motor Company, 72
hormone replacement therapy (HRT), 27, 128, 132, *table* 132, 138, 139
Horton, Jacqueline A., 116, 119, 120, 121, 130, 173, 175, 177, 178, 182, 189
hospital discharge rates, by sex and age, 140, *figure* 141
households
with female householders by tenure, type, and presence of children, *figure* 263
housing cost burden by type and tenure of, *table* 343
with unrelated partners by sex of partners and presence of children, 253, *table* 260
House of Representatives, U.S., *see* Congress, U.S., House of Representatives
housework, economic value of, 48
housing cost, *table* 343
Howard, Daniel, 62

How Schools Shortchange Girls, 52
HTLV-3, 117
Hu-DeHart, Evelyn, 168
Hudnut, Beverly B., 60
Hudnut, William H., 3d, 60
human papilloma virus (HPV), 115–16, 126
Hunt Valley conference (1991), 99
Fred Hutchinson Cancer Research Center, 70
Hutchison, Kay Bailey, 86, 346, 353, 362, *362*
Hyde, Henry, 81
Hyde amendment, 81, 88, 211
Flo Hyman Award, 52
hypertension (high blood pressure), 28, 122, *table* 132, 138–39, 164, 178–79, 192
among women age 20 to 74, by race and Hispanic origin, 178–79, *table* 179
hysterectomies, 106

IBM, 49, 68, 69, 73
illegal immigrants, 76–77, 78
immigrant women, 43–44, 53
income, 34, 45, 51, 59
age of householder and, 327, *figure* 331
of Asians and Pacific Islanders, 167
categories of, changes in size of, 53
of child care teachers, 83
of elderly, 34, *table* 148, 328, *table* 329, *table* 340–41; long-term care, 223, 224, 227, 233–37, *table* 235, 244–45, 247–48
health insurance and, *table* 145, *table* 148
median family, 327, *figure* 329, *table* 330, *figure* 332
Medicaid eligibility and, 211
of nurses, 75, *figure* 316
of preventive services' users, *table* 135; mammograms, *figure* 137; Papsmear, *table* 135, *figure* 136
sources of: for persons age 65 and over by sex, 328, *table* 339; for white, black and Hispanic women age 65 and over, *table* 340–41; for women age 15 to 64 by race and Hispanic origin, 328, *table* 333–34

Indian Health Service (IHS), 158, 159, 174, 178, 182, 184, 185, 189, 192, 193
industry(ies)
    employed women and men by, *figure* 295
    health care, *table* 299
infant birth weight, low, 162, 165, 166, 198, 206, 207
infant mortality, 29, 30, 162, 178, 191, 207
    of blacks, 165, 166, 185–86, *table* 186, 207
    by mother's race and Hispanic origin, 185–88, *table* 186
    teenage pregnancy and, 45
infertility, 128, 198, 202–3
    insurance coverage for, 210
    research on, 25, 92–93, 98, 101, 102
    STDs and, 30, 105, 198, 202–3
Infertility Prevention Act (1992), 105
influenza, *table* 114
informal care, availability of, 226, 230–32, *figure* 231, *table* 231, *table* 232
information restrictions, 217
Insley, Susan J., 72
Institute of Medicine, 206, 225
instrumental activities of daily living (IADL), limitations of, 228–29, *table* 229, *table* 243
Intel Corp., 73
interest, *table* 334, *table* 339, *table* 341
Internal Revenue Service (IRS), 52
internists, 142, 150
intrauterine devices (IUDs), 201, *table* 202, 218, 220
Inui, Thomas, 122
Iowa, Amendment 1 in, 67
Iowa, University of, 82
Ireland, female life expectancy in, *figure* 113
Ireland, Patricia, 40, 50–51

Japan, female life expectancy in, 113, *figure* 113
Japanese Americans, as physicians and providers, 194, 195
Japanese American women, 174, 177, 178, *table* 186
    hypertension of, 179
    prenatal care of, 28, 154, 176, *table* 176
Jaynes, Gerald D., 165, 176, 184, 186, 194

Jemison, Mae Carol, 68
job sharing, 45
job training, 41, 71, 77
Job Training Partnership Act (JTPA), 40–41, 59
Johns Hopkins University, 69
Johnson, Eddie Bernice, 362–63, *362*
Johnson, Jennifer C., 64–65
Johnson, J. L., 4–7
Johnson, Magic, 160
Johnson, Nancy, 363, *363*
Johnson, Norman J., 191
Johnson & Johnson, 49, 68, 84
Jones, Elaine, 79
Jones, Elise F., 205
Jones, Jean, 63
Jordan, Barbara, 63
journalists, 50
Journal of the American Medical Association, 47, 61, 66, 71, 76
judges, *table* 351
Justice Department, U.S., 42, 43, 49, 80
    Clinton nominees for, 76–77, 78
    rape figures of, 56, 57

Kannel, William B., 122, 123, 130
Kaptur, Marcy, 363, *363*
Kassebaum, Nancy Landon, 364, *364*
Kay, Herma Hill, 62
Kaye, Judith, 79
Keenan, Marianne, 242
Kelly, Patrick, 41, 42
Kelsey, Jennifer, 138
Kelso, Frank, Jr., 81–82
Kennedy, Anthony, 62
Kennedy, James H., 42
Kennedy Center, 67–68
Kennelly, Barbara, 364–65, *364*
Kenney, Genevieve, 244
Keohane, Nannerl Overholser, 52, 74
kidney disease, 130
King, Gary, 164
Kirkpatrick, Jeane, 77
Kiser, Jackson, 43
Kleiman, Carol, 64, 82
Kleinman, Joel C., 133, 134, 139
Kokmen, Emre, 131
Koonin, Lisa M., 208

Korean Americans, 170, 178, 184
Korn/Ferry International, 34, 88
Kost, Kathryn, 203, 207
Kowalski, Sharon, 51
Kraszewski, Muriel, 57
Kreps, Juanita, 54
Krone, Julie, 87
Krueger, Bob, 86
Kunin, Madeleine, 45

Labor Department, U.S., 42–43, 100, 107
    Glass Ceiling Commission of, 73–74
    Women's Bureau of, 82–83
labor force
    Hispanic, by sex and origin, *figure* 287
    wives in, by race and Hispanic origin,
        figure 302
    women in, 281, *figure* 283
labor force participation rates, 33–34
    of foreign-born women, by language
        spoken at home and English fluency,
        table 287
    of mothers with young children by
        marital status, *figure* 302
    of persons of Hispanic origin, by sex and
        origin, *table* 286
    by sex, race, and Hispanic origin, *table*
        285
    women's, by age, *table* 284
    women's, and women as percentage of
        labor force, 283, *table* 285
Labor-Health and Human Services
    appropriations bill, 88
    poverty status and, *table* 338
labor unions, 66
    white, black, and Hispanic workers with
        affiliation to, by sex, *table* 294
    workers with affiliation to, by sex,
        281–82, *figure* 293
La Guardia, Fiorello, 85
Lambert, Blanche, 365, *365*
Laotian women, 176
Larson, Rev. April Ulring, 60
Latifah, Queen, 61
law
    discrimination and, 54
    education in, *figure* 276, *table* 277
Lawrence, Wendy B., 56

Lawrence, William P., 56
law schools, 54, 62, 63, 82
lawyers, women, 51, 65, 85
Leadership Conference of Female Chiefs,
    71
Lee, Marion, 175
Leffall, LaSalle D., 164, 183
Lefkowitz, D., 133, 172, 173, 175, 192
Leigh, Wilhelmina A., 28–29, 149,
    154–96
Leimas, Stacie, 39*n*
Lerner, Debra J., 122, 123, 130
lesbians, 86
    legal guardianship of partner by, 51
    in military, 59, 84
Leung, Mingyew, 167, 168, 170, 188, 195
Levy, Jerrold E., 190
Lewis, John, 47
life expectancy, 26–27, 110
    at birth and at age 65 by race and sex,
        111, *table* 112, 113
    at birth by sex, race, and Hispanic origin,
        171, *table* 171
    at birth in selected industrialized
        countries, 113, *figure* 113
    of black women, 27, 28, *table* 112, 113,
        155, 171, *table* 171
    of Hispanic women, 28, 155, 171, *table*
        171
    long-term care and, 31, 32, 226, 230,
        231
    of Native American women, 28, 155,
        171, *table* 171
Liu, Korbin, 232
Liu, William T., 165, 168, 169, 170
liver disease, 28, *table* 114, 159, 188–89,
    192
living arrangements
    of children under age 18 with working
        parents, *table* 303
    of persons age 65 and over by sex, 254,
        figure 264
    of women age 65 and over by age, race,
        and Hispanic origin, 230–32, *table*
        231
    see also households
living together couples, households of, 232,
    253, *table* 260

Lloyd, Marilyn, 105, 365, *365*
local government, family leave and, 308,
    table 316
Long, Jill, 366, *366*
long-term care, 31–33, 223–50
    availability and use of services for,
        240–44, *table* 241, *table* 243
    community-based, 32, 224, 225, 238,
        242, *table* 243
    costs of, 31, 32, 223, 224, 227, 232–36
    defining, 32, 225–26
    financial assets and, 234–37, 247–48
    future of, 33, 240
    highlights of, 223–24
    identified with women, 226
    in-home, 32, 224, 225, 232–33, 236,
        figure 237, 238, 242, *table* 243, 244,
        247–48
    life expectancy and, 31, 32, 226, 230,
        231
    Medicaid and, 32, 33, 224, 227,
        235–38, *figure* 237, 240, 242, 244–46,
        248–49
    Medicare and, 235–36, *figure* 237, 242
    nature of problem, 227
    need for, 228–40; affordability, 232–36,
        table 235; availability of informal care,
        230–31, 276, *figure* 231, *table* 231, *table*
        232; health and functional status,
        228–29, *table* 229, *table* 230; private
        insurance, 238–39, 240; prospects for
        the future, 240; public programs, 227,
        236–38, *figure* 237
    reform options for, 33, 244–49; limited
        social insurance, 247–48; other
        possible expansions, 248–49; private
        insurance/Medicaid expansion,
        245–46; social insurance, 227, 247
    see also nursing homes
Lopez, Nancy, 52
Lowey, Nita, 366, *366*
Lu, Michael C., 167, 168, 170, 188, 195
lung cancer, 29, 175
    breast cancer compared with, 26, 103,
        109, 124, *figure* 124
    female mortality from, 124–25, *figure*
        124, 189

incidence and death rates for, 123, *table*
    123
lupus, 53, 107, 121
Lutheranism, 60

McClendon, Sarah, 45
McClintock, Barbara, 67
McKinney, Cynthia, 368, *368*
McLeod, Rev. Mary Adelia, 86
McMillan, Terry, 63
Mahoney, Kevin, 245
Makuc, Diane M., 133, 134, 139
Malcolm, Ellen, 48
Maloney, Carolyn, 367, *367*
mammography, 26, 29, 81, 109–10, 126,
        132, *table* 132, 136–37, 151, 155, 175
    guidelines for, 136–37, 192
    Medicare and, 102, 103, 140
    poor women and, 26, 110
    users, by selected characteristics, *figure*
        132
Mammography Quality Assurance Act
    (1992), 104–5
managed care, 31, 213, 220–21
managed competition, 151
management, glass ceiling in, 42, 43, 54,
        65–66, 71, 73–74
Mankiller, Wilma, 43
Manpower Demonstration Research
    Corporation (MDRC), 41
Manson, JoAnn E., 138
Manton, Kenneth G., 166, 232, 240
March for Women's Lives, 56
Margolies-Mezvinsky, Marjorie, 367, *367*
Marine Corps, U.S., 60, 62, 66, 83, *table*
    301
marital status
    contraceptive failure during first 12
        months of use by poverty status, age,
        and, 203–4, *table* 204
    economic security and, 327–28, *figure*
        329, *table* 330, *figure* 332, *figure* 336,
        table 337, *figure* 342, *table* 343
    labor force participation of mothers with
        young children by, *figure* 302
    by sex, race, and Hispanic origin, *table*
        257

Markides, Kyriakos, 162
marriage, 44, 74
   first, median age at, by sex, 253, *figure*
      258
married women, contraception of, 201,
   table 204
Marshall, Thurgood, 40
Martin, Janella Sue, 46, 64
Martin, Keller, 119
Martin, Lynn, 42–43, 54, 65–66
Mason, James, 99
Massion, Charlea T., 150
Maternal and Child Health block grant, 212
maternity care, 30, 210–11, 214
maternity leave, 53, 308, *table* 316
   see also family leave
mathematics, 50, 70
Mattel, Inc., 70
Mayeno, Laurin, 154*n*
Medicaid, 28, 29, 52, 140, 144, *table* 145,
      146–49, *table* 148, 183–84, *figure* 323
   access to services and, 213, 214
   cost of, 32
   eligibility for, 147, 211–12, 236–37,
      245
   health care reform and, 220–21
   long-term care and, 32, 33, 224, 227,
      235–38, *figure* 237, 240, 242, 244–46,
      248–49
   of men vs. women, 34, 110
   reproductive health and, 31, 211–14
   state-funded, reduction of, 149
medical leave, 46, 49, 55
medical schools and education, 45, 108,
      266, *figure* 276, *table* 277
   graduates, by sex, *figure* 278
   new entrants to, and graduates from, by
      sex, *table* 278
medical technology and research,
   restrictions on, 217–18
Medicare, 79, 140, 144, 147–49, *table* 148,
      150, 156, 183, *figure* 323
   long-term care and, 32, 224, 235–36,
      figure 237, 242
Medicare Catastrophic Coverage Act
   (1988), 102–3, 236*n*
medicine, sexual harassment and, 77–78

"Medigap" insurance, 147–48
Meek, Carrie, 368, *368*
Melton, L. Joseph, 139
menarche, 198, *figure* 198
men compared with women
   AIDS, 26, 110, 118
   as caregivers, 32, 61, 223, 226, 232
   cerebrovascular disease, *table* 115, *table*
      230
   demographics, 253, *table* 254, *figure* 255,
      figure 256, *table* 257, *figure* 258, *table*
      259–60, *table* 261, *table* 264
   depression, 50, 119
   diabetes, 229, *table* 230
   earnings and benefits, 307–8, *figure* 309,
      table 309, *table* 310–11, *figure* 312,
      figure 313, *figure* 314, *table* 314, *table*
      315, *table* 316, *table* 317; health
      insurance, 308, *figure* 320, *table* 321,
      figure 322, *figure* 323, *figure* 324, *figure*
      325, *table* 326; pension plans, *table* 318,
      table 319
   education, 266, *table* 267, *table* 270, *figure*
      271, *table* 273, *figure* 275, *figure* 276,
      table 278, *figure* 278, *figure* 279
   employment, *table* 285, *table* 286, *figure*
      287, *table* 288, *figure* 290, *table* 291,
      figure 292, *figure* 293, *table* 294, *figure*
      295, *figure* 296
   health care use, 110
   health insurance, 34, 110, *table* 145
   heart disease, 26, 42, 80, 106, 109, *table*
      114, 122–23, 229, *table* 230
   income, 34, 44, 50, 82
   life expectancy, 27, 32, 110, 111, 226,
      230, 232–33
   long-term care, 223, 224, 226, 233, 240,
      242; health and functional status,
      228–29, *table* 229
   osteoporosis, 130, 229
   poverty, 142–43, *table* 143
   prisoners of war, 62
   smoking, 109, 133, 134
   suicide, 119
   utilization of services, 140, *table* 141,
      figure 141, 142
Menendez, Barbara S., 163

menopause, 27, 199, *figure* 198
  heart disease and, 26, 110, 122, 138
*Menopause, Hormone Therapy, and Women's
  Health, The,* 107
mental retardation, 229, *table* 230
Merit Systems Protection Board, U.S., 49,
  71
Merlis, Mark, 152
Messinger, Ruth, 57
Mettlin, Curtis, 126
Mexicans, 160, 161, 190
  employment of, *table* 286, *figure* 287
  health insurance of, 183
  high cholesterol of, 172–73
  mortality rates for, 188
  physicians, 194
Mexican women, 162, *table* 172, 174, 176,
  184, *table* 186
  diabetes in, 129, *figure* 129, 178
  high cholesterol of, 172
  hypertension in, 178, *table* 179
  prenatal care of, 176, *table* 176
  preventive health measures of, 175, 176
  smoking of, *table* 173
Meyers, Jan, 369, *369*
Michelman, Kate, 45
Michelson v. *Leser,* 42
Michigan Supreme Court, 40
middle-aged women
  as caregivers, 226
  osteoporosis prevention in, 139
Mikulski, Barbara, 54, 64, 80, 98, 369, *369*
military, 58, 69
  abortion and, 76
  education and, 43, 49, 60, 67, 70, 86,
    table 274
  homosexuals in, 59–60, 84
  memorials to honor women in, 49, 59
  sexual harassment in, 44, 47, 48, 53,
    57–58, 61–62, 68, 69, 80, 84
  U.S. active duty servicewomen by
    branch of service, rank, race, and
    Hispanic origin, *table* 301
  see also specific branches
Miller, Anthony B., 136
Miller, S. M., 165, 166, 167
Mink, Patsy, 102, 370, *370*
Minkoff, Howard L., 118, 119

minorities
  glass ceiling and, 42, 43, 73–74
  long-term care for, 223, 231, *table*
    231, 233, 234, 241, *table* 241
  NIH policy on, 97
  see also specific ethnic and racial groups
miscarriage, 69, 73, 121, *table* 205
Mississippi, abortion in, 65, 73
Mitchell, Janet B., 147
Molinari, Susan, 74, 370, *370*
Moon, Marilyn, 31–33, 223–50
Moore, Demi, 40
Morella, Constance A., 77, 102, 371,
  371
Morrison, Toni, 63
mortality rates, mortality
  U.S. leading causes of, 114–15, *table*
    114
  for whites and blacks, 114–15, *table* 114
  for women of color, 28, 187–89, *table*
    188
  see also infant mortality; *specific conditions*
Moseley-Braun, Carol, 55, 63, 75, 371,
  371
Mosher, William D., 201
mothers
  drug use of, 47, 64–65
  "resource," 45
  single, 59, 69
  welfare, 41, 51–52
  see also working mothers
Motorola, 68
Ms. Foundation for Women, 84
Ms. magazine, 41
Mulinare, Joseph, 191
multi-infarct dementia, 128
Multiple Risk Factor Intervention Trial
  (Mr. Fit), 25, 95
multiple sclerosis, *table* 230
"Murphy Brown" (TV show), 59, 69
Murray, Patty, 372, *372*
music, 67–68

NAACP Legal Defense and Education
  Fund, 79
Nancy Drew conference (1993), 82
Nannygate, 76–77, 79
National Abortion Federation (NAF), 215

National Academy of Sciences, 57
National Aeronautics and Space
    Administration (NASA), 56
National Association for the Education of
    Young Children, 49
National Association of Women Business
    Owners (NAWBO), 64
National Black Women's Health Project,
    193
National Cancer Institute (NCI), 101–2,
    103
National Capital Memorial Commission,
    59
National Center for Health Statistics
    (NCHS), 44, 114, 124, 129, 138, 172,
    177, 205, 206, 207, 241
National Coalition for Life, 59
National Coalition of 100 Black Women,
    61
National Collegiate Athletic Association,
    54–55
National Commission to Prevent Infant
    Mortality, 45
National Committee on Pay Equity, 51
National Conference of Catholic Bishops,
    72
National Council of Juvenile and Family
    Court Justices, 80–81
National Council of La Raza, 183
National Council of Negro Women
    (NCNW), 175
National Council of Teachers of
    Mathematics, 70
National Girls and Women in Sports Day,
    52, 78
National Governors' Association (NGA),
    77, 211, 212, 214
National Guard, 59
National Institute on Aging, 95, 99
National Institutes of Health (NIH), 25, 61,
    70, 81, 84, 88, 91–102, 161, 192
  contraceptive research of, 92–93
  GAO report on, 95–97, 100
  Office of Research on Women's Health
    of, 25, 91, 97–98, 100, 101, 102
  reauthorization bill of, 98, 100, 101
  National Institutes of Health (GAO report),
    95–97, 100

National Institutes of Health (NIH)
    Revitalization Act (1993), 91
National Latina Health Network, 193
National Medical Expenditure Survey for
    1987, 143, 184, 191
National Nurse Survey, 75
National Organization for Women, 40,
    50–51
National Public Radio, 46
National Republican Coalition for Choice,
    59
National Science Foundation, 67
National Women's Law Center, 43
National Women's Political Caucus, 40,
    47, 56, 58, 72
National Women's Study, 57
Native American men, 159
  demographics on, *table* 254, *figure* 256
  life expectancy of, 171
Native Americans
  data collection problems for, 191
  education of, *table* 270
  health care system of, 184–85, 193
  infant, neonatal, and postneonatal,
    mortality rates for, 29, *table* 186, 187,
    191
  physicians, 194
  use of term, 156*n*–57*n*
Native American women, 43, 71
  AIDS and, 159–60, 180, *table* 180, 181,
    table 181, 182, 191
  alcoholism and alcohol-related diseases
    of, 28, 155, 159, 188–89, 192
  births of, 206
  cancer in, 189; cervical, 29, 125, 175,
    189
  demographics on, *table* 254, *figure* 256
  diabetes in, 154, 155, 177–78, 192
  drug abuse of, 159
  education of, *table* 273, *table* 277
  fetal alcohol syndrome and, 174
  health status of, 28–29, 154, 155,
    157–60, 171–82, 184–95
  high cholesterol of, 172
  hypertension of, 179
  infant, neonatal and postneonatal
    mortality rates and, 29, *table* 186, 187,
    191

Native American women (*continued*)
  life expectancy of, 28, 155, 171, *table* 171
  mortality rates for, 188–89
  obesity of, 29, 155, 172
  poverty status of, *table* 143, 144
  prenatal care of, 175, *table* 176, 206
  preventive health measures of, 175
  smoking by, 133, 173, *table* 173
Native Hawaiians, 168–69, 193
Native Hawaiian women, 172, 174,
    177–78
  cancer in, 155, 177, 188
  diabetes of, 155
  hypertension of, 179, 192
Naval Investigative Service (NIS), 47,
    57–58, 63, 69
Navy, U.S., 50, 60, 62, 66, 81–82, *table*
    274, *table* 301
  sexual harassment in, 44, 47, 48, 53,
    57–58, 61–62, 68, 69, 83, 85
neonatal mortality rates, by mother's race
    and Hispanic origin, *table* 186
never-married men, *table* 257, *figure*
    258
never-married women, *table* 257, *figure* 258
  abortions of, 208
  contraception of, 201, *table* 204
  employment of, *figure* 302
newborns
  AIDS in, 118, 119
  fetal alcohol syndrome and, 173–74
  mortality rates, by mother's race and
    Hispanic origin, *table* 186
  STDs and, 116
New England Journal of Medicine, 42, 56,
    77–78
New Jersey, welfare system in, 51–52, 64
New Our Bodies, Ourselves, The, 70
New York County Lawyers' Association,
    51
New York Stock Exchange, 62
New York Times, 41–45, 49, 51, 52, 55, 56,
    58, 60, 62, 67, 69–70, 76, 85, 87
Nicholson, Heather Johnston, 45
NIH, *see* National Institutes of Health
NIH Guide for Grants and Contracts, 94, 96
9to5, 52
Nordyke, Eleanor C., 174

Normal Human Aging, 95
Norplant, 49, 70, 92, 201, 205, 212, 220
  access to, 213–14
North Dakota, abortion in, 81
Norton, Eleanor Holmes, 353, 372, *372*
Notices, 50
Novello, Antonia C., 48, 83
nurse midwives, 106, 216
nurse practitioners, 106, 216
nurses, 75, 91, 226
  median weekly earnings of, *figure* 316
nursing homes, 225, 237, 240–41, 248
  cost of, 31, 32, 223, 224, 232
  decline in use of, 224
  funding sources for care in, 236, *figure*
    237
  residents over age 55 by sex, race, and
    age, 241, *table* 241
Nussbaum, Karen, 52, 82–83
nutritional counseling, 212, 214
Nyamathi, Adeline, 163, 164, 181

Oakar, Mary Rose, 93, 102, 103
Oakland (Calif.) Tribune, 71
obesity, 29, 128
  of Asians and Pacific Islanders, 155, 169,
    172
  in women age 20 to 74 by race and
    Hispanic origin, 172, *table* 172
O'Brien, Marilyn O., 188
obstetricians, 142, 147, 150, 213, 214
occupation(s)
  earnings and benefits by, 307, *figure* 312,
    table 317
  earnings and benefits by, median weekly,
    table 310–11
  employed white, black, and Hispanic
    women by, 282, *figure* 297
  employed women and men by, 282,
    figure 296
  health care, *table* 300, *table* 315, *figure* 316
  women as percentage of workers in
    selected, 282, *table* 298
O'Conner, Gerald, 123
O'Connor, Sandra Day, 62
O'Dell, Gloria, 63
Office of Employment Discrimination
    Complaints Resolution, 84

Office of Population Censuses and Surveys, 221
officials, 345–51
  women, selected years, 346, *table* 350
  women on federal bench, *table* 351
  women presidential appointees to Senate-confirmed positions, 346, *table* 351
  see also voter participation
O'Hagan, Patricia, 174
Okazaki, Haruo, 131
Oklahoma, University of, Law Center, 82
older women, health concerns of, 122–31
  Alzheimer's disease, 130–31
  cancer, 123–28, *table* 123, *figure* 124, *figure* 126, *figure* 127, *figure* 128
  cerebrovascular disease, 128–29
  diabetes, 129–30
  heart disease, 122–23
  hypertension, 138–39
  osteoporosis, 130
Older Women's League, 146
O'Leary, Hazel R., 75, 76
Olympic Games, 53, 65
Omnibus Budget Reconciliation Act (1990), 213
Omnibus Budget Reconciliation Act (1991), 103
Operation Rescue, 40, 41, 42, 44, 58, 76
Opportunities for Research on Women's Health, 99
oral contraceptives, *see* birth control pills
Oregonians for Ethical Representation, 74
Ortho Pharmaceuticals, 43
osteoporosis, 27, 110, 130
  exercise and, 27, 139
  long-term care and, 31, 226, 229
  prevention of, *table* 132, 138, 139
  risk factors for, 130
  studies and research of, 25, 98, 101
ovarian cancer, 126
  incidence and death rates for, 123, *table* 123
  research on, 98, 101–2
ovulation, failure of, 128

Pacific Islander women, *see* Asian and Pacific Islander women

Packwood, Bob, 72–73, 74, 78, 86
Padian, Nancy, 117
Papa Ola Lokahi, 169, 179
Pappaioanou, Marguerite, 180
Pap smears, 29, 81, 104, 109–10, 125, 132, *table* 132, 134–35, 151, 155
  Medicare and, 140
  poor women and, 26, 110, 134
  users: by age and income, *figure* 136; characteristics, *table* 135
  by women of color, 175–76
Parade magazine, 43
paralysis, 229, *table* 230
part-time workers
  health insurance for, 105
  by sex and age, *table* 292
  by sex and race, *table* 291
paternity leave, 53, 308, *table* 316
  see also family leave
Payne, LaRah D., 192
Peace Corps, 44
Pearson, Cynthia A., 52
Pell grants, 64
Pelosi, Nancy, 373, *373*
pelvic inflammatory disease (PID), 27, 30, 105, 116–17, 118, 202
Pennsylvania, abortion rights in, 51, 62, 65
pensions, 34, 234, *table* 318, *table* 319, *table* 339, *table* 340
Pepper Commission, 238, 239, 246, 247, 248
peripheral vascular disease, 130
Perot, Ross, 60
Persian Gulf War, 62
Peterson, Shirley D., 52
Petrakis, Nicholas, 177
Petronis, Kenneth R., 120
Pettiti, Diana, 138
Pfeiffer, Naomi, 118, 119
Phelan, Richard J., 61
physicians, 147, 149, 213
  abortion counseling and, 55, 76
  allied health providers/practitioners and, 216–17
  domestic violence and, 60–61, 122
  in heart disease study, 25, 91
  minority, 194–95

physicians (continued)
  primary-care, 28, 106, 149
  sex segregation of, 44–45
  specialized, 106
  visits to, by sex and age, 140, table 141
Piacentini, Joseph S., 146, 149
Piani, A., 133, 134, 138
Planned Parenthood, 71
Planned Parenthood of Southeastern
    Pennsylvania v. Casey, 51, 62, 65,
    215–16
pneumonia, table 114, 116
poetry, poets, 73, 85
political polls, 60
politics of women's health, 24–26, 91–108
  breast cancer and, 102–4
  extension beyond research and, 104–5
  GAO report and, 95–97
  health agenda expansion and, 92–93
  legislative strategy and, 100–102
  reform principles and, 105–6
  research need identified and, 93–94
Ponce, Ninez, 167, 191
poor children, 34, 63
poor women, 28, 29, 158, 164–65, 200
  abortions for, 61, 211
  cervical cancer in, 125
  clinics used by, 213, 214
  as head of family, 34
  health care access and, 27, 29, 31, 104,
    110, 142–43
  health insurance and, 110, 146–49, table
    148
  inadequate cancer screening and, 26
  long-term care for, 223, 224, 233–34,
    table 235
  prenatal care and, 31
Pope, Barbara Spyridon, 85
population, U.S., 253–64
  by age and sex, 253, figure 255
  in 1990 by race and sex, table 254
  by sex, race, and Hispanic origin, figure
    256
  see also demographics
Population Council, 83
postneonatal mortality rates, by
    mother's race and Hispanic origin,
    table 186

poverty status and rates
  contraceptive failure during the first 12
    months of use by marital status, age
    and, 203–4, table 204
  economic security and, 328, table 335,
    figure 336, table 337, table 338
  of families by family type and presence of
    children, 328, figure 336
  labor market problems and, table 338
  of unrelated individuals by sex and age,
    table 338
  of white, black and Hispanic families by
    type and presence of children, 328,
    table 337
  of women and men by age, race, and
    Hispanic origin, 142–43, table 143
pregnancy, 40, 57, 203–5
  AIDS and, 119
  autoimmune disorders and, 121
  diabetes and, 178
  discrimination and, 41
  drug treatment and, 84
  Medicaid eligibility and, 211–12
  miscarriage and, 69, 73, 121, table 205
  outcome by age of woman, 204, table
    205
  teenage, 41, 44, 45, 139, 200, 203, table
    205, 208
  unintentional, 30, 197, 202, 203, 207;
    risk of, by contraceptive type and age,
    200–201, table 201; U.S. incidence of,
    30
  violence and, 26, 110, 121, 122
Pregnancy Discrimination Act (PDA), 210
prenatal care, 28, 30–31, 81, 142, 206
  access to, 214
  lack of, 198, 206, 207
  live births by age of mother and start of,
    206, table 207
  Medicaid and, 146, 211
  for mothers with live births by race and
    Hispanic origin, 176, table 176
Presbyterian Church (U.S.A.), 60
Presidential Commission on the
    Assignment of Women in the Armed
    Forces, 62, 68, 71–72
preventive measures, 131–39, 151
  access to, 139–40

characteristics of women users of, 1990, *table* 135
heart disease, 138
osteoporosis, 138–39
smoking cessation, 133–34
women of color and, 155, 175–76
see also blood pressure, measurement of;
    hormone replacement therapy;
    mammography; Pap smears
prisoners of war, 62
Pritchard, M. H., 121
professional jobs, 34
Pryce, Deborah, 373, *373*
psychiatrists, female, 45
Public Health Service (PHS), 94, 99, 158, 230
Public Health Service Task Force, 120
Public law, 102–90
Puerto Ricans, 160, 161, 163, 170
    employment of, *table* 286, *figure* 287
    health insurance of, 183
    mortality rates for, 188
    physicians, 194
    smoking by, 133
Puerto Rican women, 161, 174, 175, 184
    AIDS and, 155, 180–81
    diabetes in, 129, *figure* 129
    high cholesterol of, 172
    hypertension in, 178, *table* 179
    infant mortality rates of, 29, *table* 186
    obesity of, *table* 172
    smoking by, 133, *table* 173

Quayle, J. Danforth, 59, 69
Quayle, Marilyn, 66, 67

race
    child support by, *table* 335
    currently married and never married
        adults by sex, Hispanic origin and,
        figure 258
    divorce ratios by sex, Hispanic origin,
        and, 254, *table* 261
    earnings and benefits, 308, *table* 309, *table*
        318; health insurance, *table* 321;
        median annual, *table* 314
    economic security and, *table* 333–34,
        table 335

education and, 265, *table* 267, *table* 269;
    college, 265, *table* 270, *table* 273, *table*
    277
employment and, *table* 285, *table* 291,
    table 299, *figure* 302; military, *table* 301;
    unemployment, 281, *table* 288, *figure*
    289
families by family type, Hispanic origin,
    and, 253, *table* 259–60
infant, neonatal, and postneonatal
    mortality rates by Hispanic origin and,
    185–87, *table* 186
life expectancy and, *table* 112, 113, 171,
    table 171
living arrangements of women age 65
    and over by age, Hispanic origin and,
    230–31, *table* 231
mammogram use by, *figure* 137
marital status by sex, Hispanic origin and,
    table 257
nursing home residents over age 55 by
    sex, age, and, 241, *table* 241
overweight women age 20 to 74 by
    Hispanic origin and, 172, *table* 172
population by sex, Hispanic origin, and,
    figure 256
population in 1990 by sex and, *table* 254
poverty status and, 143, *table* 143, 234,
    table 235
prenatal care for mothers with live births
    by Hispanic origin and, 176, *table* 176
of preventive services' users, *table* 135
voter participation by, 345, *figure* 346,
    table 347
see also specific ethnic and racial groups
racism, 154, 158, 165–67
radio broadcasting licenses, 53
Ran, Shulamit, 67–68
rape, 45, 51, 56, 57, 64, 121
Raub, William, 96, 97
Ray, Laura A., 161
Reagan, Ronald, 77, 79, *table* 351
Reality, 85
Redel, Donna, 55
"Refugee and Immigrant Women's Right
    to Know," 53
Refugee Women Council, 53
Rehnquist, William H., 62

Reno, Janet, 78, 80, 85
rents and royalties, *table* 389, *table* 341
reproductive health, 30–31, 197–222
 future of, 219–22
 highlights of, 197–98
 issues, 209–19; access to services and
  sources of care, 213–16;
  appropriateness of care, 216–19;
  financial access and insurance
  coverage, 209–12
 stages of, 198–200, *figure* 200
 status of care, 200–209; abortion, 207–9,
  table 208; birth, 204, 206–7, *table* 205,
  table 207; contraceptive use, 200–202,
  table 201, *table* 202, *table* 204;
  pregnancy, 203–4, *table* 204; STDs
  and infertility, 202–3
 see also abortion; abortion rights;
  contraception; pregnancy; prenatal
  care; sexually transmitted diseases
  (STDs)
Republicans, Republican party, U.S., 47,
 56, 57, 86
 abortion rights and, 59, 60, 66
 1992 Convention of, 66–67
Rescue America, 80
Resnick, Neil M., 130
RESOLVE, Inc., 202
rheumatoid arthritis, *see* arthritis
Rhodes Scholars, 73
Rice, Bridget, 253*n*
Rice, Haynes, 192
Rice, Mitchell F., 183
Rice, Thomas, 239
Richards, Ann, 63, 64, 69
Richards, Cory L., 30–31, 197–222
Rivlin, Alice, 232, 240
Robertson, Rev. Pat, 67
Roe v. *Wade,* 45, 51, 76, 86, 215
Rogot, Eugene, 191
Roll Call, 48
Roman Catholics, 81
Romer, Roy, 82
Rosenbach, Margo L., 162
Ros-Lehtinen, Ileana, 374, *374*
Rosoff, Jeannine I., 220
Roukema, Marge, 374, *374*
Roussel-Uclaf, 63, 79, 80, 83, 218

Rowland, Diane, 26–28, 109–53
Roybal-Allard, Lucille, 374–75, *374*
RU-486 (abortion pill), 46, 70, 76
 Benten case and, 63, 64
 U.S. availability of, 79, 80, 83, 218
Ruggles, Patricia, 234*n*, 235
Ryan White Comprehensive Resources
 Emergency (CARE) Act (1990),
 193

Sakiz, Edouard, 79
Salganicoff, Alina, 26–28, 109–53
same sex partnerships, households with,
 253, *table* 260
Samoan women, 172, 176
Scalia, Antonin, 62
Scanlon, William, 236
Schenk, Lynn, 375, *375*
Schlafly, Phyllis, 59
Schoenberg, Bruce S., 131
Schoenborn, C., 133, 134, 138
Schoendorf, Kenneth C., 166, 185
Schroeder, Patricia, 25–26, 66, 91–108,
 375–76, *375*
Schumer, Charles E., 77
Schwartz, Felice N., 87
Science, 96
Scott, Sheri, 157, 158, 172, 175, 185, 189,
 191, 194
Scrimshaw, Susan C. M., 162
self-employment, 328, *table* 333
Selik, Richard M., 179, 182
semiconductor chips, 69, 73
Semiconductor Industry Association,
 73
Senate, U.S., *see* Congress, U.S., Senate
septicemia, mortality rates for, *table* 114,
 115
Service Employees International Union
 (SEIU), 75
service-producing workers
 by industry, *figure* 295
 by sex, *figure* 293
sewing, 55–56
sex
 currently married and never married
  adults by race, Hispanic origin and,
  figure 258

discrimination and, 40–41, 42, 46, 52–55, 57, 60, 61, 63, 64, 67, 70–74, 84, 86, 87
divorce ratios by race, Hispanic origin, and, 254, *table* 261
earnings and benefits by, 307, *figure* 312, *table* 317; health insurance, *figure* 320, *table* 321, *figure* 324, *figure* 325; median annual, *table* 314; median weekly, *figure* 309, *table* 310, *table* 315; pension plans, *table* 318, *table* 319
economic security and, 328, *table* 338, *table* 339
education and, 265, *table* 267, *figure* 279; college, 265, 266, *table* 270, *figure* 271, *table* 273, *figure* 275, *figure* 276, *figure* 278
employment and, 281, *figure* 287, *table* 291, *figure* 292, *table* 292, *figure* 293; labor force participation rates, *table* 285, *table* 286; unemployment, *table* 286, *table* 288, *figure* 290; union affiliation, 281–82, *figure* 293, *table* 294
health insurance of elderly by income and, *table* 148
hospital discharge rates by age and, 140, *figure* 141
life expectancy and, 111, *table* 112, 113, 171, *table* 171; at birth and at age 65 by race and, 111, *table* 112, 113
living arrangements of persons age 65 and over by, 254, *figure* 264
marital status by race, Hispanic origin and, *table* 257
nursing home residents over age 55 by race, age and, 241, *table* 241
physician visits and usual source of care by age and, 140, *table* 141
population in 1990 by race and, *table* 254
population by age and, 253, *figure* 255
population by race, Hispanic origin and, *figure* 256
prevalence of selected chronic conditions by, 229, *table* 230
voter participation by, 345, *figure* 346, *table* 347, *figure* 348, *table* 349
sex education, 31, 198, 219

sexual harassment, 39, 57, 77–80, 84, 87
in education, 52, 53–54
in federal court system, 65
Hill-Thomas case and, 46, 47–48, 72, 75
increase in reports of, 52
medicine and, 77–78
in Navy, 44, 47, 48, 53, 57–58, 61–62, 68, 69, 83, 85
Packwood case and, 72–73, 74, 78, 86
poll on, 74, 78–79
of teenagers, 86
sexual intercourse, first, *figure* 198, 199
sexually transmitted diseases (STDs), 27, 30, 52, 115–16, 202–3, 209
infertility and, 30, 105, 198, 202–3
see also HIV/AIDS (human immunodeficiency virus/Acquired Immune Deficiency Syndrome); pelvic inflammatory disease (PID)
Shalala, Donna E., 74, 76, 107
Shepherd, Karen, 376, *376*
Short, Pamela F., 183
Siebert, Muriel F., 62
silicone breast implants, 53, 56, 75
Silverman, Jane, 208
Singh, Susheela, 201, 206, 214
single-payer plan, 150
Skull and Bones, 42
Slaughter, Louise, 43, 75, 376, *376*
Smith, George D., 165
Smith, Jack C., 208
Smith, Mark Scott, 120
smoking, 27, 76, 109, 130
cessation of, 133–34
heart disease and, 122
lung cancer and, 26, 125
passive, 134
prevention of, 108, 134
women, by age, 133, *figure* 133
among women age 18 and over by race and Hispanic origin, 173, *table* 173
Snowe, Olympia J., 25–26, 81, 91–108, 377, *377*
Snyder, John W., 44, 47, 48
soccer, 49–50, 63
social insurance, 227, 245, 247
limited, 247–48

Social Security, 77, 78, 79, 234, *table* 339, *table* 340
Social Security Administration, 234
Social Service block grants, 238
Society for the Advancement of Women's Health Research, 94
Solis, Julia M., 161, 175, 184
Somogyi, John, 52
Somogyi, Kristen, 52
Sorlie, Paul D., 191
Sosa, Socorro, 154*n*
Sotomayor, Sonia, 70
Souter, David, 62
specialization, among health care providers, 106, 110
Specter, Arlen, 47, 57
Spence, Denise, 241
spermicide, *table* 204, 205
sports, 52, 53, 68, 78, 87
    discrimination and, 54–55, 63
    Olympics and, 53, 65
    see also specific sports
Squires, Teresa S., 127
stalkers, 80
Stallard, Eric, 240
Stampfer, Meir J., 138
State Farm Insurance of California, 57
state government
    family leave and, 308, *table* 316
    workplace changes in, 44
Staurowsky, Ellen, 44
Steinem, Gloria, 57
sterilization, 30, 199, 201, *table* 201, *table* 202, 205
    access to, 213, 214
    Medicaid and, 211, 212
Stevens, John Paul, 62
Stewart, Pearl, 71
Stone, Anne J., 23–35
stroke, 27, 76, *table* 114, 115, 128, 130, 138, 188
Suagee, Mary, 157, 158, 185, 189, 191, 194
Sugg, Nancy K., 122
suicide, 119, 121
    mortality rates for, *table* 114, 115
Sullivan, Louis, 41, 64, 98–99
Summer, Laura, 149

Supplemental Security Income (SSI), 146, *table* 339, *table* 340
Supreme Court, Florida, 64–65
Supreme Court, Michigan, 40
Supreme Court, U.S., 79, 87, 345, *table* 351
    abortion rights and, 39, 62, 64, 73, 81, 92; *Bray* v. *Alexandria Women's Health Clinic,* 76, 77; *Planned Parenthood of Southeastern Pennsylvania* v. *Casey,* 65, 215–16; *Roe* v. *Wade* and, 45, 51, 86, 215
    Thomas and, 40, 43, 45–48, 55
survivors' benefits, *table* 339, *table* 340
Swank, David, 82
Sweden, life expectancy in, 113–14, *figure* 113
swimming, 54
syphilis, 115–16
systemic lupus erythematosus (SLE), 53, 107, 121

Tailhook Association, 68
Tailhook Conventions, 44, 47, 48, 57–58, 60–63, 68, 85
    Defense Dept. investigation of, 61, 69, 83
Take Our Daughters to Work Day, 84
Tannen, Deborah, 54
tax credits, 77, 249
taxes, 70, 150
    Social Security, 77, 78, 79
Taylor, Amy K., 146
teenage girls, 119, 120, 213
    abortions of, 44, *table* 205, 208
    contraceptive use of, 200–201, *table* 201
    osteoporosis prevention in, 138–39
    pregnancies of, 41, 44, 45, 159, 200, 203, *table* 205, 208
    prenatal care of, 206, *table* 207
    smoking by, 133
    STDs and, 30, 116, 203, 219
teenagers
    sexual activity of, 41, 116
    sexual harassment and, 86
Teen Talk Barbie, 70
television broadcasting licenses, 53

Teutsch, Steven M., 191
Texaco, Inc., 46, 64
Texas, University of, 63
Texas Railroad Commission, 69
Thomas, Clarence, 40, 43, 45–48, 53, 55,
    62, 72, 75
Thomas, Helen, 50
Thomas, Kathleen, 239
Thompson, Jenny, 54
Thompson, Karen, 51
Thompson, Lawrence H., 40–41
Thurman, Karen, 377, *377*
Title X Family Planning program, 212
Time magazine, 40
Times Mirror Center for the People and
    the Press, 50
Time Warner, 81
"Tomcat Follies," 66
Tong, Tony, 127
Torres, Aida, 206, 209, 214
traffic accidents, 55
Travelers, 68
Treves, Therese A., 131
Trevino, Fernando M., 161, 173, 177, 178,
    184, 188
Trudeau, Garry, 69
tuberculosis, 83, 176–77, 192
Tucker, Michael, 47
Tyler, Sonya, 87
Tyson, Laura D'Andrea, 74, 78

Underwood, C., 133, 172, 173, 175, 192
unemployment, unemployment rate, 34,
    table 333
    of foreign-born women, by language
        spoken at home and English fluency,
        table 287
    of persons of Hispanic origin by sex and
        origin, *table* 286
    by sex, race, and Hispanic origin, *table*
        288
    women's, by race and Hispanic origin,
        281, *figure* 289
    workers age 20 and over by sex and
        reason, *figure* 290
uninsured, 27, 34, 110, 144, 149, 308
    by family relationship, 308, *table* 326

people of color as, 28–29, 182–83
reproductive health and, 212
by sex, race, and Hispanic origin, 308,
    table 321
by sex and age, 308, *figure* 324
by sex and work experience, 308, *figure*
    325
unions, *see* labor unions
United Kingdom, female life expectancy in,
    figure 113
United Methodist Church, 59
United Nations, 76, 87
United Nations Development Fund for
    Women (Unifem), 55
universities, *see* colleges and universities
Unsoeld, Jolene, 378, *378*
U.S. Preventive Services Task Force
    (USPSTF), 134–35, 138
uterine cancer, *see* endometrial
    cancer

vaginal pouches, 52
Valdez, Joe, 85
Valk, Elizabeth P., 40
Vanek, Jerome, 188
Vanity Fair magazine, 40
Van Vort, Jennifer, 207–8, 215, 221
Vaught, Wilma, 59
Vegega, Maria, 55
Velazquez, Nydia, 378, *378*
Veterans Affairs Department, U.S. (VA),
    80, 84, 87, 107, 183
    Women's Bureau in, 87
Veuve Clicquot Business Woman of the
    Year Award, 62
Vietnamese women, 176
Vietnam War, women in, 49
violence, *see* domestic violence
Virginia Military Institute (VMI), 43, 49,
    70, 86
Virginia Tech, 86
volunteer workers by sex and type of
    organization, *figure* 306
voter participation
    in national elections: sex and age,
        345–46, *table* 349; sex, race, and
        Hispanic origin, *table* 347

voter participation (*continued*)
 in 1992 election: sex, race, and Hispanic
  origin, 345, *figure* 346; sex and age,
  figure 348
Vucanovich, Barbara, 379, *379*

wages, *see* earnings and benefits; income
Walden, Daniel, 233
Waldron, Ingrid, 134
Walker, Alice, 63
Washington Post, 44, 45, 50, 56, 61, 63, 64,
  67, 72–76, 78–79
Washington Post-ABC News poll, 74
Wasserheit, Judith N., 116
Waters, Alice, 58
Waters, Maxine, 61, 87, 379, *379*
Wattleton, Faye, 45
Waxman, Henry, 95
Weddington, Sarah, 45
Weissert, William, 239
Weissman, Myrna M., 119
Weld, William, 56
welfare, 70, 77, 211
 job training and, 41, 77
 in New Jersey, 51–52, 64
Wellesley College, 52
Wellington, Sheila W., 87
Welper, Leigh, 188
Western Electric, 41
West Germany, female life expectancy in,
  figure 113
White, Byron R., 62, 87
White, Catherine C., 194
white men, 230
 earnings and benefits of, 308, *table* 309,
  table 314, *table* 321
 leading causes of mortality for, 114, *table*
  114
 life expectancy of, *table* 112, *table* 171
whites
 demographics on, 254, *table* 254, *figure*
  256, *table* 257, *figure* 258, *table* 259,
  table 261, *table* 262
 education of, 265, *table* 267, *table* 270
 employment of, *table* 285, *table* 288, *table*
  291, *table* 294
 families, *table* 330, *table* 337
 hypertension of, 164

 mortality rates for, 188
 voter participation of, 345, *table* 346,
  table 347
white women, 34, 183
 AIDS and, *figure* 117, *figure* 118, 180,
  table 180, 181, *table* 181; mortality
  rates, 187, *table* 188
 alcohol use of, 174
 births of, 206
 cancer in, 29, 123, *table* 123, 155; breast,
  123, *table* 123, 124, 126–27, *figure* 127,
  figure 128, 137, 177; cervical, 123, *table*
  123, 125, *figure* 126, 175, 177; lung,
  123, *table* 123, 124; ovarian, 123, *table*
  123, 126
 cerebrovascular disease in, *table* 114,
  128–29
 contraception of, 201
 depression in, 119
 diabetes in, *table* 115, 129, *figure* 129,
  177–78
 drug use of, 174
 earnings and benefits of, *table* 309, *figure*
  313, *table* 314, *table* 321
 economic security of, *table* 333–34, *table*
  335, *table* 340–41
 education of, 33, *table* 269, *table* 273,
  table 277; 12 or more years, 265, *figure*
  268
 employment of, *table* 301; child care,
  282, *table* 305; health care, *table* 299,
  table 300; occupation, 282, *figure* 297,
  table 300; unemployment rate, 34,
  281, *figure* 289
 health care services used by, 184
 heart disease among, 114–15
 high cholesterol of, 172
 hypertension of, 138–39, 179, *table*
  179
 infant mortality rates for, 185, *table* 186
 leading causes of mortality for, 113–14,
  table 114
 life expectancy of, 27, *table* 112, 113,
  table 171
 living arrangements of, age 65 and over,
  table 231, 232
 as nursing home residents over age 55,
  table 241

obesity of, 172, *table* 172
osteoporosis in, 130
prenatal care of, *table* 176, 206
preventive services used by, 1990, *table* 135
smoking by, 133, 173, *table* 173
uninsured, 29, 182
widows, 234, *table* 257
Wiener, Joshua, 232, 240, 241
Wilkinson, Doris Y., 164
Williams, Robin M., 164, 165, 176, 184, 186, 194
Wilson, Elizabeth Xan, 85
Winn, Mylon, 183
Winter Olympics (1992), 53
Wisconsin Pharmacal, 85
Woman-Church conference (1993), 81
Women in Apprenticeship and Nontraditional Occupations Act, 70–71
Women in Crisis, 55
Women in Military Service for America Memorial Foundation, 59
"Women in the Military" (conference), 58
women of color, health concerns of, 28–29, 154–96
    access to health insurance and services, 182–85
    alcohol consumption, 173–74
    data collection problems, 189–90
    diseases, 155, 176–82
    facilities to serve, 192–93
    factors, 156–71
    high cholesterol, 172–73
    highlights, 154–55
    issues related to improvement, 155, 189–95
    life expectancy, 155, 171–72
    mortality rates for, 185–90, *table* 188; infant, neonatal, and post-neonatal, 185–87, *table* 186
    need for minority physicians and providers, 194–95
    obesity, 155, 172
    preventive health measures, 155, 175–76
    research and treatment needs, 192
    smoking, 173

substance abuse, 174–75
see also specific ethnic and racial groups
Women's Campaign Fund, 72
Women's Equal Rights, Legal Defense and Education Committee, 73
Women's Health Advisory Committee, 94
Women's Health Equity Act (WHEA), 25, 93, 96–97, 98, 100–105, 107–8
Women's Health Initiative, 25, 70, 88, 100
Women's Health Report of the Public Health Service Task Force on Women's Health Issues, 93–94
Women's Health Task Force, 107
Women's Initiative, 82
women's policy agenda,
    Hartmann-Bergmann proposal for, 70
Women's Research and Education Institute (WREI), 42, 45, 58, 68
Women's Sports Foundation, 52
"Women Tell the Truth" (conference), 57
Wood, George, 43
Wood, Kimba M., 78
Woods, Harriett, 58
Woolsey, Lynn, 380, *380*
workforce, contingent, 82
Working Mother magazine, 45
working mothers, 34, *figure* 302, *figure* 303
    child care and, *table* 305, *table* 306
    children's living arrangements and, *table* 303
    by full-time work status and age of children, 281, *table* 304
working wives, 34, 51, *figure* 302
    economic security and, 327, *figure* 329, *table* 330
workplace
    family issues and, 44, 45, 49, 53, 57, 81, 83–84
    sexual harassment in, 74
"World Conference on Human Rights" (1993), 87
World Health Organization, 114
Worthy Wage Coalition, 83
"Worthy Wage Day," 83
Wyeth-Ayerst, 213

Xerox, 68

Yale University, 42
Yard, Molly, 50
Yeakel, Lynn, 57, 63
Yeas, Martynas, 234
yeast infections, 118
Yorkin, Peg, 45–46
You Just Don't Understand (Tannen), 54
younger women, health concerns of,
    115–22
  abortions of, 208, 209
  AIDS, 117–19
  autoimmune diseases, 121

depression, 119–20, 121
eating disorders, 120
osteoporosis prevention, 138–39
pelvic inflammatory disease, 116–17
sexually transmitted diseases, 115–16
violence, 121–22
see also teenage girls
Yu, Elena S.H., 154*n,* 165, 168, 169, 170,
    188, 191

Zambrana, Ruth, 154*n,* 160–61, 162
Zedlewski, Sheila, 234

About the Editors

CYNTHIA COSTELLO, PH.D., is WREI's director of research. Before coming to WREI, Dr. Costello was the director of employment policy at Families U.S.A. She also served as director of the Committee on Women's Employment at the National Academy of Sciences. Dr. Costello is the author of a book on organizing among clerical workers entitled *We're Worth It! Women and Collective Action in the Insurance Workplace.* She lives in Washington, DC with her husband, Peter Caulkins, and their son Michael.

ANNE J. STONE is senior research associate at WREI, where she has authored and coauthored policy analyses on various subjects, including the federal budget, employment issues for women, and women in the military. She has also worked on the four previous editions of *The American Woman,* and was the coeditor of the fourth edition. Ms. Stone lives in Washington, DC with her husband, Herbert Stone. They have two daughters and two granddaughters.